AMERICAN MARRIAGE AND DIVORCE

Wedlock, as old men note, hath likened been
Unto a publick crowd or common rout,
Where those that are without would fain get in
And those that are within would fain get out.

—*Poor Richard's Almanack*

AMERICAN MARRIAGE
AND DIVORCE

Paul H. Jacobson, Ph.D.

in collaboration with
PAULINE F. JACOBSON

RINEHART & COMPANY, INC., New York

Composed at
Vance Weaver Composition, Inc.
New York, New York

To Edith and Howard

PREFACE

THIS book deals with the *occurrence*, *duration*, and *dissolution* of marriage in the United States. For the first time, nationwide data are made available on such topics as the chances of marriage and of remarriage, the frequency of religious ceremonies, the duration of marriage and of widowhood, the chances of celebrating wedding anniversaries, the frequency of racial intermarriage, and the probabilities of divorce and of widowhood. Other topics are Gretna Greens, effectiveness of premarital regulations, seasonal pattern of marriage, interval between divorce and remarriage, stability of war and of depression marriages, causes of divorce, children in divorce, orphanhood, divorce proceedings, and alimony. Divorce and annulment in South Carolina and New York, and migratory divorce are reviewed in detail. Also highlighted are the changes in trend engendered by the depression of the 1930's and by World War II. Most subjects cover events of the twentieth century; some antedate the Civil War.

The author was stimulated to undertake this extensive research by an awareness of the paucity of statistics on marriage and divorce, despite the importance of such information. The United States is the only major country without a system of centralized collection of marriage and divorce records. Yet, comprehensive information is required if we are to understand the trends in family formation and dissolution, and if we are to promote the well-being of American families. Persons in many fields and professions—for example, child welfare, demography, education, housing, insurance, law, psychiatry, public affairs, religion, and sociology—all share in the concern over the lack of adequate information on the various phases of family life. In recognition of this situation, the Bureau of the Census has recently enlarged the scope of its work to include more data on the status and composition of American families. The National Office of Vital Statistics has also expanded its activities, with the aim of eventually providing nationwide statistics on marriage and divorce. Meanwhile there remains an immediate need for such data, the absence of which cannot be remedied by statistics for future years. This volume is intended to meet the present needs for information on the more important aspects of American marriage and divorce.

So far as possible, the basic data for this book were gathered from published national, state, and local reports. In addition, tabulated statistics were requested from states having centralized records; otherwise county, city, or court offices were contacted. In those areas where these offices were unable to cooperate, arrangements were made with universities, family organizations, or other agencies to transcribe the required information from the official records. In all, several thousand inquiries were directed to officials throughout the country in order to collect the basic statistics.

The author is indebted to hundreds of persons and organizations whose cooperation and assistance over a period of almost a decade helped make this book possible. Included are the state registrars of vital statistics and other state and county officials, as well as personnel of the Bureau of the Census and of the

National Office of Vital Statistics. Special thanks are due the staff of the Economics Division, Reference Department of the New York Public Library, for the many courtesies extended to me and to my wife in our search for publications of the past century. Grateful acknowledgment is also made to the Family Service Association of America and its member agencies for lightening the task of collecting information in South Carolina and several other areas of the country.

This book would not have been undertaken without the encouragement and assistance of Professor Kingsley Davis, formerly of Columbia University and now of the University of California. I am also obligated to him and to Professors Paul F. Lazarsfeld and David Donald of Columbia for constructive criticism of the initial version of the Introduction and Chapters 1-3, which was used as the author's doctoral dissertation at Columbia University. In addition, Mortimer Spiegelman of the Metropolitan Life Insurance Company gave advice on the construction of the nuptiality tables and reviewed the final manuscript; Mary E. Ryan and Amanda K. Schmitt lent timely assistance. My thanks also to Dr. John S. Bradway of Duke University and Dr. Clyde V. Kiser of the Milbank Memorial Fund for their encouragement and interest.

Finally, it is a pleasure to acknowledge indebtedness to my wife for her invaluable assistance with the collection and processing of the basic data, and for her collaboration in the preparation of the manuscript. My heartfelt thanks also to our children, Howard and Edith, for their understanding during the many years devoted to this book and for their assistance in its completion.

Paul H. Jacobson

New York, N. Y.
March, 1959

CONTENTS

Page

FIGURES

TABLES

Table   *Page*

AMERICAN MARRIAGE AND DIVORCE

THE NATIONAL SYSTEM OF MARRIAGE AND DIVORCE STATISTICS

IT has been said that Americans are the most fact-minded individuals in the world. Considering the immensity of statistical reports on almost every conceivable subject which are turned out each year in the United States, one would hardly expect to have to qualify this statement. Yet, with respect to marriage and divorce, the information available for our country is woefully inadequate. This is in sharp contrast to the situation in most countries, where marriage and divorce statistics are compiled and published routinely together with other national vital data.

From the earliest days, vital records including those of marriage and divorce were filed in some of the colonies, so that they would be available for legal and official purposes. When the Constitution of the United States was drawn up, it contained no provision for national registration of vital events. It did, however, include a clause which became the basis for our decennial censuses and it was in connection with the latter that the first attempts were made to collect national statistics on vital events.

THE FEDERAL CENSUS

The United States was the first nation to make constitutional or legal provision for a regular periodic census of its inhabitants. In 1790, less than a decade after the American colonies had achieved their independence, and within a year from the date of the inauguration of President Washington and the assembling of the First Congress of the United States, there was begun the first enumeration of our population. The constitutional requirement for a decennial census is found in Article I, Section 2, Paragraph 3, which reads in part:

Representatives and direct taxes shall be apportioned among the several States which may be included within this Union according to their respective numbers, which shall be determined by adding to the whole number of free persons, including those bound to service for a term of years, and excluding Indians not taxed, three-fifths of all other persons. The actual enumeration shall be made within three years after the first meeting of the Congress of the United States and within every subsequent term of ten years, in such manner as they shall by law direct.

The first census, conducted in 1790, related solely to population; its scope, although very limited, was somewhat greater than that required by the Constitution. The name of the head of each family was taken together with the total number of persons in the family, classified as free or slave. The free persons were further classified as white or other, the free whites as male or female, and the free white males as under or over 16. This first census was taken under the supervision of seventeen United States marshals, with about 650 assistants performing the actual enumeration. The marshals transmitted their reports directly to the President; and the reports were printed without review, verification, or analysis.

Subsequently from time to time the field covered by the census has been enlarged. In more recent years information has been obtained regarding such characteristics of the population as age, sex, race, birthplace, employment status, occupation, industry, and marital status.

Vital Statistics. Not all lines of investigation pursued in the decennial censuses have proved successful. In 1800 two groups urged Congress to broaden the field of the census to a much larger number of facts than had been obtained in 1790. One of the memorials submitted was signed by Thomas Jefferson, then president of the American Philosophical Society. It included a suggestion that the number of births occurring during the year be enumerated and tabulated.[1] It was not until 1850, however, that the collection of

[1] Sam Shapiro, "Development of Birth Registration and Birth Statistics in the United States," *Population Studies*, 4:88, June, 1950.

vital statistics on a national basis was first attempted. In that year, a schedule was provided to obtain data for each birth, death, and marriage that occurred within the year before the census date. Similar collections were made at each census through 1900, after which the procedure was discontinued. Although the statistics were published, it was apparent that they were incomplete.[2] This was attributed to the time interval between the occurrence of these events and the census enumeration. However, it is likely that there were other contributory factors.

Population by Marital Status. Inquiry regarding the marital status of the population in the United States was first made in connection with the 1880 Census. The results were not tabulated, however, so that the earliest national figures on marital status are those from the 1890 Census. For earlier years, this information is available for only a handful of states which included such inquiry in their state censuses—Michigan starting in 1854; New York in 1855; and Kansas, Massachusetts, and Rhode Island in 1875.[3]

Each of the federal censuses from 1890 to 1940 included the item, "whether single, married, widowed, or divorced." In addition, all but the 1920 Census contained one or more supplementary items. It is also noteworthy that the 1890 Census, for the only time in our history, used a separate

schedule for each family enumerated. In some communities the schedule was filled in by each family prior to the enumerator's visit.[4]

In connection with the 1900 Census, inquiry was made as to the "number of years married," but the data were not published. In 1910 the schedule called for "number of years of present marriage," and "whether married before." None of this information was published until after the 1940 Census, and then only for a sample of the native white and Negro women aged 15-74.[5]

In 1930 "age at first marriage" was obtained for only those persons who were reported as married (existing marriages), so that the information was not very useful and the nationwide data were never tabulated.

In 1940 every twentieth person, if a woman who was or had been married, was asked whether "married more than once" and "age at first marriage." The 1940 Census reports on fertility made available some of the 1910 and 1940 data on duration of marriage.[5] These data have limited value, however, since they are restricted to native white and Negro women aged 15-74 who were married once and living with their husband.

More useful and more comprehensive data on this subject were published by the Bureau of the Census as a product of its April, 1948, sample survey of the population. In that survey, persons who had ever been married were asked to report the number of years they had been in their present marital status. Thus, married persons were asked how many years it had been since their (last) marriage; widowed persons were asked how many years it had been since their (last) spouse died; and divorced persons were asked how many years it had been since they and their (last) spouse were divorced. These data are available for both men and women, classified by three broad age groups, by number of times married, and other characteristics.[6] It should be noted that the Bureau's monthly survey of population in 1948 consisted of a sample of approximately 25,000 households, or

---

[2]For example, only 197,029 persons (excluding slaves) of the total enumerated on June 1, 1850, were reported to have married during the preceding year (Census Office, *Statistical View of the United States: Compendium of the 7th Census*, Washington, 1854, p. 111). Similarly, 224,682 were reported to have married during the year ended June 1, 1860 (Census Office, *Population of the United States in 1860*, Washington, 1864, p. xxxvi). By comparison, on the basis of registration data, the author estimates that 256,000 marriages occurred in 1860 (Table 2). In other words, 512,000 persons married during that year — more than twice the number reported in the Census.

Despite greater emphasis on the enumeration of marriages in the 1870-1890 Censuses, including the reporting of the month of marriage in 1870 (Census Office, *The Statistics of the Population of the United States, 1870*, Vol. I, Washington, 1872, p. xxix), the returns remained far short of their expected number. In consequence, the data were not published, and the item was omitted from the 1900 Census. The enumerated births and deaths were also incomplete, but by a much smaller margin. These data were published in detail, and the items were not dropped from the census until after 1900.

[3]Walter F. Willcox, *The Divorce Problem, A Study in Statistics*, Columbia University Studies, 1891, p. 17.

[4]Carroll D. Wright, *The History and Growth of the United States Census*, Washington, 1900, pp. 71-72.

[5]Bureau of the Census, *Population: Differential Fertility, 1940 and 1910; Fertility by Duration of Marriage; Women by Number of Children Ever Born;* and *Fertility for States and Large Cities*, Washington, 1943-1947.

[6]Bureau of the Census, *Current Population Reports*, Series P-20, Nos. 21 and 23.

about 85,000 persons.[7] Since the statistics are estimates based on a sample, they are subject to sampling variability. In addition, like data from a complete enumeration, the estimates are subject to certain biases due to errors of response and to nonreporting. The latter bias could not have seriously affected the data from the April, 1948, survey, since only about 1.5 per cent of all persons ever married failed to report on duration of present marital status. However, there is every indication that the number of newly married couples is materially understated in the estimates.[8]

In 1950, as in each decade since 1880, the census schedule called for the marital condition of each person in the population. In one respect, however, the item was different. In 1940, for example, it was necessary to estimate the number of separated couples from the number of married men and women with spouse absent.[9] Since such estimates had to allow for spouses absent for reasons other than marital discord, they were at best only gross approximations. Encouraged by Canada's "success" in enumerating its separated population in 1941, the United States census schedule in 1950 asked whether the individual is "now married, widowed, divorced, *separated,* or never married."

Information for two items on marital status was obtained on a sample basis in the 1950 Census. Every thirtieth person, if ever married, was asked whether married more than once, and also the number of years in the present marital status. Since "separated" was treated as a status in 1950, the census made available information on the length of time such persons had been sepa-

rated, but did not provide data on the number of years since separated persons were (last) married.

Limitations. Very few persons are ignorant of their own marital status. However, when data concerning any person are obtained from some one other than the person enumerated, incorrect information may be supplied.

Not all errors, of course, arise through ignorance; in certain cases incorrect replies may be given to the enumerator with intent to deceive. Men who disown or who desert their families may report themselves as single. On the other hand, the unmarried mother of an illegitimate child may report herself as married, widowed, or divorced. Another source of error, in former years, arose from the fact that some foreign-born men, while their wife was still in the home country, reported themselves as single. Factors of even greater importance which affect the data are discussed in the two sections which follow.

Classification of Annullees. It is not generally known that it is census practice to classify persons with an annulled marriage as single, that is, as having never been married. Prior to 1950, the Bureau of the Census never revealed this practice in their reports, or even in their instructions to enumerators.[10]

The Bureau justifies its procedure on the ground that "Classifying such persons as single has the advantage from the point of view of relations between the enumerators and respondents of not imputing that the person with an annulled marriage is divorced." Moreover, the Bureau believes that the procedure is "...in conformity with the interpretation of the person's status that is given by religious organizations."[11] How valid is the Bureau's justification for its policy?

No doubt some persons consider their civil status as determined by their religious status, and will continue to so report themselves regardless of census practice. It is very unlikely, however, that the Bureau of the Census would suggest that all persons report themselves to the

---

[7]The current sample design, instituted in May, 1956, covers about 40,000 households. For details, see Bureau of the Census, *Current Population Reports,* Series P-20, No. 83, p. 7, and No. 84, p. 6.

[8]The Bureau of the Census reported 1,280,000 women married less than one year, and 1,559,000 married between one and two years (P-20, No. 23, p. 12). By comparison, 1,937,000 marriages were performed in the year ended March 31, 1948, and 2,189,000 in the preceding year (Table 3). Allowing for migration changes and for dissolutions by death and divorce, on April 1, 1948, there probably were about 1,910,000 women married less than one year and 2,090,000 married one year. Thus, the Bureau's estimates accounted for only two thirds of the women in the first year of marriage and for three fourths of those in the second.

[9]Bureau of the Census, *Population: 1940,* Vol. IV, Part 1, Washington, 1943, p. 4 and various tables.

[10]For example, see Bureau of the Census, *Instructions to Enumerators: Population and Agriculture, 1940,* p. 45, paragraph 465.

[11]The Technical Advisory Committee on Population for the 1950 Census endorsed this practice. Personal communications, dated June 10, 1949, and July 21, 1949, from Mr. Howard G. Brunsman, Chief, Population Division, Bureau of the Census.

census enumerator on this basis. The fact is that persons who do so err in failing to differentiate between the two statuses. Religious status depends upon a person's spiritual beliefs; civil status is determined by our laws. Just as the law cannot destroy or impair the individual's religious status, for example, his right to regard his union as a spiritual one; his creed cannot create his civil status.

The Bureau's justification of its policy infers a public preference for annulment over divorce. Recall the words, "...of not imputing that the person with an annulled marriage is divorced." The writer knows of no study which has indicated such a public attitude. Indeed, if we judge by available information, namely, statistics on annulment and divorce, we would have to accept the contrary opinion. For example, in states where marriages can be legally dissolved as readily by either means, even among childless couples married less than five years, divorces far outnumber annulments. Actually, most persons make no special distinction between absolute divorce and annulment. The particular remedy sought in formally dissolving a broken marriage probably depends on the laws and the couple's circumstances.

Is there a legal or practical basis for the Bureau's policy? Theoretically, there is a significant difference between an annulment and an absolute divorce, but in civil practice the differentiation hardly exists. For one thing, an increasing number of states have included the grounds for annulment in their divorce law.[12] More important, New York State and California together account for two thirds of the annulments granted in the country as a whole. It is common knowledge that annulments in these states serve to circumvent certain aspects of their divorce laws. In other words, if not for special circumstances, the large preponderance of their broken marriages would also be legally dissolved by absolute divorce rather than by annulment. Curiously enough, the Bureau of the Census itself has recognized the lack of statistical or social justification for a distinction between annulment and divorce,[13] yet

it adheres to its policy of classifying as single, persons *who report themselves* as annullees. Despite this policy, it is likely that approximately the same proportion of persons with an annulled marriage report themselves as divorced (or as married more than once if they have subsequently married), as do those whose marriage was dissolved by absolute divorce.

The fact that the Bureau had not publicized its policy prior to the 1950 Census is as important to demographers and other social scientists as the policy itself. Owing to the mistaken belief that census data treat the annulled and the divorced in a similar manner, data from other sources have been classified on this basis, supposedly to make them comparable to census data.[14] Moreover, it is likely that the marriage or death of most persons with an annulled marriage is included with the divorced.[15] This misunderstanding of census procedure may be resolved somewhat in the future, since at the author's suggestion the instructions to enumerators in 1950,[16] for the first time, stated that a person with an annulled marriage should be reported as "never married." At the same time, it is not likely that the quality of the data was materially improved thereby. Accordingly, the addition of the term "marriage annulled" on future census schedules would appear to be advisable. In this way, a larger proportion of such persons might be reported (and classified) in a uniform manner.

Census data on the number of divorced persons in New York and California may be seriously deficient as an index of marital discord due to the relatively large number of annulments granted in these states. For the country as a whole, however, annulments constitute no problem; of much greater consequence is the underenumeration of persons whose last marriage was dissolved by absolute divorce.

[12]National Conference on Family Life, May, 1948, *The American Family: A Factual Background*, Report of the Inter-Agency Committee on Background Materials, Washington, 1949, p. 368.

[13]Bureau of the Census, *Marriage and Divorce, 1926*, Washington, 1929, pp. 43 and 47.

[14]For example, see Clyde V. Kiser and Nathalie L. Schacter, "Demographic Characteristics of Women in 'Who's Who'," *Milbank Memorial Fund Quarterly*, 27:416, October, 1949.

[15]This is the procedure which has always been followed by the New York State Department of Health. Personal communication, dated July 21, 1950, from Dr. Joseph V. DePorte, Director, Office of Vital Statistics.

[16]Bureau of the Census, *Urban and Rural Enumerator's Reference Manual: 1950 Census of the United States*, p. 34, paragraph 126; see also, *1950 U.S. Census of Population*, P-B1, Washington, 1952, p. XII.

Are Divorced Persons Underenumerated? It is widely believed that the number of divorced persons is understated in decennial censuses. Despite the absence of adequate documentation, writers have a ready explanation. They say that the attitude that divorce is shameful is still widespread. In consequence, it is stated, many persons who have experienced divorce are ashamed to admit it even to the impersonal census enumerator. In view of the prevalence of this attitude, it is important to explore the subject thoroughly.

First, it should be noted that the terms "single," "married," "widowed," and "divorced" refer to a person's marital status at the time the census is taken. A divorced (or widowed) individual who has remarried is reported as married, so that the returns for divorced (or widowed) persons *are not supposed to represent* the total who have ever been divorced (or widowed). Thus, the question resolves itself into whether the enumerated number of divorced persons is less than the actual number who have been divorced and not remarried. The Bureau of the Census has always held to the opinion that divorced persons are underenumerated (or misreported). Thus, the Bureau has stated that "it is probable that the number of persons reported as divorced in 1910 was considerably less than the actual number." In connection with the 1930, 1940, and 1950 Censuses,[17] likewise, it was stated that the "returns doubtless understate somewhat the actual number of divorced persons who have not remarried."

In the past, due to the absence or inadequacies of pertinent data, it was almost impossible to investigate this question. Now, however, with the aid of the statistics summarized in Table 1, it is possible to make a reasonably accurate evaluation.

The table reveals a number of interesting details regarding our population statistics. Note, for example, the large "undercount" of total males and females in 1920 and other censuses.[18] More important to the present inquiry, however, are the discrepancies for the individual marital classes. These errors are relatively small for single and married persons, and possibly also for the widowed; for the divorced population, on the other hand, they are relatively large and have increased numerically at each successive census.

Apparently, divorced persons are underenumerated (or misreported), but it is unlikely that the errors are as large as the differences between the expected and reported figures shown in the table. For example, note that the 1,108,000 divorced men reported in the 1950 Census constitute only 56 per cent of the "expected" total of 1,966,000. This could reflect the actual degree of completeness of enumeration only if the intercensal numbers of divorces, migrants, remarriages, and deaths were substantially correct. However, if they were, the decennial population errors would be cumulative, and the 1950 Census count would represent only one fourth of the men who were ever divorced and not remarried. But this is highly improbable, since it would attribute to divorced persons an unrealistically low death rate. Thus one must conclude that there are errors in some or all of the estimated components of population change, as well as in the census counts themselves.

It is likely that the relative errors for divorced persons are smallest on death certificates and largest on census schedules, with those on marriage licenses of an intermediate degree. However, since there is no direct evidence on the true magnitude of the errors, the annual number of divorced persons has been estimated on the assumption that the relative errors are of the same magnitude for all three factors. These adjusted estimates for the period from 1890 to 1950 are shown in the right-hand columns of Table A6; the details regarding their derivation are given in Appendix Note 3. Even these adjusted estimates, however, indicate that the errors in the census data are relatively large. The ratios of the reported to the adjusted numbers of divorced persons, per 100, are as follows:

	1890	1900	1910	1920	1930	1940	1950
Male	41	42	48	59	67	71	80
Female	62	59	59	68	74	73	79

Thus, about one fifth of the divorced population was not enumerated (or was misreported) in the 1950 Census. Moreover, it would appear that the extent of underenumeration was much greater in the earlier censuses. In 1920, for example, about two fifths of the divorced men were not enumerated;

[17] See, for example, Bureau of the Census, *1950 United States Census of Population*, Special Report P-E No. 2D, Washington, 1953, p. 4.

[18] Several other studies have indicated census undercounts. See Mortimer Spiegelman, *Introduction to Demography*, Society of Actuaries, Chicago, 1955, pp. 33-38.

Table 1. Population by Sex and Marital Status, and Estimated Components of Change, United States, 1900-1950

(Number in Thousands)

Marital Status, and Component of Change	MALE					FEMALE				
	1900-1910	1910-1920	1920-1930	1930-1940	1940-1950	1900-1910	1910-1920	1920-1930	1930-1940	1940-1950
SINGLE										
Population at start of interval — census enumeration	23,493	27,456	29,944	33,209	33,101	20,491	23,522	26,244	29,103	28,994
Allowance for persons with status unknown‡	47	79	43	36	—	13	33	14	16	—
Armed forces overseas	—	—	—	—	83	—	—	—	—	—
Births	13,247	14,383	15,034	12,488	16,388	12,548	13,617	14,213	11,851	15,531
Annulments	*	*	37	54	134	*	*	37	54	134
Migrants	1,992	1,076	1,412	- 62	513	1,212	1,045	1,087	70	331
Marriages	- 7,265	- 8,763	-10,275	-10,383	-13,907	- 7,314	- 8,756	-10,250	-10,470	-13,890
Deaths	- 3,803	- 3,537	- 2,997	- 2,397	- 2,196	- 2,764	- 2,358	- 2,002	- 1,539	- 1,257
Population at end of interval — expected	27,710	30,694	33,198	32,945	34,116	24,186	27,103	29,342	29,084	29,844
Reported§	27,535	29,987	33,245	33,184	34,329	23,555	26,257	29,119	28,994	30,278
Difference, expected minus reported	175	707	- 47	- 239	- 214	631	845	224	90	- 434
MARRIED										
Population at start of interval — census enumeration	13,956	18,093	21,852	26,328	30,192	13,814	17,688	21,324	26,175	30,090
Allowance for persons with status unknown‡	53	68	61	44	—	21	29	29	29	—
Armed forces overseas	—	—	—	—	67	—	—	—	—	—
Marriages	8,265	10,062	12,272	12,442	17,405	8,265	10,062	12,272	12,442	17,405
Migrants	626	13	185	- 142	473	256	317	467	36	522
Divorces and annulments	- 683	- 1,032	- 1,839	- 2,132	- 4,110	- 683	- 1,032	- 1,839	- 2,132	- 4,110
Deaths of husbands and wives	- 4,049	- 4,883	- 5,545	- 6,148	- 6,645	- 4,049	- 4,883	- 5,545	- 6,148	- 6,645
Population at end of interval — expected	18,167	22,322	26,986	30,393	37,382	17,623	22,181	26,708	30,403	37,263
Reported§	18,161	21,913	26,372	30,259	37,522	17,717	21,353	26,204	30,090	37,504
Difference, expected minus reported	6	409	614	134	- 140	- 93	828	504	312	- 242
WIDOWED										
Population at start of interval — census enumeration	1,178	1,471	1,758	2,025	2,144	2,718	3,176	3,918	4,734	5,700
Allowance for persons with status unknown‡	5	8	6	5	—	7	7	8	8	—
Armed forces overseas	—	—	—	—	1	—	—	—	—	—
Deaths of spouse	1,733	2,037	2,348	2,368	2,251	2,317	2,845	3,197	3,779	4,395
Migrants	27	14	25	—	27	66	72	116	36	67
Marriages	- 783	- 888	- 1,163	- 941	- 1,072	- 648	- 775	- 1,055	- 810	- 1,093
Deaths	- 831	- 1,067	- 1,234	- 1,391	- 1,543	- 1,400	- 1,739	- 2,070	- 2,275	- 2,580
Population at end of interval — expected	1,329	1,575	1,740	2,066	1,807	3,059	3,586	4,114	5,472	6,489
Reported§	1,479	1,764	2,030	2,144	2,307	3,183	3,926	4,742	5,700	6,711
Difference, expected minus reported	- 150	- 189	- 289	- 78	- 500	- 124	- 340	- 628	- 228	- 222
DIVORCED										
Population at start of interval — census enumeration	84	156	235	489	624	115	185	273	573	823
Allowance for persons with status unknown‡	†	1	1	1	—	†	†	†	1	—
Armed forces overseas	—	—	—	—	1	—	—	—	—	—
Divorces	683	1,032	1,802	2,078	3,976	683	1,032	1,802	2,078	3,976
Migrants	1	1	2	3	10	1	1	6	8	17
Marriages	- 217	- 411	- 834	- 1,119	- 2,426	- 303	- 531	- 967	- 1,162	- 2,423
Deaths	- 29	- 59	- 89	- 152	- 220	- 21	- 36	- 51	- 78	- 104
Population at end of interval — expected	522	720	1,118	1,301	1,966	475	652	1,065	1,419	2,289
Reported§	157	236	491	626	1,108	185	274	574	823	1,374
Difference, expected minus reported	365	484	627	675	857	290	378	491	597	915
TOTAL										
Population at start of interval — census enumeration	38,816	47,332	53,900	62,137	66,062	37,178	44,640	51,810	60,638	65,608
Armed forces overseas	—	—	—	—	151	—	—	—	—	—
Births	13,247	14,383	15,034	12,488	16,388	12,548	13,617	14,213	11,851	15,531
Migrants	2,646	1,104	1,624	- 201	1,023	1,535	1,435	1,676	150	937
Deaths	- 6,981	- 7,509	- 7,517	- 7,719	- 8,354	- 5,918	- 6,171	- 6,470	- 6,261	- 6,192
Population at end of interval — expected	47,729	55,310	63,042	66,705	75,270	45,343	53,521	61,229	66,378	75,884
Reported§	47,332	53,900	62,137	66,213	75,266	44,640	51,810	60,638	65,608	75,867
Difference, expected minus reported	396	1,410	905	492	4	703	1,711	591	770	18

*Not available.   †Less than 500.

‡1900-1930 estimated by the author according to the distribution of persons reported by age and marital status; 1940 and 1950 estimated by the Bureau of the Census and included with the enumerated.

§Sum of census enumeration, allowance for persons with status unknown, and armed forces overseas.

Note: Individual figures have been independently rounded; hence the sums of parts may differ slightly from the totals.

in 1890 and 1900, the proportion was almost three fifths.[19] Each census has reported more divorced women than men, but prior to 1930 this may have been due to the fact that divorced women were more accurately enumerated than men. Even so, the number of divorced women was understated by about two fifths in the censuses of 1890 to 1910.

No doubt some divorced persons are hesitant to reveal their status to the census enumerator, but other factors may also be involved. The average man at the time of divorce is relatively young and tends to associate with other young unmarried men, most of whom are bachelors. Since he is unlikely to have children in his care, he may reside in a rooming house or other quasi household. Very likely, too, he is living in a new neighborhood where his status is not known. Living alone and associating with other unmarried people, he is classed by his neighbors as "single" —a term popularly used for "unmarried." Thus the census enumerator often records such an individual as "single"—sometimes, because the respondent is a caretaker or other neighbor who does not know the individual's true status; other times, because the individual himself without intending to deceive may so report.[20]

The better reporting for divorcees is also understandable. If there are children of the dissolved marriage, the mother would most likely have them in her care. Under these circumstances, a home is important, and thus such divorced women are found in better living quarters. As a consequence, too, she is more often correctly enumerated. Moreover, if an error is made, the divorced woman with children may be reported as "widowed." However, most underenumerated divorcees are probably reported as spinsters. No doubt this is a common error among the childless for reasons similar to those for divorced men.

The fact that many divorced men and women may be included with the single in census reports is a serious problem for consumers of census statistics. Due to the large number of single adults in the population, the effect on the statistics for the single is relatively unimportant, except possibly at the older ages. For the divorced, however, the magnitude of the distortion appears to be so large that the statistics should be used with extreme caution.

BIRTH AND DEATH STATISTICS

Development of National Registration. The registration of vital events in this country has a long history. In 1632, the Grand Assembly of Virginia required ministers or wardens from every parish to present themselves annually at court on June 1 and provide a register of all burials, christenings, and marriages.[21] In 1639 the Massachusetts Bay Colony passed a law which marked a departure from past practice by requiring government officers to record births, deaths, and marriages instead of the ecclesiastical ceremonies of baptisms, burials, and weddings. As time went on, other colonies placed similar measures into effect. In 1646 the Plymouth Colony,

[19]It is interesting to compare these estimates with those previously derived by other investigators. On the basis of statistics for prison inmates, Alfred Cahen concluded that the number of men reported as divorced in the 1920 Census was only one fourth of their actual number (*Statistical Analysis of American Divorce*, Columbia University Press, New York, 1932, p. 107). E. R. Groves and W. F. Ogburn also demonstrated that divorced persons are underenumerated, but did not estimate its extent (*American Marriage and Family Relationships*, Henry Holt and Company, New York, 1928, pp. 362-366). I. M. Rubinow, by contrast, was of the opinion that divorced persons were not materially understated in census data (*Some Statistical Aspects of Marriage and Divorce*, American Academy of Political and Social Science, Pamphlet Series, No. 3, 1936, pp. 28-32). Nor is the distortion limited to United States data. Enid Charles, for example, estimated that the number of divorced persons in Canada was about three times the number recorded in their 1941 Census (*A Statistical Note on Divorce*, Dominion Bureau of Statistics, Canada, Undated, p. 3).

[20]Census coding procedures for 1940 and 1950 also contributed somewhat to the undercount of divorced persons. In 1940, persons with marital status not reported, who were not obviously married, were classified as single. Similarly, in 1950, although a more complicated coding procedure was used for distributing persons with marital status not re-

ported, none of these persons were assigned to the divorced category. If the spouse or children were present, the person was coded as married; otherwise the marital status assigned was single, married, or widowed, whichever was the modal category for the age group. In 1930, only the "unknowns" under age 18 were tabulated with the single; all others were left as status not reported. Prior to 1930, the latter procedure was used for persons of all ages.

[21]U.S. Congress, *Measures Relating to Vital Records and Vital Statistics*, House Document No. 242, 78th Congress, 1st Session, Union Calendar No. 214, Washington, 1943, p. 40.

for example, designated the town clerk to keep a record of all such events. The Connecticut Court of Election ordered town clerks or registrars to record births and marriages in 1644, and added the registration of deaths in 1650.[22]

Further important steps toward modern registration procedure were taken in the years ahead by the Massachusetts Bay Colony, but it was not until 1842 that the way to central registration was formulated. In that year, Massachusetts required the town clerks to submit annually in May certified copies of all births, deaths, and marriages on forms provided by the Secretary of the Commonwealth. It is noteworthy that the registration system in Massachusetts was devised and perfected long before the establishment of organized public health work on either the state or local level. Indeed, its registration system has continued under the auspices of the Secretary of the Commonwealth; Massachusetts is now the only state in which records of births and deaths are not under health department jurisdiction.

The Civil War halted enactment of legislation, but further gains were recorded almost immediately afterward, when both Michigan and Ohio passed registration laws. The work of numerous scientific conferences in the latter part of the nineteenth century, calling for further and more efficient registration laws, culminated in three important advances shortly after the turn of the century. The first was the establishment of the Bureau of the Census as a permanent office in 1902. Equally important, on February 11, 1903, Congress adopted a joint resolution memorializing the states to cooperate with the Bureau toward securing a uniform system of birth and death registration in the United States. Another significant step occurred when the federal government began the annual collection, from those states and cities with reliable registration systems, of death statistics starting with 1900 and of birth statistics starting with 1915.

When Congress passed its resolution in 1903, only fifteen states and the District of Columbia had central files for birth records, and one additional state had a law relating to a central file for deaths. In the years thereafter, statutes were

enacted in state after state as the use of birth and death certificates for statistical purposes gained impetus from the requirements of public health for statistics to evaluate the effectiveness of health programs. Thus, by 1919, with the passage of laws in Georgia and New Mexico, all states had registration statutes, but the laws were not strictly enforced in all of them. Indeed, it was not until 1933 that the reporting systems were deemed sufficiently complete in all states to warrant their inclusion in the Birth and Death Registration Areas.

Deaths by Marital Status. The use of birth and death certificates as a potential source for supplementary statistics on the family has hardly been explored in the United States. No state or city, for example, obtains information on the duration of the present marital status of the deceased or of the mother at the time of a birth or fetal death. Nor does any death certificate ask for the number of children ever born or the number surviving. Moreover, while marital status is called for on every state's death certificate, little use has been made of the information.

Shattuck, father of American vital statistics, probably compiled the first mortality data by marital status for our country. These related to Massachusetts for the period 1844-1848 for persons at least 20 years of age. In the absence of population data by marital status, the only analysis possible was to compare the marital classes by their average age at death. For this reason, nothing further was done in the United States until 1890. In connection with the federal census of that year, deaths[23] and population were enumerated by marital status, and the information was published for both the Death Registration States and the country as a whole.

This procedure was repeated in the 1900 Census, but little use was made of the data. Willcox, one of the pioneers in American vital statistics, reviewed the data available for 1890, and concluded that they were of little value since rates could be computed for only three broad age groups, namely, 15-44, 45-64, and 65 or over. He was, of course, referring to the data for the Death Registration States; those for the country as a whole were

---

[22]Connecticut Department of Health, *100th Registration Report, (1947)*, Public Document No. 9, Hartford, 1949, p. 11.

[23]Census Office, *Report on Vital and Social Statistics in the United States at the Eleventh Census: 1890, Part IV — Statistics of Deaths*, Washington, 1895, pp. 24-25, 38, 50-136.

available by more detailed age groups but were
valueless since they were obtained by census
enumeration, which as we have already noted were
materially incomplete. Willcox mistakenly assumed that the same situation existed for 1900.[24]
Actually, however, it was possible to compile
deaths and population by marital status, sex, and
detailed age groups for the Death Registration
States of 1900.[25]

In 1912, the Bureau of the Census published
deaths by marital status, but not by age, for the
Death Registration States of 1910. Nothing further
was done until 1924, when at the request of Willcox
the Bureau began to tabulate deaths in the Death
Registration Area by sex, age, and marital condition. This was discontinued five years later without any of the results being published. The data,
however, were made available to Willcox, who
computed and published the death rates for the
five-year period.[26]

This work was resumed by the Bureau in 1935,
and for each of the years through 1939 the reports
included deaths by marital status according to
sex, but not by age, for each of the states. The
details were expanded for 1940 when, for the first
time in our history, deaths according to marital
status were made available by age, sex, color,
and cause; but no information at all was tabulated
for the individual states.

The National Office of Vital Statistics tabulated,
but did not publish, the number of deaths by marital status according to age, sex, and color for
1943. Starting with 1949, however, that Office
inaugurated a plan to publish at intervals these
essential details regarding deaths in the United
States.

MARRIAGE AND DIVORCE STATISTICS

Marriage and divorce statistics are today the
least developed branch of American vital statistics,

yet national data, on divorce in particular, were
available for many years before information on
births and deaths. To understand this situation,
it is necessary to review the programs by which
marriage and divorce data have been collected.

Past Programs. Interest in national statistics
on marriage and divorce was first aroused by
individuals and organizations who regarded
"divorce as a social menace to be investigated,"
and migratory divorce as an abuse to be curbed.
Seeking adequate information on which to base an
effective appeal for a federal law on marriage
and divorce, the New England Divorce Reform
League (later known as the National League for
the Protection of the Family), organized in Boston
in 1881, began the task of collecting from the
states and counties their statistical records of
marriage and divorce. At the same time, under
the leadership of its secretary, the Rev. Samuel W.
Dike, agitation was begun for a comprehensive
federal investigation.

This drive succeeded in 1887 when, by act of
Congress on March 3 of that year, the Commissioner of Labor was authorized to "collect and
report to Congress the statistics of and relating
to marriage and divorce in the several States
and Territories and in the District of Columbia."
The report of the investigation, which covered the
years 1867-1886, was published in 1889.[27] In the
introduction, the report declared that the results
with regard to marriage were thoroughly incomplete and unsatisfactory. Due to the wretched
condition of marriage records at that time in
most areas of the country, the statistics were
confined simply to the number of marriages
performed in 1,728 counties, or not quite two
thirds of the total. In only five states (Vermont,
Massachusetts, Rhode Island, Connecticut, Ohio)
and the District of Columbia, was it possible to
obtain marriage statistics for the twenty years
with practical completeness. Even in one or two
of these states the number reported was thought
to be perhaps 10 per cent deficient. For six
other states (Maryland, Michigan, Illinois,
Wisconsin, Minnesota, Kansas), the statistics
were also fairly complete from 1870 forward.

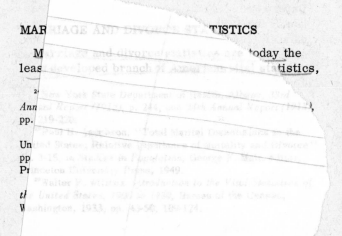

[24] New York State Department of Health, 22nd
Annual Report ..., p. 244, and 32nd Annual Report ...,
pp. 116-123.

[25] Paul H. Jacobson, "Total Marital Expectancy in the
United States, Relative Importance of Mortality and Divorce
..., p. 115, in Studies in Population, George F. Mair, editor,
Princeton University Press, 1949.

[26] Walter F. Willcox, Introduction to the Vital Statistics of
the United States, 1900 to 1930, Bureau of the Census,
Washington, 1933, pp. 42-50, 180-124.

[27] U.S. Commissioner of Labor, *A Report on Marriage and
Divorce in the United States, 1867 to 1886*, Washington, 1889
(Vol. 1, Special Report of the Commissioner, U.S. Labor
Bureau — revised in 1891 and reprinted in 1897), 1074 pp.

The divorce statistics in this first report, by contrast, were practically complete and included, in addition to the number granted by county, various details such as legal grounds, to whom granted, and duration of marriage, by state and year; also included were some statistics regarding alimony for 45 counties in 11 states. These data were obtained mainly by government field workers from the court records in 95 per cent of the counties; in the balance, covering less than 2 per cent of the country's population, the records had been destroyed, either partially or totally. For most cases, the agents of the Commissioner of Labor had to examine not only the libels but often the dockets and whatever evidence was on file; pending cases and decrees nisi were not considered.

The story is very much similar for the next federal investigation made two decades later. The movement for reform of marriage and divorce laws, not having made any progress toward federal legislation, was interested in bringing the figures of the first report up to date. At the request of Rev. Dike, the Interchurch Committee on Marriage and Divorce, and numerous other petitioners, President Theodore Roosevelt sent a special message to Congress on January 30, 1905, requesting that a second investigation be made. This was approved by a joint resolution of Congress on February 9, authorizing the Director of the Census to "collect and publish the statistics of and relating to marriage and divorce in the several states and territories and in the District of Columbia since January 1, 1887." The report of this investigation for the years 1887-1906 was transmitted to Congress in 1908-1909.[28] Since the first report was out of print, it summarized much of the data for 1867-1886 and was thus virtually a report for the period from 1867 to 1906. The details were fairly similar to those for the earlier period, but the coverage was more extensive. It included the number of marriages performed in more than nine tenths of the counties, and data on divorces for all but six of the counties with a few others known to be incomplete.

Nothing further was done thereafter for several years. In 1914, however, a drive was begun to collect statistics for the years which had elapsed since 1906. This campaign was also motivated by the groups seeking federal legislation on marriage and divorce, spearheaded this time by the International Committee on Marriage and Divorce. The drive culminated successfully in July, 1917, when Congress appropriated funds sufficient for a complete census of marriage and divorce during 1907-1916. Owing to war conditions, however, it was decided to limit the survey to the single year 1916. The report of this survey[29] contained somewhat fewer details on divorce than the preceding one, and was also more deficient in coverage. For one thing, the abnormal conditions due to the war and to the administration of selective service considerably hampered the collection of reports from the counties. Equally important is the fact that, for the first time, the statistics were collected wholly by correspondence.[30]

The report for 1916 was planned as the first of a series which would provide statistics annually. Our entrance into World War I, however, delayed the inauguration of this program until 1922. Then, for a period of eleven years, information was obtained annually through correspondence, following the general pattern of the 1916 report. In these annual reports, the marriage returns (limited to number by county) were apparently complete.[31] For divorce, on the other hand, detailed data were missing for a small number of counties. We also know now that the reports omitted a few courts in counties where more than one court had jurisdiction. Nevertheless, the divorce statistics published for 1922-1932 are probably as complete as those for any previous year. Moreover, in one respect the data from 1926 forward are superior; starting with that year, for the first time, the Bureau included statistics on annulments. The report for 1926 also contained estimates of the number of marriages and divorces in the country as a whole for years not covered by any previous report, namely, 1907-1915 and 1917-1921.

The annual series on marriage and divorce was discontinued in the economy program of 1933—at

[28]Bureau of the Census, *Marriage and Divorce, 1867-1906*, Washington, Part I, 1909, 535 pp.; Part II, 1908, 840 pp.

[29]Bureau of the Census, *Marriage and Divorce, 1916*, Washington, 1919, 47 pp.

[30]In some southern counties where the court clerks failed to make the returns, mainly on divorce, special agents of the Bureau of the Census did the work.

[31]Bureau of the Census, *Marriage and Divorce* (Annual Reports, 1922-1932), Washington, 1925-1934.

the very time when the data were more valuable than ever before—and nothing further was done for several years. In response to public demand for such data, the Bureau launched a twofold program in connection with the 1940 Census. First, the national summaries from 1887 forward were published, together with some new material.[32] Data were also collected from which estimates were made of the state and national figures for 1937-1940.[33]

The second, and more important, part of the program consisted of a project to obtain detailed statistics from those states with central registration which were willing to provide transcripts of the individual records in their files. These included twenty-seven states and the District of Columbia for marriage, but only twelve states for divorce. At the time, it was hoped to develop the project into a permanent function of the Bureau to supplement its work on births and deaths. With the outbreak of World War II, these plans were curtailed and later discontinued. It is noteworthy, however, that the program was successful in collecting and publishing the first detailed data on marriage for a large segment of our country. The reports for 1939 and 1940 (chiefly those for 1940) included statistics for brides and grooms by such details as age, color, previous marital status, place of residence, type of ceremony, and month of marriage.[34] In contrast, divorce statistics were published for 1939 only, and were much less comprehensive in scope than those for earlier years.[35]

In 1944, the Bureau of the Census resumed a limited program of marriage and divorce statistics. Two years later, in July, 1946, all of the vital statistics functions of the Bureau were transferred to the newly created National Office of Vital Statistics in the U.S. Public Health Service, where this work has continued. Since 1944 three series of statistics have been published: (1) monthly marriage licenses for major cities; (2) monthly marriages or marriage licenses for each state; and (3) annual estimates of marriages

and divorces for the country. Two reports of the latter annual series are worthy of special mention. The report for 1945 is the first in which divorce statistics for 1941-1944 are shown for some of the states,[36] and the report for 1946 is the first to give estimates of the total number of marriages in the United States from 1867 to 1906.[37]

Such was the status of marriage and divorce statistics for the United States at the end of World War II. Three points should be noted about these past programs and the published statistics. First, no details on marriage, other than their total, had ever been published for the country as a whole. Second, although nationwide statistics on divorce are available for many of the years prior to 1932, both limited and absolute divorces are combined in the data.[38] Since the only reference ever made by the Bureau of the Census to the limited decrees was that "less than 1 divorce in 100 is a limited divorce,"[39] we do not know the actual number of absolute divorces in former years. For some states, estimates can be made from the statistics on legal grounds, e.g., New York, North Carolina. For others, we know that limited decrees were never granted, e.g., Texas. For most states, however, there is no satisfactory method of estimating the number of legal separations included in the national divorce statistics.

The inclusion of limited decrees results in overstatement of the divorce (absolute) rate for former years and also distorts the relative distribution of such variables as legal grounds, duration of marriage, and children affected. It is encouraging that the situation has improved somewhat in recent years—more and more states have excluded limited decrees from their reports or have tabulated them separately. Such decrees have been excluded from the author's data for the years 1940 forward; in the reports by the National Office of Vital Statistics, however, they are still included in the statistics for several states.

The final point to be noted—possibly the most

[32]Bureau of the Census, *Vital Statistics—Special Reports*, Vol. 9, No. 60.

[33]*Ibid.*, Vol. 15, Nos. 13 and 18.

[34]*Ibid.*, Vol. 15, Nos. 8 and 19; and Vol. 17, Nos. 9, 13, 14, 22, and 23.

[35]*Ibid.*, Vol. 17, No. 25.

[36]National Office of Vital Statistics, *Vital Statistics—Special Reports*, Vol. 23, No. 9.

[37]*Ibid.*, Vol. 27, No. 10.

[38]Bureau of the Census, *Marriage and Divorce, 1931*, Washington, 1933, p. 10.

[39]Bureau of the Census, *Marriage and Divorce, 1867-1906*, Part I, Washington, 1909, p. 19.

important one to emerge from a review of the
past—is that no permanent system was developed
which could provide continuously and currently
nationwide statistics on marriage and divorce.
For this reason, the present program of the
National Office of Vital Statistics lays great
stress on the building and perfecting of state
registration systems at the same time that some
essential statistics are provided currently. It is
now clear that the foundation for an enduring program must be built upon central registers of
marriage and divorce records at the state level,
following the general pattern which proved so
successful in providing national birth and death
statistics.

Status of State Registration Systems. Local
filing of marriage records shares a common
heritage with that of births and deaths, dating
back to the seventeenth century in many of the
colonies. Indeed, by the time the United States
was established, two states, Massachusetts and
Vermont, already had some form of marriage
registration. In the ensuing decades, however,
little progress was made. At the start of the
twentieth century only a dozen states and the
District of Columbia had central files. It is noteworthy that all of the New England states fell into
this group.

The early history of central registration does
not have the same significance for divorce. From
the earliest times, divorces were generally
granted by the governors in council and, as the
legislatures took their place, the practice of divorce by private statute evolved. After the United
States gained her independence, this practice continued for more than a half century in the majority
of the states. Gradually, however, the grounds
for absolute divorce began to be defined by the
state legislatures and jurisdiction transferred to
the state courts. For about five decades now these
courts have had sole jurisdiction in all states.
Thus, in large measure, the early history of
central files for divorce records was determined
by the year in which jurisdiction was transferred
from the legislature to the courts. The unique
divorce law enacted early in our history by New
Jersey gives that state the distinction of having
the first state file. In 1795 the Court of Chancery
(now the Chancery Division of the Superior Court)
located in the state capitol, was given sole

jurisdiction over divorce. By 1900 five states
and the District of Columbia maintained a central
file for divorce records.

In the past half century, progress toward state
registration of marriage and divorce records has
been greatly accelerated (Table A11). Today,
three fourths of the states and the District of
Columbia have central files for marriage records;
the last state to enact such legislation was
Kentucky in 1958. Divorce files continue to lag
behind those for marriage, but in recent years
the gap has been reduced. With the file started
in Kentucky on July 1, 1958, two thirds of the
jurisdictions now have central registration.

The fact that a statute exists in a particular
state does not necessarily mean that the law is
enforced, or that the state tabulates and publishes
detailed marriage and divorce statistics. On the
other hand, a few states without central files collect detailed statistics and publish marriage or
divorce data annually. Massachusetts is no doubt
the most outstanding example; the annual vital
statistics report published by the Secretary of
the Commonwealth contains detailed statistics
on divorce and annulment dating back to 1860.[40]
The State Department of Health in Rhode Island
also compiles an annual report on divorce which
includes some detailed statistics, but these facts
have not been published regularly in recent years.

Divorce statistics, dating back to the Civil War,
were also compiled in some detail in both Connecticut and Ohio prior to the establishment of
their state files. In Ohio the reports were compiled and published by the Secretary of State on a
fiscal year basis and included detailed divorce
statistics as well as marriages by county, color,
and month. The Connecticut divorce data were
published together with their marriage registration statistics in the annual vital statistics reports
of the State Department of Health. It should also
be noted that since 1927 the State Judicial Council
of Kansas has published statistics on divorce by
fiscal year. These data, including some details
other than number by county, have appeared in
the October issues of their Bulletin.

In reviewing the history of the first half of
this century, it is evident that while progress
toward nationwide state registration systems for

[40]See Table A11, footnote (e).

marriage and divorce has been accelerated, not enough has been accomplished. The program has lacked the coordinated efforts which proved so successful in establishing national birth and death registration areas. It should be recalled that at the turn of the century the situation was not much more favorable for the latter than for marriage and divorce, yet by 1919 all states had laws with regard to registration of births and deaths and by 1933 these laws were satisfactorily enforced throughout the country. It is apparent that the Joint Resolution by Congress in 1903, urging the states to cooperate with the federal government, played a vital role in bringing about national statistics on births and deaths. The cooperative state-federal efforts which followed brought success within three decades. The two elements of the program were the building of state registration systems and the annual publication of statistics for the expanding registration areas. Each element was necessary; neither alone would have been sufficient. The central files provided the source from which statistics could be gathered; the annual statistics gave a certain degree of prestige to states in the registration area and thus stimulated the others to attain the same distinction.

Many organizations and individuals have now come to the realization that similar action must be taken if we are to have adequate national statistics on marriage and divorce. The Association of State and Territorial Health Officers, in December, 1946, endorsed the central registration of marriage and divorce records or official abstracts in state health departments. The American Sociological Society at its 1947 Annual Meeting took action to express its concern over the need for more adequate marriage and divorce data. The American Public Health Association, The Population Association of America, the Technical Advisory Committee on Population for the 17th Decennial Census, and several other professional groups have also taken action recently. The Public Health Conference on Records and Statistics has also shown an active interest in this area, and has a Working Group investigating the problem.

Recognition of the need for state statutes is not new, however. As early as 1906 the National Congress on Uniform Divorce Laws passed a resolution calling upon the states to enact legislation providing for the annual collection and publication of uniform statistics on marriage and divorce. This proposal placed a dual burden on the states, namely, that of collecting the records or statistics from the local areas and of summarizing and publishing them. If one considers the diversity of the statistics on births and deaths made available by the states even today, it is apparent that national detailed data on marriage and divorce will never become available if the responsibility is placed wholly on state initiative. Accordingly, present plans call for a pattern similar to that followed with regard to births and deaths.

As in the case of births and deaths, aside from providing a source of statistical data, the basic records of marriage and divorce have many legal, personal, social, health, and welfare uses. Just as birth and death registrations indicate the beginning or ending of the life of an individual, so do the marriage and divorce registrations indicate the beginning or ending of the life of a family. Documentary proof of marriage may be required as evidence of marital status and of family relationship—for example, to prove legitimacy of offspring or responsibility for support, the right to receive insurance or pension benefits, the right to an inheritance, ability to establish citizenship, or to establish exemption from liability to military service. The administration of the social security program, veterans' benefits, workmen's compensation, and other public welfare and health programs require, at some stage of operation, proof of marriage or its termination. The divorce certificate, or other proof of the termination of a marriage, may also be needed to prove the right to remarry, to obtain release from financial obligation to the former spouse, or to establish the right of the wife and children to alimony and support. In the absence of central files, an individual needing copies of marriage or divorce records may be confronted with the task of inquiring among hundreds of local offices to discover the one in which his records are filed. Moreover, until every state has central registers of both marriage and divorce records, there can be no effective provisions for endorsing the fact of divorce upon the central record of marriage, thus leaving open an avenue of fraud.

RECORDS AND PROCEDURE

All states have marriage-recording statutes of some kind. These statutes universally require the issuing officer to record the license at the time of issuance, and generally prescribe that the officiant return the license or certificate to the issuing officer after the marriage is performed. Beyond these essentials, there are wide variations in practice among the states. There are also serious deficiencies in the completeness of reporting and in the accuracy and quality of the information given on reports which are filed at both the local and state levels. At one extreme, in Texas for example, the law does not require the issuing officer to ascertain the ages of the parties or even to file the original license (which in many counties is given to the couple). In several other states, the situation is not much better, with the result that only the number of licenses issued can be ascertained—a figure which is generally 2 per cent greater than the number of marriages occurring.[41] Moreover, in but few states do the laws, records, and procedures conform to those required for efficient registration and/or tabulation of meaningful statistics. Indeed, judged by two states with better than average procedures (New Jersey[42] and New York[43]), the number of marriages in the United States may be overstated by almost 1 per cent a year due to the treatment of second ceremonies as if they were original marriages.

To remove these discrepancies and differences and to ensure an adequate foundation for nationwide efficient registration and comprehensive statistics, various proposals have been made from time to time. Those which follow are based largely on the tentative recommendations made by the Bureau of the Census in 1943,[44] and by the current Working Group on Marriage and Divorce of the Public Health Conference on Records and Statistics.[45]

Registration Areas. The National Office of Vital Statistics should establish, supervise, and promote registration areas for marriage and divorce comparable to the birth and death registration areas. To be eligible for admission to the registration area, a state should meet four minimum requirements:

1. Adopt the standard definition of the event.
2. Use an approved certificate or certified transcript. This should include the essential details about the event and the personal particulars of the participants. In addition to the standard items required for administrative purposes and routine statistical tabulations, states should be encouraged to include on their record forms such other details as will enable the central file to serve as a depository of information for special intensive analyses of the events.
3. All local areas transmit completed records to the state agency within a specified time interval after the event.
4. Attain a minimum percentage of completeness of registration (approximately 90 per cent).

In addition, a state once admitted to the registration area should continue to administer its laws conscientiously. The state should also file marriage and divorce records in an orderly manner, exercising the same care and observing the same standards for their receipt, filing, and indexing as it does with birth and death records.

Marriage. Under the Constitution of the United States, authority to regulate marriage is left to the jurisdiction of the several states. In consequence, the legal definition of marriage varies from state to state. For purposes of nationwide registration and statistics, however, it is necessary and sufficient to define marriage as that procedure which is licensed and recorded by a particular state and which inaugurates the status (or relationship) of husband and wife. By the very nature of the event, a marriage which is not

---

[41]National Office of Vital Statistics, "Comparison of marriages with marriage licenses," *Vital Statistics—Special Reports*, Vol. 31, No. 16, p. 222; Vol. 36, No. 2, p. 15; Vol. 37, No. 3, p. 53.

[42]In 1947, records of second marriage ceremonies accounted for more than one in 100 of the total marriage records filed with the New Jersey State Registrar. See Thomas P. Monahan, *The Pattern of Age at Marriage in the United States*, Stephenson-Brothers, Philadelphia, 1951, Vol. I, p. 182.

[43]See Appendix Note 1.

[44]U.S. Congress, *Measures Relating to Vital Records and Vital Statistics*, House Document No. 242, 78th Congress, 1st Session, Union Calendar No. 214, Washington, 1943, pp. 165-176.

[45]See also report of U.S. National Committee on Vital and Health Statistics, "National Vital Statistics Needs," in National Office of Vital Statistics, *Vital Statistics—Special Reports*, Vol. 45, No. 11, pp. 219-269, and report of Committee on Marriage and Divorce Statistics, American Sociological Society, "The Need for Nationwide Marriage and Divorce Statistics," *American Sociological Review*, 23: 306-312, June, 1958.

licensed and recorded, e.g., common law, is excluded. Of much greater significance is the fact that the definition also excludes second marriage ceremonies. Many of these are religious ceremonies conducted under authority of the original license (see Appendix Note 1). However, the second ceremony should be excluded even if it is performed under authorization of a new license from a different jurisdiction, since the status of husband and wife did not arise from the second ceremony but existed since its inauguration by the first ceremony. Moreover, the fact that there may be some question regarding the legality of the original marriage does not alter the situation as to how the second marriage ceremony should be treated.[46] Indeed, if we did not accept the license to marry as evidence of the legality of a marriage, registration and enumeration would be almost impossible, since some void or voidable marriages are not so declared for years and others never are.

How should second marriage ceremonies be processed? Obviously, there is no problem if the second ceremony is to take place under authorization of the license from the original issuing office. In such cases, the second certificate should be given the same license and state file numbers as the original certificate and be filed with it, as is done in Connecticut, in preference to the practice in some jurisdictions of maintaining a separate file for second ceremony records. The fact that the certificate is for a second (or subsequent) ceremony should be clearly indicated on its face, possibly by the use of a rubber stamp reading:

SECOND CEREMONY
Original Marriage on (date) at (place)

The situation is somewhat more complicated when a couple planning a second ceremony make the mistake of applying for a new license. In such a case, the first problem is to detect the true situation. If the couple do not report that they are already married, the information may be disclosed by two items on the application. These are

"number of previous marriages" and "last marriage ended by." If for no other reason, it is urgent that these items be included on the marriage record (Figure 1). Once the true situation is ascertained, it is possible in most cases to direct the couple to the original issuing office for a copy of the original license. When for any reason this is not possible, but the couple can produce proof of marriage and they also meet the marriage regulations of the jurisdiction in which they are applying, a license may be issued in accordance with the procedure for an original marriage.[47] Such marriage records, however, should be identified with the "Second Ceremony" stamp. It should also be so identified in the local and state indexes. Moreover, like all other second ceremonies, it should be excluded from the marriage statistics.

In the great preponderance of applications, an original marriage is involved. In such cases, it is desirable that both the prospective bride and groom appear before the local licensing authority and there prepare and sign the application for the marriage license (see Appendix Note 2). This form should show the personal particulars of the parties corresponding to those eventually entered on the standard marriage record (Figure 1). The couple are given any forms that need to be filled in before the license is issued. These may include proof of identity, residence, and age; doctor's certification as to physical condition; consent of parents or guardian for underage persons; and proof of dissolution of last marriage, if previously married.

After having acquired the necessary documents in compliance with the law, the prospective bride and groom return to the local marriage office.[48] All forms required by the state are left with the authorizing officer and he affixes his signature to the marriage license granting authority for the performance of the marriage ceremony.

Following the marriage ceremony, which should be performed within thirty days after issuance of the license,[49] the officiant endorses the place and

---

[46]For example, some persons who are divorced in Massachusetts avoid the two-year ban on remarriage for defendants by marrying in New Hampshire. Then, to "assure" the legality of their marital status, after the two-year period has elapsed, the couple is "married a second time" in Massachusetts.

[47]New York's attorney general has ruled that such "marriages" cannot be forbidden.

[48]The licensing officer should have authority to take such steps as he deems necessary to verify the facts about the applicants prior to issuance of the license.

[49]A time limit is generally set between the medical examination and the application for issuance of the marriage

DEPARTMENT OF PUBLIC HEALTH

_____ (State) _____

OF VITAL STATISTICS

_____ (Division)

STANDARD RECORD OF MARRIAGE

FORM APPROVED
BUDGET BUREAU NO. 68-R546

| COUNTY | STATE FILE NO. |

APPLICATION FOR MARRIAGE LICENSE — **GROOM**

| 1. NAME a. (First) b. (Middle) c. (Last) | 2. DATE OF BIRTH (Month) (Day) (Year) |

| 3. USUAL RESIDENCE a. STATE b. COUNTY | 4. PLACE OF BIRTH (State or foreign country) |

| c. CITY OR TOWN (If outside corporate limits write RURAL and give township) | 5. PREVIOUS MARITAL STATUS NEVER MARRIED ☐ LAST MARRIAGE ENDED BY: DEATH ☐ DIVORCE ☐ ANNULMENT ☐ |

| 6. NUMBER OF PREVIOUS MARRIAGES____ ☐ NONE | 7. COLOR OR RACE WHITE ☐ NEGRO ☐ OTHER ☐ (specify)____ | 8a. USUAL OCCUPATION | 8b. KIND OF BUSINESS OR INDUSTRY |

BRIDE

| 9a. NAME a. (First) b. (Middle) c. (Last) | 10. DATE OF BIRTH (Month) (Day) (Year) |

9b. MAIDEN NAME IF DIFFERENT

| 11. USUAL RESIDENCE a. STATE b. COUNTY | 12. PLACE OF BIRTH (State or foreign country) |

| c. CITY OR TOWN (If outside corporate limits write RURAL and give township) | 13. PREVIOUS MARITAL STATUS NEVER MARRIED ☐ LAST MARRIAGE ENDED BY: DEATH ☐ DIVORCE ☐ ANNULMENT ☐ |

| 14. NUMBER OF PREVIOUS MARRIAGES____ ☐ NONE | 15. COLOR OR RACE WHITE ☐ NEGRO ☐ OTHER ☐ (specify)____ | 16a. USUAL OCCUPATION | 16b. KIND OF BUSINESS OR INDUSTRY |

| DATE | SIGNATURE(S) OF APPLICANT(S) |

CERTIFICATION

| DATE OF MARRIAGE (Month) (Day) (Year) | PLACE OF MARRIAGE (County) (State) |

| DATE OF RECORDING | SIGNATURE AND TITLE OF OFFICIAL MAKING RETURN TO STATE DEPARTMENT OF HEALTH |

(left margin: NEW-LEX., KY. DEPARTMENT OF HEALTH, EDUCATION, AND WELFARE · · PUBLIC HEALTH SERVICE 6-54 PHS-2039)

Figure 1. Standard Record of Marriage

Other desirable items:
a) Type of marriage ceremony—Religious, Civil, or Other (specify)
b) If previously married—
  (1) date when last marriage ended
  (2) number of children under age 18

date of marriage on the marriage form and he and the witnesses affix their signatures as provided by law. The officiant then gives a marriage certificate to the couple, and sends the official marriage record to the proper local authority within

seven days after the ceremony.[50] The local officer completes his record of the marriage and sends a copy of the completed marriage certificate, or transcript thereof, to the state registrar no later than ten days after the calendar month in which he received the marriage certificate.

license, and this purpose is defeated unless a time limit is also set for validity of the license after its issuance. A relatively short period also improves the chances of following up unreported marriages and thus makes for more complete registration.

[50]To assist with the follow-up of unreported marriages, the issuing officer could give the couple a post card form, to be returned after the marriage with the name of the officiant and the date of marriage entered thereon. It is also recommended that the officiant maintain his own record of the marriage for at least three months.

The issuing officer should be paid a specified fee for each certificate or transcript forwarded by him to the state office—the fee to be paid by the applicants for the license together with the license fee. It would also appear advisable, expecially in states which attract a large number of nonresident marriages, to levy an additional fee to cover the expense of maintaining the state file and publishing statistics.

Divorce. The procedures with regard to divorce, of necessity, are very different from those for marriage. The original divorce records are never filed elsewhere than in the office of the court which granted the decree. Thus the records in existing state files are at best certified copies from the clerk of the court and may merely be unverified transcripts. In addition, the final decrees filed by our courts are generally devoid of personal particulars about the participants. In most actions, the judgment includes only the names and such other information as is deemed sufficient to identify the parties. Yet, in view of the court action required for a divorce, it should be comparatively easy to obtain, in almost every case, and quite accurately, the facts needed for administrative and statistical purposes.

One other factor complicates the situation that exists today, namely, the lack of a definition of divorce for registration and statistical purposes. The problem has two aspects. On the one hand, most jurisdictions which now have central files do not distinguish between decrees which dissolve (or nullify) a marriage and those which legalize separation of the spouses. At the same time, due to the fact that the law varies from state to state, and also because of the unrestricted mobility of our population, one or both spouses may petition and obtain decrees from different jurisdictions. It is clear that both aspects of the problem result in overstatement of the national divorce rate.

In view of the above, for purposes of nationwide registration and statistics, it is necessary and sufficient to define divorce as the first decree by any jurisdiction which either dissolves the marriage bond or declares it void. Thus final decrees of absolute divorce (divorce *a vinculo matrimonii*),[51] annulment, or dissolution of marriage

(Enoch Arden decrees in New York State) fall within the definition. On the other hand, all forms of separations or limited decrees are excluded— for example, decrees variously termed divorce *a mensa et thoro*, separate maintenance, legal separation, bed and board, alimony, or limited divorce.[52] The definition also excludes a final decree of absolute divorce if the defendant had previously obtained an annulment or absolute divorce from the plaintiff. At present, the fact that the defendant has obtained a divorce from the plaintiff in another jurisdiction is in itself a legal ground for divorce in Florida, Michigan, and Ohio. In all other states, a "second" decree must be obtained on some other ground, such as desertion, adultery, cruelty, etc.

All forms for a "second" decree should be prepared at the local office as if for a "first" decree. However, the fact that it is for a "second" decree should be clearly indicated on its face, possibly by the use of a rubber stamp reading:

Defendant Obtained		Absolute Divorce Annulment	Decree
on	(date)	at	(place)

The records for these decrees, with appropriate identification, should be included in the state's divorce file and index, but excluded from the divorce statistics. However, because of the value of such information, it is recommended that states publish the number of "second" decrees, classified by year versus place of the "first" decree.

As a general principle, the information required for preparing the divorce record (Figure 2) should be a statutory prerequisite to the granting of the decree. The filing of the record, in a manner approved by the state registrar, should be a duty of the clerk of court in which the decree is granted. He should have authority to obtain and verify the personal particulars of the parties from the plaintiff or his attorney and, if possible, also from the defendant. When the decree becomes final, the court clerk should enter the facts regarding the decree on the state record and send

[51] This is true whether or not the decree of absolute divorce specifies certain restrictions on remarriage, for example, the three-year-remarriage ban on defendants in New York State actions.

[52] If limited decrees are reported to the state agency, it is desirable that the form used be clearly distinguishable from that for absolute decrees. Also, such forms should be kept in a separate file until such time, if ever, that a certificate of absolute divorce is filed. Finally, if statistics on limited decrees are desired by the state, they should be tabulated and published separately.

_____ DEPARTMENT OF PUBLIC HEALTH
(State)

_____ OF VITAL STATISTICS
(Division)

FORM APPROVED
BUDGET BUREAU NO. 68-R547

STATE FILE NO.

| COUNTY | STANDARD RECORD OF | LOCAL FILE NO. |
| ☐ DIVORCE OR ☐ ANNULMENT |

HUSBAND

1. NAME a. (First) b. (Middle) c. (Last)	2. DATE (Month) (Day) (Year) OF BIRTH
3. USUAL RESIDENCE a. (City) b. (County) c. (State)	4. PLACE (State or foreign country) OF BIRTH
5. NUMBER OF THIS MARRIAGE	6. RACE OR COLOR WHITE ☐ NEGRO ☐ OTHER ☐ (specify)_____	7a. USUAL OCCUPATION	7b. KIND OF BUSINESS OR INDUSTRY

WIFE

8. MAIDEN NAME a. (First) b. (Middle) c. (Last)	9. DATE (Month) (Day) (Year) OF BIRTH
10. USUAL RESIDENCE a. (City) b. (County) c. (State)	11. PLACE (State or foreign country) OF BIRTH
11. NUMBER OF THIS MARRIAGE	13. COLOR OR RACE WHITE ☐ NEGRO ☐ OTHER ☐ (specify)_____	14a. USUAL OCCUPATION	14b. KIND OF BUSINESS OR INDUSTRY

| 15. PLACE OF THIS MARRIAGE   a. (County)   b. (State or foreign country) | 16. DATE OF (Month) (Day) (Year) MARRIAGE |
| 17. NUMBER OF CHILDREN UNDER 18 | 18. PLAINTIFF   HUSBAND ☐ WIFE ☐ ____ | 19. DECREE GRANTED TO   HUSBAND ☐ WIFE ☐ ____ | 20. LEGAL GROUNDS FOR DECREE |

I hereby certify that the above persons were divorced on: (Month)   (Day)   (Year) | DATE OF RECORDING   (Month)   (Day)   (Year) |

| SIGNATURE OF COURT OFFICIAL | TITLE OF COURT OFFICIAL |

(left margin vertical text) HEW-LS., KY. • PUBLIC HEALTH SERVICE • DEPARTMENT OF HEALTH, EDUCATION, AND WELFARE • 6-54 • PHS-2040

Figure 2. Standard Record of Divorce or Annulment

Other desirable items:
a) Number of children awarded to custody of Husband, Wife, or Other (specify)
b) Date and place last lived together

it to the state agency no later than ten days after the calendar month in which the decree became final.

The clerk of court should be paid a specified fee for each record prepared and forwarded by him to the state office. This fee should be assessed by the court as part of the costs for the absolute divorce or annulment. In addition, the court should assess a sum to cover the expense of maintaining the state file, cross-indexing the decree to the marriage record, and publishing statistics.

FUTURE OUTLOOK

It is encouraging that an increasing number of states have provided by law for centralizing their marriage and divorce records, and have also taken steps to furnish current detailed statistics on these vital events. However, much more will have to be accomplished before a nationwide program of comprehensive statistics is in operation.

To throw light on some of the problems involved, in 1949 the National Office of Vital

Statistics made a survey of the status of state marriage and divorce records. Such problems as degree of registration, definition and comparability of items, and completeness of entries for items on certificates were explored. The information from this survey has proved valuable in initiating an interim, state-federal program for providing some detailed statistics on marriage and divorce. The program represents a new approach to the problem; those states which are able and willing to cooperate furnish prepared tables of statistics to the National Office, which consolidates and publishes them in *Vital Statistics of the United States* and *Vital Statistics—Special Reports*. Statistics on marriages and divorces by place of occurrence have since been published starting with data for 1948; the reports have also included such details as county and month of occurrence, age, race, marital and residence status, grounds for divorce, number of children, and duration of the marriages dissolved.[53]

What are the prospects for national statistics on a regular basis? It should be recalled that the two basic ingredients which helped establish national statistics on births and deaths were:

1. The Joint Resolution by Congress in 1903 which led to a comprehensive nationwide policy, and resulted in coordinated efforts toward state registration systems.

2. Authorization for the Bureau of the Census to tabulate and publish statistics for the expanding registration areas on a regular basis.

No doubt passage of a congressional resolution with regard to marriage and divorce would accelerate enactment of fundamentally uniform registration laws by all states. It is also likely that such statutes would ultimately be legislated in all states, without a resolution by Congress, provided the National Office of Vital Statistics continued its current program. However, this is dependent on two conditions.

First, unlike the program for births and deaths, there is no "legal" basis for Congress to continue to authorize the National Office to carry on this work. Passage of a joint resolution by Congress would change this; but, until such or similar action is taken, the National Office's program will remain a year-to-year project.[54] In this connection, it should be recalled that prior to World War II similar plans were launched for a continuing program but these were soon curtailed and then completely abandoned because of the war.

Second, and equally important, the present marriage and divorce program places too much responsibility for its success on the states. No doubt, better results would be obtained if the states were instructed to classify, code, and punch their data on IBM cards according to uniform specifications. The National Office could then compile statistics from these cards. Also, some characteristics could be tabulated on a sample basis. Nevertheless, it is not likely that a permanent and comprehensive program could ever be established in this manner.

Our objective must remain, therefore, to follow the path which proved so successful for births and deaths. Each state should be responsible for maintaining an efficient central file and for forwarding transcripts of their records to the National Office of Vital Statistics, on the same basis as applies to birth and death records. The National Office, in turn, should be authorized by Congress to compile and publish the statistics derived therefrom. Not until such a program has been started can we look forward to accurate, complete, and detailed annual statistics on marriage and divorce for the United States.

[53] The National Office of Vital Statistics has also explored the possibility of obtaining marriage data through the Current Population Surveys of the Bureau of the Census. See Hugh Carter, P. C. Glick, and S. Lewit, "Some Demographic Characteristics of Recently Married Persons: Comparisons of Registration Data and Sample Survey Data," *American Sociological Review*, 20:165-172, April, 1955.

[54] A good "straw in the wind" is furnished by the District of Columbia, since it is the only area of the country in which marriage and divorce are under federal jurisdiction. To date, the clerk of the District Court for the District of Columbia has not participated in the current program of supplying pretabulated marriage and divorce statistics.

Chapter 1

THE TREND OF MARRIAGE

IN "normal" years, the marriage rate in the United States is higher than in most countries of the world. But "normal" years may be elusive. A number of factors such as war and the state of the economy affect the marriage rate, which in turn affects the supply of marriage eligibles. Thus the marriage record for a specific year must be considered in relation to these factors and to the marriage rate of preceding years.

THE CRUDE RATE AND OTHER INDICES OF MARRIAGE

A rate is a measure of the relative frequency with which an event occurs. Mathematically speaking, it has a chance or probability meaning, e.g., the chance that a marriage will occur among a defined group of persons eligible to marry. However, it is not always possible or desirable to use such an index. In some circumstances, it may be sufficient that the index, usually a ratio, indicate approximately how the relative frequency of the event has changed from one year to the next, or how it varies from group to group.

The computation of the former type of rate requires detailed data on both the event and the population exposed. Primarily due to the absence of such detailed statistics for marriages, but also because such information cannot be made available until some time after the event, a less specific, gross measure is generally employed as the index of the current marriage rate.

The most common index, for this purpose, is the number of marriages per 1,000 total population—sometimes called the crude marriage rate. To compute this rate for the United States in 1930, for example, it is necessary to know only the number of marriages performed during 1930 and the total population of the country at midyear. Thus, with 1,126,856 marriages reported in the United States during 1930 and the total population estimated at 123,077,000 on July 1, 1930, the rate

was 9.2 per 1,000. These rates for the years since 1860 are given in Table 2. Obviously, this index measures the frequency with which marriages occurred; to obtain the rate at which people married, it is necessary to double the above figure. In other words, the rate at which persons married in 1930 was 18.4 per 1,000.

The latter refinement, however, adds little to our knowledge of the event. Moreover, neither index measures the propensity to marry; each one is based on the total population, a large proportion of which is already married or under the legal age for marriage. The marriage rate per 1,000 eligible persons serves this purpose, and is easily computed since the only additional information required is the number of the divorced, the widowed, and the single who have attained a specified age. This age is generally taken as 15 years,[1] since relatively few females and only an occasional male marry at an earlier age in the United States. According to this definition, there were about 17,575,000 eligible males in the United States in 1930. Thus, the marriage rate for eligible males was 64 per 1,000. The comparable rate for eligible females, who were somewhat fewer in number, was 67 per 1,000. In other words, about $6\frac{1}{2}$ per cent of the eligibles married during 1930.

How closely does the crude marriage rate parallel the rates based on the eligible population? As may be seen from Table 2, the over-all pattern is fairly similar; the crude rate, however, is a less sensitive index. This was particularly true in periods of general upswing or decline, and also in years immediately following sharp fluctuations. The deviations between the two types of rates were especially marked in the years after World War II. This resulted from the high birth rate, which increased the total population, at the

---

[1] The legal minimum age is not used since it varies from state to state and is frequently circumvented by "migration" from a state with a high minimum to one with a lower age.

same time that the high marriage rate decreased the eligible population. Thus eligibles as a proportion of the total population declined. Prior to World War I, by contrast, the decline in eligibles resulting from the upswing in marriages was offset by the increasing number of persons attaining the eligible ages and by immigrant adults. Accordingly, the ratio of eligibles to the total population remained fairly constant, and in consequence the crude marriage rate closely paralleled the refined rate.

The marriage rate is also affected by trends in other components of the population, such as the balance of the sexes. This subject is discussed in a later section of this chapter. At this point, however, it should be noted that as a result of the relatively greater increase of females in our adult population, the marriage rate for eligible females, although higher than for males, was converging prior to 1939; since that year the male rate has been higher and the two rates have been diverging. Thus, in a comprehensive analysis of the trend of marriage, the rates for both eligible males and females must be considered. For some purposes, however, the rate may be computed for the two sexes combined, as the number of persons marrying per 1,000 eligibles. It is also possible to compute the rates for each sex and combine them by means of a standard weighting factor, such as the proportionate distribution of the two sexes at the last census. Obviously, simplification of the index results in loss of some information.

Since changes in the composition of our population completely determine the efficiency of the crude marriage rate as a measure of the trend

Table 2. Number of Marriages and Marriage Rates, United States, 1860-1956

Year	Number	Rate per 1,000 Total Population	Marriage Eligibles Male	Marriage Eligibles Female	Year	Number	Rate per 1,000 Total Population	Marriage Eligibles Male	Marriage Eligibles Female
1860	256,000	9.3	71	83	1909	897,354	9.9	64	74
1861	232,000	8.2	61	69					
1862	236,000	7.9	58	65	1910	948,166	10.3	66	77
1863	256,000	7.7	60	66	1911	955,287	10.2	66	76
1864	282,000	8.2	62	68	1912	1,004,602	10.5	69	79
1865	334,000	9.4	71	77	1913	1,021,398	10.5	69	79
1866	354,000	9.7	73	78	1914	1,025,092	10.3	69	78
1867	357,000	9.6	71	76	1915	1,007,595	10.0	68	76
1868	345,000	9.0	67	71	1916	1,075,775	10.6	72	80
1869	348,000	8.9	66	69	1917	1,144,200	11.1	77	84
					1918	1,000,109	9.6	67	73
1870	352,000	8.8	66	68	1919	1,150,186	10.9	77	83
1871	359,000	8.8	65	68					
1872	378,000	9.0	66	69	1920	1,274,476	12.0	84	92
1873	386,000	9.0	66	69	1921	1,163,863	10.7	76	83
1874	385,000	8.7	64	67	1922	1,134,151	10.3	74	79
1875	409,000	9.1	66	70	1923	1,229,784	11.0	79	85
1876	405,000	8.8	64	68	1924	1,184,574	10.4	74	80
1877	411,000	8.7	63	67	1925	1,188,334	10.3	74	79
1878	423,000	8.8	63	68	1926	1,202,574	10.2	73	78
1879	438,000	8.9	64	69	1927	1,201,053	10.1	72	77
					1928	1,182,497	9.8	70	74
1880	453,000	9.0	65	71	1929	1,232,559	10.1	71	76
1881	464,000	9.0	64	70					
1882	484,000	9.2	64	70	1930	1,126,856	9.2	64	67
1883	501,000	9.3	64	70	1931	1,060,914	8.6	59	62
1884	485,000	8.8	60	66	1932	981,903	7.9	54	56
1885	507,000	8.9	60	67	1933	1,098,000	8.7	59	62
1886	534,000	9.2	62	69	1934	1,302,000	10.3	70	72
1887	513,000	8.7	58	64	1935	1,327,000	10.4	71	72
1888	535,000	8.8	58	65	1936	1,369,000	10.7	73	74
1889	563,000	9.1	60	67	1937	1,451,296	11.3	77	78
					1938	1,330,780	10.3	70	71
1890	570,000	9.0	59	67	1939	1,403,633	10.7	74	74
1891	592,000	9.2	60	67					
1892	601,000	9.2	60	67	1940	1,595,879	12.1	84	83
1893	601,000	9.0	59	66	1941	1,695,999	12.7	90	89
1894	588,000	8.6	56	63	1942	1,772,132	13.1	95	94
1895	620,000	8.9	58	65	1943	1,577,050	11.5	85	84
1896	635,000	9.0	58	65	1944	1,452,394	10.5	78	76
1897	643,000	8.9	58	65	1945	1,612,992	11.5	87	84
1898	647,000	8.8	57	64	1946	2,291,045	16.2	126	120
1899	673,000	9.0	59	66	1947	1,991,878	13.8	113	107
					1948	1,811,155	12.4	104	98
1900	709,000	9.3	61	68	1949	1,579,798	10.6	92	86
1901	742,000	9.6	62	70					
1902	776,000	9.8	64	72	1950	1,667,231	11.0	98	91
1903	818,000	10.1	66	74	1951	1,594,694	10.3	95	87
1904	815,000	9.9	64	73	1952	1,539,318	9.8	92	84
1905	842,000	10.0	65	74	1953	1,545,234	9.7	93	84
1906	895,000	10.5	68	77	1954	1,490,897	9.2	89	80
1907	936,936	10.8	70	80	1955	1,541,485	9.3	93	82
1908	857,461	9.7	62	72	1956	1,585,076	9.4	95	84

Note: Population excludes slaves prior to 1865; includes armed forces overseas during 1917-1919 and 1940-1956. All population figures for 1951-1956 are provisional. Marriage eligibles include single persons aged 15 years or over and all divorced or widowed persons.

Source: Number of marriages for 1867-1956 are largely from the National Office of Vital Statistics; those for 1860-1866 are estimated by the author.

of marriage, it is possible to project our evaluation into the near future. Until about 1970, there will be an increasing proportion of children in our population. Thus, should the marriage rate per 1,000 eligibles rise, the crude index will understate the magnitude of the increase. More likely, however, the rate based on marriage eligibles will remain virtually stationary or even decline somewhat further. In the former contingency (virtually stationary), the crude rate will fall; in the latter case, the crude rate will overstate the extent of the decrease. In other words, the crude rate will not be too reliable an index in the years immediately ahead.

HISTORICAL REVIEW OF THE MARRIAGE TREND

Over the past 100 years, the marriage rate has varied widely from year to year but has shown a general upswing. In 1860, when the country stood on the threshold of the war between the states, only about 256,000 marriages occurred during the year. Currently, five times that number would represent an off year for marriage. In 1956, for example, there were as many as 1,585,000 marriages in the country, despite the fact that the supply of eligible men and women had been markedly reduced by the unusually high marriage rates of the preceding decade.

While the long-term trend has been upward, the pattern has not been uniform. As may be seen from Table 2, the turn of the century delineates two distinct periods. Prior to 1900, the annual rate hovered close to 9 marriages per 1,000 total population. Since that time, the rate has been definitely upward and subject to increasingly marked fluctuations.

At first glance, the stability of the marriage rate during the earlier period appears unbelievable; from 1868 to 1900, the crude rate never fell below 8.6 or rose above 9.3. This occurred in an era of reconstruction, expansion, and transition, the equal of which had never previously been experienced by any country in the world. Almost each year, billions of dollars of new wealth were added to the national output as our industrial enterprises grew by leaps and bounds and our population spread westward occupying practically every acre of arable or grazing land. These were

years also in which immigrants were flowing into our eastern ports. Some moved westward to occupy the free lands, but by far the larger number settled in cities and sought employment in industries and commerce. In consequence, our urban communities grew rapidly. In fact, despite the widespread movement to farms in the West and Midwest, the urban population increased from 25.7 per cent of the country's total in 1870 to 39.7 per cent in 1900.

No doubt marriages were less completely recorded prior to 1900 than after that year. It is also likely that common-law marriages, which are not included in the marriage statistics, were more frequent. However, while these eventualities may have contributed to the relatively low recorded marriage rate, they cannot account for the absence of marked annual fluctuations. The only explanation seems to be that the events of that era, despite their magnitude, did not affect a sufficiently large segment of the population. This judgment appears to be supported by the marriage trend during the Civil War. Here was one event during this period which markedly affected almost all of the country's population. From all the evidence that is available (Tables 2 and A12), its effect on marriage was immediate and marked; the rate per 1,000 total population dropped from 9.3 in 1860 to about 7.7 in 1863 at the height of the conflict. Moreover, in compensation for the marriages postponed during hostilities, the rate climbed to a postwar high of 9.7 in 1866. It is noteworthy that the crude rate during the Civil War, which may have been the lowest in our history, was not approached again until the depression year of 1932.

The twentieth century ushered in a new phase in the marriage trend. Within a few years, by 1903, the annual rate climbed above 10 marriages per 1,000 total population and it remained at that level with few exceptions through 1951. This second period is also notable for increasingly marked fluctuations in the annual marriage rate. Several factors have contributed to this situation, but fundamentally they are all interrelated. The past half century was an era in which man gained partial mastery over his physical environment, but in doing so he became increasingly dependent on his fellow man. In consequence, fluctuations in the economy have become more intense and international conflicts have broadened in scope. Thus, it is not the marital habits or attitudes of the population that have changed, but rather the character of events—each new war, depression, or boom has affected in a similar manner the personal outlook of more and more young people. It is still true that young people marry when times are good and postpone marriage when conditions are unfavorable.

MARRIAGE AND THE ECONOMY

That the level of the marriage rate is influenced by economic conditions has been known for a long time.[2] When the harvest was good, which meant prosperity for agricultural communities, the marriage rate rose; poor crops, on the other hand, were followed by fewer marriages. Early in the industrial revolution, the harvest lost its exclusive role in determining economic well-being. Nevertheless, for many years up to about the middle of the last century, the price of such provisions as wheat, corn, and rye remained a useful measure of economic prosperity. More recently, as industrialization has progressed, business failures, unemployment, industrial production, and other more complex indices have proved to be excellent barometers of the economy.[3] Regardless of the measure used, these indices invariably show a close parallel between business conditions and the marriage rate. When the contrast between depression and prosperity is not very marked, as was generally true in former years, the effects on the marriage rate are relatively slight. On the other hand, in a widespread and severe depression such as that of the 1930's, the effects are likely to be very pronounced. This relationship is well illustrated by the experience in the United States.

Although the effects of depressions on the national marriage rate were not very marked prior to 1930, it is likely that the rate declined substantially in some areas and components of the population. From a review of marriages in the United States between 1870 and 1930, it has been shown[4] that the fluctuations of the rate for eligible persons were wider in a group of highly industrialized states (Connecticut, Massachusetts, Ohio, Rhode Island, Vermont, and the District of Columbia) than in a group with lesser industrialization (Illinois, Kansas, Maryland, Michigan, Minnesota, and Wisconsin). For example, during the depression of 1873-1877, the rate dropped by 19 per cent in the former group but only by 14 per cent in the latter.[5] Moreover, since the decrease for the country as a whole was of much smaller magnitude (Table 2), the South and other areas of the country must have been even less affected if at all. Our frontier areas, in particular, were probably unaffected. In fact, it is possible that the recurrent business reverses in the industrialized areas may have contributed to the development of the West. Faced with the need to postpone marriage due to the lack of employment opportunities in their own communities, many young people may have elected to move westward to take possession of the new lands.

In 1923, a year of prosperity following World War I, the marriage rate rose to 11.0 per 1,000 total population. In the next few years, there was a general decline to about 10 per 1,000. On October 29, 1929, however, the collapse of the stock market in New York marked the beginning of the severest and most prolonged depression in our history. With millions of persons thrown out of work, the marriage rate plunged downward for three consecutive years to a low of 7.9 in 1932. Although this may not have been the lowest crude rate in our history, it is unlikely that a decline of similar magnitude had ever previously occurred. Moreover, only $5\frac{1}{2}$ per cent of the eligible population married during that year, which is a lower proportion than at any time since before the Civil War (Table 2).

As business recovered, after the 1932 presidential election inaugurated the "Roosevelt Era," the marriage rate rebounded. It was above 10 per 1,000 by 1934, and continued upward to 11.3

[2]For reference to studies on this relationship, dating back to Süszmilch's in 1775, see J. H. van Zanten and T. van den Brink, "Population Phenomena in Amsterdam," *Population*, December, 1937, pp. 7-11.

[3]See, for example, "The Marriage Rate and the Business Cycle," *Statistical Bulletin* (Metropolitan Life Insurance Company), July, 1938, pp. 1-3, which compares the marriage rate in selected states with business failures in the country.

[4]Walter F. Willcox, *Introduction to the Vital Statistics of the United States, 1900 to 1930*, Bureau of the Census, Washington, 1933, pp. 83-84, 135-137.

[5]During the 1930's, by contrast, marriages per 1,000 eligibles fell off by about 25 per cent in the country as a whole.

in 1937. Then followed a decline to 10.3 during the recession of 1938, after which it again rose sharply with the increased economic activity resulting from our defense efforts.

One aspect of the decline in marriages during a depression has long been of concern to sociologists, that is, the loss of marriages which results therefrom. Unfortunately, most statistical investigations have been restricted to the deficit during the event and have not considered the long-term effect. Thus, it has been stated that one million marriages were postponed during 1930-1932,[6] and another study estimated the net deficit at about 700,000 for the years 1930 to 1935 inclusive.[7] We know that this deficit was wiped out by the upsurge of marriages after the depression. However, the question which has not been answered by previous research is whether any component of the population suffered a permanent loss of marriage.

Although detailed statistics on marriage are presented in a later chapter, there is one finding which appears worthy of note at this point, namely, the effect of the depression on the chances of remarriage for the widowed. The indications are that the marriage rate declined most sharply for widows and widowers from 1929 to 1932. This is in agreement with other reports that the decline in marriage was marked at the older ages,[8] and it also conforms with the fact that the economic impact of the depression was particularly severe on older persons.[9]

Equally significant was the relatively small upswing in the marriage rate for the widowed after the depression. In fact, their 1929 rate was equaled in only one year since then and that was during the all-time record marriage boom of 1946. Apparently, thousands of widows lost their

chances for marriage due to the depression of the 1930's. This is understandable since a widow's chances for marriage are generally most favorable in the years immediately after her bereavement. Moreover, for most women of middle age, delay in marriage for even a few years soon brings them to an age when the men they would have married pass them by to marry younger women. This is particularly true today, due to the growing excess of women over men at the older ages.

WAR AND THE MARRIAGE RATE

The effects of war on a country's marriage rate are necessarily related to the proximity of the actual conflict and to the nature and intensity of its impact on the population. Thus a conflict of short duration, which hardly disturbs the normal activities of a country, occasions no more than a dent in the marriage rate—for example, the Spanish-American War in 1898. On the other hand, when a country is overrun as was France in 1914, the reaction of the marriage rate is both immediate and pronounced.[10]

The level of marriages also varies with the changing phases of a conflict. The fluctuations during our own Civil War are a case in point. The highlights have already been discussed; the available data are shown in Table A12.

World War I. With our entrance into the war on April 6, 1917, marriages rose sharply (Table 3) and remained at an unusually high level through June when registration for military service began and our first troops landed in France. The upswing, though short-lived, was sufficient to push the rate for the year to its highest point on record up to that time—about 8 marriages per 100 eligibles (Table 2). The next year, when many of our young men were overseas or in active military service at home, marriages were much less frequent. After the Armistice on November 11, 1918, however, the rate again swung upward and reached a new peak of almost 9 marriages per 100 eligibles in 1920.

In reviewing the marriage record for World

[6]"Better Times – More Marriages," *Statistical Bulletin* (Metropolitan Life Insurance Company), June, 1934, p. 2.

[7]Samuel A. Stouffer and Lyle M. Spencer, "Marriage and Divorce in Recent Years," *Annals of the American Academy of Political and Social Science*, 188:63-64, November, 1936.

[8]Jessie Bernard, "The Differential Influence of the Business Cycle on the Number of Marriages in Several Age Groupings," *Social Forces*, 18:549, May, 1940; and James H. S. Bossard, "Depression and Pre-Depression Marriage Rates," *American Sociological Review*, 2:695, October, 1937.

[9]Samuel A. Stouffer and Paul F. Lazarsfeld, *Research Memorandum on the Family in the Depression*, Bulletin 29, Social Science Research Council, New York, 1937, p. 35.

[10]For marriage rates in nineteen foreign countries during World War I, see "The Marriage Rate in Wartime," *Statistical Bulletin* (Metropolitan Life Insurance Company), November, 1939, p. 6.

War I, it is noteworthy that the rate for widowed persons was only slightly affected, if at all, by the course of hostilities (Table 28, p. 68). No doubt this resulted from the fact that active participation in the conflict was limited primarily to young men in their twenties. In addition, it should be recalled that the influenza pandemic which struck in the autumn of 1918 took its heaviest toll among persons 25 to 34 years of age.[11] Thus the pandemic may have contributed to the decline of marriages among single and divorced persons.

The postwar marriage record for the widowed is also of special interest, since the increase in the rate during 1919-1921 was greater for them than for the other classes of unmarried persons. This, too, may have resulted in part from the 1918 pandemic which left in its wake almost 200,000 relatively young widowed persons. Husbands who died while with the expeditionary forces overseas contributed to the supply of young widows (Table A27), but the latter probably represented only about one out of every four women widowed by the war and pandemic combined.

World War II. The pattern during World War II was fairly similar to the trend during the previous world conflict. The marriage rate rose during the early period, declined during its course, increased sharply in the immediate postwar years, and then reverted more or less to its prewar level. How and why the marriage rate was so greatly influenced by the war will be apparent from the review which follows.

[11] Forrest E. Linder and Robert D. Grove, *Vital Statistics Rates in the United States, 1900-1940*, Bureau of the Census, Washington, 1943, p. 254.

Table 3. Marriages and Marriage Rate by Month, United States, 1917-1919 and 1939-1955

Year	Jan.	Feb.	March	April	May	June	July	Aug.	Sept.	Oct.	Nov.	Dec.
					Number in Thousands*							
1917	80	75	67	112	93	130	88	90	94	96	101	116
1918	80	70	70	84	86	113	85	95	97	70	73	77
1919	76	70	73	83	81	123	92	96	108	113	116	119
1939	84	84	79	110	113	161	117	123	146	127	127	134
1940	86	87	96	104	118	191	129	175	175	175	135	126
1941	94	103	102	132	157	192	141	165	142	145	143	180
1942	149	133	116	145	146	178	142	155	152	159	153	145
1943	120	117	121	128	133	164	137	132	133	131	129	131
1944	115	113	112	124	122	143	119	119	121	120	117	128
1945	116	103	112	113	118	150	135	137	137	149	161	182
1946	179	176	168	184	198	255	181	212	194	183	187	174
1947	148	139	134	161	176	230	157	184	182	164	160	156
1948	129	113	125	140	156	215	158	171	170	152	143	139
1949	111	111	95	128	133	185	138	148	148	133	122	127
1950	97	103	94	128	130	186	155	171	177	145	133	149
1951	120	104	124	119	127	190	128	145	148	128	123	140
1952	96	108	98	115	134	177	127	153	134	131	133	134
1953	109	104	98	124	132	183	128	147	137	134	122	127
1954	101	104	90	110	130	173	136	136	137	130	118	126
1955	102	99	89	124	125	182	141	144	144	135	122	135
					Rate per 1,000 Total Population							
1917	9.2	9.5	7.7	13.2	10.7	15.3	10.1	10.3	11.0	10.9	11.9	13.1
1918	9.0	8.8	7.9	9.8	9.7	13.1	9.6	10.7	11.3	7.9	8.4	8.7
1919	8.6	8.8	8.2	9.6	9.1	14.3	10.3	10.7	12.4	12.6	13.4	13.3
1939	7.6	8.4	7.1	10.2	10.2	14.9	10.5	11.0	13.5	11.4	11.8	12.0
1940	7.7	8.3	8.6	9.6	10.6	17.6	11.5	15.6	16.1	15.6	12.4	11.2
1941	8.3	10.1	9.0	12.0	13.9	17.5	12.4	14.6	12.9	12.7	13.0	15.8
1942	13.1	12.9	10.2	13.1	12.8	16.1	12.4	13.5	13.7	13.8	13.7	12.5
1943	10.4	11.2	10.4	11.4	11.5	14.6	11.8	11.3	11.8	11.3	11.4	11.2
1944	9.8	10.3	9.6	11.0	10.4	12.6	10.2	10.2	10.6	10.2	10.3	10.9
1945	9.8	9.7	9.4	9.8	9.9	13.1	11.3	11.5	11.9	12.5	14.0	15.3
1946	15.0	16.3	14.0	15.9	16.5	21.9	15.1	17.6	16.7	15.2	15.9	14.3
1947	12.1	12.7	11.0	13.6	14.4	19.4	12.8	15.0	15.3	13.3	13.4	12.6
1948	10.5	9.8	10.1	11.7	12.6	17.9	12.7	13.7	14.1	12.2	11.8	11.1
1949	8.8	8.8	7.6	10.5	10.5	15.1	10.8	11.6	12.0	11.0	9.9	10.0
1950	7.6	8.9	7.3	10.3	10.1	14.9	12.0	13.3	14.1	11.2	10.6	11.5
1951	9.2	8.8	9.5	9.4	9.7	15.0	9.7	11.0	11.6	9.7	9.6	10.6
1952	7.3	8.7	7.4	9.0	10.1	13.8	9.5	11.4	10.3	9.8	10.3	10.0
1953	8.1	8.6	7.2	9.5	9.8	14.0	9.4	10.8	10.4	9.8	9.2	9.3
1954	7.4	8.4	6.6	8.3	9.5	13.0	9.8	9.8	10.2	9.3	8.8	9.0
1955	7.3	7.9	6.4	9.1	8.9	13.4	10.1	10.3	10.5	9.5	8.9	9.5

*Independently rounded; hence the sums of monthly figures may differ slightly from the annual totals shown in Table 2.

Note: Rates are adjusted to annual basis; population includes armed forces overseas. Source: Estimated by the author.

When Germany invaded Poland on September 1, 1939, few Americans foresaw this event as the opening gun of what was to be the most extensive and most costly war in world history. Like most other industrialized countries of the world, we had only recently recovered from a prolonged and severe economic depression. We had heard of political unrest in Europe. We knew of Hitler's rise to power and of his vast armaments program.

But we just could not believe that Germany had the strength to plunge the world again into war. Moreover, most people felt that even if affairs did deteriorate in Europe, it was none of our business and we would not again be drawn into her conflicts.

These mistaken beliefs were not completely dispelled, despite the rapid march of events in Europe, until the Japanese attack on Pearl Harbor brought us into the war. Nevertheless, even before that date, the war in Europe was having a significant effect on our country. At first, this was restricted to increased industrial activity resulting from foreign war orders. Later, as the country adopted a defense program of its own, industries were converted and expanded for war. At the same time, a military training program was started and this together with improved economic conditions gave a strong impetus to marriage. A better indication of the role of each of these factors can be gained by comparing

events with the simultaneous movement of the marriage rate. In making this comparison, it should be kept in mind that a large backlog of marriage eligibles had accumulated during the depression (Tables A6 and A8), and that many of these young men and women would have married in the early 1940's even without the turn of international events.

A graphic picture of the month-to-month variation in the crude marriage rate, from January, 1939, to December, 1950, is presented in Figure 3 (the horizontal dotted lines represent the annual rates); the number of marriages and rate for each month are given in Table 3. It is quite evident from the graph that the marriage rate reacted sharply to the major events of this period. As early as September, 1939, the outbreak of war in Europe and the President's declaration of a limited national emergency were accompanied by an upswing in marriages. Reflecting the attitudes of the times, the rise was not

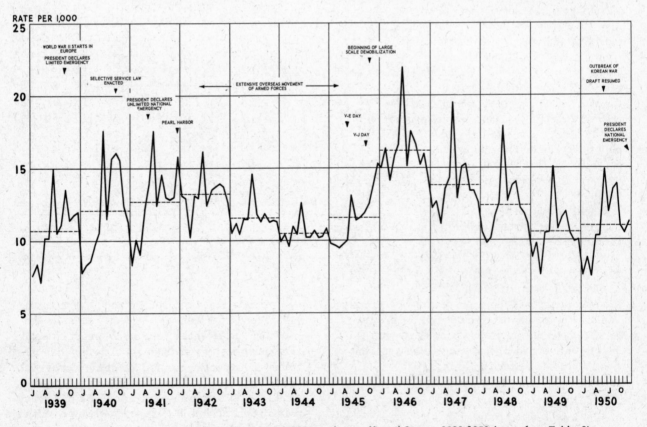

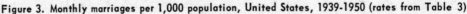

Figure 3. Monthly marriages per 1,000 population, United States, 1939-1950 (rates from Table 3)

sustained; in two of the early months of 1940 the rate actually fell below its level for the same period of 1939.

By mid-1940, however, attitudes were starting to change and marriages were becoming more frequent. In Europe, the German army had almost completed its lightning sweep westward, and in our own country increasing consideration was being given to the creation of a conscripted peace-time army. These considerations culminated in the Burke-Wadsworth Bill, which was introduced in Congress on June 20. Discussion of the Bill continued through the summer until the Selective Service and Training Act was signed on September 16. Registration under the Act followed a month later and the first inductees were selected on October 29. Marriages rose sharply during this period, reflecting the desire of thousands of young men to establish some basis for claiming deferred status.[12]

Marriages again swung upward after May 21, 1941, when the President proclaimed an unlimited state of national emergency. Nevertheless, despite the rapid march of events overseas, even as late as August, 1941, it was not generally believed that we would eventually become active combatants. Thus, in that month, deferment from the draft was decreed for men over age 27 and provision was made for the release of those already inducted. In fact, renewal of the Selective Service Act itself passed through Congress by only one vote.

On December 7, 1941, the Japanese attack on the American fleet and shore installations at Pearl Harbor stimulated another marriage rush. The rate rose sharply in December and remained relatively high for months thereafter. In fact, the rate for 1942 was at a new peak of 13.1 per 1,000 population; three years earlier it had been 10.7.

With our active participation in the war, the marriage pattern was reversed. From late 1942 through the early months of 1945, marriages fell off and the month-to-month fluctuations became

[12]From the very start of Selective Service, its administrators recognized the importance of the family and granted deferment to married men. Strictly speaking, this regulation covered only those cases in which the wife was dependent on the registrant's income for support. However, in line with the national policy of resolving all reasonable doubts in favor of the registrant, many draft boards deferred men solely on the basis of the marriage relationship itself.

less pronounced. As is evident from Figure 4, this was the period in which increasing numbers of young men were entering the armed forces, and thousands were being transferred overseas. By March, 1945, when our forces were close to maximum, the rate was down to 9.4 marriages per 1,000 population—the lowest for any month in four years. No doubt the rate would have dropped even lower during this period but for two factors.

First, the civilian population was experiencing a period of unprecedented prosperity due to the war effort. With wages high and unemployment at a minimum, the marriage rate remained at a high level among certain components of the population, for example, the widowed and the divorced.

Two acts of Congress affecting servicemen also contributed to wartime marriages. In February, 1942, the National Service Life Insurance Act was amended, increasing the amount to which the life of a serviceman could be financially protected. Four months later, the Servicemen's Dependency Act added considerably to his income. Regardless of the extent to which these acts stimulated marriages, it is clear that thousands of men married either in anticipation of entering the armed forces or before leaving for overseas service. Thus, all during the war, marriages continued at a high level in Miami, Norfolk, San Diego, and in other cities near large military or naval establishments.

The end of hostilities, with V-E Day on May 8, 1945, and V-J Day on September 1, was followed by an exceedingly sharp upsweep in marriages, which carried the rate to its highest point in our history. Comparison of Figures 3 and 4 clearly indicates the close relationship between the demobilization of our armed forces and this unprecedented marriage boom. By the time Germany surrendered, the armed forces of the United States had grown to $12\frac{1}{3}$ million officers and enlisted men. In the next few months, our forces declined somewhat from this peak strength but they still consisted of more than 12 million men at the time of Japan's surrender. Soon thereafter, however, demobilization was begun on a large scale and within a few months about 5 million men had been discharged. During this period, the marriage rate increased by 50 per cent, reaching 15.3 per 1,000 in December. Thereafter, as

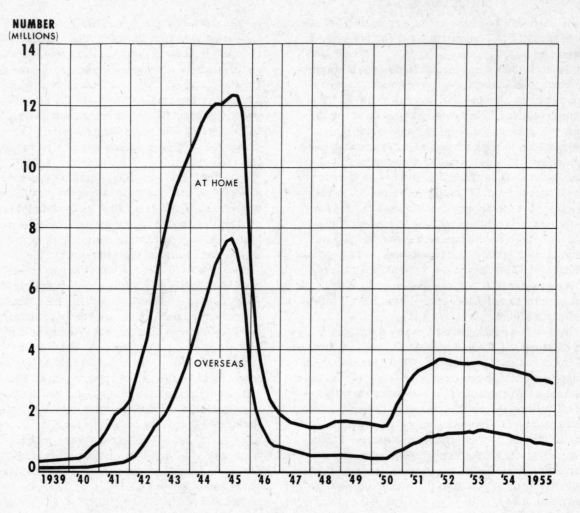

NUMBER
(MILLIONS)

Figure 4. Armed Forces Strength, United States, 1939-1955

demobilization continued to progress rapidly, marriages continued upward. Within a little more than a year, by the close of 1946, our forces had actually fallen below their prewar strength. Accompanying this return of millions of young men to civilian life, business conditions remained favorable. In consequence, close to 2,300,000 marriages occurred in 1946 alone.

An indication of the magnitude of the marriage boom can be gained from the fact that almost one out of every eight persons eligible to marry did so during 1946—more than twice the proportion (5½ per cent) recorded at the depth of the depression only fourteen years earlier (Table 2). Nor did the influence of demobilization end in 1946. Marriages fell off in the months that

followed, but it was not until 1949 that their number had receded to the prewar level. Moreover, although the supply of eligible men and women had been appreciably reduced (Table A8), the marriage rate remained high; even in 1949, close to 9 per cent of the eligibles married. This was at a rate in excess of that experienced in any year for at least three quarters of a century prior to Pearl Harbor. Clearly the marriage record established after World War II will not be equaled again for many years to come.

Korea. In the early months of 1950 there was every indication that the decline in marriages would continue for the fourth successive year. During March, for example, the rate was down to 7.3 marriages per 1,000 total population, the lowest in a decade. In fact, for the first half of the year the marriage rate averaged $5\frac{1}{2}$ per cent below the level of the year before.

Then, on June 25 Communist forces of North Korea invaded the Republic of Korea south of the thirty-eighth parallel of latitude. The United Nations immediately ordered a cease-fire and, when this failed to halt the hostilities, on June 27 inaugurated counter military measures with United States forces carrying the brunt of the action. This, accompanied by a resumption of the draft, brought a sharp reversal in the marriage picture. Beginning with July, each month in the second half of 1950 recorded a larger number of marriages than the corresponding month of 1949. The boom in marriages was particularly marked in August and September, when the rate was not much below that for June—the usual seasonal high month. By October, however, the peak had already passed and marriages were again declining.

Although the entry of Chinese Communist forces on the side of the North Koreans in November and the President's declaration of a national emergency in December occasioned another small upswing in marriages, the boom was over in the early months of 1951. By April the marriage rate had already fallen below its previous year's level and, except for June, it remained lower throughout the balance of the year. The start of truce negotiations may have contributed to the decline; its effect, however, was undoubtedly negligible since hostilities and the drafting of young men continued uninterrupted. Of greater importance was the fact that the available supply of eligibles was not sufficient to sustain any prolonged rise in marriages. For this reason, too, the signing of the Korean armistice on July 27, 1953, occasioned no perceptible alteration in the downswing of marriages.

International Trends. It is evident from the preceding sections that throughout our history the rise and fall in the marriage rate has been strongly influenced by war and its aftermath. This relationship has been fairly similar in most other countries of the world, as is well illustrated by the experience during World War II.

As would be expected, the effects of the war were most pronounced in the occupied countries and in those which participated actively in the hostilities. In the neutral countries of Europe,

on the other hand, marriage rates were relatively little affected. These trends are shown in Table 4.

In general, the marriage rates for the English-speaking countries followed courses much like our own. The high point in the early period of the war (1939-1942) was followed by lower rates for two or three years. The cessation of hostilities brought a new rise, the peak occurring in 1945 in the British Isles[13] and one year later in the other countries.

Most overrun European countries suffered severely depressed marriage rates during the later years of the war. A common pattern is observed in the cases of Belgium, France, Italy, Luxembourg, and Romania. Contrary to the experience of all other warring nations, their marriage rates were continually below the prewar level up through 1944; rates of about 5 per 1,000 were not uncommon. However, the end of the war brought a sharp rebound in each instance. In France, for example, the rate almost doubled within a year, rising from 5.4 per 1,000 in 1944 to 10.1 in 1945, and increasing further to 12.8 in 1946. Even as late as 1950, France's marriage rate was higher than in prewar years. Belgium and Luxembourg also exceeded their prewar levels.

Another pattern for the overrun countries is seen in the record for Austria, Czechoslovakia, the Netherlands, and Norway. Each experienced a rise in marriages in the early war years which then gave way to a decline. The decrease was particularly pronounced in Austria and the Netherlands. The latter reached its nadir in 1944, after it had been under German domination for several years; Austria had its lowest point in 1945, when it was occupied by the Allies. For these countries, too, 1946 brought a sharp upturn in the marriage rate, and for each of them the rate in 1950 was still somewhat higher than in 1935-1938.

During and after the war years, the marriage rate in Denmark alone of the occupied countries pursued a course of its own—one closely paralleling that of the neutral nations. This may have resulted from the fact that Denmark's agricultural

---

[13] The earlier peak was undoubtedly due to the fact that the siege of the British Isles ended well before V-E Day. Also, her forces were closer to home, and relatively few were engaged in the Pacific.

Table 4. Marriages Per 1,000 Population, Selected Countries, 1935-1950

Country	1935-1938	1939-1942	1943	1944	1945	1946	1947	1948	1949	1950
North and South America										
United States	10.7	12.2	11.5	10.5	11.5	16.2	13.8	12.4	10.6	11.0
Canada	7.6	10.4	9.4	8.5	9.0	10.9	10.1	9.6	9.2	9.1
Chile	7.6	8.6	8.3	8.2	7.9	7.8	8.2	8.3	8.1	7.9
Costa Rica	6.6	6.3	5.8	6.9	6.9	6.0	7.6	4.7	7.3	7.8
Mexico	6.7	7.4	7.6	6.9	6.8	6.0	5.9	6.3	5.7	6.9
Nicaragua	1.4	2.2	3.7	3.9	3.9	4.4	4.5	4.3	4.2	4.2
Puerto Rico	6.9	8.1	7.1	7.9	8.3	9.5	7.8	7.0	7.4	9.3
Venezuela	3.5	4.3	4.2	3.9	4.1	4.5	4.4	4.6	4.9	5.0
Europe — Neutral (World War II)										
Ireland	5.0	5.3	5.9	5.7	5.9	5.9	5.5	5.4	5.4	5.4
Portugal	6.5	6.8	7.4	7.5	7.6	7.7	8.2	7.8	7.8	7.8
Spain	5.5	7.1	6.6	7.1	7.2	7.5	8.3	7.8	7.1	7.5
Sweden	8.7	9.5	9.7	9.9	9.7	9.5	8.8	8.4	7.9	7.7
Switzerland	7.3	8.1	8.3	8.0	8.1	8.7	8.7	8.6	8.0	7.9
Europe — Other										
Austria	8.5	11.4	7.1	6.0	4.6	9.0	10.9	10.3	9.9	9.3
Belgium	7.6	6.2	6.3	5.5	10.0	10.9	9.9	9.3	8.5	8.3
Bulgaria	8.2	9.4	10.1	9.2	11.9	11.0	10.9	*	*	*
Czechoslovakia	8.0	9.6	7.9	6.8	7.5	10.1	11.1	10.7	10.4	*
Denmark	9.2	9.1	9.3	9.4	9.0	9.8	9.6	9.4	8.9	9.1
England and Wales	8.7	10.0	7.0	7.1	9.3	9.0	9.3	9.1	8.6	8.2
Finland	8.6	8.5	8.6	8.4	11.8	13.1	11.3	10.0	8.8	8.5
France	6.8	5.9	5.7	5.4	10.1	12.8	10.5	9.0	8.2	7.9
Germany	9.3	8.7	7.3	*	*	*	*	*	*	*
Berlin	11.0	11.3	9.6	8.7	6.9	6.7	8.2	9.3	8.9	9.2
Western Germany	*	*	*	*	*	8.8	10.0	10.6	10.1	10.6
Hungary	8.5	8.2	7.9	8.0†	8.1	10.9	10.8	10.4	11.0†	*
Italy	7.6	6.7	4.8	4.8	6.9	9.2	9.7	8.4	7.8	7.7
Luxembourg	8.0	6.8	4.5	4.2	7.8	10.0	9.0	8.8	8.7	8.7
Netherlands	7.5	8.5	7.2	5.5	7.8	11.4	10.2	9.0	8.3	8.2
Northern Ireland	6.9	8.1	7.6	7.0	7.7	7.3	7.0	6.9	6.7	6.6
Norway	7.8	9.0‡	7.9	7.2	7.6	9.5	9.5	9.2	8.5	8.3
Romania	9.1	8.1	6.9	5.2	10.6	11.3	9.4	*	*	*
Scotland	7.7	9.6	7.4	7.1	9.4	8.9	8.6	8.5	8.1	7.9
Trieste	8.2	8.1	5.6	5.5	5.0	7.9	8.6	9.6	8.1	7.9
Africa, Asia, and Oceania										
Australia	8.7	10.7	9.4	9.3	8.5	10.6	10.1	9.7	9.2	9.2
Ceylon	5.4	6.3	8.2	7.5	6.8	6.4	6.2	6.3	6.3	6.8
Cyprus	8.1	7.2	9.9	8.0	9.4	9.3	9.5	6.4	6.9	7.1
Egypt	13.1	12.9	15.6	15.4	14.9	15.2	13.7	14.0	14.1	13.4
Israel§	12.3	13.0	10.5	9.2	9.2	13.0	13.0	10.9	13.4	14.5
Japan	8.2	9.2	10.0	*	*	*	12.0	12.0	10.3	8.6
New Zealand	9.3	9.8	7.5	8.4	10.1	12.4	10.9	9.7	9.5	9.0
Union of South Africa+	11.0	11.2	10.8	10.0	10.3	11.9	11.0	11.1	10.5	9.9

*Not available.   †Estimated by the author from data available for part of the year.   ‡1939-1941 only.
§Jewish population only.   +Europeans only.

Source: United States, from Table 2; most other countries, from the United Nations.

economy was little disturbed by German control. In the neutral nations of Europe, the marriage rates fluctuated somewhat above the 1935-1938 level throughout the period of hostilities, undoubtedly because of war-induced economic prosperity.

Marriages Overseas. Statistics are not available on the number of marriages contracted abroad each year by members of the armed forces stationed outside continental United States. Nor for that matter is the marriage overseas of any resident included in the country's marriage statistics.[14] For this reason, the National Office of Vital Statistics relates the number of marriages in the United States to our population

[14]It should be relatively simple to obtain certificates of marriage for citizens who marry outside the borders of the United States. Men in the armed forces, for example, are generally required to secure approval from their superior officers; civilians apply to our consulate offices abroad for entry visas, if the spouse is an alien. For documentary and statistical purposes, some unit of the federal government should be designated by law as the depository for certified evidence of marriages (and other vital events) occurring to citizens while located or residing abroad.

excluding armed forces overseas. However, this policy does not appear to be justified. Marriages do occur outside the country, but the indications are that their rate of occurrence is relatively low. As will be shown below, this was true even during World Wars I and II, when thousands of our young men were overseas. Moreover, some of these overseas marriages are followed by second ceremonies in the United States, and these are included in our marriage statistics. Finally, it is likely that in most years the overstatement of our marriage totals due to inefficient national registration procedures is greater than the understatement resulting from the omission of overseas marriages. Thus, exclusion of the armed forces overseas from the population base contributes to the overstatement of the "true" marriage rate. Preferably, marriages in the United States should be related to our population including armed forces overseas, which is the procedure used in this book.

Although statistics on overseas marriages are not available, minimum estimates thereof are afforded by information from several sources, principally statistics by the U. S. Immigration and Naturalization Service on aliens admitted under the "War Brides" Act.[15] From April, 1946, when the first ships carrying war brides arrived in the United States, until three years later when the Act expired, 113,135 wives, 327 husbands, and 4,537 children were admitted to the country.[16]

These 117,999 persons came from

practically every part of the world where our armed forces were stationed. The principal countries (according to birth) from which the war brides came were Great Britain (34,894), Germany (13,315), Italy (8,873), France (8,531), Canada (7,236), and Australia (6,649). It is also noteworthy that as many as 5,099 had been born in China, 752 in Japan, and about 780 in the Union of Soviet Socialist Republics. Of the total, close to one half were from English-speaking countries. The reasons for this are self-evident. Not only were thousands of our armed forces stationed in the British Isles and Australia throughout the war, but there was also the facility of communication due to a common language.

It is of interest to compare the marriages overseas with the number in the United States

Table 5. Marriages in the United States and Among Armed Forces Overseas, World War II

Period	Marriages in the United States	Marriages Among Armed Forces Overseas		
		Number*	Per Cent of Total†	Annual Rate per 1,000‡
December, 1941–June, 1946	7,754,807	44,836	0.6	3
July, 1946–June, 1947	2,118,375	25,837	1.2	29
July, 1947–December, 1948	2,815,486	42,789	1.5	50
Total	12,688,668	113,462	0.9	6

*Based on alien wives and husbands admitted to the United States under the "War Brides" Act. U. S. Department of Justice, Immigration and Naturalization Service, Washington, *Annual Report, 1949*, p. 14.
†Total represents sum of marriages in the United States and those overseas.
‡Based on mean strength of armed forces overseas, estimated by the author from monthly population data in various reports by the Bureau of the Census.

[15]The "War Brides" Act consists of two laws that were designed to ease the problems of members of the armed forces who married nationals of foreign countries. Public Law 271, passed December 28, 1945, facilitated the entry into the United States of alien wives, husbands, and children of members of the armed forces of this country, by waiving visa requirements and the excluding provisions concerning physical and mental defectives. On July 22, 1947, Public Law 213 extended these benefits to racially ineligible spouses, provided they were married to United States citizens prior to or within thirty days after passage of the law.

[16]Includes 88 wives and 26 children who started from their homes but failed to reach the United States by midnight of December 28, 1948.

during World War II and the immediate postwar years. It is clear from Table 5 that those overseas represented only about 1 per cent of our total marriages during the entire period from Pearl Harbor through 1948. Moreover, it was not until late in the postwar period that marriages overseas approached the rate at which marriages were occurring in the United States. For July, 1947, to December, 1948, the rate overseas was 50 marriages per 1,000. However, considering the age and marital status composition of the armed forces overseas, this was only about two thirds of the marriage rate in the United

States.[17] It is also important to note that the statistics in Table 5 overstate the overseas marriage rate for the later periods, since many of the alien wives were admitted to the United States a long time after the marriage occurred. The interval after marriage must have been particularly long for wives admitted during November and December of 1948, when thousands who had hesitated or who had been delayed raced to beat the December 28 deadline.

The tendency of men in the expeditionary forces to marry foreign brides would have been greater but for the rigid regulations concerning these marriages which were set up by the armed forces. In the early months of World War II, the armed forces prohibited personnel on duty in any foreign country or possession of the United States from marrying without the consent of the commanding officer. More difficult matrimonial hurdles were added thereafter, when it was found that the earlier regulations were not deterring marriages overseas of our Army and Navy personnel. Moreover, a number of countries in which our troops were stationed publicized the general difficulties involved in such marriages, and attempted to discourage them until hostilities were over. In general, too, the very circumstances of war were not conducive to the formation of permanent relationships.

Although marriages were not too frequent during the course of hostilities, men on occupation duty in both the European and Pacific areas have been favorably disposed toward foreign brides. The record for alien wives admitted under the "War Brides" Act is only one indication of this. In addition, 8,312 alien fiancees or fiances of members of the armed forces were admitted to the United States within three years after the 1946 act authorizing such entries.[18] Marriages

have also continued to occur in appreciable numbers among our armed forces stationed in Germany, Italy, and Japan.[19]

Another item of interest is a comparison of the number of overseas marriages during the two world conflicts. Unfortunately, statistical estimates are even less adequate for World War I, since at that time a foreign bride automatically attained citizenship upon marriage to an American. It is known, however, that about 3,700 war brides were brought to the United States in army transports and that an unknown number came on commercial vessels. In addition, it has been estimated that upward of 8,000 arrived in the years immediately after World War I.[20]

The number of marriages overseas is not known with too great a degree of accuracy for either of the two world wars, but it is apparent that a much greater number of men married foreign brides during World War II. This does not necessarily mean that the tendency to marry overseas was much different in the two global conflicts. For one thing, American participation in World War II lasted $2\frac{1}{2}$ times as long as in the earlier war. Then, too, the number of our armed forces abroad was almost four times as great.

INFLUENCE OF THE SEX RATIO AND OF FLUCTUATIONS IN THE BIRTH RATE

The balance of the sexes exerts an important influence on the marriage rate. In general, the number of marriages is greater if the sexes at the adult ages are numerically equal than if either sex outnumbers the other. In the latter case, obviously, the marriage rate would be higher for the sex that is in short supply. At one time it was believed that women were more dependent than men upon a favorable sex ratio.[21]

[17]The method used to evaluate the significance of the overseas marriage rate is given in Paul H. Jacobson, *Some Statistical Patterns of Marriage in the United States*, Ph.D. dissertation, Faculty of Political Science, Columbia University, 1952, pp. 167-168.

[18]Reflecting the postwar shift in location of the armed forces, the greatest number of these *intended spouses* were born in Germany (1,862), Italy (1,326), France (1,090), Greece (824), and Austria (729). By contrast, the number from Great Britain (105) and Canada (12) was negligible. (U.S. Department of Justice, Immigration and Naturalization Service, Washington, *Annual Report, 1949*, Table 9A.)

[19]Despite the fact that military personnel must obtain permission from their commanding officers to marry Japanese girls, thousands have married in Japan. Most of the brides eventually come to the United States under provisions of Public Law 717 of August 19, 1950, which permits entry of racially inadmissible alien spouses and minor children of members of our armed forces.

[20]"Foreign War Brides of American Servicemen," *Statistical Bulletin* (Metropolitan Life Insurance Company), June, 1946, p. 2.

[21]Ernest R. Groves and William F. Ogburn, *American Marriage and Family Relationships*, Henry Holt and Company, New York, 1928, p. 199.

More recently it has been shown that neither sex derives any special advantage from an imbalance of the sexes.[22]

Until the late 1930's, females in the United States were favored by an excess of unmarried men (Tables A6-8). This was due primarily to the large volume of immigration prior to World War I and during the immediate postwar years, in which the men greatly outnumbered the women. The restricted immigration of recent years, by contrast, has consisted of a greater number of unmarried women, thus contributing to the long-term decline in the ratio of male to female marriage eligibles (Tables A2-3).

Although there now are more eligible females than males in the population, this excess is found only at the middle and older ages, and is due largely to the fact that women outlive men. At birth, males exceed females by about 6 per cent. However, throughout life, males experience a higher death rate than females; as a result the initial excess of males is steadily reduced with advance in age, and is eventually changed into a growing deficit.

Even though the sexes are balanced numerically at specified ages, this is not sufficient since men generally marry women somewhat younger than themselves. For this reason, changes in the birth rate also affect the balance of marriage eligibles. This is particularly true at the younger ages when marriage is most common. As is evident from Table 6, the number of men aged 20-25 per 100 women aged 18-23 rose to a peak of 105 in 1952, and has since declined. The recent upswing was

a direct result of the decline in births up through 1933 (Table A1); the current decrease of the sex ratio is due to the war and postwar rise in births. In consequence of these trends, unmarried men aged 20-25 have recently had a relatively small number of women aged 18-23 from whom to choose a bride; since 1957 the situation has been reversed. These changes affect the marriage rate to the extent that they are not offset by variations in the proportion of bachelors who select a bride 2 to 4 years younger as compared with one of some other age.

The birth rate has another, more important, effect on the marriage rate in that it determines the number of men and women who will become eligible for marriage approximately two decades later. It is clear from Figure 5 that one of the factors which contributed to the marriage boom in the United States during the 1940's was the record number of men and women attaining the age for marriage. However, the numbers of men at ages 20-25 and women at ages 18-23, who usually comprise about half of our grooms and brides, have declined in the present decade—a result of the decrease in births during the 1930's. The number of men aged 20-25, for example, has fallen from an all-time high of $7\frac{1}{4}$ million in 1945 to $6\frac{1}{2}$ million in 1957. In consequence of this and the fact that the ranks of single men were markedly reduced by the high marriage rates of recent years, the number of bachelor marriages has decreased. After 1960, however, the situation will change as more and more of the war and postwar babies reach the adult ages. By 1965 there may be 8 million men aged 20-25 years—almost one fourth more than in 1957 and one tenth above their previous peak in 1945. Moreover, their number should continue to rise until the late 1970's, since the baby boom has not yet abated. Thus, in the absence of a major depression, it is likely that marriages will climb rapidly to new high levels after the late 1960's.

LONG-TERM TREND OF MARRIAGE

The number of married men and women in the United States has increased without interruption for at least a century (Tables A6-7). In the 1940-1950 decade alone, $14\frac{1}{2}$ million were added to our married population, bringing the total

Table 6. Males Aged 20-25 per 100 Females Aged 18-23, United States, 1890-1957, and Forecasts to 1965

Year	Ratio	Year	Ratio	Year	Ratio	Year	Ratio
1890	96	1940	96	1949	101	1957	99
		1941	97	1950	102	1958	99
1900	96	1942	97	1951	104	1959	99
		1943	97	1952	105	1960	98
1910	101	1944	98	1953	104	1961	95
		1945	99	1954	104	1962	94
1920	96	1946	99	1955	103	1963	97
		1947	98	1956	101	1964	97
1930	93	1948	99			1965	92

Source of basic data: Various reports by the Bureau of the Census; figures include population in the armed forces overseas.

[22]Elizabeth R. Kramm and Dorothy S. Thomas, "Rural and Urban Marriage in Relation to the Sex Ratio," *Rural Sociology*, 7:39, March, 1942.

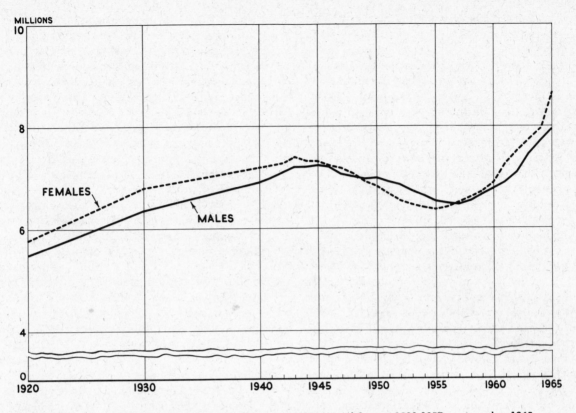

Figure 5. Number of males aged 20-25 and females aged 18-23, United States, 1920-1957; projected to 1965 (includes population in the armed forces overseas)

(including those in the armed forces overseas) to 75½ million by July, 1950. Although the growth has been slower since then, due to the decline of marriages and the relatively large number of marital dissolutions, the married population exceeded 82 million toward the close of 1956 and will probably reach 86 million in 1960.

Married people have risen not only in absolute number but also in proportion to the adult population. In 1950 somewhat more than two thirds of the population at ages 15 and over were married; by contrast, for at least a half century prior to 1940, the proportion married was three fifths or less. Among men, for example, the proportion had been rising slowly from 54.1 per cent in 1900 to 61.6 per cent in 1940. During the 1940's, however, the increase was greatly accelerated, so that by 1950 the proportion had climbed to 69.0 per cent (Table 7). The trend has been upward among women also, but the rise has been less

Table 7. Per Cent Married at Ages 15 Years and Over, By Sex and Age, United States, 1890-1950

Sex and Age	1890	1900	1910	1920	1930	1940	1950
Male							
15 and over	54.1	54.7	56.1	59.4	60.1	61.6	69.0
15 – 19	.5	1.0	1.2	2.1	1.7	1.8	3.1
20 – 24	18.9	21.6	24.2	28.4	28.2	28.0	39.5
25 – 34	61.6	60.7	63.0	65.9	68.5	70.3	79.0
35 – 44	81.0	78.9	79.3	80.1	81.6	82.8	87.0
45 – 54	84.4	82.3	81.6	81.2	81.7	83.1	85.8
55 – 64	82.4	79.8	79.0	78.0	78.1	78.9	81.6
65 and over	70.6	67.3	65.7	64.9	63.7	64.2	66.0
Female							
15 and over	56.8	57.1	59.0	60.9	61.1	61.4	67.3
15 – 19	9.5	10.9	11.4	12.6	12.6	11.9	16.8
20 – 24	46.8	46.6	49.9	52.5	51.6	52.1	65.8
25 – 34	75.3	73.2	75.2	76.8	77.7	77.6	84.8
35 – 44	80.7	79.6	80.2	80.5	81.5	81.4	84.5
45 – 54	74.0	73.9	74.8	74.3	75.2	76.3	77.8
55 – 64	60.4	60.5	62.1	61.4	62.0	63.4	65.3
65 and over	35.4	34.2	35.0	34.2	34.6	34.6	35.8

Note: Includes armed forces overseas during 1940 and 1950.

Source of basic data: 1890, as of June 1, from the decennial census; all other years, as of July 1, from Tables A8-9.

pronounced for them than for the men—due, in part, to the changing balance of the sexes.

The upswing in the proportion married has been most marked at the younger ages. Among women aged 20-24, the proportion rose from 47 per cent in 1890 to 52 per cent in 1940 and then spurted to about 66 per cent in 1950. In fact, at every age period under 45 years, the gains for men and women during the 1940-1950 decade were either equal to or greater than those of the prior half century. Moreover, even beyond age 45 the 1950 proportions married among women, but not among men, were at their highest points in at least six decades.

A part of the record growth of the married population is due to the long-term decline in mortality and consequent reduction in the incidence of widowhood. Of much greater importance, however, has been the increasing inclination toward marriage, which started around the turn of the century and may have been accelerated by World War II.

One indication of this is the trend of the marriage rate among single persons. Since this subject is treated in detail in a later chapter, it need only be noted here that the marriage rate for bachelors and spinsters has generally moved upward during this century. Among single men, for example, the average annual marriage rate rose from 64 per 1,000 in the 1900's to 69 in the 1910's, and to 73 in the 1920's. Although the rate dropped sharply during the depression of the 1930's, it soared upward in the next decade to the unusually high level of 92 per 1,000.

Another indication of the increased propensity toward marriage is afforded by the extent to which the single population has been depleted. Among males aged 15 and over (including those in the armed forces overseas) the proportion single declined from 42 per cent in 1890 to 33 per cent in 1940, and to less than 25 per cent in 1950. Single women experienced smaller decreases than the men, particularly around the turn of the century. However, they also benefited substantially from the recent marriage boom; the proportion single among women dropped from 25½ per cent in 1940 to 18⅓ per cent by mid-1950. Currently, the proportion single is at its lowest point since at least 1890.

These population statistics, when classified by year of birth and attained age, reveal even more clearly than those already presented that an increase in nuptiality started toward the close of the nineteenth century. As is shown in Table 8,

Table 8. Per Cent Single at Ages 25-74; Men and Women in the United States, by Attained Age and Year of Birth

Sex and Year of Birth	Attained Age, in Years				
	25-34	35-44	45-54	55-64	65-74
Men					
1815-24	*	*	*	*	6.0
1825-34	*	*	*	6.8	6.1
1835-44	*	*	9.1	7.6	6.6
1845-54	*	15.4	10.3	8.3	7.8
1855-64	36.8	17.0	11.1	9.8	9.0
1865-74	37.3	16.7	12.0	10.1	10.1
1875-84	35.1	16.2	11.4	10.7	8.6
1885-94	32.2	14.3	11.1	8.5	
1895-04	29.2	14.0	8.6		
1905-14	28.7	9.7			
1915-24	19.0				
Women					
1815-24	*	*	*	*	5.9
1825-34	*	*	*	5.8	6.2
1835-44	*	*	7.0	6.6	6.6
1845-54	*	9.9	7.8	7.1	7.4
1855-64	20.7	11.1	8.5	8.4	8.4
1865-74	22.6	11.4	9.6	8.9	9.4
1875-84	20.9	11.4	9.1	9.0	8.7
1885-94	19.3	10.0	8.7	8.0	
1895-04	17.7	10.4	7.9		
1905-14	18.9	8.4			
1915-24	11.4				

*Not available.

Note: Estimated by the author from data in various reports by the Bureau of the Census; includes armed forces overseas.

the proportion of the population that remained permanently single has been relatively small and notably constant throughout our history. Among men and women born in each ten-year period since 1815, one tenth or fewer of those who celebrated their 65th birthday had never married. However, there was a gradual decrease in the proportion ultimately marrying among persons born in successive periods up to the years immediately after the Civil War, and thereafter a gradual increase. Equally important, there appears to have been a small decline in age at marriage among the post-Civil War generations. This reversal in the trend of nuptiality corresponds with our previous findings that the pattern of marriage changed around the turn of the century. In other words, the marriage rate swung upward when persons born around 1875 reached the usual age for marriage, and this upswing has continued despite temporary postponements during depressions. It is also possible that nuptiality was further stimulated by World War II, since the proportion single among those born as recently as 1915-1924 is already at an unusually low level. At any rate, it is evident that people are now marrying at an earlier age than any other generation of the past century. It is also likely that a somewhat larger proportion of the recent generation will eventually marry.[23]

[23]In this regard, see J. Hajnal, "The Marriage Boom," *Population Index*, 19:80-100, April, 1953, and "Age at Marriage and Proportions Marrying," *Population Studies*, 7:111-138, November, 1953. International marriage trends and their implications are also reviewed in United Nations, *Recent Trends in Fertility in Industrialized Countries*, Population Studies, No. 27, New York, 1958, pp. 45-56.

Chapter 2

SEASONAL PATTERN OF MARRIAGE

RELIGIOUS customs, climate, occupation, and a variety of local and personal conditions have an important bearing on the month chosen for marriage. In consequence, the seasonal pattern of marriage varies considerably among the peoples of the world.

RELIGIOUS CUSTOMS

In seasons of religious fasting and penitence few marriages occur. Thus, during the Lenten season marriages decline sharply in Catholic countries. In Italy, for example, the marriage rate in March is usually less than half of the annual rate. This gives rise, naturally, to an unusually large number of weddings in April. Marriages are also relatively frequent in February, particularly in Bulgaria and among other Greek Orthodox Catholics whose custom it is to marry before Lent. For similar reasons, people of the Jewish faith are disinclined to marry during the period which follows Passover in spring and during the religious holidays of the late summer and early fall. Accordingly, marriages are frequent before and after the holidays; in Israel, for example, March is the favored month. Religious customs are not the most important factor in determining the seasonal pattern of marriage in the United States; the changing dates of the Lenten season, however, do affect annual variations in the February-April pattern.

CLIMATE

In most countries of the world, there is an association between climate and the seasonal incidence of marriage. For example, marriages fall off sharply at the height of winter in Canada, Finland, Norway, Sweden, and in some of our West North Central states. On the other hand, there is a sharp rise in marriages during the late spring and early summer. June is the most popular month in Canada, Sweden, and the United States; and May is preferred in Austria, Denmark, Germany, the Netherlands, and Switzerland. Similarly, in the southern latitudes, where the seasons are the reverse of our own, a large increase occurs in December in Australia, Chile, and New Zealand.

That climate should have a bearing on the season chosen for marriage is understandable. Periods of extreme weather conditions, such as monsoons, very low temperatures, and the like, generally result in social isolation of the population and make difficult the assembling of family and other guests. Even within more moderate limits, climate influences a series of social and economic activities, and it is within the framework of the latter that young people generally find it appropriate to plan their wedding date. Several European countries, for example, still retain the ancient custom of celebrating the spring festival during May, which makes this period the preferred time for young couples to start life together. Then too, in the United States and in many other industrialized countries, the start of the vacation season and the close of the school year correspond with the end of spring. Since weather conditions are also generally ideal, this season affords young people an opportune time for an elaborate wedding and a honeymoon trip.

OCCUPATION

It is natural that people dependent upon agriculture should prefer autumn weddings. This is the season when the profits of months of labor are acquired. With food and money on hand, the young farmer finds the period of leisure which follows the harvest an opportune time for taking a wife. For much the same reason, in communities where fishing is the principal industry, the return of the fleets is generally accompanied by a rise in marriages. Thus December has been a popular month for nuptials in Norway and Scotland.

The influence of financial considerations on the month chosen for marriage is also evident from the recent experience in England and Wales. Since World War II there has been a marked transfer of their marriages from the second to the first quarter of the year, with March now the most popular month. This shift has apparently resulted from the British system of income tax assessment, under which a husband can claim a full year's allowance for his wife even if they marry just before the end of the fiscal year. With the start of the tax year in early April, and the potential amount of tax relief comparable to a wedding gift of about $250 for the average couple, it is not

spring and summer. Even in the United States, the proverbial June bride was not always the fashionable one. Prior to the twentieth century, autumn marriages were much more popular. However, at the turn of the century, as the population swung away from agricultural pursuits,[1] June came to the fore in the urban Northeast and then spread to other northern areas. June replaced autumn as early as 1892 in Philadelphia; 1893 in New York City and Massachusetts; 1898 in Pittsburgh and Maine; 1899 in New Hampshire; 1900 in Connecticut; and 1902 in Rhode Island, Michigan, and Ohio. Similar changes occurred shortly thereafter in Seattle, Wisconsin, Indiana, New Jersey, Kansas, and in many other sections of the country. By 1917, June was already well

Table 9. Monthly Variation in Marriages, United States, Regions and Divisions, 1917 and 1948

Area	Daily Average in Each Month as Per Cent of Daily Average for Year											
	Jan.	Feb.	March	April	May	June	July	Aug.	Sept.	Oct.	Nov.	Dec.
1917												
UNITED STATES	82	86	69	119	96	138	91	93	100	99	108	119
Northeast	94	93	61	126	100	159	94	88	98	102	101	86
North Central	77	84	70	123	105	147	91	95	102	94	106	108
South	81	82	75	113	85	119	88	92	98	102	114	152
West	75	82	69	111	97	120	94	108	104	98	111	130
1948												
UNITED STATES	84	79	81	95	101	145	103	112	115	99	96	91
Northeast	81	68	71	102	110	162	101	110	129	105	96	66
North Central	81	74	72	93	106	164	101	119	117	102	94	78
South	89	85	93	92	96	123	104	105	104	97	97	115
West	85	89	87	92	92	136	106	115	114	94	97	93
New England	72	68	46	105	109	168	115	99	143	117	103	57
Middle Atlantic	83	67	79	101	110	160	97	114	125	100	94	68
East North Central	81	73	71	94	107	161	106	118	117	102	95	75
West North Central	80	77	74	90	104	170	89	122	118	101	93	83
South Atlantic	87	83	94	93	94	126	105	105	107	95	97	112
East South Central	87	87	91	90	97	118	104	104	102	99	96	123
West South Central	93	84	92	92	99	122	102	106	101	97	98	113
Mountain	87	86	89	91	102	121	108	112	111	101	99	94
Pacific	84	92	86	93	83	150	105	118	117	87	95	92

Source of basic data: Marriages by month, estimated by the author.

surprising that March now has a strong appeal to couples who would otherwise have married at a somewhat later date.

THE PATTERN IN THE UNITED STATES

In most countries, industrialization and urbanization have been accompanied by a transfer of marriages from the fall and winter months to the

established as the country's most popular month for marriage, as is evident from the data in the upper tier of Table 9.

Since World War I, the appeal of June weddings has become even more widespread in the United States. No doubt, this has also resulted from

[1]It is noteworthy that public education was extended and summer vacations became popular among young people at about this time.

changes in socioeconomic conditions. Agriculture has become less and less a family enterprise; mechanization and diversification of crops have become commonplace. Thus, most farming activities now are on a year-round industrial basis. Moreover, even in states still primarily dependent on one harvest in autumn, such as the Dakotas, small industries now provide employment for some young people. Finally, the automobile and other means of transportation, and radio and television have broken the social isolation of rural communities. In consequence, more and more young farm people are receiving the same kind of education and training as city youths, and they are being exposed to the same kind of motivations and social propaganda—particularly the commercialization and popularization of June as the traditional month for marriage.

Although June weddings have increased in rural areas, December still is the most popular month for marriage in a large part of the deep South, namely, Alabama, Arkansas, Georgia, Mississippi, South Carolina, and Tennessee. The agricultural aspect of rural life in the South is an important factor in this situation. However, it may also be due in part to the sociocultural lag among the Negro population. Among white persons in Mississippi, for example, June has been the preferred wedding month for about two decades; by contrast, even as late as the 1930's, autumn was the favored season among Negroes in New York City. Thus, it is likely that changes in the social and economic conditions of the rural South will also eventually result in a shift from December to June marriages.

For more than four decades now, June has been the most popular month for marriage in the United States as a whole. Indeed, despite the marked fluctuations in the annual marriage rate during the 1940's, June was the peak month in all but one year (Table 3).

June weddings are most popular, particularly in the Northeast and North Central states. In these areas, the daily number of marriages in June of 1948, for example, was from 60 to 70 per cent greater than the daily average for the year; this compared with 45 per cent for the country as a whole (Table 9). In the Dakotas and Wisconsin, June marriages averaged twice the daily number for the year. In six other states scattered throughout the northern half of the country—Oregon, Vermont, Minnesota, Iowa, Massachusetts, and Nebraska—June marriages were at least 70 per cent above the annual average.

The areas where the marriage curve reaches a pronounced peak in June also show a secondary peak in late summer or early fall. This is particularly the case in New England. Secondary peaks in August or September, but of smaller magnitude, are likewise observed in the Middle Atlantic, North Central, and Pacific states. In most of these areas, relatively few marriages occur during the winter months.

FIRST MARRIAGE AND REMARRIAGE

The relatively large number of marriages in June in the United States reflects the popularity of that month among single girls, who constitute

Table 10. Monthly Variation in Marriages; Brides by Previous Marital Status and by Age, United States, 1948

Status; Age	Daily Average in Each Month as Per Cent of Daily Average for Year											
	Jan.	Feb.	March	April	May	June	July	Aug.	Sept.	Oct.	Nov.	Dec.
All Brides	84	79	81	95	101	145	103	112	115	99	96	91
First Marriage	82	76	73	94	102	156	100	116	121	101	95	84
Remarriage	94	89	109	96	99	105	110	96	92	95	99	115
Divorcee	94	92	114	97	99	105	113	94	89	91	96	115
Widow	94	81	95	93	99	107	105	103	100	104	105	113
Under 20	85	74	80	92	97	147	105	116	117	98	97	92
20 – 24	84	81	78	90	103	162	93	120	119	96	91	84
25 – 34	86	81	85	104	107	131	106	102	109	99	99	92
35 – 54	82	79	87	98	101	115	122	95	104	108	103	104
55 and over	75	62	85	84	92	109	111	95	123	142	108	111

Source: Estimated by the author from data for selected areas.

a large majority of our brides. Their choice of month for marriage, as compared with that of women remarrying, is shown in Table 10.

Among single brides, the daily average of June marriages is 56 per cent above the daily average for the year. By contrast, the weddings of remarrying brides are much more evenly distributed over the year. In fact, widows prefer December over June, and divorcees are more likely to choose March, July, or December.

That June does not have a marked appeal for those who undertake a "second" matrimonial venture may be due to a number of factors. Remarriage ceremonies are generally small private affairs; thus, weather conditions and the possibility of assembling guests may not influence the selection of a wedding date. More practical considerations may also be involved. The groom may be a widower with children from his previous marriage, and the pressure for a homemaker may dictate a marriage date soon after the decision to marry is made. Then too, some divorcees remarry shortly after the dissolution of their previous marriage, whatever the month may be. This may explain the absence of a pronounced seasonal pattern for marriage in Nevada (a small rise occurs during the summer months), where one third of the brides are divorcees and almost a tenth are widows (Table 31, p. 72).

THE AGE FACTOR

The seasonal distribution of marriages is also influenced by the age of the bride. As is evident from the data in Table 10, the preference for June decreases progressively with advance in age. Thus, the June index in 1948 was 162 for brides aged 20-24 years, 131 for brides aged 25-34 years, 115 for those 35-54 years, and 109 for those of older age.

Until mid-life this pattern is determined largely by the growing proportion of remarriages; the preference of single women for a June wedding lessens only gradually with age. At the older ages, however, the preference for autumn increases sharply among women of all marital classes, with the result that after age 55, October marriages outrank those of any other month by a considerable margin. In fact, autumn weddings seem to have a greater appeal to spinsters than to widows or divorcees at these ages.

Chapter 3

GEOGRAPHIC VARIATIONS IN MARRIAGE AND THE LAW

MANY of the factors which affect the seasonal distribution of marriages also influence the extent to which people marry. As a result of variations in the demographic characteristics of populations, their stage of socioeconomic development, and also because of religious attitudes, taboos, and other special conditions, there are marked differences in the level of the marriage rate among the countries of the world. A good indication of this may be gained from the rates shown in Table 4.

INTERNATIONAL DIFFERENCES

The marriage rate in the United States is higher than in most countries of the world. From 1944 to 1948, for example, there were 13 marriages annually for every 1,000 population. During this period, only Egypt exceeded our record; the rate in that country was about 14½ marriages per 1,000 population. Three other countries also had relatively high rates; Israel, Finland, and New Zealand each averaged more than 10 marriages per 1,000 population. At the other extreme, the rate was less than 7 per 1,000 in Ceylon, Mexico, Costa Rica, Ireland, Venezuela, and Nicaragua. The low marriage rates in the Latin American republics are explained, in part, by the prevalence of unrecorded common-law unions, and also by the fact that the registration of formal marriages is far from complete.

The situation in Ireland presents a special phenomenon which is worthy of more extended consideration than can be allotted in this book. Suffice it to note that, pressed with misfortune and poverty during the second half of the nineteenth century, thousands of Irish emigrated from the country and those who stayed behind elected to postpone marriage—many remained single throughout life. In consequence, the frequency of marriage decreased sharply. For example, among Irish women aged 35-44, the proportion ever

married dropped from 85 per cent in 1841 to 72 per cent in 1901, and it has remained close to this lower level up to the present.

GEOGRAPHIC PATTERN IN THE UNITED STATES

Just as the marriage rate differs from one country to another, there are variations within the United States. In fact, although the rate has not always followed a parallel trend in all parts of the country, a distinct geographic pattern has been evident throughout the years. In general, marriages tend to be relatively more frequent as one moves from north to south and from east to west. There are exceptions to this pattern, but the absence of comprehensive data precludes the possibility of adequately evaluating their significance. The available data represent enumerations by place of occurrence and are thus affected by migratory marriages. In view of the relatively high frequency of the latter and the fact that their geographic distribution changes with the enactment of new state regulations, available marriage statistics afford a very poor index for evaluating the marital behavior of a state's population. However, the data do provide the basis for constructing the national pattern and they are useful for other purposes, such as for evaluating the effects of our diverse state marriage regulations.

Number of Marriages by State. Each year more marriages are performed in New York than in any other state of the country. In 1949, for example, 134,115 marriages were reported in New York. This exceeded by a wide margin the number performed in Texas, which ranked second with 96,214 marriages. Illinois (88,020), Pennsylvania (83,995), and California (77,873) also contributed a substantial number. By contrast, although two of the country's most popular marriage centers are located in Nevada, only

Table 11. Number of Marriages by State of Occurrence, United States, 1939-1950

Geographic Division and State	1939	1940	1941	1942	1943	1944	1945	1946	1947	1948	1949	1950
UNITED STATES	1,403,633	1,595,879	1,695,999	1,772,132	1,577,050	1,452,394	1,612,992	2,291,045	1,991,878	1,811,155	1,579,798	1,667,231
New England	76,571	89,526	102,413	98,135	75,757	70,784	79,939	122,191	108,194	98,876	84,176	88,503
Maine	9,062	10,202	9,892	9,724	7,248	6,849	8,173	13,519	11,152	10,293	8,085	8,617
New Hampshire	5,065	6,036	6,648	6,973	4,549	4,542	5,859	10,288	9,268	8,427	7,428	7,631
Vermont	4,369	4,906	4,424	3,527	2,734	2,438	3,087	4,939	4,340	3,889	3,385	3,569
Massachusetts	38,784	44,836	52,992	48,098	37,232	34,681	38,197	56,498	49,803	45,940	39,639	41,711
Rhode Island	5,509	6,172	7,845	7,894	6,812	6,799	7,579	10,628	9,337	8,716	7,098	7,501
Connecticut	13,782	17,374	20,612	21,919	17,182	15,475	17,044	26,319	24,294	21,611	18,541	19,474
Middle Atlantic	228,988	258,914	275,650	273,990	232,600	208,251	235,804	366,395	329,551	306,304	262,579	277,035
New York	104,820	132,501	144,368	140,686	121,655	107,939	120,314	182,981	165,431	156,024	134,115	141,075
New Jersey	31,895	41,059	46,538	50,498	41,045	36,084	39,711	61,020	55,802	51,913	44,469	46,291
Pennsylvania	92,273	85,354	84,744	82,806	69,900	64,228	75,779	122,394	108,318	98,367	83,995	89,669
East North Central	231,717	256,847	295,496	261,687	226,133	220,957	263,196	412,329	367,653	333,149	276,793	317,344
Ohio	62,624	83,781	102,552	77,846	59,577	56,148	67,524	106,092	93,779	83,146	59,600	75,136
Indiana	58,800	39,900	41,000	40,000	36,000	35,388	42,868	66,750	58,537	54,387	48,282	61,659
Illinois	51,181	63,445	72,139	67,399	63,778	66,553	79,206	121,715	108,461	101,051	88,020	93,288
Michigan	37,836	46,342	50,989	51,582	44,385	41,678	48,329	78,808	71,319	61,986	53,109	58,180
Wisconsin	21,276	23,379	28,816	24,860	22,393	21,190	25,269	38,964	35,557	32,579	27,782	29,081
West North Central	165,088	193,272	204,191	187,627	144,181	117,692	141,459	214,684	175,643	152,243	132,915	137,285
Minnesota	24,488	27,500	30,385	26,883	22,703	21,559	25,935	38,239	35,991	33,085	28,659	30,991
Iowa	36,862	48,350	25,936	13,085	13,531	17,121	21,264	32,434	30,002	28,585	25,515	27,603
Missouri	60,600	71,800	95,000	96,000	60,000	26,182	31,660	46,497	43,613	42,534	37,113	34,300
North Dakota	4,220	4,174	4,158	3,074	2,984	3,032	3,633	5,531	5,559	5,488	4,828	5,108
South Dakota	6,421	4,138	4,576	4,225	5,071	5,057	5,641	8,393	7,905	7,330	6,519	6,969
Nebraska	12,866	15,977	18,802	18,462	13,818	9,115	10,358	14,130	14,726	14,938	12,743	13,828
Kansas	19,631	21,333	25,334	25,898	26,074	35,626	42,968	69,460	37,847	20,283	17,538	18,486
South Atlantic	210,545	242,927	274,403	308,848	288,871	271,071	281,371	368,013	310,202	290,585	250,091	265,061
Delaware	2,277	4,825	6,332	7,789	7,052	6,251	6,164	8,271	5,161	2,662	2,597	2,635
Maryland	25,096	39,305	59,077	59,002	43,888	42,271	47,529	69,472	60,181	56,177	47,842	50,661
District of Columbia	5,680	7,727	10,554	14,873	13,294	11,304	12,013	15,059	12,775	11,591	9,991	10,198
Virginia	52,719	52,680	35,180	40,443	33,654	30,175	34,104	46,475	40,350	37,423	33,174	36,732
West Virginia	9,983	8,181	15,870	17,802	11,599	13,410	15,236	23,242	18,655	16,495	13,739	17,199
North Carolina	15,700	15,100	17,613	20,411	24,472	23,269	26,200	38,800	32,049	29,773	27,275	29,751
South Carolina	35,000	43,200	52,000	54,000	52,000	51,689	48,134	58,519	48,357	46,748	39,509	46,175
Georgia	36,100	39,200	41,000	46,000	49,000	44,595	53,154	78,219	68,715	68,206	53,925	44,122
Florida	27,990	32,709	36,777	48,528	53,912	48,107	38,837	29,956	23,959	21,510	22,039	27,588
East South Central	145,577	175,098	136,566	154,943	156,109	135,288	153,412	224,682	188,804	154,119	145,821	134,272
Kentucky	56,500	76,300	31,180	42,501	38,548	40,477	51,886	82,569	71,563	64,232	58,621	33,019
Tennessee	25,700	30,700	24,000	17,000	16,000	14,626	15,900	21,574	17,232	15,316	15,024	21,692
Alabama	31,421	34,010	39,244	45,877	55,531	38,626	40,755	56,335	46,425	20,926	19,411	22,823
Mississippi	31,956	34,088	42,142	49,565	46,030	41,559	44,871	64,204	53,584	53,645	52,765	56,738
West South Central	176,834	190,906	185,572	215,950	218,467	205,162	204,828	259,479	221,542	206,024	184,743	190,039
Arkansas	43,160	43,600	37,116	42,290	39,267	40,945	37,052	51,514	43,652	43,490	44,043	51,584
Louisiana	25,327	27,487	27,000	33,000	34,000	33,153	33,000	41,081	32,909	29,000	26,000	26,900
Oklahoma	31,547	33,319	32,000	35,000	33,000	31,558	26,666	23,792	21,183	20,636	18,486	22,400
Texas	76,800	86,500	89,456	105,660	112,200	99,506	108,110	143,092	123,798	112,898	96,214	89,155
Mountain	80,161	111,022	131,776	141,270	95,952	85,682	101,972	154,867	143,290	134,233	121,687	132,594
Montana	7,500	8,700	8,000	7,000	8,000	6,433	8,147	12,974	9,769	7,131	6,981	7,235
Idaho	6,313	8,892	11,213	11,700	5,900	5,171	4,377	7,394	8,029	8,354	7,565	8,345
Wyoming	2,422	2,935	3,200	3,889	2,747	2,666	2,566	3,858	3,696	3,736	3,414	3,549
Colorado	11,942	7,407	10,000	12,000	12,000	11,102	12,172	16,230	15,188	14,009	12,639	13,735
New Mexico	9,125	12,170	12,200	12,000	11,400	11,372	12,115	18,144	15,986	16,492	16,392	22,717
Arizona	14,585	23,643	26,700	33,300	21,200	17,083	20,700	27,300	25,101	24,824	23,139	20,031
Utah	7,488	8,245	7,263	6,081	6,705	6,262	7,034	9,781	7,965	7,327	6,402	7,110
Nevada	20,786	39,030	53,200	55,300	28,000	25,593	34,861	59,186	57,556	52,360	45,155	49,872
Pacific	88,152	77,367	89,932	129,682	138,980	137,507	151,011	168,405	146,999	135,622	120,993	125,098
Washington	25,327	26,300	33,600	44,900	37,900	34,315	38,385	45,736	39,659	35,007	32,374	34,438
Oregon	4,932	5,998	7,445	8,768	9,272	8,675	9,764	14,674	12,881	12,373	10,746	11,300
California	57,893	45,069	48,887	76,014	91,808	94,517	102,862	107,995	94,459	88,242	77,873	79,360

Note: For some states, includes partial estimates based on number of marriage licenses issued; the author's state estimates for 1941-1943 were deflated in order that the state figures add to the United States estimates published by the National Office of Vital Statistics.

Source of basic data: Various reports by the National Office of Vital Statistics, except as follows: Ohio, 1942, from annual report of Secretary of State; Missouri, 1941-1943, from Committee on Marriage and Divorce of the Missouri Bar; and Indiana, South Carolina, Georgia, Tennessee, Louisiana, Oklahoma, Texas, Montana, Colorado, and New Mexico for 1941-1943, from local marriage registrars.

45,155 marriages took place in that state in 1949. As is evident from Table 11, this was less than the number reported in twelve states.

Marriage Rates by Area. State marriage rates vary over an extremely wide range. In 1949, as in other recent years, Nevada stood in a class by itself with a rate of 287.6 marriages per 1,000 population. This was almost nine times the

Table 12. Marriages by State of Occurrence per 1,000 Resident Population, United States, 1939-1950

Geographic Division and State	1939	1940	1941	1942	1943	1944	1945	1946	1947	1948	1949	1950
UNITED STATES	10.7	12.1	12.7	13.2	11.7	10.9	12.2	16.4	13.9	12.4	10.6	11.0
New England	9.1	10.6	12.0	11.4	9.0	8.5	9.6	13.8	12.0	10.7	9.0	9.5
Maine	10.7	12.0	11.6	11.6	9.0	8.6	10.2	16.2	13.1	11.7	9.0	9.4
New Hampshire	10.3	12.3	13.6	14.5	9.8	10.0	12.8	20.8	18.3	16.2	13.9	14.3
Vermont	12.2	13.5	12.7	10.3	8.4	7.8	9.8	14.4	12.3	10.8	9.2	9.4
Massachusetts	8.9	10.4	12.1	11.0	8.7	8.3	9.1	12.6	10.9	9.8	8.4	8.9
Rhode Island	7.9	8.6	10.7	10.6	9.0	8.6	9.8	13.8	12.0	11.1	8.9	9.5
Connecticut	8.1	10.2	11.8	12.2	9.6	8.7	9.6	13.8	12.4	10.7	9.1	9.6
Middle Atlantic	8.3	9.4	10.0	10.1	8.8	8.0	9.2	13.2	11.4	10.4	8.7	9.2
New York	7.8	9.8	10.9	10.8	9.5	8.5	9.6	13.7	11.8	10.8	9.0	9.5
New Jersey	7.7	9.8	10.9	11.8	9.7	8.7	9.7	13.6	12.1	10.9	9.1	9.5
Pennsylvania	9.3	8.6	8.6	8.5	7.4	7.0	8.3	12.4	10.6	9.6	8.1	8.5
East North Central	8.8	9.6	10.9	9.6	8.5	8.3	10.0	14.5	12.6	11.2	9.1	10.4
Ohio	9.1	12.1	14.7	11.2	8.7	8.1	9.8	14.1	12.2	10.6	7.5	9.4
Indiana	17.3	11.6	11.8	11.4	10.4	10.3	12.5	18.0	15.5	14.0	12.2	15.6
Illinois	6.5	8.0	9.0	8.4	8.2	8.6	10.4	14.9	13.0	11.8	10.2	10.7
Michigan	7.3	8.7	9.3	9.3	8.2	7.6	8.8	13.4	11.7	10.0	8.4	9.1
Wisconsin	6.8	7.4	9.2	8.1	7.4	7.1	8.5	12.3	10.9	9.8	8.2	8.4
West North Central	12.2	14.3	15.4	14.3	11.3	9.4	11.4	16.3	13.1	11.2	9.6	9.7
Minnesota	8.8	9.9	11.2	10.1	8.8	8.5	10.2	14.0	12.9	11.5	9.8	10.3
Iowa	14.6	19.1	10.4	5.4	5.8	7.4	9.2	13.1	12.0	11.2	9.9	10.5
Missouri	16.0	19.0	24.9	25.1	16.2	7.4	9.0	12.4	11.3	11.1	9.6	8.7
North Dakota	6.6	6.5	6.8	5.3	5.5	5.7	6.7	9.7	9.6	9.5	8.1	8.2
South Dakota	10.0	6.5	7.5	7.2	8.6	9.0	9.7	14.3	13.2	12.0	10.3	10.6
Nebraska	9.8	12.1	14.8	14.9	11.1	7.5	8.6	11.3	11.6	11.8	9.8	10.4
Kansas	10.8	11.9	14.4	14.7	14.5	20.0	24.8	38.5	20.4	10.7	9.1	9.6
South Atlantic	12.0	13.5	14.9	16.3	14.8	14.0	14.6	18.6	15.4	14.4	12.1	12.5
Delaware	8.7	17.9	23.0	27.9	25.0	21.9	21.6	27.7	16.9	8.5	8.2	8.2
Maryland	14.0	21.4	30.9	29.5	21.0	20.0	22.7	31.4	26.8	24.7	20.5	21.5
District of Columbia	8.6	11.2	13.8	17.5	14.8	12.8	13.7	16.8	14.4	13.8	12.4	12.7
Virginia	19.7	19.4	12.3	13.3	10.8	9.3	10.7	14.5	12.6	11.7	10.1	11.1
West Virginia	5.3	4.3	8.4	9.7	6.7	7.9	8.9	12.7	9.9	8.7	7.1	8.6
North Carolina	4.5	4.2	4.9	5.7	6.7	6.5	7.4	10.5	8.5	7.8	7.0	7.3
South Carolina	18.7	22.7	26.5	26.9	26.4	26.6	24.9	30.2	24.3	23.4	19.5	21.8
Georgia	11.6	12.6	12.9	14.3	15.1	14.0	17.0	24.1	21.0	20.9	16.2	12.8
Florida	15.2	17.1	18.2	22.6	22.0	19.9	15.8	12.3	9.5	8.3	8.3	9.9
East South Central	13.6	16.2	12.5	14.2	14.4	12.9	14.8	20.8	17.1	13.9	13.1	11.7
Kentucky	20.0	26.7	11.0	15.2	14.3	15.4	20.0	29.9	25.5	22.8	20.6	11.2
Tennessee	8.9	10.5	8.1	5.8	5.4	5.1	5.5	7.0	5.4	4.8	4.6	6.6
Alabama	11.2	12.0	13.5	15.6	19.1	19.2	14.7	19.4	15.8	7.0	6.5	7.5
Mississippi	14.7	15.7	19.3	22.4	20.2	19.2	21.5	31.1	25.4	25.8	25.3	26.1
West South Central	13.6	14.6	14.0	16.1	16.0	15.5	15.7	19.0	15.9	14.6	13.0	13.0
Arkansas	22.2	22.3	18.9	21.4	21.3	23.2	21.0	28.7	23.8	23.8	23.9	26.9
Louisiana	10.9	11.6	10.9	13.0	13.3	13.2	13.6	16.1	12.8	11.2	9.9	9.9
Oklahoma	13.5	14.3	14.1	15.8	15.0	15.4	13.1	11.2	9.9	9.9	8.8	10.0
Texas	12.1	13.5	13.6	15.7	16.0	14.5	15.8	19.9	16.8	14.8	12.6	11.5
Mountain	19.6	26.7	32.3	34.5	21.8	20.1	24.2	34.9	31.4	28.4	24.9	26.0
Montana	13.5	15.6	14.7	13.5	16.5	13.7	17.1	25.2	18.4	13.2	12.3	12.2
Idaho	12.1	17.0	22.4	24.5	11.8	9.8	8.6	14.5	15.4	15.2	13.3	14.2
Wyoming	9.8	11.7	13.0	15.5	11.1	11.0	10.7	15.2	14.3	13.9	12.3	12.2
Colorado	10.7	6.6	8.9	10.8	10.4	9.8	10.9	13.5	12.3	11.1	9.8	10.3
New Mexico	17.5	22.9	24.1	23.9	21.3	21.6	22.6	32.3	27.5	27.3	25.5	33.2
Arizona	30.2	47.4	54.5	63.5	30.6	28.0	34.8	44.3	38.4	36.0	32.4	26.6
Utah	13.8	14.9	13.2	10.6	10.6	10.4	11.9	15.3	12.5	11.2	9.5	10.3
Nevada	193.8	345.4	443.3	403.6	185.4	167.3	234.0	413.9	386.3	335.6	287.6	311.7
Pacific	9.2	7.9	8.9	12.1	11.8	11.2	11.8	12.8	11.0	9.9	8.6	8.6
Washington	14.8	15.1	18.8	23.6	18.7	16.4	17.4	20.0	17.9	15.5	14.1	14.5
Oregon	4.6	5.5	7.0	7.9	7.6	7.0	7.8	11.0	9.5	8.8	7.5	7.4
California	8.5	6.5	6.8	9.8	10.8	10.6	11.0	11.3	9.6	8.8	7.5	7.5

figure for the next highest state, Arizona, where the rate was 32.4 per 1,000. Unusually high rates were also recorded in five other states: New Mexico (25.5), Mississippi (25.3), Arkansas (23.9), Kentucky (20.6), and Maryland (20.5). At the other extreme, Tennessee, with only 4.6 marriages per 1,000 population, registered the lowest rate in the country. Alabama and North Carolina also experienced rates far below the national average in 1949.

The crude marriage rates for 1939 to 1950 are shown for each state in Table 12. Several sharp deviations from the national pattern are apparent. These resulted from fluctuations in nonresident marriages—a subject which will be considered in subsequent sections of this chapter. Discounting these marked digressions, the trend of the marriage rate appears to have been similar in all parts of the country. This uniformity is also indicated by population data, which show that every region of the country experienced a decline in single persons from 1940 to 1950 (Table 13).

Table 13. Per Cent Single,* Males and Females Aged 14 and Over, United States by Geographic Region and Urban-Rural Area, 1940-1950

Area	Male			Female		
	1940	1947†	1950	1940	1947†	1950
United States	34.9	31.0	29.5	27.5	24.1	22.9
Region						
Northeast	38.3	33.7	32.9	32.7	28.4	28.0
North Central	35.5	31.1	29.6	27.6	23.8	22.8
South	30.9	28.4	26.8	23.8	20.6	20.0
West	36.4	27.7	29.1	24.2	18.8	19.9
Urban-Rural						
Urban	35.5	30.9	29.5	30.0	25.0	24.5
Rural nonfarm	33.1	27.4	28.6	23.8	19.9	19.4
Rural farm	35.1	33.2	31.2	23.2	22.7	19.9

*Standardized according to the age distribution of the total population in the United States, April 1, 1940.
†Civilian population.

Source of basic data: Various reports by the Bureau of the Census.

The proportion single also decreased in both urban and rural communities.

In view of the magnitude of the recent marriage boom, and the data in the accompanying table, it is likely that there has been a reduction in the marriage differential among communities of the country. In other words, the "pushing ahead" of marriage was probably greatest among population groups, such as urban residents, who generally marry at a somewhat later age. However, no precise measure of such change is available; population data reflect the effects of migration as well as of marriage. Thus the farm girl who marries at an early age is likely to remain in a rural community. Her unmarried sister, on the other hand, may be lured away from the farm or village by the more favorable opportunities for employment and social contacts offered by the city. Accordingly, census data show that the proportion single is highest for women who reside in urban areas. By contrast, young men are needed in agricultural areas to perform the heavy manual labor, with the result that among men the proportion single differs by only a small margin between urban and rural areas and is likely to be higher on farms. The selective effects of migration also influence geographic comparisons, since the relative importance of the urban population varies from one region to another.

STATE MARRIAGE LAWS

Under the Constitution of the United States, the regulation of marriage is a matter within the exclusive province of the individual states. Congress has authority only in our territories and possessions, such as Hawaii, the Virgin Islands, and the District of Columbia. In consequence, the laws differ widely in detail, but there is some agreement on fundamentals. In all states there is a common policy requiring persons who intend to marry to first secure the permission of the state. A license is not, however, essential to the validity of a marriage in all states. A few states allow banns to be published as a substitute for a license and exempt Quaker marriages from the law both as to license and ceremony. Moreover, common-law marriages are still recognized, though deprecated, in eighteen states and the District of Columbia.[1]

[1]John W. Morland, *Keezer on the Law of Marriage and Divorce*, Third Edition, Bobbs-Merrill Company, Indianapolis, 1946, pp. 34 and 1076. Since the pioneer conditions which fostered common-law marriage have disappeared, an increasing number of states have prohibited such marriages.

State laws include numerous details concerning the administrative procedure for issuance of a license and performance of the marriage ceremony. Emphasis on the prevention of undesirable marriages has also resulted in an increasing variety of requirements and qualifications which must be met before a license is issued. These have mostly to do with the relationship of the contracting parties, and their health and mental condition. All states forbid marriage with a parent, brother or sister, grandparent, and uncle or aunt.[2] All set the minimum age at which a person may marry, and bar subsequent marriages if a prior marriage still exists. There is an additional miscellany of impediments to marriage in some states, such as that the parties be not of different races, be not under the influence of intoxicants or narcotics, or be not habitual criminals.

Waiting Period. During our early history, it was customary for couples to announce their intended marriage by posting a notice in a public place or by having it proclaimed in their church. This was usually done on three successive Sundays or on festival days; or, in the Roman Catholic Church, during the celebration of the mass. The purpose of these banns was to enable public objection to the proposed marriage by anyone who was aware of an existing impediment. However, as our population grew and became urbanized, this procedure proved impractical and thus rapidly lost favor. Today, it is virtually obsolete in civil marriages, and it occurs as a matter of form only in certain religions. However, among some segments of the population the public form has been perpetuated by the practice of announcing engagements.

Our state legislatures have also attempted to fill this void. At one time, about a half dozen states required the prospective bride and groom to post a bond conditioned on the fact that no impediment to the marriage existed and that the parties would comply with the provisions of the law. In Tennessee, for example, the parties had to post a bond of $1,250. However, such laws never achieved a measure of success. The problem of preventing hasty or ill-considered marriages was thus attacked by a different approach. Since applicants for marriage licenses did not have to be legal residents of the state where the license was issued, many "elopement" marriages occurred outside the state of the couple's residence. To curtail these, several states enacted regulations requiring nonresidents to give several days' notice to the local registrar before receiving a marriage license. Connecticut enacted such a law on October 1, 1913, and immediately thereafter the number of marriages declined in its towns bordering New York and Massachusetts. Although a few states enacted special regulations for nonresident couples, the requirement generally proved ineffective. For one thing, couples could give a fictitious address, particularly in a large city, or else they could use the local address at which they were temporarily staying. Equally important, such laws did not affect hasty marriages of resident couples. Accordingly, a more popular procedure was the enactment of laws prescribing a minimum waiting period for all applicants. Such laws proved extremely popular during the 1920's and 1930's, with one state after another adding a waiting period to its marriage regulations. To date, more than three fourths of the states have had such a requirement, but in nine the law has subsequently been repealed (Table 14).

Premarital Examination. The question of fitness for marriage has received relatively little attention from state legislatures. Since marriage requires the intelligent assent of both parties, in all states marriages of insane persons, idiots, and the feeble-minded are void or voidable. In addition, marriage of epileptics is prohibited in nineteen states; in seven of these, the restriction applies only when the intended bride is under 45 years of age, whether or not she is the epileptic.[3]

[2] An interesting exception exists in the state of Rhode Island, where the law expressly declares that persons professing the Jewish religion may contract valid marriages, though related, provided the marriage is within the degrees of relationship allowed by their respective rites and ceremonies. Thus a Jewish man may marry his niece, since in Leviticus there is an injunction against a nephew marrying an aunt but none against a niece marrying an uncle. Moreover, such Rhode Island marriages have been recognized by other states on the ground that the marriages were valid where contracted.

[3] The law is restricted to couples where the bride is of reproductive age in Connecticut, Kansas, New Hampshire, North Dakota, Utah (marriage is permitted in this state, however, if the epileptic has been sterilized), Virginia, and

Table 14. States Requiring Waiting Period or Premarital Examination

(As of August 1958)

State	Minimum Waiting Period* (Days)	Premarital Examination (Date Law Effective)	State	Minimum Waiting Period* (Days)	Premarital Examination (Date Law Effective)
Alabama	- -	1-48	Nebraska	- -	8-43
Arizona	2	12-56	Nevada	- -	- -
Arkansas	3	7-53	New Hampshire	5	10-38
California	(a)	9-39	New Jersey	3	7-38
Colorado	(a)	10-39	New Mexico	- -	5-57
Connecticut	5	1-36	New York	1(e)	7-38
Delaware	1(b)	7-47	North Carolina	(a)	4-39
Dist. of Columbia	3	- -	North Dakota	- -	7-39
Florida	3	10-45	Ohio	5	8-41
Georgia	(c)	8-49	Oklahoma	- -	5-45
Idaho	(a)	4-43	Oregon	3	12-38
Illinois	(a)	7-37	Pennsylvania	3	5-40
Indiana	3	3-40	Rhode Island	(f)	4-38
Iowa	(a)	4-41	South Carolina	1	- -
Kansas	3	7-47	South Dakota	- -	7-39
Kentucky	3	1-41	Tennessee	3	7-41
Louisiana	3	1924(d)	Texas	(a)	10-49
Maine	5	7-41	Utah	- -	7-41
Maryland	2	- -	Vermont	5	7-41
Massachusetts	5	6-43	Virginia	- -	8-40
Michigan	3	10-37	Washington	3	(g)
Minnesota	5	- -	West Virginia	3	5-39
Mississippi	3	7-58	Wisconsin	5	8-37
Missouri	3	1-44	Wyoming	(a)	5-43
Montana	(a)	7-47			

(a) Law repealed after enactment.
(b) Four days if both applicants are nonresidents.
(c) Five days if one or both applicants are under age.
(d) Certificate of examination from groom only; since July 30, 1958, bride also.
(e) Marriage ceremony cannot be performed until three days after serological test.
(f) Five days if bride is nonresident.
(g) Both applicants swear to health status, but only groom must submit affidavit stating he is free from contagious venereal disease.

*Refers to period between application for and issuance of license, except in Delaware, Louisiana, New York, Rhode Island, and Vermont where it refers to period between issuance of the license and performance of the marriage.
In most states, judges are empowered to waive the waiting period in whole or part under certain conditions.

Source: State reports and statutes, and correspondence from state registrars.

Incurable physical incapacity (impotency) is also generally an impediment to contracting marriage. Such marriages, however, are not void, but must be dissolved by annulment or divorce. Five states (Delaware, North Dakota, Ohio, Oregon, and Washington) expressly bar marriage of habitual or common drunkards, and three (North Carolina, North Dakota, and Washington) rule against persons with pulmonary tuberculosis in an advanced stage.

Venereal infections are essentially the only

Washington; it is unlimited in Delaware, Indiana, Michigan, Minnesota, Missouri, Nebraska, New Jersey, North Carolina, Ohio, Oregon, West Virginia, and Wisconsin.

other diseases to which any specific reference is made in state marriage regulations. Laws requiring the male applicant to furnish a medical certificate showing freedom from venereal disease were first enacted over forty years ago. However, because these so-called "eugenic laws" were poorly drawn and failed to receive public support, they were generally unsuccessful. The situation changed completely in the 1930's with inauguration of the nationwide campaign to control syphilis. Starting with Connecticut, which passed the first of the newer premarital examination laws in 1936, public approval and interest in such laws led to their speedy adoption in state after state. By 1958, there were forty-three states with laws making an examination and/or serologic test for venereal disease a prerequisite to issuance of the marriage license. In addition, Washington requires an affidavit by the prospective groom stating that he is free from such infection. Thus, only four states and the District of Columbia do not have any legislation in this regard (Table 14).

EFFECT OF STATE REGULATIONS

One effect of premarital legislation is immediate and often very pronounced, e.g., marriages fall off in the state which enacts such legislation. At the same time, however, there is usually a countertrend in neighboring states. Apparently, new laws induce some residents to travel to nearby states to avoid the inconveniences of the new regulations. Equally important, such legislation reduces sharply the number of nonresidents who come to the state to avoid the laws of their home state. Eventually, however, the new statute loses some of its deterring effect on residents, whereas the number of nonresident marriages remains at a lower level.

Fluctuations in State Marriage Totals. Although marriages generally decline in a state which enacts new legislation, the effect may not be very obvious when the national trend is downward and the state has other regulations which deter nonresident couples. This is illustrated by the situation in Massachusetts after premarital examinations were required in June, 1943. The decline may also be relatively minor when the national trend is upward. This was true in Maine, Vermont, and Utah, where laws became effective in July, 1941, as well as in Pennsylvania (May, 1940), Oklahoma (May, 1945) and Texas (October, 1949).

South Carolina presents a somewhat different set of circumstances which resulted in a not too marked decline in marriages. Enactment of a one-day waiting period, effective July 1, 1945, coincided with the start of the postwar marriage boom. Nevertheless, South Carolina lost some of its marriage "trade" to Georgia (Table 11). However, because South Carolina's marriage statutes were still relatively lenient, as soon as Georgia required a premarital examination (August, 1949), South Carolina regained the marriages she had formerly attracted from nearby states.

The data in Table 11 also reveal numerous examples of sharp reactions to new legislation; for example, the declines in Tennessee and Idaho after laws were enacted in July, 1941, and April, 1943, respectively. Even more dramatic was the experience of several other states, where the statutes shifted nonresident marriages from one state to others in the immediate vicinity. Thus new requirements in Florida, which became effective in October, 1945, were followed by a marked decline in marriages even though marriages were booming elsewhere in the country. Simultaneously, marriages rose sharply in the contiguous states of Georgia and Alabama. With the law of January 2, 1948, in Alabama, however, marriages dropped by more than one half in that state. This added further to the number of nonresident couples marrying in Mississippi and Georgia. Subsequent legislation in the latter state (August, 1949) caused another realignment of marriages in the South.

Several years earlier, a similar redirection of marriages occurred farther north on the Atlantic seaboard. In 1940 Virginia had enacted premarital

legislation which became operative in August of that year. Usually June is the peak month for marriage, but the rush to avoid the blood-test law was so great that marriages continued upward in July. However, they dropped sharply in August, and remained at a lower level thereafter. In direct consequence, marriages swung upward in Maryland, West Virginia, the District of Columbia, and Delaware. They continued at a relatively high rate in Delaware until its own premarital law became effective on July 1, 1947, after which only one half as many marriages were performed.[4]

The experience in Arkansas is also noteworthy. In February, 1945, when a three-day waiting period became effective in that state, marriages fell off by one tenth. The reaction was even more marked after premarital serologic tests were required on July 1, 1953; marriages dropped by about three fifths in the months immediately following, and continued falling at a slower pace through 1954 and 1955. However, contrary to the downswing in the rest of the state, marriages increased in Little Rock.

[4]Also outstanding was the experience of our North Central states during the 1940's. Essentially, it consisted of two phases. The first started with Indiana's law in March, 1940. In consequence of this law, between 1939 and 1940 marriages dropped from 58,800 to 39,900 in Indiana and rose markedly in the contiguous states of Ohio and Kentucky. The rise in the latter state was short-lived, however, for on the first of the next year its own law took effect. This slashed marriages by more than one half in Kentucky, and added to the rise in Ohio. The latter in turn sustained a drop several months later, when in August, 1941, premarital examinations became mandatory in Ohio. This effected a partial rebound of marriages in Kentucky, the rate remaining above the national average all during the war years. In 1946, moreover, marriages climbed sharply to a new peak in Kentucky, and remained relatively high until January 1, 1950, when a three-day waiting period became effective. This again slashed marriages by almost one half in Kentucky, their number falling from 58,621 in 1949 to 33,019 in 1950. Not only did some Kentucky couples now avail themselves of the absence of a waiting period in Indiana, but Kentucky also lost its postwar marriage "trade" from Ohio. In consequence, marriages swung upward in both Indiana and Ohio.

The second phase of "disturbed" marriage rates in the North Central states can also be traced to the 1940 law in Indiana. In this phase, however, Indiana served as a transfer agent only. Some Illinois residents, who prior to 1940 had availed themselves of the marriage centers in Indiana, shifted westward to Iowa. A year later, in April, 1941, when a premarital examination became mandatory in Iowa, Illinois couples remained in their own state or went elsewhere. At

Table 15. Marriages by Resident Status of Groom, Iowa and Virginia, 1939-1954

	IOWA				VIRGINIA			
Year	Total	Resident	Non-resident	Per Cent Non-resident	Total	Resident	Non-resident	Per Cent Non-resident
1939	36,862	18,498	18,364	49.8	52,719	25,593	27,126	51.5
1940	48,350	20,605	27,745	57.4	52,680	24,443	28,237	53.6
1941	25,936	14,463	11,473	44.2	35,180	24,301	10,879	30.9
1942	13,085	9,317	3,768	28.8	40,443	29,681	10,762	26.6
1943	13,531	10,626	2,905	21.5	33,654	25,281	8,373	24.9
1944	17,121	*	*	*	30,175	22,491	7,684	25.5
1945	21,264	16,880	4,384	20.6	34,104	24,661	9,443	27.7
1946	32,434	25,597	6,837	21.1	46,475	34,392	12,083	26.0
1947	30,002	23,891	6,111	20.4	40,350	30,634	9,716	24.1
1948	28,585	23,119	5,466	19.1	37,423	28,186	9,237	24.7
1949	25,515	19,977	5,538	21.7	33,174	24,264	8,910	26.9
1950	27,603	21,522	6,081	22.0	36,732	26,045	10,687	29.1
1951	24,301	18,515	5,786	23.8	36,825	23,371	13,454	36.5
1952	22,600	16,630	5,970	26.4	37,049	23,003	14,046	37.9
1953	23,180	16,890	6,290	27.1	37,261	23,048	14,213	38.1
1954	23,228	16,743	6,485	27.9	36,150	21,738	14,412	39.9

*Not available.

These diverse trends undoubtedly resulted from the fact that the border counties, which had by frequent waiver of the waiting period built up a large marriage "trade" from Little Rock and states adjacent to Arkansas, lost their attractiveness after premarital examinations were required.

Nonresident Marriages. The decline in marriages, which accompanies new premarital regulations, results primarily from the loss of nonresident couples. In Wyoming, for example, nonresident grooms constituted 59 per cent of

the same time, many couples from Iowa migrated across the state borders, with the result that marriages fell off sharply in Iowa but rose in some of the adjacent states. In Missouri, for example, nonresident marriages had been mounting ever since the law of July, 1937, in Illinois. Indeed, by 1942 many border counties of Missouri were averaging more than fifty marriages per 1,000 population. These high marriage rates diminished rapidly with enactment of legislation in Missouri—a three-day waiting period took effect in 1943 and a premarital examination was required after January 1, 1944. In Nebraska also, which had built up a sizable number of nonresident marriages as a result of Iowa's law, enactment of legislation (August, 1943) reversed the flow of migratory couples. Accordingly, marriages dropped sharply in Nebraska but they climbed rapidly in Kansas. The latter state in turn sustained a sharp break in marriages after its own laws of July 1, 1947, halted the influx of nonresidents from Iowa, Nebraska, and Missouri.

the total in 1942, the year before premarital examinations were required. Thereafter, the proportion fell off steadily to 31 per cent in 1947, and it has remained close to that level since then. Similarly, in Montana 40 per cent of the grooms were nonresidents in 1946. The proportion dropped to 31 per cent, coincident with their new law in 1947, and fell off still further to 20 per cent in 1948.

The experience in New York is another good illustration of the decline in nonresident marriages following premarital legislation. Nonresidents had been marrying in increasing numbers in New York ever since World War I, due to the enactment of legislation in neighboring states. In upstate New York, for example, nonresident brides accounted for only 6 per cent of the total in 1916-1918. Thereafter the proportion swung upward, reaching 12 per cent in 1926, 22 per cent in 1932, and almost 34 per cent in 1936—the year premarital examinations were required in Connecticut. To cope with this situation, a waiting period of three days became effective in New York on September 1, 1937. The number of nonresident marriages declined immediately; the proportion for the year dropped to 27 per cent. Inauguration of premarital blood tests on July 1, 1938, further deterred nonresidents; among brides the proportion nonresident fell to 10 per cent in 1938, and to 4 per cent in 1939.

It is also noteworthy that, as states in the neighborhood of Massachusetts successively adopted laws requiring a premarital examination, nonresident marriages climbed in Massachusetts despite its compulsory five-day waiting period. In fact, nonresident grooms increased to 22 per cent of the total by the time the state's own blood-test law became effective in 1943.

A state which enacts new legislation generally loses resident as well as nonresident marriages. This is well illustrated by the experience in Iowa, where premarital examinations were required in April, 1941. As is evident from Table 15, both resident and nonresident marriages fell off in 1941 and 1942, but the decline was much greater for nonresidents. Moreover, nonresident marriages continued downward in 1943, whereas resident marriages swung upward in that year. In consequence, the index—nonresident marriages as a proportion of total marriages—did not immediately reflect the full effect of the new legislation. For grooms, it dropped from 57.4 per cent in 1940 to 44.2 per cent in 1941. Thereafter, however, it declined to 28.8 per cent in 1942, and to 21.5 per cent in 1943.

The situation was fairly similar in Virginia after its law became effective in August, 1940. As in Iowa, nonresident marriages were slashed by more than one half. On the other hand, resident marriages appear to have been only little affected. In consequence, nonresidents as a percentage of the total fell more quickly in Virginia than in Iowa, but in each the proportion eventually dropped by more than one half. Nevertheless, thousands of nonresident couples continue to marry in both states. In 1948, for example, 9,237 nonresident grooms married in Virginia. These included 2,587 from Pennsylvania, 1,549 from North Carolina, 1,095 from West Virginia, 813 from the District of Columbia, 494 from New York, 471 from Tennessee, and 455 from Maryland.

A relatively large proportion of nonresident marriages continues to occur in most states after passage of premarital legislation. This is evident from Table 16, which shows nonresident grooms as a proportion of the total. For example, despite Maine's law in 1941, even as late as 1949, about 12 per cent of the marriages in that state involved nonresident grooms. The experience is similar for Vermont, South Dakota, Nebraska, and Delaware.

With so many states having enacted premarital legislation during the 1940's, the question naturally arises whether there has been any change in the frequency of out-of-state marriages in

the country as a whole. On the basis of the data for reporting states (Table 16), it would appear that there has actually been an increase in nonresident marriages. However, it is not very likely that these data reflect the actual trend. In fact, if we make reasonable allowance for the missing states (All Other States in Table 16), the indications are that there has been practically no change. This is not unexpected since a decline in one state is usually accompanied by a rise in another. Thus in at least five states, namely, New Hampshire, Connecticut, Maryland, Mississippi, and California, the nonresident proportion was higher in 1949 than a decade earlier. It should also be noted that some nonresident marriages occur in every state, regardless of circumstances. Then too, the proportion is usually high in states which lose residents to contiguous states. This is particularly true in the Mountain states, where two-way "migration" prevails on a large scale according to the convenience of travel and the proximity of populated communities.

Statistics on residence derived from marriage records are not always meaningful. During World War II, for example, many servicemen

Table 16. Nonresident Grooms as Per Cent of Total Marriages, United States and Specified States, 1939, 1940, 1948, and 1949

Area	1939	1940	1948	1949	Area	1939	1940	1948	1949
United States	19.1	20.2	17.3	18.8	South Atlantic				
Reporting states	18.0	19.9	19.2	24.0	Delaware	27.7	52.1	*	23.0
All other states†	20.3	20.6	16.9	16.6	Maryland	42.2	51.1	*	56.5†
					Dist. of Columbia	36.7	44.9	*	*
New England					Virginia	51.5	53.6	24.7	26.9
Maine	17.4	19.6	*	12.1	West Virginia	36.2	40.0	*	*
New Hampshire	41.8	41.9	45.1	49.0	Florida	9.0	8.8	*	*
Vermont	31.2	33.2	*	20.1					
Massachusetts	17.9	19.5	*	*	South Central				
Rhode Island	*	11.2	*	*	Tennessee	*	*	8.8	13.9
Connecticut	13.5	12.5	18.4	19.2	Alabama	7.8	9.2	*	7.0†
					Mississippi	14.7	17.9	43.5	48.7
Middle Atlantic					Arkansas	18.4	22.6	*	*
New York‡	4.9	4.8	6.8	7.4	Louisiana§	*	*	8.4	8.1
New Jersey	12.7	12.4	*	*	Oklahoma	18.4	19.1	*	*
Pennsylvania	13.3	9.7	*	*					
North Central					West				
Michigan	3.0	3.1	*	*	Montana	*	*	20.3	22.2
Wisconsin	6.5	6.7	3.1	*	Idaho	39.9	49.0	38.4	39.2
Iowa	49.8	57.4	19.1	21.7	Wyoming	*	*	30.8	32.8
North Dakota	*	*	*	10.1	New Mexico	*	*	*	57.8
South Dakota	32.9	16.9	10.1	26.1	Utah	25.5	28.4	*	*
Nebraska	25.1	32.2	*	18.1	Oregon	7.7	7.9	*	*
Kansas	*	*	15.3	19.6	California	2.8	2.2	*	4.3

*Not available.   †Estimated.
‡1948 and 1949, excludes New York City; proportion for comparable area in 1939 and 1940 was close to 7 per cent.
§Includes estimate for New Orleans.

Source of basic data: 1939 and 1940, primarily from reports by the Bureau of the Census; 1948 and 1949, from state registrars.

listed their base or camp, rather than their home town, as their residence on applications for marriage licenses. In communities with large military or naval installations, such as the Hampton Roads-Peninsula Area,[5] this resulted in a substantial overstatement of residents. The problem is of much smaller magnitude today, but it still exists wherever armed forces are stationed.

Despite the limitations of the available data, it would appear that one of every five grooms marries outside of the state in which he resides; currently this is true in about 300,000 marriages a year. The proportion is about 2 per cent less for brides, who are more likely to marry in their state of residence. Marriages in which both bride and groom are nonresidents are even less frequent; they probably account for one of every six marriages in the country.

Gretna Greens. In 1754, when England enacted legislation prohibiting marriage without parental consent, many young couples traveled to the village of Gretna Green which is located just across the border in Scotland. There, couples were quickly and legally married, without formality or obstacle, by merely declaring themselves man and wife before any two witnesses. Although the frequency of such marriages was sharply curtailed by enactment of residence requirements in 1876, even to this date Gretna Green continues to attract "runaway" couples.

In the United States today, it is not generally possible for couples to be married by merely declaring themselves. However, there are places which are noted for the large number of nonresident couples who secure licenses and are married. Have the number of these places decreased as more and more states have enacted restrictive legislation? A simple answer is not readily available. For one thing, comparisons between periods of time, generations apart, involve qualitative as well as quantitative consideration. Obviously,

transportation is an important factor. Today, it may be more convenient to travel fifty miles to the next state than it was at the turn of the century to get to the next town five miles away. Then too, years ago, common-law marriages were fairly frequent in our frontier areas; today, couples generally obtain a marriage license at the closest county seat. In sparsely settled areas, however, this often is in an adjoining state. Shifts in the population and the growth of urban communities also affect such long-time comparisons.

Aside from such considerations, evaluation of the question for short periods is hindered by the lack of adequate data, with the result that these so-called "Gretna Greens" have to be identified primarily on the basis of the number (or rate) of marriages occurring in a county. The Bureau of the Census, in its former reports, used the criterion "counties having a marriage rate at least three times the rate of the state in which located."[6] The limitations of this definition are apparent from the fact that Washoe County (Reno) with 5,102 marriages in 1931 was excluded; it accounted for two thirds of the marriages in Nevada and thus practically determined the state marriage rate. At the same time, counties with relatively few marriages were included—for example, Flagler County (Florida), with only 108 marriages in 1931.

It would appear more appropriate to consider both the absolute number and the rate of marriage in identifying "Gretna Greens." First, it is essential that such a place have a relatively large number of marriages. For recent years, this might be set at a minimum of 1,000 marriages a year for the county in which the marriage center is located. In 1948, for example, about 337 counties (or independent cities) met this requirement. Obviously the number of marriages in a typical community depends on the size of its population, so that a high marriage rate is also a necessary condition. Moreover, the rate should be related to the national average rather than to the rate in the state in which the county is located. With 12.4 marriages per 1,000 population for the country as a whole in 1948, at what level was a rate high? Examination of the rates for the 337

---

[5]Members of the armed forces accounted for 53.8 per cent of the grooms who applied for marriage licenses during 1942-1945 (see Rigdon W. Kernodle, *The Effect of World War II on the Incidence of Marriage in the Hampton Roads-Peninsula Area*, Ph.D. dissertation, University of North Carolina, Chapel Hill, 1949, p. 156). In New Jersey, more than 50 per cent of the marriages in 1944 involved soldiers (Thomas P. Monahan, *The Pattern of Age at Marriage in the United States*, Stephenson-Brothers, Philadelphia, 1951, Vol. II, p. 272).

[6]Bureau of the Census, *Marriage and Divorce, 1931*, Washington, 1933, p. 8.

counties with 1,000 or more marriages in 1948 indicates that most were below 20 per 1,000 population; the rate was less than 10 in 64 counties, 10-19 in 188 counties, 20-29 in 13 counties, 30-39 in 10 counties, 40-49 in 12 counties, and 50 or more in 50 counties. Clearly, there is no scientific basis for selecting a particular rate as the criterion; apparently a rate twice the national average would suffice for the purpose. However, a more conservative measure has been selected, namely, a rate of at least 50 marriages per 1,000 population—approximately four times the national rate. The counties classed as "Gretna Greens" in 1948, according to this definition, are shown in Table 17.

These "Gretna Greens" were located in 18 states, scattered primarily throughout the South and West, with the principal concentration lying along a band stretching in a southwesterly direction from Maryland to Texas. Mississippi and Arkansas, with six in each state, had the largest number. In Mississippi these centers were not in the resort part of the state; they were located on the Tennessee and Alabama borders, from which states a total of 20,000 couples annually marry in Mississippi. It seems apparent, therefore, that the "Gretna Greens" in Mississippi owed their existence to the fact that during 1948 licenses could be obtained without a waiting period or premarital examination. The popularity of the centers in Arizona, Nevada, Georgia,[7] and Colfax County (New Mexico) also resulted in part at least from their location on state borders and from the absence of restrictive marriage regulations. Similarly, relatively lenient laws account for the "Gretna Greens" along the northern boundary in South Carolina and for the two in Texas[8] (Clay and Cooke counties) on the Oklahoma border.

Variations in the laws of contiguous states explain the popularity of marriage centers in several other states. Thus, although both Oregon and Washington have a three-day waiting period,

[7]Although 1948 data are not available for Walker County, it too probably fell within the definition of "Gretna Green" (Table 17). Rossville, in that county, is just across the state border from Chattanooga in east Tennessee. It is noteworthy that, when Georgia passed its blood-test law, facilities were hastily set up in Rossville to provide rapid blood testing — thus assuring survival of its marriage "trade."

[8]In 1948 only males were required to have a premarital examination.

Table 17. Gretna Greens* in the United States, 1948

Area	Recorded Marriages		Area	Recorded Marriages	
	Number	Rate		Number	Rate
North Central			South (continued)		
Indiana					
Clark	2,758	57	North Carolina		
Steuben	1,136	67	Pasquotank	1,664	69
Iowa			South Carolina		
Chickasaw	1,398	92	Cherokee	2,468	71
Ohio			Darlington	3,163	63
Meigs	1,608	69	Marlboro	2,120	67
			York	5,545	77
South			Texas		
			Clay	1,175	119
Arkansas			Cooke	1,547	70
Benton	2,485	65	Guadalupe	1,297	51
Boone	1,012	62	Parker	1,985	92
Clay	4,324	162	Rockwall	2,730	446
Crawford	1,288	57	Virginia		
Randolph	1,546	89	Frederick	1,034	59
Saline	2,430	102	Greensville	1,138	70
Georgia			Winchester†	1,688	123
Camden	1,526	208			
Rabun	1,437	195			
Kentucky			West		
Campbell	7,150	95			
Greenup	7,456	300	Arizona		
Kenton	5,658	54	Yuma	15,460	570
Mason	1,280	70	Idaho		
Simpson	2,839	244	Kootenai	2,376	95
Louisiana			Nevada		
St. Bernard	2,100	189	Clark	19,197	404
Maryland			Douglas	1,392	697
Cecil	12,602	378	Elko	2,034	175
Garrett	2,423	114	Ormsby	3,026	739
Mississippi			Washoe	24,511	495
Alcorn	5,586	207	New Mexico		
De Soto	6,220	253	Colfax	1,947	119
George	2,097	210	Hidalgo	1,802	353
Jackson	1,899	61	Washington		
Lowndes	2,350	62	Clark	4,772	56
Tishomingo	1,598	103	Skamania	1,469	306

*Counties with at least 1,000 recorded marriages which had 50 or more recorded marriages per 1,000 resident population.
†Independent city.

thousands of residents of Portland and its environs cross the Columbia River into Washington and marry in Vancouver and Skamania in order to avoid the blood test required by Oregon. The explanation is fairly similar for the five centers in Kentucky. In 1948, this state required an examination but had no waiting period,[9] whereas the adjoining states of Ohio and Tennessee had both regulations.

Not all of the counties shown in Table 17 owe their popularity to differences in state marriage laws. Some are on highways leading out of, or are adjacent to, large cities. These include Saline in Arkansas; Kootenai in Idaho; Clark in Indiana; Saint Bernard in Louisiana; Pasquotank

[9]A three-day waiting period became effective in Kentucky on January 1, 1950.

in North Carolina; and Guadalupe, Parker, and Rockwall in Texas. Chickasaw County, Iowa, is also an exception to the general rule; a romantic interest has attached itself to the locality ever since The Little Brown Church near Nashua was popularized by song more than four decades ago.

Currently the most popular marriage centers in the country are those in Washoe (Reno) and Clark (Las Vegas) counties, Nevada; and Cecil County (Elkton), Maryland. For years, Elkton, a small town in Maryland adjoining Delaware, regularly attracted thousands of nonresident couples from five or more states. On November 8, 1938, Maryland imposed a two-day waiting period and immediately the number of marriage licenses issued in Elkton fell off sharply. Only 4,532 marriages were performed during 1939 in Cecil County, compared with 16,054 in 1938. In 1940, however, the trend was reversed, and by 1941 Elkton had regained most of its former patronage. In 1948, for example, more than 25,000 persons were married in Cecil County. This corresponds to three fourths of their resident population. More than nine of every ten couples who marry in Elkton are residents of other states; two fifths of the nonresidents come from Pennsylvania, another two fifths from New York and New Jersey, and most of the balance from Delaware and Connecticut.[10] The continued popularity of Elkton is all the more remarkable in view of the fact that all marriages in Maryland must be performed by religious officiants.

The other two outstanding "Gretna Greens"— Reno and Las Vegas—owe their origin to the enactment of premarital legislation in the neighboring state of California. Effective July 29, 1927, a wait of three days was required in California between the application for a marriage license and its issuance. This resulted in an immediate decline in marriages in California, from 56,664 in 1926 to 53,487 in 1927 and to 46,945 in 1928.

At the same time, however, marriages rose rapidly in Nevada and Arizona. In Yuma, the marriage rate jumped from 16 per 1,000 population in 1926 to 45 in 1927, and to 102 in 1929. By 1932 the rate had passed 200 per 1,000 and was still climbing. Sharp upswings also occurred in

Reno, Las Vegas, and other small towns in Nevada, as thousands of California couples crossed the border to avoid the marriage law of their home state. Almost overnight, wedding chapels and billboards advertising these chapels sprung up on all roads leading out of California. A new and very lucrative business enterprise had started, for which no capital but only a room with an appearance of dignity was needed.

In September, 1939, premarital blood tests were required in California, causing the marriage rate to fall to a record low of 6.5 per 1,000 in 1940 and resulting in further increases in Nevada and Arizona. During World War II, however, migration of couples out of California was sharply curtailed. For one thing, difficulties in transportation arose due to the rationing of gasoline. Then too, many young people in the armed forces and civilians engaged in war work found it necessary to marry where they were stationed or employed. Equally important, California's three-day waiting period was repealed early in 1943. The end of the war again witnessed an upswing of marriages at the centers in Nevada and Arizona. In 1948, more than 400 marriages per 1,000 population occurred in Las Vegas, Reno, and Yuma.[11]

The reasons for the continued popularity of the centers in Nevada are readily apparent. Foremost, of course, is the ease and convenience with which couples can be married at any time of night or day. In fact, couples can fly from Los Angeles to Las Vegas, be married, and return within hours. However, even if restrictive laws were enacted in Nevada, it is likely that its marriage centers would retain at least part of their "trade." This is particularly true of Reno and Las Vegas, which have become famous for their gambling casinos and vacation facilities. The

---

[10]Based on sample of 2,065 marriages in 1950, classified by residence of the groom (statistics supplied by the Registrar of Vital Statistics, Maryland Department of Health).

[11]Marriages plunged downward in Arizona after December 7, 1956, as a result of legislation requiring a premarital serologic test and a waiting period of 48 hours. Although Arizona formerly attracted a large number of California couples, many of its own residents married outside the state. For example, Hidalgo County in New Mexico issued four fifths of its marriage licenses to Arizona residents. The county clerk attributes this to the fact that, when a divorce is granted in Arizona, both parties must wait one year before they can remarry in the state. As a result, those people who marry soon after their divorce do so in New Mexico.

remarriage in Nevada of persons divorced there would also keep the marriage rate at a relatively high level.

Evaluation. It is clear that premarital examinations and waiting periods depress the marriage rate, at least temporarily, in states which enact such regulations, but it is equally evident that there is generally a compensating upswing in neighboring states. Accordingly, it is unlikely that such laws have any measurable effect on the frequency of marriage in the country as a whole. Some couples fail to return for their marriage license after applying for it, but this is not evidence[12] that waiting periods are effective deterrents to "hasty" marriages. There are a host of reasons why couples fail to go through with a contemplated marriage, and this may occur at any stage of the procedure. In fact, in states with or without restrictive regulations, each year hundreds of marriage applications do not culminate in marriage.

Premarital regulations are relatively ineffective because they often conflict with public policy. For example, after Pearl Harbor, when the marriage rush was on and there were daily lineups at the marriage bureaus in most communities, men in the armed forces or merchant marine were moved ahead. It was also common policy to waive premarital regulations in favor of these men. In fact, in some cities committees were formed by bar associations and other groups of the citizenry to expedite the issuance of licenses to soldiers and sailors. Moreover, at all times, in almost every state, marital regulations can be waived in case the prospective bride is pregnant or for other reasons acceptable to the responsible official.

There may not be any better solution than to waive the law in such cases, despite the fact that many of these marriages are the very ones which are supposed to be deterred by restrictive legislation. Under the circumstances, it is possible that nothing would be lost by the country as a whole if premarital waiting periods were repealed in all states, as has been done to date in nine states. Obviously, if such laws were re-pealed, there would be further shifting of non-resident marriages from one state to another. Such shifts may also occur in the future because the laws as they now exist effect a concentration of marriages in "isolated" states, and this may ultimately force these states to enact legislation for "protective" purposes.

More likely, however, the major shifts of the future will result from repeal or modification of existing laws requiring premarital examinations. In a number of states, the law or administration thereof has overemphasized the importance and value of serologic tests. In consequence, several articles have already appeared in the public health and medical literature stressing the fact that these laws are not intended to prevent permanently the marriage of persons with venereal infection, but only to delay the marriage of those with communicable or potentially communicable disease until the disease has been rendered permanently noninfectious.[13] More important, the very basis for this type of legislation is now being challenged by public health officers. Most notable has been the position taken by Maryland officials, with the result that such legislation has not been enacted in that state. These persons question whether the premarital blood-test law is a sound approach to the venereal disease problem, let alone to the whole subject of pre-marital public education and fitness for marriage.

There is no question but that everyone should try to determine, before marriage, whether he is fit to marry. Do I have tuberculosis? Am I mentally sound? Are we compatible in all essential relationships? Can I make an adequate living for a family? Do I have syphilis or gonorrhea, or any other condition which would make me unsuitable for marriage? There is, however, no legal process by which the answers to these questions can be forced. People must learn to want to know whether they are fit to marry. When they really want to know, they will go to the most competent doctor they can find, tell the truth and submit to exhaustive study. The physician will make the best examination of which he is capable, and will give his opinion as to the result. It will not be a legal guarantee of fitness to marry, and it should not be, for it will still depend upon how much of the truth has been told, upon how well trained and experienced the physician may be in all the medical factors to be

---

[12]Paul Popenoe and Roswell H. Johnson, *Applied Eugenics*, Revised Edition, The Macmillan Company, New York, 1933, p. 183.

[13]For example, see "Premarital Examination for Syphilis," *Journal of American Medical Association*, 139:310-311, January 29, 1949.

considered and upon how capable the best of medical science may be of providing the answers.[14]

Currently most states apply one inconclusive test for a single disease to the whole question of fitness to marry. Clearly, this is unsound. It should be equally obvious from the earlier sections of this chapter that our state borders are boundaries, not barriers, and that no type of marital legislation can effectively alter this situation. Nor is there any particular "magic" in requiring a waiting period of one, two, or even

[14]Baltimore City Health Department, "Why Is A Pre-Marital Blood Test Law Unsound Legislation?" Baltimore *Health News*, 24:131, May, 1947. See also, Maryland State Department of Health *Monthly Bulletin*, 27:2-3, October, 1955, and A. W. Hedrich and Charlotte Silverman, "Should The Premarital Blood Test Be Compulsory?" *American Journal of Public Health*, 48:125-132, February, 1958. Due to the marked decrease in the number of unknown cases of infectious syphilis, even former proponents of premarital examination laws now recommend reevaluation of their case-finding and control value. See Philip K. Condit and A. Frank Brewer, "Premarital Examination Laws — Are They Worth While?" *American Journal of Public Health*, 43:880-887, July, 1953.

seven days. Such requirement has meaning only if something is done during this period. Those who are intent on a hasty marriage will find some devious way to circumvent the law. On the other hand, in the more typical cases, the prospective groom and bride will be no more prepared after the lapse of a few days than they were before. Preparation for marriage is the result of a lifetime of training, guidance, and experience —by the home, by the church, and by educational and other public institutions. In only one respect can couples be aided by the state at the last moment, and that is in possibly preventing the perpetration of fraud. Yet this is the very area in which most states are completely remiss.

It is possible, of course, that premarital regulations have some beneficial educational value and that this cannot be measured by available marriage (or divorce) statistics. If this is so, the effects are undoubtedly slight. At any rate, despite recent legislation, there is no evidence that nonresident marriages have declined in frequency.

Chapter *4*

MARRIAGES BY TYPE OF CEREMONY

MARRIAGE by religious ceremony has been favored over the civil throughout most of our history. In early colonial days, however, the Puritan idea that marriage was a purely civil contract was shared by the founders of the church and commonwealths in New England, with the result that only magistrates could legalize marriages.

Toward the close of the seventeenth century, the colonists lost sympathy with this complete secularization of marriage. Accordingly, in 1692 the Massachusetts Province laws were amended to enable the Congregational clergy to solemnize marriages, and shortly thereafter it became the universal custom to permit ministers of all denominations to perform the ceremony.

In most states, the law now clearly sets forth how and by whom a marriage may be celebrated. Usually this may be by a magistrate or other civil official, or by an ordained minister of the gospel. It is important to note, however, that clergymen in our country have always performed the marriage ceremony, not in their capacity as ministers, but as civil officers constituted for the purpose by the state.

GENERAL PATTERN

Currently, about three out of every four marriages in the United States are celebrated with a religious ceremony (Table 18). The proportion of couples who eventually have a religious ceremony is somewhat higher, however, since a considerable number of civil ceremonies are followed by a religious one (Appendix Note 1).

Little is known about the actual frequency of religious and civil ceremonies during most of our history. There are indications, however, that the pattern has not changed much during this century. In Rhode Island and Philadelphia, for example, the proportion of marriages by religious ceremony declined by 2 per cent up to the end of World War I

Table 18. Marriages by Type of Ceremony, United States, 1939-1948

Year	Religious		Civil	
	Number (1,000's)	Per Cent	Number (1,000's)	Per Cent
1939	1,046	74.5	358	25.5
1940	1,183	74.1	413	25.9
1941	1,306	77.0	390	23.0
1942	1,348	76.1	424	23.9
1943	1,148	72.8	429	27.2
1944	1,041	71.7	411	28.3
1945	1,150	71.3	463	28.7
1946	1,650	72.0	641	28.0
1947	1,476	74.1	516	25.9
1948	1,354	74.8	457	25.2

Source: Estimated by the author. Figures for 1941-1947 were approximated from data for areas which reported one tenth of the total marriages in the country as a whole.

and by about an equal amount in the next two decades.[1]

The national picture for more recent years is shown in Table 18. It is clear that the frequency of religious ceremonies in 1948 was approximately the same as in 1939. In both years religious officiants performed almost 75 per cent of the country's total marriages. By contrast, around the turn of the century, they may have performed closer to 80 per cent of the total.

WORLD WAR II

The number of marriages by civil ceremony remained relatively unchanged at somewhat above

[1]During this period, the decrease in the proportion of marriages by religious ceremony also averaged close to 2 per cent a decade in Australia, but was much less in New Zealand. However, in both countries, religious ceremonies are relatively more frequent than in the United States. In Australia the clergy officiate in somewhat more than nine tenths of all marriages; in New Zealand the proportion exceeds four fifths.

400,000 per year during most of the period of our active participation in World War II. However, the number by religious ceremony was affected somewhat more, and largely determined the trend of total marriages during the conflict. Church weddings as a proportion of the total rose from 74 per cent in 1940 to a peak of 77 per cent in 1941, and then declined to a low of 71.3 per cent in 1945. Thereafter the proportion swung upward to the prewar level.

The decrease in religious ceremonies during hostilities probably resulted from a number of factors. Many servicemen had little opportunity to arrange for a church wedding. This was particularly true for men who married hastily before "shipping" overseas. Often in such cases the intended bride visited the general area of the military or naval station only long enough for the ceremony to be performed by a civil officiant. In fact, were it not for the considerable number of couples who were married by service chaplains, religious ceremonies would have been much less frequent.

Many civilians also found it inconvenient to have a church wedding, either because they were employed away from home and thus few relatives or friends could attend the affair, or because the pressure of war work did not afford sufficient time for the necessary preparations.

It is noteworthy that in Australia religious marriages increased from $91\frac{1}{2}$ per cent of the total in 1939-1940 to almost 93 per cent in 1943-1944, when large numbers of military personnel from the United States and other countries were stationed there. By contrast, during World War I, the proportion of marriages by religious ceremony declined slightly in Australia.[2]

ECONOMIC CONDITIONS

Church weddings are usually performed in the presence of relatives and acquaintances, and often entail considerable expense for the families of the bride and groom and for the invited guests. It is therefore not surprising that religious cere-

monies fall off during economic depressions. In Australia, for example, the proportion of marriages by religious officiants declined from 92.4 per cent in 1929 to a low of 90 per cent in 1931, and then in the next four years climbed back to the predepression level. The pattern was similar in New Zealand, religious ceremonies dropping from 80.7 to 77.4 per cent between 1929 and 1931.

Available data for selected areas in the United States indicate a similar pattern. New York City marriages in which the clergy officiated fell from 69 per cent of the total in 1929 to 67 per cent in 1932. In Milwaukee and Philadelphia, the declines were even greater. The proportion dropped from about 82 per cent to somewhat less than 78 per cent in Milwaukee, and from about 94 per cent to 90 per cent in Philadelphia.

The effects of an economic depression on the proportion of marriages by religious ceremony appear to be twofold. Some of the couples, who would have had a church wedding,[3] postpone their marriage until better times; others are wed by a civil officiant. The latter couples, apparently, help to maintain the number of civil ceremonies at about their normal level. In some areas—for example, Philadelphia—their number actually increased during the 1930's.

GEOGRAPHIC VARIATIONS

The proportion of marriages by religious officiants varies considerably from one area of the country to another. In general, religious ceremonies are most frequent in the Middle Atlantic and West North Central divisions, and least frequent in the Mountain states. This is evident from Table 19, which shows the figures for every state in 1948 and for about one half of the states in 1939 and 1940.

Several states deviate from the national pattern by a wide margin. In Maryland[4] and West Virginia

---

[2]The effect of the first World War may also have been negligible in our own country. In Rhode Island and Philadelphia, for example, religious ceremonies as a proportion of the total fell by about one per cent from 1917 to 1918 and then rebounded in 1919.

[3]Even the word "wedding" has an economic connotation. The word is derived from the ancient custom of marriage by purchase. The intended groom gave a "wed" of money or cattle as the price for purchasing his bride. The word "groom" also has an interesting history. On the wedding day in early England, it was customary for the man to wait upon his intended bride at the table. Since such a servitor was called a groom, the husband-to-be became known as the "bride's groom."

[4]Marriage is recognized as a "civil contract" and not a "sacrament" in Maryland, yet the 1871 decision of their

Table 19. Per Cent of Marriages by Religious Ceremony, by State of Occurrence, United States, 1939, 1940, and 1948

Geographic Division and State	1939	1940	1948
United States	74.5	74.2	74.8
New England	*	85.3	82.5
Maine	82.5	80.9	82.2
New Hampshire	69.4	68.1	59.2
Vermont	83.2	80.2	85.4
Massachusetts	89.3	87.8	86.4
Rhode Island	*	94.9	86.4
Connecticut	86.2	85.3	81.2
Middle Atlantic	86.1	85.5	85.6
New York	88.7	85.2	85.3
New Jersey	85.8	84.4	87.0
Pennsylvania	83.0	86.5	85.2
East North Central	*	*	80.5
Ohio	*	*	85.4
Indiana	*	*	76.6
Illinois	*	*	75.2
Michigan	89.2	88.1	81.7
Wisconsin	88.9	90.5	88.0
West North Central	*	*	85.0
Minnesota	*	*	83.7
Iowa	67.5	63.4	85.9
Missouri	*	*	91.1
North Dakota	*	*	92.0
South Dakota	74.2	86.4	81.6
Nebraska	56.0	51.6	79.4
Kansas	*	*	76.8
South Atlantic	*	*	72.4
Delaware	96.0	92.0	99.5
Maryland	100.0	100.0	100.0
District of Columbia	96.4	93.9	95.0
Virginia	88.1	86.4	87.0
West Virginia	100.0	100.0	100.0
North Carolina	*	*	71.8
South Carolina	*	*	41.2
Georgia	*	*	55.0
Florida	37.9	36.4	62.6
East South Central	*	*	66.5
Kentucky	*	*	70.5
Tennessee	*	*	79.4
Alabama	71.6	70.9	72.8
Mississippi	74.0	73.2	55.7
West South Central	*	*	64.8
Arkansas	64.8	66.4	43.5
Louisiana	*	*	77.4
Oklahoma	73.0	73.1	73.4
Texas	*	*	68.2
Mountain	*	*	45.0
Montana	*	*	66.1
Idaho	62.5	66.0	61.3
Wyoming	*	*	66.6
Colorado	*	*	76.6
New Mexico	*	*	35.6
Arizona	*	*	39.3
Utah	*	*	84.9
Nevada	*	*	29.5
Pacific	*	*	78.1
Washington	*	*	71.3
Oregon	90.4	*	84.3
California	79.9	84.3	79.9

*Not available.
Source: State figures for 1939 and 1940 are largely from reports by the Bureau of the Census; all other data are from surveys by the author.

court of appeals is still in effect so that it is necessary to have a religious ceremony in order to contract a valid marriage in that state.

only religious ceremonies are permitted, and in Delaware the mayor of Wilmington is the only civil officiant who can perform a marriage.[5] Religious ceremonies also predominate strongly in six other areas. In 1948, they represented more than nine tenths of the total in the District of Columbia, North Dakota, and Missouri, and were only slightly below that proportion in Wisconsin, New Jersey, and Virginia.

At the other extreme, marriages by civil ceremony outnumber the religious in five states—Nevada, New Mexico, Arizona, South Carolina, and Arkansas. In Nevada the clergy officiate in only 30 per cent of the marriages. In fact, more civil ceremonies are performed in that state than in any other. In 1948, for example, there were about 36,900 in Nevada; by contrast, New York State had less than 23,000, even though its population was almost a hundred times greater.

RACIAL INFLUENCE

Despite the special legal requirements in Delaware, Maryland, and West Virginia, less than 69 per cent of all marriages in the South are performed by the clergy. The extent to which the white and nonwhite races contribute to this situation cannot be ascertained from available data. There are indications, however, that religious ceremonies may be relatively more frequent among Negroes than whites in the rural areas of the deep South but less frequent elsewhere. In Alabama during 1940, for example, the proportion of marriages by religious ceremony was 79 per cent for the nonwhite population compared with 67 per cent for the white. In Mississippi the annual differential was even greater between 1936 and 1942; the proportion averaged 80.7 per cent for the Negro population and 63.4 per cent for the white. On the other hand, in Virginia during 1936, about 95 per cent of the white couples had a religious ceremony compared with 93 per cent of the nonwhite. Then too, eight southern counties[6] with about 4,640 marriages in 1948 recorded a marked difference

[5] Civil ceremonies have been permitted in Kentucky since 1932.
[6] Baldwin, Bibb, DeKalb, Washington, and Worth counties, Georgia; Cumberland and Nash counties, North Carolina; and Lee County, South Carolina.

in favor of white couples; their proportion was close to three fourths compared with only one half for the nonwhite.

RELATION TO RESIDENT STATUS

The extent to which nonresident couples marry in a state has an important bearing on the relative frequency of religious ceremonies in that area. In Iowa, for example, religious ceremonies increased from 63.4 per cent of the total in 1940 to 85.9 per cent in 1948, at the same time that their number of nonresident marriages fell off sharply. This is not surprising since only one half of the nonresident marriages in Iowa are by religious ceremony, whereas the proportion is nine tenths for marriages in which one or both of the intended spouses is a resident.

The relationship to resident status is also evident from the experience in Mississippi where religious ceremonies dropped from 73.2 per cent of the total in 1940 to 55.7 per cent in 1948 and the proportion of marriages by nonresident couples more than doubled.

Nationwide statistics also confirm this relationship. As may be seen from Table 20, the proportion by religious officiants is much higher for residents than for nonresidents. Thus, in 1939-40 the proportion was 77.2 per cent for the resident grooms, but only 62.6 per cent for the nonresident. For brides the differential was even greater. It is also noteworthy that religious ceremonies are most frequent for marriages between a resident bride and a nonresident groom, and least frequent if both are nonresidents.

Table 20. Marriages by Type of Ceremony and Resident Status, United States, 1939-40

Resident Status*	Per Cent by Religious Ceremony	Per Cent by Resident Status		
		All Marriages	Marriages by Religious Ceremony	Marriages by Civil Ceremony
Total	74.3	100.0	100.0	100.0
Resident groom	77.2	80.3	83.4	71.3
Resident bride	77.6	78.0	81.5	68.1
Nonresident bride	63.6	2.3	1.9	3.2
Nonresident groom	62.6	19.7	16.6	28.7
Resident bride	81.3	4.1	4.5	3.0
Nonresident bride	57.7	15.6	12.1	25.7
Resident bride	77.8	82.1	86.0	71.1
Nonresident bride	58.5	17.9	14.0	28.9

*In state where marriage occurred.
Source: Estimated by the author from data for selected areas.

As would be expected, civil marriage ceremonies predominate in Gretna Greens. The 1948 situation in Nevada has already been cited. However, the proportion of marriages by civil ceremony was even higher in several counties in other states. For example, they represented about nine tenths of the total in York (South Carolina) and Hidalgo (New Mexico), and exceeded seven tenths in such widely scattered counties as Guadalupe (Texas), Clay (Arkansas), Meigs (Ohio), and Kootenai (Idaho).

FIRST MARRIAGE AND REMARRIAGE

The type of ceremony chosen by a couple is related to their marital status. In 1948 about 81 per cent of all first marriages in the United States were performed by the clergy; among remarriages, the proportion was 55 per cent for grooms and 51 per cent for brides. Moreover, the proportion varied considerably between the widowed and the divorced, as is evident from Table 21. Two thirds of the widowed had a religious ceremony, compared with less than one half of the divorced.

Table 21. Per Cent of Marriages by Religious Ceremony, by Previous Marital Status of Grooms and Brides and by Age of Brides, United States, 1948

Status	Groom	Bride	Age	Bride
Total	74.8	74.8	Total	74.8
			Under 20	81.9
First Marriage	80.5	81.6	20 - 24	81.8
Remarriage	54.6	51.1	25 - 29	70.1
			30 - 39	55.4
Widowed	67.6	65.1	40 - 49	50.9
Divorced	49.8	45.6	50 - 59	61.7
			60 and over	68.7

Note: Estimated by the author.

The relatively large proportion of marriages by civil ceremony among persons who have been previously wed results from a number of factors. Foremost is the prohibition by some faiths against remarriage within the church of divorced persons. Thus in Connecticut during 1949, Roman Catholic ceremonies represented about three fifths of all religious ceremonies for persons entering their first marriage compared with somewhat less than one fourth for those who were remarrying—the great majority of whom had been previously divorced. That civil ceremonies predominate among divorced Catholics who re-marry is also indicated by Iowa statistics.[7]

Aside from religious considerations, church weddings are less frequent among those who re-marry because many widowed and older persons in general prefer a simple affair and the civil ceremony often suffices for this purpose. In fact, even single persons are more likely to have a civil ceremony if they marry late in life.[8]

DIFFERENTIALS BY AGE

Most young couples have a church wedding. At the middle and older ages, religious ceremonies

are much less frequent, reflecting the increased importance of remarriages in the total picture. The age pattern for brides in the United States during 1948 is shown in the right-hand column of Table 21. At ages under 25, about 82 per cent were married by religious ceremony. With advance in age the proportion fell off to a mini-mum of 51 per cent for those in their forties, and then swung upward for the older brides. At ages 60 and over, when widows predominate, about 69 per cent were married by the clergy.

In view of the above, it is not surprising to find that couples who are married by a civil officiant are older on the average than those who have a religious ceremony. In 1948 about 53 per cent of the brides who had a civil ceremony were 25 years of age or older; for those married by the clergy, the corresponding proportion was less than 29 per cent.

[7]Thomas P. Monahan and Loren E. Chancellor, "Statis-tical Aspects of Marriage and Divorce by Religious Denomi-nation in Iowa," *Eugenics Quarterly*, 2:166-167, September, 1955.

[8]Joseph V. DePorte, "Civil Marriage in New York State, Apart from New York City," *American Sociological Review*, 17:234, April, 1952. Data for Bronx County in New York City show a similar pattern.

Chapter 5

PATTERNS IN MARRIAGE

THE present chapter considers the patterns in marriage with regard to such demographic characteristics as race, age, and previous marital status.

DIFFERENTIALS BY RACE

Marriage Rate. The marriage rate for the non-white population is higher than the rate for the white. This is evident from Table 22, which shows the estimated number of registered marriages per 1,000 male eligibles during each year since 1900. In the first decade of this century, the rate for the nonwhites averaged less than one fifth above that for the whites. Since then, however, although the rate for both groups moved upward, the differential in favor of the nonwhites has been much more pronounced. Their rate averaged one third above that of the whites during the 1910's and 1940's; between the two world wars it was about one half higher.

The comparatively low rate for the nonwhites around the turn of the century may reflect, in part, the incompleteness with which their marriages were registered at that time. Of much greater consequence, no doubt, was the fact that during those years common-law marriage without license or ceremony was still frequent among Negroes in the deep South and in some urban areas.

It is clear from the accompanying table that the marriage rate for total males is largely determined by that for the white. In fact, during the entire period under review, the rate for the white eligibles was only about 2 or 3 per 1,000 less than that for the total, and never dropped below it by more than 5 per 1,000. This close agreement between the two series of rates is understandable, since the white eligibles constitute a very large proportion of the total. Thus the rate for the total could be used as an approximation of the rate for the whites.

The situation is quite different for the nonwhite population. Most noteworthy is their experience during the depression of the 1930's and the periods of armed conflict. Thus between 1929 and 1932 the marriage rate for both groups decreased by one fourth. The decline for the nonwhites, however, was the more precipitous—almost all of it occurred by 1931. Nevertheless, even in 1931-32, when only 8.1 per cent of the nonwhite eligibles married, their rate was not exceptionally low. It had been lower in most years prior to World War I, and the rate for the whites had been that high only in 1920. For white males, on the other hand, the rate in 1932 (51 per 1,000 eligibles) may have been the lowest in our history.

During World War I, the rate for nonwhite males increased without interruption from 82 per 1,000 eligibles in 1915 to a peak of about 119 per 1,000 in 1919-20. The rate for the whites, by contrast, dropped sharply in 1918 at the height of our participation in the hostilities and did not reach its postwar peak until 1920.

The outbreak of the second world conflict was also accompanied by an upsurge of marriages which carried the rates for whites and nonwhites to new high levels. The two groups, however, reacted differently to the course of events. During the period prior to Pearl Harbor, there was no definite policy concerning the assimilation of Negroes into the armed forces, with the result that they were less likely to be selected by local draft boards. Our military preparations thus had less influence on the nonwhite population. In consequence, while the marriage rate for white males rose from 71 per 1,000 in 1939 to 87 in 1941, or by 23 per cent, the nonwhite rate increased by only 15 per cent. In 1942, however, with the increased tempo of the draft and favorable opportunities for employment in war industries, the rise in the marriage rate was much more marked for the nonwhites than for the whites. In fact, the rate for the nonwhites remained at a wartime peak of 132 marriages per 1,000 eligibles in 1942 and 1943, and dropped only to about 117 per 1,000 in the next two years.

At the close of World War II, the rates for both groups soared to all-time highs. However, the up-swing started earlier and was relatively more pronounced for white males. Moreover, only the rate for the whites rose in 1950, when the Korean conflict started. As a result of these recent trends, the relative difference in the mar-riage rate between the whites and nonwhites has narrowed consider-ably; in 1950 it was the smallest since the turn of the century.

Age at Marriage. The best avail-able information on age at mar-riage for the white and nonwhite population are the decennial census statistics showing the proportion of young people who have ever married. These data for the period since 1890 are summarized in Table 23. Clearly, the higher mar-riage rate of the nonwhite popula-tion is related, in part at least, to the earlier age at which they marry. Thus, at ages under 25, the proportion ever married has been consistently higher for the non-white population than for the white. In 1890, for example, among men aged 20-24 years, about 34 per cent of the nonwhites were or had been married compared with only about 17 per cent of the whites. Moreover, although the increase in this proportion has since been greater for white persons, particu-larly in recent years, the non-whites still had a somewhat higher proportion than the whites in 1950.

Remarriage. Another important factor in the relatively high marriage rate for nonwhite persons is the greater frequency of remarriage among them. Census data for 1940 and 1910 show that persons married more than once constitute a larger propor-tion of the total number of married Negro couples than of the native white. Thus, among married women at ages 15-74 years in 1940, the propor-tion who had been previously married was 18.5 per cent for the Negroes but only 9.4 per cent for

Table 22. Marriages, Marriage Eligibles, and Marriage Rate, by Color of Groom, United States, 1900-1950

Year	Number of Marriages (1,000's)		Marriage Eligibles (1,000's)		Marriages per 1,000 Eligibles		
	White	Non-white	White	Non-white	Total	White	Non-white
1900	628	81	10,323	1,299	61	61	62
1901	655	87	10,573	1,314	62	62	66
1902	679	97	10,825	1,327	64	63	73
1903	710	108	11,052	1,338	66	64	81
1904	716	99	11,306	1,350	64	63	73
1905	736	106	11,588	1,365	65	64	78
1906	788	107	11,845	1,376	68	67	78
1907	819	118	12,075	1,385	70	68	85
1908	754	103	12,350	1,397	62	61	74
1909	784	113	12,638	1,409	64	62	80
1910	847	101	12,890	1,420	66	66	71
1911	852	103	13,021	1,427	66	65	72
1912	890	115	13,134	1,432	69	68	80
1913	898	123	13,266	1,440	69	68	85
1914	906	119	13,388	1,445	69	68	82
1915	889	119	13,457	1,446	68	66	82
1916	931	145	13,500	1,444	72	69	100
1917	995	149	13,513	1,437	77	74	104
1918	838	162	13,450	1,423	67	62	114
1919	980	170	13,596	1,430	77	72	119
1920	1,105	169	13,664	1,438	84	81	118
1921	1,020	144	13,847	1,460	76	74	99
1922	985	149	13,899	1,471	74	71	101
1923	1,060	170	14,119	1,498	79	75	113
1924	1,018	167	14,399	1,533	74	71	109
1925	1,027	161	14,604	1,560	74	70	103
1926	1,045	158	14,831	1,588	73	70	99
1927	1,025	176	15,078	1,620	72	68	109
1928	1,006	176	15,335	1,653	70	66	106
1929	1,056	177	15,565	1,682	71	68	105
1930	975	152	15,858	1,717	64	61	89
1931	918	143	16,121	1,742	59	57	82
1932	841	141	16,409	1,769	54	51	80
1933	936	162	16,667	1,795	59	56	90
1934	1,117	185	16,831	1,808	70	66	102
1935	1,145	182	16,923	1,814	71	68	100
1936	1,177	192	17,004	1,820	73	69	105
1937	1,251	200	17,054	1,821	77	73	110
1938	1,142	189	17,115	1,824	70	67	104
1939	1,224	180	17,191	1,830	74	71	98
1940	1,396	200	17,228	1,836	84	81	109
1941	1,488	208	17,040	1,837	90	87	113
1942	1,530	242	16,802	1,830	95	91	132
1943	1,335	242	16,629	1,831	85	80	132
1944	1,234	218	16,706	1,860	78	74	117
1945	1,395	218	16,641	1,874	87	84	116
1946	2,010	281	16,328	1,859	126	123	151
1947	1,746	246	15,838	1,821	113	110	135
1948	1,595	216	15,539	1,806	104	103	120
1949	1,386	194	15,348	1,802	92	90	108
1950	1,479	188	15,196	1,804	98	97	104

Note: Marriage eligibles represent single men aged 15 years or over and all divorced or widowed men, including those in the armed forces overseas during 1917-1919 and 1940-1950, as of July 1 of each year.
Source: Estimated by the author.

Table 23. Per Cent Ever Married According to Age, by Color and Sex, United States, 1890-1950

Age	White							Nonwhite						
	1890	1900	1910	1920	1930	1940	1950	1890	1900	1910	1920	1930	1940	1950
	Male													
15-19	0.5	0.9	1.0	1.9	1.5	1.6	3.2	0.9	1.8	2.3	4.0	3.6	3.2	4.4
20-24	17.3	20.2	22.9	27.2	27.1	26.5	40.5	33.5	34.8	38.8	44.0	41.7	39.6	45.3
25-29	52.4	52.6	55.8	59.4	62.4	63.3	76.4	66.8	65.6	67.7	69.8	68.5	69.5	74.8
30-34	73.1	71.8	73.4	75.6	78.8	79.3	86.9	76.8	77.0	78.4	78.8	78.8	78.7	85.6
35-44	84.7	82.9	83.0	83.6	85.7	86.2	90.4	84.3	83.7	86.1	85.8	85.7	84.5	90.2
45-54	90.8	89.6	88.6	87.6	88.3	88.9	91.4	91.3	90.4	91.2	91.4	90.9	89.2	92.3
55-64	93.1	92.3	91.5	90.0	89.6	89.2	91.4	93.6	93.1	93.1	93.0	93.1	91.3	93.8
65 and over	94.4	94.2	93.6	92.5	91.4	89.9	91.4	94.2	94.9	95.3	94.3	94.0	93.0	94.5
	Female													
15-19	8.8	10.4	10.7	11.8	11.8	10.9	16.5	15.1	16.8	18.4	21.2	21.9	19.0	21.1
20-24	46.2	46.4	49.6	52.4	51.9	51.6	67.6	61.9	60.3	65.1	68.5	66.9	62.8	68.8
25-29	73.6	71.5	73.9	76.0	77.3	76.8	86.8	82.5	79.6	83.0	84.5	84.4	80.6	85.9
30-34	84.5	82.9	83.2	84.6	86.3	85.0	90.7	88.4	87.2	89.1	89.7	90.4	87.4	91.1
35-44	89.8	88.5	88.1	88.1	89.5	89.3	91.5	92.6	92.2	93.0	93.1	93.8	92.1	93.6
45-54	92.7	91.8	91.1	90.0	90.4	91.0	91.8	95.2	95.0	95.4	95.1	95.5	94.8	95.4
55-64	94.1	93.1	92.7	91.3	90.7	90.7	91.8	95.9	95.9	96.2	95.8	96.1	95.5	95.9
65 and over	94.2	93.9	93.4	92.7	91.6	90.3	90.7	95.7	95.7	96.4	95.9	96.3	95.9	95.6

Source of basic data: Population enumerated at the decennial censuses. Figures exclude armed forces overseas.

the whites. As is evident from Table A17, this differential is found at every age period, and was even greater in 1910 than in 1940.

These differences for the whites and nonwhites may arise in part from the relative quality of the census data on marital status for the two groups (see Introduction). It should be noted, however, that the findings are consistent with available marriage statistics for selected states which show that the widowed as a proportion of all brides and grooms is higher for the nonwhite population than for the white. Thus it is likely that there are racial differences in remarriage, and that these result largely from the higher incidence of widowhood among Negroes. It is also likely that these differences have lessened, and will continue to do so, as progress is made in reducing the excess mortality among Negroes.

Intermarriage. Marriages between white persons and Negroes or members of other nonwhite races are relatively infrequent in the United States. In 1939, the only year for which data are available, such interracial marriages accounted for only 8 out of every 10,000 marriages in the country.[1]

Of the total marriages between whites and nonwhites in 1939, slightly more than one half (51 per cent) took place between white men and non-

[1] The frequency of interracial marriages may have increased somewhat after World War II, when soldiers stationed overseas married girls from Japan and other Far East countries. See section, "Marriages Overseas," in Chapter 1.

white women, as may be seen from Table 24. The proportion is not uniform throughout the country, however; in fact, in some cities and states a majority of the intermarriages take place between Negro men and white women. This geographic variation, which is due largely to the relative infrequency of mixed marriages, probably explains the diversity of findings in previous studies based on the marriage experience in local areas.[2]

Table 24. Number of Marriages by Color of Bride According to Color of Groom, United States, 1939

Color of Groom	Total	Color of Bride	
		White	Nonwhite
Total	1,403,633	1,223,609	180,024
White	1,223,633	1,223,050	583
Nonwhite	180,000	559	179,441

Source: Estimated by the author from data for selected areas.

Intermarriage between white and nonwhite has been prohibited in many of our states since before the Civil War. Although such laws were omitted from some state codes during Reconstruction, they remained in effect in some areas of the North as well as in the South.[3] Currently,

[2] Joseph Golden, "Characteristics of the Negro-White Intermarried in Philadelphia," *American Sociological Review*, 18:177-183, April, 1953.

[3] John H. Franklin, "History of Racial Segregation in the United States," *Annals of the American Academy of Political and Social Science*, 304:5, March, 1956.

miscegenation statutes exist in 29 states, including all those in the South where our Negro population is concentrated.[4] In addition to the laws against Caucasians marrying Negroes, 17 states also prohibit marital unions between whites and one or more of the other nonwhite races.

AGE DIFFERENTIALS IN MATE SELECTION

American men generally marry in their twenties, choosing a bride who is within a few years of their own age. However, men who marry later in life prefer women several years their junior. These age differences are evident from Tables 25 and A13, which are derived from data on marriages in the United States during 1948.

Relatively few boys marry before age 18; those who do, tend to select a bride who is several months their senior. Aside from these teen-age grooms, however, men marry women younger than themselves. Moreover, the average difference in the ages of the couple increases rapidly with advance in age of the groom. At their 20th birthday men marry women whose median age is 19.0 years, a difference of only one year, but at age 25 they take brides three years their junior. The disparity increases to five years for a man who marries at age 31, and to about eight years where he is close to age 50. In the few marriages where the groom is past 75, the average age of the bride is almost 14 years less than his.

The pattern according to age of bride is quite different, as may be seen from the right-hand columns of Table 25. The typical bride chooses a mate older than herself, and the number of years she is younger than her spouse fluctuates with the period of life in which she marries. For brides 15 years of age, the median age of the grooms is 20.5 years, a difference of 5.5 years. Among those who become brides at age 18, the groom averages 3.6 years older; the difference is 2.3 years at age 21 and falls to only 1.6 years at age 28. Women who are 30 or older take a groom who is two to four years their senior, on an average. Elderly women, however, have no particular preference as to the age of their groom—brides past age 67 choose almost equally between younger and older men. It is also evident that the median age of grooms increases more rapidly with advancing age of brides than does the average age of brides for the older grooms.

The average bride is 2¼ years younger than her groom. However, in only a small proportion

Table 25. Median Age of Marital Partner, by Age of Groom and by Age of Bride, Marriages in the United States, 1948

Exact Age of Groom	Median Age of Bride	Exact Age of Groom	Median Age of Bride	Exact Age of Bride	Median Age of Groom	Exact Age of Bride	Median Age of Groom
16	17.9	48	40.1	15	20.5	47	51.5
17	17.2	49	41.1	16	21.2	48	51.4
18	17.8			17	21.3	49	51.7
19	18.5	50	42.5	18	21.6		
		51	42.7	19	22.1	50	53.6
20	19.0	52	43.8			51	54.7
21	19.3	53	45.6	20	22.7	52	55.7
22	20.0	54	46.0	21	23.3	53	56.2
23	20.8	55	46.8	22	24.2	54	58.1
24	21.4	56	46.7	23	25.1	55	59.8
25	22.0	57	46.8	24	26.0	56	59.1
26	22.5	58	48.2	25	26.9	57	60.2
27	23.0	59	49.9	26	27.7	58	61.4
28	23.7			27	28.7	59	61.1
29	24.6	60	51.2	28	29.6		
		61	51.6	29	30.9	60	62.0
30	25.4	62	52.7			61	63.6
31	26.0	63	53.4	30	32.1	62	65.2
32	26.8	64	53.9	31	33.1	63	65.9
33	27.9	65	55.9	32	34.2	64	66.1
34	28.8	66	57.4	33	35.0	65	66.2
35	30.1	67	54.8	34	35.9	66	66.7
36	31.2	68	55.2	35	37.1	67	67.8
37	31.0	69	58.4	36	38.1	68	68.2
38	31.4			37	39.2	69	68.9
39	32.9	70	60.5	38	40.3		
		71	61.5	39	40.8	70	70.4
40	34.1	72	62.8			71	71.8
41	35.7	73	62.0	40	42.3	72	72.0
42	36.7	74	61.6	41	44.1	73	72.8
43	37.1	75	62.5	42	45.0	74	74.6
44	37.9	76	62.0	43	45.5	75	76.2
45	38.0	77	64.9	44	46.4	76	76.6
46	38.5	78	66.6	45	47.7	77	76.0
47	39.6	79	65.0	46	49.6	78	78.7

Source: Data on marriages compiled by the author.

[4] Interracial marriages are not legally forbidden in any of the New England or Middle Atlantic states. Illinois, Iowa, Kansas, Michigan, Minnesota, Ohio, South Dakota, and Wisconsin in the North Central region are also free of restrictions. Mixed marriages are also permitted in the District of Columbia, and in Alaska, New Mexico and Washington.

of marriages—less than 12 per cent of the total—do the ages of the spouses differ by that exact amount. In three fourths of all marriages the bride is younger than the groom, in one tenth the spouses are of the same age, and in one seventh the bride is older than the groom (Table A13).

In almost two out of every three marriages, the ages of the couple differ by less than five years. In the remainder, the differences scatter over a wide range, with occasional marriages involving disparities of as much as 60 years. Moreover, the dispersion of relative ages becomes greater with advance in the age of the groom. Thus the proportion of grooms whose bride differs in age by five years or more increases from about 5 per cent for grooms under 18 years of age, to 15 per cent for those aged 20-24, and to about 75 per cent after age 50.

The young bride, on the other hand, chooses her partner from a relatively wide range of ages. Also, unlike the pattern for grooms, the dispersion is smaller for brides in their early twenties than for the teen-agers.

In most of the marriages in which the bride is older than the groom, only a small difference in age is involved. In fact, less than 4 per cent of all brides are older than their groom by five years or more. However, such marriages are much more frequent among older brides. They represent almost 10 per cent of the total where the bride is 30 years of age and exceed 20 per cent for those past age 65.

Variations by Race. The average disparity between the ages of groom and bride is somewhat greater for the Negro population than for the white. This is evident from Table A14, which is based upon marriages in 1940—the only year for which such detailed data are available for an extensive area of the country.

White men in the age group 20-24 years—averaging about $22\frac{1}{2}$ years—marry women whose average age is 21.3 years, a difference of about one year. By comparison, Negro grooms of those ages take brides almost three years younger than themselves. At ages 25-34 years, white and Negro grooms choose brides who are about the same number of years their junior; however, at the later ages white men marry women closer to their own age. For grooms 45-49 years of age, the average white bride is two years older than

the Negro bride. This disparity exceeds three years for grooms in their 50's, and is almost seven years for those past 70. Comparable details according to age of bride are also shown in Table A14.

Influence of Marital Status. Spouses tend to be about two years farther apart in age if either or both are remarrying than if neither partner was previously married.[5] This is due largely to the fact that remarriages occur at a later age, when wide age gaps are more common.

The previous marital status of a groom has little influence on the age of the bride he chooses. This is evident from Table 26, which is based upon marriages in Massachusetts. For example, during 1947-51 bachelors 20-24 years of age took brides whose average age was 21.5 years,

Table 26. Median Age of Bride According to Age of Groom and Previous Marital Status of the Couple, Marriages in Massachusetts, 1947-51 and 1921-25

| Age of Groom (Years) | All Marriages | Median Age of Bride | | | | | |
| | | Single Groom | | | Remarrying Groom | | |
		Total	Single Bride	Remarrying Bride	Total	Single Bride	Remarrying Bride
				1947-50			
20 - 24	21.5	21.5	21.4	25.1	21.9	21.4	24.0
25 - 29	23.9	23.9	23.7	28.1	24.8	23.8	27.6
30 - 34	27.8	27.7	27.2	31.5	28.4	26.6	31.2
35 - 39	32.2	32.1	31.2	35.5	32.6	30.1	34.9
40 - 44	36.6	36.5	35.5	39.1	36.7	34.1	38.5
45 - 49	40.6	40.8	39.3	43.3	40.5	37.7	42.2
50 - 54	44.9	44.5	42.5	47.2	45.0	41.8	46.6
55 - 59	49.4	49.0	47.0	50.9	49.5	45.1	51.2
60 - 64	53.6	54.3	51.5	55.7	53.5	48.5	55.0
65 - 69	58.0	58.2	54.8	61.1	58.0	52.2	59.0
70 - 74	61.8	63.8	62.5	*	61.8	57.0	62.9
				1921-25			
20 - 24	21.5	21.5	21.5	25.6	22.0	21.7	24.6
25 - 29	24.0	23.9	23.8	28.4	24.5	23.6	28.6
30 - 34	27.3	27.2	26.7	32.1	27.8	26.6	31.3
35 - 39	31.0	30.8	29.7	35.4	31.4	29.2	34.5
40 - 44	35.7	35.5	33.9	39.6	35.9	33.0	38.5
45 - 49	39.6	39.4	37.7	42.8	39.7	37.0	42.0
50 - 54	44.0	43.8	41.5	46.8	44.1	40.5	46.3
55 - 59	47.9	47.4	44.9	51.3	48.0	42.9	50.5
60 - 64	51.4	51.6	47.1	55.8	51.4	45.9	54.0
65 - 69	55.4	53.2	*	*	55.5	48.6	58.0
70 - 74	58.6	*	*	*	58.9	51.0	60.9

*Number of marriages too few to warrant computation.
Source of basic data: Annual reports of vital statistics, Secretary of the Commonwealth of Massachusetts.

[5]Bureau of the Census, *Current Population Reports*, Series P-20, No. 26, p. 18. See also Paul C. Glick and Emanuel Landau, "Age as a Factor in Marriage," *American Sociological Review*, 15:517-519, August, 1950.

which compares with 21.9 years for brides of the men who had been wed before. However, the average age of brides varies appreciably with their prior marital status. To illustrate, spinsters who married bachelors in the age group 20-24 years were 21.4 years old, on an average, whereas the corresponding divorcees and widows were 25.1 years of age. These figures undoubtedly overstate somewhat the actual age differences; within each age group, the average groom who chooses a previously married woman is somewhat older than the groom who marries a single girl. However, it is also likely that where men marry women older than themselves the proportion of divorcees or widows is higher than in couples where the bride is younger than the groom.

Trend. Where the groom is under age 30, the difference in age between the bride and groom is about the same now as a generation ago. On the other hand, men marrying later in life now choose brides somewhat closer to their own age, and increasingly so as the age at marriage rises.

In Massachusetts, for example, where the man is 30-34 years at marriage, the median age of his bride increased from 27.3 years to 27.8 years between 1921-25 and 1947-51, thereby decreasing the difference in the age of such newlyweds by one half year. Where the groom is at midlife, the disparity in age has been reduced by one year, and where he is past age 65, the reduction has been at least two years (Table 26).

Marriages involving marked age differences between spouses may also have become less

frequent over the years, judged by the experience in upstate New York. Thus marriages with the groom 15 or more years older than the bride declined from 3.7 per cent of the total in 1919 to 2.4 per cent in 1948. Also noteworthy, as may be seen from Figure 6, was the sharp decline immediately prior to our entrance into World War II and the even more marked upswing at the height of the hostilities. No doubt these deviations resulted largely from the fluctuations in the relative importance of the younger and older persons who married in the two periods.

How closely the marriage trends in Massachusetts and New York reflect the national pattern cannot be determined in the absence of nationwide statistics. No doubt one factor in the Massachusetts and New York patterns has been the declining number of foreign born, among whom large age differences between spouses are relatively common. However, there are indications that the age of the bride has become more like the groom's even among our native population. In fact, the current tendency to marry early

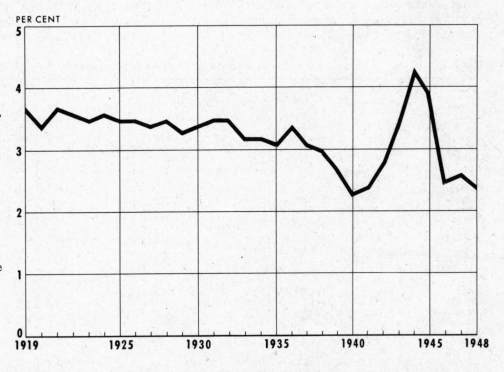

Figure 6. Marriages in which the groom is at least 15 years older than the bride, as a per cent of all marriages in New York State (exclusive of New York City), 1919-1948

in life, when the difference between the groom's age and that of his bride is at a minimum, has in itself lessened the age disparity of the average American couple.

INFLUENCE OF MARITAL STATUS ON MATE SELECTION

About seven out of every ten marriages in our country during 1948 were between persons who had not previously been married. However, this proportion prevailed only in the North Central states and in the South. In the Northeast, marriages between single persons represented almost eight tenths of the total, and in the West less than six tenths. These figures are derived from Table 27, which shows statistics on marriages in the United States during 1948—the only year for which such nationwide information is available. The data also indicate that people tend to marry individuals with similar marital backgrounds, with the single marrying the single, and the widowed and divorced marrying persons who have been wed before.

First Marriage. The great majority of bachelors marry single women, and vice versa. The actual proportion varies somewhat from one geographic area of the country to another. In 1948 it was as high as 91.8 per cent for the single brides in the Northeast and as low as 86.7 per cent for those in the West. The proportion for the men was about equal to that for the women in every region but the West, where only 83.4 per cent of the single grooms took single brides. Also noteworthy is the pattern of marriages between single persons and those who had previously been married. In such cases, the chances that the remarrying spouse was previously divorced rather than widowed were about three to one in the Northeast and much greater elsewhere.

Remarriage. Somewhat more than two fifths of the widows and widowers who remarried in 1948 selected as their mate someone who had also been previously widowed; the balance chose almost equally between single and divorced persons. In the case of the divorced, close to one half (48 per cent) took as their new mate another who had been divorced, and about two fifths entered their remarriage with a single person. Thus divorced persons, more often than widows or widowers, selected as their mate a person who had not been married before.

Factors. The differentials in mate selection by

Table 27. Marriages by Previous Marital Status of the Couple, by Region of Occurrence, United States, 1948

Region; Status of Groom	Status of Bride											
	Number				Per Cent							
	Total	Single	Widowed	Divorced	Total	Single	Widowed	Divorced	Total	Single	Widowed	Divorced
United States	1,811,155	1,402,413	116,175	292,567	100.0	77.4	6.4	16.2	100.0	100.0	100.0	100.0
Single	1,410,796	1,254,935	33,545	122,316	100.0	88.9	2.4	8.7	77.9	89.5	28.9	41.8
Widowed	107,205	29,829	47,411	29,965	100.0	27.8	44.2	28.0	5.9	2.1	40.8	10.2
Divorced	293,154	117,649	35,219	140,286	100.0	40.1	12.0	47.9	16.2	8.4	30.3	48.0
Northeast	405,180	343,389	20,696	41,095	100.0	84.8	5.1	10.1	100.0	100.0	100.0	100.0
Single	345,096	315,253	7,549	22,294	100.0	91.3	2.2	6.5	85.2	91.8	36.5	54.3
Widowed	20,800	7,114	8,572	5,114	100.0	34.2	41.2	24.6	5.1	2.1	41.4	12.4
Divorced	39,284	21,022	4,575	13,687	100.0	53.5	11.7	34.8	9.7	6.1	22.1	33.3
North Central	485,392	376,116	27,255	82,021	100.0	77.5	5.6	16.9	100.0	100.0	100.0	100.0
Single	378,465	338,541	7,827	32,097	100.0	89.4	2.1	8.5	78.0	90.0	28.7	39.1
Widowed	25,559	6,135	10,614	8,810	100.0	24.0	41.5	34.5	5.3	1.6	39.0	10.8
Divorced	81,368	31,440	8,814	41,114	100.0	38.7	10.8	50.5	16.7	8.4	32.3	50.1
South	650,728	501,377	47,214	102,137	100.0	77.0	7.3	15.7	100.0	100.0	100.0	100.0
Single	498,431	443,719	13,122	41,590	100.0	89.0	2.6	8.4	76.6	88.5	27.8	40.7
Widowed	45,312	13,376	20,768	11,168	100.0	29.5	45.8	24.7	7.0	2.7	44.0	10.9
Divorced	106,985	44,282	13,324	49,379	100.0	41.4	12.4	46.2	16.4	8.8	28.2	48.4
West	269,855	181,531	21,010	67,314	100.0	67.3	7.8	24.9	100.0	100.0	100.0	100.0
Single	188,804	157,422	5,047	26,335	100.0	83.4	2.7	13.9	70.0	86.7	24.0	39.1
Widowed	15,534	3,204	7,457	4,873	100.0	20.6	48.0	31.4	5.7	1.8	35.5	7.3
Divorced	65,517	20,905	8,506	36,106	100.0	31.9	13.0	55.1	24.3	11.5	40.5	53.6

Source: Compiled by the author.

marital status arise from a number of factors. For one thing, the conditions which influence persons entering a second marriage are necessarily different from those which govern individuals embarking on a first marriage. There is usually a different psychological outlook, habits may be different, economic circumstances are often different, and young children from the earlier marriage may be present.

Equally important, the average age of remarrying persons is higher than that of persons marrying for the first time. Hence, in seeking a mate, a widowed or divorced person has a smaller proportion of single persons and a larger proportion of the widowed and divorced to choose from than the average single person has. For this reason, too, individuals who have been married more than once, and venture still again, are even more likely to wed someone who has been previously married.[6]

Trend. The present tendency toward assortative mating is not unlike that of generations ago. Around the turn of the century, in Massachusetts for example, the proportion of grooms who took spinsters as their consort was as high as 95 per cent in first marriages but fell to 65 per cent in second marriages, and to less than 50 per cent in those of higher order. Of course, years ago, unlike today, widowed persons had a more prominent role than the divorced in the remarriage picture.

Remarriage of Divorced Couples to Each Other. A legal dissolution of marriage does not always terminate all contact between the spouses. This is especially true when there are children involved or alimony payments to be made, but there are other reasons as well. In consequence, the divorced mates may continue to have dealings with each other, and these sometimes culminate in remarriage. Although nationwide statistics on this subject are lacking, the available data appear to indicate that such remarriages constitute a significant proportion of the divorced persons who

take mates of like marital status. This is evident from a review of 3,100 marriage records in five different counties.[7] If these records are typical of the situation in the United States, it would mean that about 9,500 marriages occurred in 1948 between couples who had been previously married to each other. In other words, about one out of every fifteen divorced men who married a divorced woman remarried his former spouse. It is also noteworthy that not all such remarriages are successful. For example, in one case, a groom had been married, divorced, remarried, and divorced a second time from the same wife, and then at age 22 took a single bride aged 21.

MARRIAGE AND REMARRIAGE

Annual marriage rates for single, widowed and divorced persons during the period 1900-1950 are shown in Table 28. The figures are based on the marriage estimates in Table A15 and the population estimates in Table A6.

Rate for Single Persons. The marriage rate for bachelors and spinsters has been increasing since the turn of the century. Among men, for example, the average annual rate rose from 64 per 1,000 eligibles in the 1900's to 69 in the 1910's, and to 73 in the 1920's. The frequency of marriages fell off sharply during the depression, but the downswing was more than compensated for by the marriage boom which started with World War II.[8] In fact, the average annual rate for the twenty-one years from 1930 through 1950, namely, 79 per 1,000 single men, was previously exceeded only in 1920.

Several other details disclosed by the data in Table 28 are also noteworthy. The rate for men and women climbed to a peak immediately after World War I, and then declined gradually. Nevertheless, as late as 1929 it still was about one eighth above the 1900 level. After 1929, however, during the depression, the marriage rate plunged downward, declining one fourth by 1932, when it

[6]See, for example, "Whom Do the Widowed and the Divorced Marry?" *Statistical Bulletin* (Metropolitan Life Insurance Company), December, 1936, pp. 4-5.

For indications of the effect of age on the relationship of marital status to mate selection, see Charles E. Bowerman, "Assortative Mating by Previous Marital Status: Seattle, 1939-1946," *American Sociological Review*, 18: 170-177, April, 1953.

[7]Marriages during 1948 in Pinal County, Arizona; Muscogee and Richmond counties, Georgia; and Bronx and New York counties, New York.

[8]Among men, each major occupational group, with the notable exception of farmers, shared in the upswing in marriages after 1940. See "Marriage Trends by Occupational Class," *Statistical Bulletin* (Metropolitan Life Insurance Company), January, 1958, pp. 6-8.

Table 28. Marriages per 1,000 Population, Grooms and Brides by Previous Marital Status, United States, 1900-1950

Year	Groom				Bride			
	Total	Single	Wid-owed	Di-vorced	Total	Single	Wid-owed	Di-vorced
1900	61	60	62	190	68	83	22	202
1901	62	61	62	193	70	85	22	218
1902	64	63	62	204	72	87	23	220
1903	66	65	63	216	74	90	23	228
1904	64	64	60	206	73	88	23	227
1905	65	65	59	194	74	90	23	217
1906	68	68	54	198	77	95	22	221
1907	70	70	58	198	80	98	23	219
1908	62	62	57	182	72	87	22	206
1909	64	63	57	181	74	90	21	203
1910	66	66	59	200	77	93	22	216
1911	66	66	56	204	76	92	22	216
1912	69	68	58	217	79	97	22	218
1913	69	69	57	235	79	96	22	243
1914	69	69	55	238	78	95	21	248
1915	68	67	51	253	76	93	20	248
1916	72	72	55	251	80	98	22	262
1917	77	76	56	264	84	103	23	284
1918	67	66	57	240	73	88	23	263
1919	77	75	67	257	83	100	28	284
1920	84	83	70	279	92	111	30	307
1921	76	74	67	255	83	99	28	277
1922	74	72	61	247	79	96	25	264
1923	79	77	64	262	85	103	26	276
1924	74	72	61	252	80	97	25	262
1925	74	71	60	242	79	96	24	244
1926	73	71	58	234	78	95	23	232
1927	72	70	56	221	77	94	22	217
1928	70	68	55	206	74	90	21	199
1929	71	69	56	203	76	93	21	192
1930	64	62	50	181	67	82	19	169
1931	59	58	46	168	62	76	17	153
1932	54	52	40	154	56	69	14	139
1933	59	58	42	175	62	76	15	153
1934	70	68	47	208	72	89	16	177
1935	71	69	45	221	72	90	16	185
1936	73	71	47	231	74	92	16	189
1937	77	75	48	246	78	97	16	199
1938	70	68	44	228	71	88	15	180
1939	74	72	45	238	74	93	15	182
1940	84	82	46	253	83	107	16	196
1941	90	88	47	284	89	115	16	215
1942	95	92	49	338	94	119	17	257
1943	85	81	48	325	84	105	17	247
1944	78	73	45	297	76	96	16	228
1945	87	82	47	294	84	106	18	231
1946	126	122	57	357	120	156	23	285
1947	113	109	51	294	107	142	20	239
1948	104	101	47	268	98	132	18	219
1949	92	88	43	247	86	115	16	199
1950	98	95	43	249	91	124	16	203

Note: Rates based on population estimates which exclude single persons under 15 years of age.
Source of basic data: Tables A6 and A15.

may have been at its lowest point in our history. Within two years thereafter, the rate rebounded to its predepression level. It then continued upward, reaching new record highs in 1942 and 1946. In fact, 12.2 per cent of all bachelors and

15.6 per cent of all spinsters married during 1946. This was more than two fifths above the peak rate after the first world conflict.

The marriage rate for single men is very much like that for total male eligibles. During the period from 1900 to 1950, the annual rate for bachelors averaged only 1.7 per 1,000 less than that for all unmarried men, and never dropped below it by more than 5 per 1,000. Thus, in the absence of statistics on marriages by previous marital status, the marriage rate for bachelors could be approximated from the rate for total male eligibles. Then, from this rate and the number of single males at ages 15 and over, the total number of single men who married could be estimated. Moreover, since there is close agreement annually between the number of bachelors and spinsters who marry (Table A15), the marriage rate for single women could also be approximated. For this purpose, however, only the experience after World War II should be used, since there now are somewhat fewer single brides than single grooms whereas the reverse was generally true in earlier years.

Rate for the Widowed. Unlike the long-term upswing in the marriage rate for single persons, the rate for the widowed is now well below its level of earlier decades. Among men in 1900, for example, the marriage rate for the widowed was slightly higher than that for the single; in 1950, by contrast, the rate for bachelors was more than double that for widowers. This change has resulted largely from the reduced incidence of widowhood at the early adult and middle ages, with the result that the widowed population is much older today than at the turn of the century. For this reason the rates for the widowed shown in Table 28 are primarily useful for evaluating short-term trends.

The marriage rate for widowed persons declined generally in the first two decades of this century, being only slightly affected by our participation in World War I. However, the widowed appear to have benefited more than any other marital class from the marriage boom which followed the close of hostilities. In fact, from 1919 through 1921, the rates for widowers and widows were at their highest levels for this century. No doubt this was effected in part by the influenza pandemic which struck in the autumn of 1918 and took its heaviest toll among young adults. Thus the pandemic may have contributed to the decline in marriages of single and divorced persons during 1918. Equally significant, it left in its wake almost 200,000 relatively young widowed persons. Married men who died in service overseas also contributed to the postwar supply of young widows, but the latter probably represented only about one out of every four women widowed by the war and pandemic combined.

Also noteworthy is the effect of the depression on the marriage rate for the widowed. For one thing, their rate declined somewhat more sharply from 1929 to 1932 than did the rate for single or divorced persons. Of much greater consequence was the relatively small upswing in the marriage rate for the widowed after the depression. In fact, the 1929 rate for the widowed was equaled in only one year since then and that was during the record-breaking marriage boom of 1946. Apparently thousands of widows and widowers failed to remarry due to the depression. This is understandable since the remarriage rate is highest in the years immediately after a bereavement. Moreover, for most women of middle age, delay in marriage for even a few years soon brings them to an age when the men they might have married pass them by to marry younger women. This is particularly true for recent years, due to the growing excess of women over men at the older ages.

The widowed shared in the marriage boom at the close of World War II. The upswing was especially marked for widows; the relative rise for them was equal to that for single women and divorcees. No doubt the remarriage of war widows was a factor in this situation, since almost 140,000 of our married men died overseas from 1941 through 1945 (Table A27).

Rate for the Divorced. The marriage rate for divorced persons is also greatly influenced by war and economic depression. During the two world conflicts and the years immediately thereafter, the rates for men and women were at unusually high levels. The rate among men, for example, never dropped below 240 per 1,000 from 1915 through 1925, and reached as high as 279 per 1,000 in 1920. Moreover, it was above the 1920 peak during all of World War II, and soared to a record high of 357 per 1,000 in 1946.

The remarriage rate for divorcees followed a similar course during the first three decades of the century. After the depression, however, the upswing in their rate was less pronounced than that for the men. In fact, even during the recent marriage boom, the rate for divorced women fell short of its former level. Thus, in the 1940 decade the rate for divorcees averaged only 232 marriages per 1,000, whereas during the 1910's and 1920's the average annual rate was close to 250 per 1,000.[9]

Since men generally bear the economic costs of divorce, those who remarry often face the necessity of supporting two families. For this reason, during the depression of the 1930's one might have expected the marriage rate for divorced men to have declined more markedly than the rate for other eligibles. Judged by the data in Table 28, this did not occur. The indications are that the relative decrease for divorced men approximated that for bachelors and was somewhat less marked than that for divorcees.

The decline in remarriages of divorced persons during the depression resulted primarily from the sharp reduction in the number of divorce decrees. The remarriage rate also fell off, but the decrease among persons classified by years elapsed since their divorce appears to have been relatively small and restricted largely to the early period of the depression. The proportion of men who remarried within a year after divorce, for example, declined from about 19.3 per cent in the late 1920's to a low of 18.6 per cent for those divorced in 1931 and then rose above the predepression level. Equally noteworthy is the unusually high proportion who eventually remarried among persons divorced at the depth of the depression, as is evident from the data in Table 29.

Interval between Divorce and Remarriage. Most persons who remarry after divorce do so in a relatively short period after their marriage is dissolved. Among women, for example, one third remarry within a year, almost one half within the space of two years, and about two

[9]The long-term upswing in the remarriage rate for divorced men has probably been greater than that indicated by the data in Table 28, due to the decreasing understatement in census enumerations of the divorced male population. The rates for divorcees are similarly affected, but to a lesser extent. For details, see the Introduction.

Table 29. Per Cent Remarried Among Men and Women Divorced in the United States during 1919-1934, by Years Elapsed Since Divorce According to Year of Divorce

Sex; Year of Divorce	Years Elapsed Since Divorce								
	1	2	3	4	5	10	15	20	More Than 20†
Male									
1919	19.5	27.8	33.0	37.0	39.9	48	50	52	54
1920	20.1	28.5	33.6	38.1	41.7	52	56	58	60
1921	20.4	29.9	35.3	39.1	42.3	51	55	57	60
1922	19.5	28.5	33.7	37.8	41.3	50	54	56	59
1923	20.7	29.3	34.5	38.4	41.6	49	53	54	57
1924	19.5	27.9	32.9	36.8	39.9	47	49	*	54
1925	20.4	28.4	32.8	36.8	39.8	47	51	*	57
1926	19.3	27.0	31.8	35.5	38.1	46	51	*	58
1927	19.2	27.0	31.7	35.3	38.1	47	53	*	61
1928	19.4	26.8	31.4	34.9	37.8	47	53	*	60
1929	19.3	26.9	31.3	34.7	37.7	47	*	*	58
1930	18.9	25.9	30.5	34.7	38.3	49	*	*	64
1931	18.6	26.3	32.1	37.1	41.1	54	*	*	70
1932	19.9	29.0	35.4	40.8	45.5	59	*	*	76
1933	21.3	31.2	37.7	43.1	47.2	62	*	*	79
1934	21.8	30.6	36.3	41.1	45.5	*	*	*	78
Female									
1919	25.1	35.3	40.8	44.9	47.8	55	57	58	60
1920	26.2	36.7	43.1	47.4	50.9	60	64	66	69
1921	26.8	38.1	44.9	49.3	52.6	61	65	67	71
1922	25.9	37.4	44.6	49.3	52.6	61	65	67	70
1923	25.6	35.6	41.5	45.5	48.2	55	58	60	63
1924	24.5	34.3	39.9	44.1	47.1	54	57	*	61
1925	23.3	32.3	37.7	41.7	44.7	53	57	*	63
1926	23.9	33.2	38.7	42.7	45.3	53	57	*	63
1927	24.5	34.4	40.0	43.7	46.6	55	59	*	64
1928	22.1	31.4	35.9	39.2	41.9	51	57	*	61
1929	21.5	29.7	34.4	37.9	41.2	50	*	*	58
1930	22.4	30.6	35.3	39.2	42.6	52	*	*	61
1931	21.4	30.2	36.3	41.5	45.6	58	*	*	69
1932	21.8	31.9	38.8	44.2	48.4	60	*	*	70
1933	25.8	36.5	42.9	48.1	52.1	65	*	*	75
1934	23.9	33.8	40.1	44.5	47.5	*	*	*	71

*Not available.
†Represents proportion expected to eventually marry.
Note: Estimated by the author from remarriages by year of divorce in upstate New York during 1919-1938 and a sampling of those in New York City during 1948, and remarriages of divorced persons in the United States during 1919-1948.

thirds before the lapse of five years. The comparable proportions are somewhat smaller for men; nevertheless, close to three fifths of those who eventually remarry do so within five years.[10]

[10]Due to the absence of requisite data, it is not possible to estimate the interval between widowhood and remarriage in the United States. However, judged by data from other sources, it is likely that this interval is not too different from that for divorced persons. In France, for example, among men widowed before age 50, almost three fourths of those who remarry do so within five years. For women aged 20-44 years at the time of widowhood, the comparable proportion is about three fifths. (See Roland Pressat, "Le Remariage Des Veufs Et Des Veuves," *Population*, 11:53-58, January-March, 1956.) Unlike divorced persons in the United States, however, the widowed in France are most likely to remarry during the second year. Remarriages are also most

Remarriages occur even after twenty years, but these now represent only about 3 per cent of all divorced men and women who remarry.

The average interval between divorce and remarriage has lengthened for both men and women since World War I. This has been due primarily to the younger age at which divorce occurs, with the result that the proportion who remarry five or ten years after divorce is somewhat larger now than in former years. For men the remarriage rate has also increased in the period immediately after divorce. In consequence, the proportion who eventually remarry, or are expected to, has increased from about three fifths for those divorced around 1920 to almost four fifths for those divorced in 1934 (Table 29). Moreover, there are indications that the proportion will be at least that high for the men divorced after World War II.

Largely as a result of the growing excess of women over men at the ages past midlife, the increase in the proportion of divorced persons who eventually remarry has been much smaller for women than for men. In fact, the men are now more likely to remarry than the women, whereas the reverse appears to have been true for persons divorced prior to 1930.

Increasing Importance of Remarriages. At the turn of the century, first marriages accounted for close to nine tenths of all marriages in the United States, while almost all of the balance involved widowed persons. This general pattern continued until the first world war, but since that time first marriages have decreased in relative importance. Single grooms as a proportion of the

frequent during the second year among widows receiving workmen's compensation in the United States. (See William F. Roeber and Ralph M. Marshall, "An American Remarriage Table," *Proceedings of the Casualty Actuarial Society*, XIX: 279-349, May, 1933.) The later peak for the widowed is understandable, since there is generally a period of bereavement after the loss of a husband or wife. In the case of divorced persons, on the other hand, considerable time usually elapses — for statutory or other reasons — between the breakup of the marriage and its legal dissolution. Moreover, although about one third of the states have some restrictions on remarriage after divorce, the required waiting period may be, and often is, circumvented by remarriage in a neighboring state.

It is interesting to note that none of the states requires a waiting period between widowhood and remarriage, as is true in Puerto Rico where the minimum period is 300 days.

total declined from 87.4 per cent in 1917 to 83.0 per cent in 1930, to 80.2 per cent in 1943, and to less than 78 per cent after 1947. The long-term decrease has been even greater for brides, as is evident from Table 30. In fact, first marriages now constitute a somewhat smaller proportion of

the total for brides than for grooms, whereas the reverse was true around 1900.

The character of remarriage has also changed considerably during the twentieth century. With divorce becoming more frequent and widowhood being increasingly postponed to the older ages, the remarriages of divorced persons have replaced those of the widowed in relative importance. Moreover, the upswing in the proportion for the divorced has been so marked that it has more than counterbalanced the decline for the widowed. To illustrate, of the total grooms in 1900, 10.3 per cent were widowers and only 2.3 per cent were divorced. In 1950, by contrast, 5.9 per cent were widowers but as many as 16.6 per cent were divorced. Similarly, the proportion for divorcees has increased almost without interruption from 3.3 per cent of all marriages in 1900 to 16.7 per cent in 1950; for the widows, the proportion has fallen from 8.3 per cent to 6.5 per cent.

Geographic Variations. About three fourths of those who now wed in the United States have not been married before; the remainder are being married for the second or subsequent time. The geographic divisions of the country vary markedly in the proportions single, widowed, and divorced among those getting married. The proportion of brides who married for the first time in 1948 ranged from about 85 per cent in the Middle Atlantic states to about 65 per cent in the Mountain states. These figures are inversely related to those for the divorced; their proportion among the brides ranged from less than 10 per cent in the Middle Atlantic division to almost 27 per cent in the Mountain area. The individual states reveal even greater differences, as is evident from Table 31. Most extreme is the situation in Nevada, where divorced persons represent fully one third of all brides and grooms.

These geographic variations reflect a number of factors, including the age and marital composition of the population, differences in attitudes toward divorce among various religious groups, and—even more important—the diversity in our marriage and divorce laws. Thus the high proportion for bachelors and spinsters among persons marrying in Massachusetts and New York reflects in part the tendency of many of their divorced residents to remarry in other states.

Table 30. Per Cent of Grooms and Brides by Previous Marital Status, Marriages in the United States, 1900-1950
(Total for each year equals 100%)

Year	Groom			Bride		
	Single	Widowed	Divorced	Single	Widowed	Divorced
1900	87.4	10.3	2.3	88.4	8.3	3.3
1901	87.5	10.2	2.3	88.3	8.2	3.5
1902	87.5	10.1	2.4	88.1	8.4	3.5
1903	87.6	9.8	2.6	88.4	8.1	3.5
1904	87.7	9.7	2.6	88.2	8.1	3.7
1905	88.1	9.4	2.5	88.5	7.9	3.6
1906	89.0	8.4	2.6	89.1	7.3	3.6
1907	88.6	8.7	2.7	89.0	7.4	3.6
1908	87.5	9.6	2.9	88.1	7.9	4.0
1909	87.6	9.4	3.0	88.5	7.5	4.0
1910	87.5	9.2	3.3	88.5	7.3	4.2
1911	87.8	8.9	3.3	88.1	7.6	4.3
1912	87.7	8.8	3.5	88.3	7.4	4.3
1913	87.7	8.6	3.7	88.0	7.2	4.8
1914	87.8	8.4	3.8	87.9	7.1	5.0
1915	87.7	8.0	4.3	87.7	7.0	5.3
1916	87.4	8.4	4.2	87.2	7.3	5.5
1917	87.4	8.1	4.5	86.6	7.5	5.9
1918	85.4	9.7	4.9	84.7	8.8	6.5
1919	84.9	10.2	4.9	84.2	9.4	6.4
1920	84.7	9.8	5.5	83.9	9.2	6.9
1921	83.6	10.4	6.0	83.1	9.5	7.4
1922	83.9	9.8	6.3	83.6	8.8	7.6
1923	84.1	9.5	6.4	83.6	8.8	7.6
1924	83.6	9.6	6.8	83.2	8.8	8.0
1925	83.6	9.4	7.0	83.4	8.6	8.0
1926	83.7	9.1	7.2	83.7	8.2	8.1
1927	83.6	9.1	7.3	83.6	8.2	8.2
1928	83.3	9.2	7.5	83.5	8.1	8.4
1929	83.2	9.1	7.7	83.6	8.0	8.4
1930	83.0	9.0	8.0	83.4	7.9	8.7
1931	83.0	8.8	8.2	83.7	7.5	8.8
1932	83.3	8.5	8.2	83.9	7.2	8.9
1933	83.7	8.0	8.3	84.3	6.9	8.8
1934	84.2	7.5	8.3	85.0	6.3	8.7
1935	84.0	7.2	8.8	84.6	6.2	9.2
1936	83.6	7.2	9.2	84.4	6.1	9.5
1937	83.4	7.0	9.6	84.1	6.1	9.8
1938	83.0	7.0	10.0	83.7	6.2	10.1
1939	83.0	6.8	10.2	83.9	5.9	10.2
1940	84.1	6.2	9.7	84.5	5.6	9.9
1941	83.7	6.0	10.3	84.1	5.5	10.4
1942	82.1	6.1	11.8	82.3	5.8	11.9
1943	80.2	6.7	13.1	80.3	6.5	13.2
1944	78.8	7.0	14.2	79.0	6.8	14.2
1945	78.7	6.6	14.7	78.5	6.9	14.6
1946	79.6	5.6	14.8	79.1	6.3	14.6
1947	78.6	5.8	15.6	78.2	6.3	15.5
1948	77.9	5.9	16.2	77.4	6.4	16.2
1949	76.7	6.2	17.1	76.2	6.8	17.0
1950	77.5	5.9	16.6	76.8	6.5	16.7

Source of basic data: Table A15.

Table 31. Per Cent of Grooms and Brides by Previous Marital Status, Marriages by State of Occurrence, United States, 1948

(Total for each area equals 100%)

Geographic Division and State	Groom			Bride		
	Single	Widowed	Divorced	Single	Widowed	Divorced
UNITED STATES	77.9	5.9	16.2	77.4	6.4	16.2
New England	83.5	4.7	11.8	83.5	4.8	11.7
Maine	79.5	5.0	15.5	80.1	5.2	14.7
New Hampshire	74.5	5.3	20.2	73.8	5.7	20.5
Vermont	83.4	4.9	11.7	83.0	4.6	12.4
Massachusetts	87.5	4.8	7.7	86.9	4.4	8.7
Rhode Island	85.0	4.0	11.0	84.8	4.6	10.6
Connecticut	80.0	4.3	15.7	81.1	5.1	13.8
Middle Atlantic	85.7	5.3	9.0	85.2	5.2	9.6
New York	87.2	5.7	7.1	86.7	5.3	8.0
New Jersey	81.7	5.8	12.5	82.5	5.9	11.6
Pennsylvania	85.4	4.3	10.3	84.1	4.8	11.1
East North Central	77.4	5.3	17.3	76.8	5.8	17.4
Ohio	78.0	5.3	16.7	77.9	5.7	16.4
Indiana	69.3	6.3	24.4	68.2	7.5	24.3
Illinois	75.6	5.6	18.8	75.1	5.8	19.1
Michigan†	81.6	‡	18.4*	80.3	‡	19.7*
Wisconsin	86.8	4.8	8.4	86.9	5.0	8.1
West North Central	79.3	5.1	15.6	79.0	5.2	15.8
Minnesota	‡	‡	‡	‡	‡	‡
Iowa	83.5	3.9†	12.6	82.4	4.4†	13.2
Missouri	71.4	7.0	21.6	72.1	6.4	21.5
North Dakota	‡	‡	‡	‡	‡	‡
South Dakota	83.7	3.6	12.7	81.3	4.9	13.8
Nebraska†	80.1	5.0	14.9	78.4	5.5	16.1
Kansas	77.0	5.0	18.0	76.0	5.6	18.4
South Atlantic	78.5	5.8	15.7	78.8	6.3	14.9
Delaware†	82.3	4.5	13.2	81.9	5.3	12.8
Maryland†	79.9	5.6	14.5	79.1	6.3	14.6
District of Columbia	‡	‡	‡	‡	‡	‡
Virginia	82.5	5.2	12.3	81.5	6.2	12.3
West Virginia	81.1	6.9	12.0	80.9	5.7	13.4
North Carolina	‡	‡	‡	‡	‡	‡
South Carolina	‡	‡	‡	‡	‡	‡
Georgia	74.6	6.1	19.3	76.5	7.1	16.4
Florida†	66.5	8.4	25.1	64.7	9.5	25.8
East South Central	75.2	7.6	17.2	76.5	7.4	16.1
Kentucky	74.2	6.1	19.7	75.2	6.1	18.7
Tennessee	79.8	6.1	14.1	80.5	5.9	13.6
Alabama	78.1	6.1†	15.8	79.7	5.7†	14.6
Mississippi	‡	‡	‡	‡	‡	‡
West South Central	74.9	8.2	16.9	75.0	8.5	16.5
Arkansas	‡	‡	‡	‡	‡	‡
Louisiana	78.1	5.4	16.5	77.9	5.7	16.4
Oklahoma	‡	‡	‡	‡	‡	‡
Texas	‡	‡	‡	‡	‡	‡
Mountain	67.7	5.7	26.6	65.2	8.0	26.8
Montana	74.2	4.5	21.3	68.1	6.4	25.5
Idaho	71.5	4.8†	23.7	65.8	6.9†	27.3
Wyoming	70.3	4.7	25.0	63.8	7.4	28.8
Colorado	76.6	5.5	17.9	75.7	6.8	17.5
New Mexico	‡	‡	‡	‡	‡	‡
Arizona†	66.1	7.0	26.9	63.4	8.9	27.7
Utah	85.6	4.3	10.1	84.7	4.1	11.2
Nevada	61.2	4.9	33.9	57.4	9.1	33.5
Pacific	72.2	5.8	22.0	69.4	7.6	23.0
Washington	66.2	5.7	28.1	60.8	7.8	31.4
Oregon†	76.3	4.5	19.2	74.7	5.9	19.4
California†	74.0	6.1	19.9	72.0	7.8	20.2

*Includes the widowed. †Estimated in part.
‡Insufficient sample or not available; estimate included in figures for geographic division.
Note: Persons with previous marriage annulled included with the single, except in New York where they are included with the divorced.
Source of basic data: Surveys by the author of city, county, and state registrations; the figures for some areas are based on samples.

Such a movement from Massachusetts accounts in large measure for the relatively high frequency of divorced persons among the brides and grooms in New Hampshire. Similarly, many New Yorkers, as well as persons from other states, obtain their divorce in Nevada or Florida and remarry in those areas before returning home.

Also noteworthy is the proportionately large number of widows and widowers who marry in Florida—9.5 per cent of their brides and 8.4 per cent of their grooms. While many of our elders are attracted by that state's favorable climate, it would appear that some—and the widowed in particular—also find romance and companionship for their old age. In Florida as in every other state, however, the widowed constitute the smallest group among those marrying.

Differentials by Age. The relative importance of first and later marriages varies widely according to age. Among those marrying in 1948 at ages under 20, bachelors and spinsters constituted over 98 per cent of the total. However, the proportion decreased rapidly with advance in age. For grooms, less than two thirds of those at ages 30-34 entered their first marriage; at ages 40-44, the fraction was about one third; and at ages past 50, it was less than one fifth. The proportions were about the same for spinsters five years earlier in life—reflecting the somewhat younger age at marriage for women than for men. Thus, spinsters constituted about two thirds of the brides at ages 25-29, and about one third at ages 35-39.

Among the men and women who married in 1948 at ages 25 or older, a considerable proportion had already been divorced. One quarter of all the brides at ages 25-29 were divorcees, and the proportion rose to a maximum of nearly one half at ages 35-44. Of the brides in their early 50's, divorcees represented about a third. For grooms, the proportion previously divorced increased from one seventh for those marrying at ages 25-29, to a maximum of one half for those marrying between ages 40 and 50.

With advancing age, the widowed increase in relative importance among those marrying, as is evident from Table 32. Widows in 1948, for example, constituted one quarter of the brides at ages 40-44, one half at 50-54, and more than

Table 32. Per Cent of Grooms and Brides by Previous Marital Status, by Age at Marriage, United States, 1940 and 1948

(Total for each area equals 100%)

Age	Groom			Bride		
	Single	Widowed	Divorced	Single	Widowed	Divorced
1948 Total	77.9	5.9	16.2	77.4	6.4	16.2
Under 20	99.3	.0	.7	98.1	.1	1.8
20 - 24	96.1	.2	3.7	89.9	1.1	9.0
25 - 29	84.2	1.1	14.7	68.1	5.3	26.6
30 - 34	64.8	3.4	31.8	48.3	8.6	43.1
35 - 39	46.6	8.4	45.0	35.1	17.1	47.8
40 - 44	35.9	14.6	49.5	25.5	27.6	46.9
45 - 49	25.8	26.2	48.0	17.5	43.9	38.6
50 - 54	19.9	38.7	41.4	12.5	51.5	36.0
55 - 64	11.3	59.5	29.2	10.1	65.2	24.7
65 - 74	5.5	75.2	19.3	4.9	84.4	10.7
75 and over	4.5	86.1	9.4	7.9	81.2	10.9
1940 Total	84.1	6.2	9.7	84.5	5.6	9.9
Under 20	99.8	.1	.1	99.0	.1	.9
20 - 24	98.3	.4	1.3	95.3	.6	4.1
25 - 29	92.2	1.8	6.0	81.6	3.4	15.0
30 - 34	76.1	5.9	18.0	59.3	10.3	30.4
35 - 39	57.1	10.3	32.6	40.4	22.2	37.4
40 - 44	39.6	22.2	38.2	26.5	36.9	36.6
45 - 49	27.0	33.4	39.6	18.4	51.2	30.4
50 - 54	19.3	46.5	34.2	14.1	62.8	23.1
55 - 64	10.9	67.0	22.1	10.3	75.4	14.3
65 - 74	5.4	78.9	15.7	4.5	89.7	5.8
75 and over	4.7	83.9	11.4	12.2	78.2	9.6

Source: Table A16.

broad resemblance in the pattern of the age-specific marriage rates for the single, the widowed, and the divorced. Among all three groups the marriage rate rises to a peak in early adult life—at ages 20-24 for women and at ages 25-29 for men—and then decreases with advance in age.

At almost every age, the rate is highest for men and women who have been divorced and lowest for those who are single, with the rate for the widowed intermediate. This is evident from the marriage rates for 1940 and 1948, which are shown in Table 33.

At the younger ages the remarriage rate for divorced persons is extremely high. Among the women aged 15-24, about three fifths remarried in 1948; among the men aged 20-29, the proportion was well over one half. The rate falls off rapidly after these peaks, but even in the next five years of life almost one half of the men and more than two fifths of the women remarried during 1948.

four fifths at ages 65 and over. However, because marriages at the later ages make up only a small fraction of the total, the widowed accounted for only about 6 per cent of all brides and grooms in 1948.

The pattern for grooms and brides at the different age levels changed between 1940 and 1948. Most noteworthy is the much greater relative importance of previously divorced persons among grooms and brides of almost every age, reflecting the record number of divorces during World War II and immediately thereafter. The compensating changes for the single and the widowed may be seen from a comparison of the data in the two tiers of Table 32.

Rates by Age and Previous Marital Status. There is a

Table 33. Marriages per 1,000 Population, Grooms and Brides by Previous Marital Status and Age, United States, 1940 and 1948

Age	Groom				Bride			
	Total	Single	Widowed	Divorced	Total	Single	Widowed	Divorced
1948								
14 and over	98.3	93.7	47.1	267.7	92.7	120.1	17.8	218.7
14	.0	.0	.0	.0	2.8	2.7	22.0	75.0
15 - 19	20.9	20.8	5.0	145.6	115.2	113.6	66.0	600.8
20 - 24	211.2	206.5	180.6	531.8	302.1	288.1	259.4	609.2
25 - 29	248.1	226.1	258.9	560.1	228.8	193.7	223.4	431.2
30 - 34	199.1	153.4	253.0	478.5	156.0	111.8	114.2	322.3
35 - 39	153.7	94.0	226.4	382.1	107.5	66.9	91.7	218.9
40 - 44	110.7	57.7	158.8	261.0	66.8	36.1	59.4	144.9
45 - 49	80.9	33.5	130.2	180.3	41.7	19.1	41.4	91.5
50 - 54	63.7	23.2	95.7	134.3	23.7	9.8	21.5	66.2
55 - 59	45.9	12.6	71.4	89.1	14.1	5.7	13.1	46.2
60 - 64	29.8	6.1	41.1	63.8	8.1	4.2	7.6	30.8
65 - 74	18.2	3.4	21.7	47.3	3.4	1.1	3.5	15.6
75 & over	4.7	1.3	4.9	17.0	.5	.3	.4	7.5
1940								
14 and over	78.1	75.9	46.2	247.8	78.0	96.8	15.6	192.1
14	.0	.0	.0	.0	.7	.7	.0	87.7
15 - 19	7.2	7.2	44.5	53.7	65.8	65.3	64.8	363.4
20 - 24	155.2	153.5	277.0	496.5	238.3	234.2	136.6	502.2
25 - 29	222.0	211.8	392.7	559.9	193.6	179.1	134.2	422.3
30 - 34	165.7	138.9	310.8	488.5	115.9	91.7	94.8	282.9
35 - 39	110.1	75.5	162.9	369.1	68.4	45.8	61.5	171.6
40 - 44	73.4	38.7	127.7	234.2	41.8	22.7	41.2	111.1
45 - 49	54.3	21.5	92.1	178.4	26.8	12.4	27.9	74.6
50 - 54	37.4	11.9	61.5	116.7	15.8	6.8	16.6	47.6
55 - 59	29.1	6.7	50.5	73.9	9.5	3.8	10.3	28.6
60 - 64	19.3	3.7	29.3	50.6	5.0	2.2	5.2	17.5
65 - 74	12.5	2.1	15.8	41.8	2.3	.6	2.5	8.8
75 & over	3.5	.9	3.7	21.6	.3	.3	.2	5.9

Source: Tables A10 and A16.

Before age 25, the marriage rate is higher for women than for men (except among the widowed at ages 20-24 in 1940); after age 25, the situation is reversed. Moreover, at the later ages, the decline in the marriage rate is more gradual for men than for women, particularly among the widowed, with the result that the sex disparity widens. In 1948, for example, the marriage rate for all eligible men aged 25-29 was about 248 per 1,000, or less than one tenth above that for women of the same age. Twenty years later in life, at 45-49 years, the marriage rate for men was almost twice that for women. Even after retirement age, men still marry in appreciable numbers, whereas elderly women rarely enter wedlock.

A number of factors account for the higher marriage rate among men past age 25. For one thing, men generally marry women who are somewhat younger than themselves. Also, since women tend to outlive men, their numerical preponderance at the middle and older ages lessens their chances for marriage or remarriage. Then too, a man at the head of a broken family may need a new mate to take care of his home and children, whereas a woman seeking remarriage may be handicapped by young dependents. Women may also be discouraged from remarrying by the fact that some pension and compensation plans as well as wills and alimony contracts provide that benefits terminate upon remarriage.

Bigamous Marriages. There are indications that bigamy is more frequent today than a generation ago. Although accurate information on the incidence of bigamy is not available, due to the very nature of the event, a minimum estimate can be derived from court statistics. The most common procedure for dissolving a bigamous marriage is by annulment. Bigamy is also a ground for divorce in a number of states, but such decrees account for only about one fifth of the total dissolutions due to bigamy.

According to reports by the Bureau of the Census, bigamous marriages dissolved by divorce or annulment averaged about 1,300 annually during 1926-1932. This corresponded to a rate of 115 for every 100,000 marriages contracted during those years. In the period following, the incidence probably increased. Statistics collected by the author show that there were about 3,600 decrees due to bigamy in 1948—or at a rate of about 200 out of every 100,000 marriages performed. More recent statistics, available for a group of states, indicate that the number of dissolutions due to bigamy has changed little since 1948. If this has been true for the country as a whole, it would be unlike the trend in the United Kingdom, where the incidence of bigamy decreased markedly after the close of World War II.

The recorded increase in the United States may reflect, in part, the greater frequency with which bigamous marriages are now brought under judicial purview. It is also likely that there has been a true increase in their incidence, possibly associated with the disruption of family life during World War II and the Korean conflict. Favorable economic conditions may also be a factor.

Chapter 6

CHANCES OF MARRIAGE AND REMARRIAGE

THE prospects of marriage have generally been very favorable in the United States. A large proportion of our men and women marry at an early age and, even for those who do not, the chances of eventual marriage are excellent. This situation is due in large measure to the advantageous economic conditions in our country. Young people have good opportunities for employment at relatively high wages, which make it possible for them to marry young. Then too, our traditions and social attitudes favor undertaking of family life relatively early. Boys and girls probably have more social life and mix more freely here than in most other countries, with the result that they have greater opportunities to meet marital partners. At the same time, our relatively high divorce rate indirectly contributes to the chances of first marriage in later life, since many bachelors and spinsters marry people who have been divorced.

The present chapter is based largely on tables for 1940 and 1948 (pages 78-81 and 83-86), which show the chances of marriage for single, widowed, and divorced persons in the United States.

Age at First Marriage. Early marriage, which has long been favored by people in the United States, became even more popular after World War II. Census statistics indicate that the median age at first marriage for all women who ever marry declined only slightly between 1890 and 1940, namely, from 22 years to about $21\frac{1}{2}$. After World War II, however, it dropped to about 20 years. The trend to earlier marriage has been equally pronounced among men; the median age fell from 26 years in 1890 to about 24 in 1940, and is now only about 23 years.[1]

The chances of early marriage are greater in the United States than in any other country of the Western world. For example, about one sixth of our girls aged 15-19 are married. The proportion is not much lower in Yugoslavia, but other countries lag considerably behind. The closest are Czechoslovakia, France, and Australia, where after World War II the proportion was less than 6 per cent. The girls in Germany and Ireland have the smallest chances for early marriage; less than 2 per cent of those 15-19 years are married.

Men in the United States are also likely to marry early in life. At ages 20-24, almost one half are or have been married. In Yugoslavia the proportion is about one third, and in most other European countries it is one fourth or lower. Norway and Ireland are at the other extreme, with less than one tenth of their men married at an early age.

Although Americans marry relatively young, the age at marriage in our country is not the lowest in the world. In India, for example, about nine tenths of the girls are wed before their 20th birthday. Very early marriage is also common in Mozambique and in other peasant-agricultural countries.[2]

There are also marked variations in the age at marriage within our own country. In general, people in the South marry at a relatively early age, whereas those in the Northeast do so one or two years later in life. The chances for early marriage tend to be lowest for residents of

---

[1] It is interesting to note how closely these figures for the period after 1940 compare with those computed from column 7 of the marriage tables for single persons (Tables 34-37). The latter show that the median age at first marriage for men declined from 24.0 years in 1940 to 22.9 years in 1948; for women, the corresponding figures are 21.3 and 20.2.

[2] Statistics on the marital status of the population classified by age and sex are shown for various countries of the world in the annual issues of *United Nations Demographic Yearbook*. See also, "Americans Marry Young" and "Increase in Early Marriage," in *Statistical Bulletin* (Metropolitan Life Insurance Company), February, 1947, pp. 8-10 and May, 1953, pp. 7-9; and Kingsley Davis, "Statistical Perspective on Marriage and Divorce," *Annals of the American Academy of Political and Social Science*, 272:12-15, November, 1950.

Massachusetts, and increase as one proceeds from east to west along the northern tier of the country.

Legal Age for Marriage. The minimum age for marriage depends upon the law of the state in which a marriage occurs. As is evident from Table A18, in one half of the states, a man at the age of 18 and a woman at 16 may marry if the parents or guardian approve; in the others, the age is lower—generally by one or two years. In New Hampshire, a boy need be only 14 and a girl 13; with parental consent boys may also marry at age 14 in Washington. A majority of states also have provisions for authorization of marriages under the minimum age when special circumstances prevail, such as pregnancy of the girl.

At common law, persons reaching the age of puberty—14 years for the male and 12 for the female—were considered to have the capacity to marry in their own right. Today, marriage without consent is fixed by statute at an older age, generally 21 for men and 18 for women.

MARRIAGE TABLES FOR THE SINGLE POPULATION

The chances for eventual marriage and the average remaining lifetime as a single person, as well as related information, are shown for males and females in Tables 34-37. The 1948 tables may be considered as approximations of conditions which have prevailed since the postwar marriage boom subsided; those for 1940 are representative of the experience in the years immediately prior to World War II.

Marriage Rates. Column 2 in each table shows the annual number marrying per 1,000 alive and single at the beginning of each year of age. The rates are based on marriages reported in the United States during 1940 and 1948 (Table A16) and on the population including armed forces overseas during those years (Table A10). The figures for individual ages were derived largely by interpolation of the data grouped in five-year intervals. This included ages over 75 years, for which the five-year groupings are not shown in the Appendix tables. At the younger ages, where the rate increases rapidly, marriages and population by single years of age were used so far as

was necessary to provide a smooth blend with the values obtained by interpolation. In the absence of such detail for the young persons who married in 1940, the values within five-year age groups, obtained by interpolation, were adjusted to conform with the individual age patterns for 1948. Although some age falsification probably occurs around the legal age minimums,[3] the marriage data were not adjusted for this possible bias in order to retain the marked increase in the marriage rate which actually occurs at these ages.

Before age 14 virtually the entire population is unmarried. After this age the single population is increasingly depleted as the marriage rate soars rapidly. In 1948, for example, the rate for single men rose to a maximum of 240 per 1,000 at age 21 and remained above 200 per 1,000 through age 27. For females, who marry somewhat earlier than males, a more marked peak of 301 per 1,000 occurred at age 21, and the rate exceeded 200 per 1,000 at ages 18-25. After early adult life, the rates for both men and women decline without interruption throughout the life span. Although the marriage rates were lower in 1940 than in 1948, the age pattern was similar, as is evident from Tables 34-37.[4]

Mortality Rates. Column 3 in each table shows the annual number dying while single, per 1,000 alive and single at the beginning of each year of age. The rates for the 1948 and 1940 tables are based on the mortality experienced in the United States during 1949-1951 and 1939-1941. Three sources of data were used in their derivation: (a) deaths during 1949-1951 and 1940, classified by marital status and age, from publications by the National Office of Vital Statistics, which were adjusted by distributing prorata decedents reported with status or age unknown; (b) population during 1950 and 1940, classified by marital status and age, from Table A5 and reports by the Bureau of the Census; and (c) mortality rates from the 1949-51 and 1939-41 United States life tables for total males and total females.

[3] See, for example, Harold T. Christensen, "Falsification of Age at Marriage," *Marriage and Family Living*, 15:301-304, November, 1953.

[4] See, for comparison, the marriage rates in tables for 1940 previously published by Wilson H. Grabill in "Attrition Life Tables for the Single Population," *Journal of American Statistical Association*, 40:364-375, September, 1945.

Number Living and Single at Beginning of Year of Age. Column 4 in each table (Tables 34–37) shows the number of single persons remaining at each attained age out of a cohort of 100,000 live births, among whom the marriage and death rates at each age of life are exactly those shown in columns 2 and 3. As is evident from all four tables, the cohorts are rapidly reduced after the adult ages are reached. In the 1948 tables, for example, the number of single males drops from about 91 per cent of the initial group to less than 10 per cent between ages 19 and 30. The comparable decline occurs over an even shorter span among females, namely, between the 17th and 26th birthdays.

The figures in column 4 are known as the "net nuptiality" survivors, since they escape both death and marriage. The losses due to these causes at each age are shown in columns 5 and 6. In the United States, death is the sole source of decrement before the teen-ages; thereafter, until midlife, marriage is the more important factor in reducing the number of surviving single persons. Thus, in the 1948 tables, marriages exceed deaths among single males at ages 16–52, and among females at ages 14–52.

Chances of Eventual Marriage. These figures are shown in column 10 (Tables 34–37) under the heading, "Per cent marrying for the first time in this year of age and all later years." They represent the proportion of single persons at a particular age who are expected to marry during their lifetime according to the marriage and death rates in columns 2 and 3. The figures are calculated from the accumulated number marrying for the first time (column 7) divided by the number of surviving single persons (column 4).

The probability of eventually marrying is extremely favorable in the United States. According to the 1948 tables, 92.2 per cent of newborn males and 94.6 per cent of the females may look forward to marrying during the course of their lives. Moreover, since some persons die during infancy and childhood, the chances for marriage increase after birth to a maximum in the late teens. The chances reach as high as 98.1 per cent for females at age 16 and 97.1 per cent for males at age 19, and remain close to these peaks for several years thereafter. Under age 20, the chances of eventual marriage are greater for females than for males, but beyond this age the situation is reversed.

After the mid-20's, the prospects for marriage decline with increasing rapidity throughout life. Among single men, for example, the chances of eventual marriage drop from about nine in ten at age 27 to less than one in two after age 39. Among women, the comparable decline occurs about three years earlier. After the 44th birthday for men and the 40th birthday for women, the odds are better than two to one against their eventual marriage. For this reason persons who have not married by these ages may be considered as confirmed bachelors and spinsters. However, there is no age when the hope of marriage is entirely gone. Even after the 65th birthday, about 3 per cent of the bachelors and 1 per cent of the spinsters may expect to marry.

As a result of lower death rates and higher marriage rates, the outlook for eventual marriage is considerably more favorable now than before World War II. The extent of the improvement may be illustrated by a few figures read from Tables 34–37. For a single man of age 30 the proportion expected to eventually marry increased from 74.4 per cent in 1940 to 82.2 per cent in 1948; at age 40, the rise was from 31.4 to 45.3 per cent. The gains were equally large for women about five years earlier in life.

Average Number of Years Remaining Before First Marriage or Death. These figures, shown in column 11, represent the expectation of life as a single person. In order to arrive at these values, it is first necessary to compute the total time (in years) lived while single within each year of age by the survivors from the initial cohort of 100,000 live births. The figures for any one year of age (column 8) are midway between the surviving single persons at the beginning and end of that year of age (column 4). Column 9 is constructed by accumulating the figures in column 8, and represents the total number of years lived while single by the survivors of the initial cohort after attaining a specified age. This cumulated number (of years) for a particular age divided by the number of single persons surviving to that age (column 4) gives the average remaining lifetime as a single person.

The expectation of life as a single person has declined somewhat for males at every age and for females at ages under 44. For females past midlife, on the other hand, the figure has increased due to the fact that the decline in

Table 34. Marriage Table for Single Males, United States, 1948

Age (Years)	Per 1,000 alive and single at beginning of year of age		Of 100,000 Born Alive				Stationary Population		Per cent marrying for the first time in this year of age and all later years	Average number of years remaining before first marriage or death
	Number marrying during year	Number dying during year while single	Number living and single at beginning of year of age	Number dying during year of age while single	Number marrying for the first time		In year of age	In this year of age and all later years		
					During year of age	In this year of age and all later years				
(1)	(2)	(3)	(4)	(5)	(6)	(7)	(8)	(9)	(10)	(11)
0	–	33.4	100,000	3,339	–	92,216	97,095	2,354,448	92.2	23.5
1	–	2.4	96,661	236	–	92,216	96,543	2,257,353	95.4	23.4
2	–	1.5	96,425	146	–	92,216	96,352	2,160,810	95.6	22.4
3	–	1.1	96,279	110	–	92,216	96,224	2,064,458	95.8	21.4
4	–	1.0	96,169	92	–	92,216	96,123	1,968,234	95.9	20.5
5	–	.9	96,077	83	–	92,216	96,035	1,872,111	96.0	19.5
6	–	.8	95,994	75	–	92,216	95,956	1,776,076	96.1	18.5
7	–	.7	95,919	69	–	92,216	95,884	1,680,120	96.1	17.5
8	–	.7	95,850	63	–	92,216	95,819	1,584,236	96.2	16.5
9	–	.6	95,787	61	–	92,216	95,756	1,488,417	96.3	15.5
10	–	.6	95,726	61	–	92,216	95,696	1,392,661	96.3	14.5
11	–	.7	95,665	62	–	92,216	95,634	1,296,965	96.4	13.6
12	–	.7	95,603	68	–	92,216	95,568	1,201,331	96.5	12.6
13	0.0	.8	95,535	78	0	92,216	95,497	1,105,763	96.5	11.6
14	.0	.9	95,457	91	1	92,216	95,411	1,010,266	96.6	10.6
15	.1	1.1	95,365	107	11	92,215	95,306	914,855	96.7	9.6
16	1.5	1.3	95,247	123	142	92,204	95,115	819,549	96.8	8.6
17	6.5	1.4	94,982	135	615	92,062	94,607	724,434	96.9	7.6
18	34.0	1.6	94,232	148	3,207	91,447	92,555	629,827	97.0	6.7
19	61.4	1.7	90,877	157	5,577	88,240	88,010	537,272	97.1	5.9
20	92.1	1.9	85,143	159	7,841	82,663	81,143	449,262	97.1	5.3
21	240.2	1.9	77,143	143	18,528	74,822	67,808	368,119	97.0	4.8
22	204.9	2.0	58,472	119	11,980	56,294	52,423	300,311	96.3	5.1
23	212.0	2.2	46,373	101	9,830	44,314	41,408	247,888	95.6	5.3
24	212.7	2.3	36,442	83	7,750	34,484	32,526	206,480	94.6	5.7
25	213.5	2.4	28,609	68	6,108	26,734	25,521	173,954	93.4	6.1
26	209.5	2.5	22,433	56	4,699	20,626	20,056	148,433	91.9	6.6
27	203.9	2.7	17,678	47	3,604	15,927	15,853	128,377	90.1	7.3
28	194.9	2.9	14,027	40	2,734	12,323	12,640	112,524	87.9	8.0
29	181.4	3.1	11,253	35	2,041	9,589	10,215	99,884	85.2	8.9
30	168.4	3.3	9,177	31	1,545	7,548	8,389	89,669	82.2	9.8
31	152.5	3.6	7,601	27	1,159	6,003	7,008	81,280	79.0	10.7
32	138.7	3.9	6,415	25	890	4,844	5,958	74,272	75.5	11.6
33	127.1	4.2	5,500	23	699	3,954	5,139	68,314	71.9	12.4
34	116.2	4.6	4,778	22	555	3,255	4,490	63,175	68.1	13.2
35	106.0	5.0	4,201	21	445	2,700	3,968	58,685	64.3	14.0
36	96.4	5.5	3,735	21	360	2,255	3,545	54,717	60.4	14.6
37	87.6	6.1	3,354	21	294	1,895	3,197	51,172	56.5	15.3
38	79.7	6.8	3,039	21	242	1,601	2,908	47,975	52.7	15.8
39	72.7	7.6	2,776	21	202	1,359	2,665	45,067	49.0	16.2
40	66.4	8.3	2,553	21	169	1,157	2,458	42,402	45.3	16.6
41	60.6	9.0	2,363	21	143	988	2,281	39,944	41.8	16.9
42	54.9	9.8	2,199	21	121	845	2,128	37,663	38.4	17.1
43	49.5	10.6	2,057	22	102	724	1,995	35,535	35.2	17.3
44	44.4	11.4	1,933	22	86	622	1,879	33,540	32.2	17.4
45	39.7	12.3	1,825	22	73	536	1,778	31,661	29.4	17.3
46	35.6	13.3	1,730	23	62	463	1,688	29,883	26.8	17.3
47	32.0	14.3	1,645	24	53	401	1,607	28,195	24.4	17.1
48	29.3	15.3	1,568	24	46	348	1,533	26,588	22.2	17.0
49	27.3	16.4	1,498	25	41	302	1,465	25,055	20.2	16.7
50	25.7	17.6	1,432	25	37	261	1,401	23,590	18.2	16.5
51	24.3	19.0	1,370	26	33	224	1,341	22,189	16.4	16.2
52	22.5	20.4	1,311	27	30	191	1,283	20,848	14.6	15.9
53	20.4	22.1	1,254	28	26	161	1,227	19,565	12.8	15.6
54	18.2	23.8	1,200	29	22	135	1,175	18,338	11.3	15.3
55	16.0	25.6	1,149	29	18	113	1,126	17,163	9.8	14.9
56	13.9	27.5	1,102	30	15	95	1,080	16,037	8.6	14.6
57	12.1	29.4	1,057	31	13	80	1,035	14,957	7.6	14.2
58	10.5	31.4	1,013	32	11	67	992	13,922	6.6	13.7
59	9.0	33.5	970	32	9	56	950	12,930	5.8	13.3
60	7.7	35.6	929	33	7	47	909	11,980	5.1	12.9
61	6.6	37.9	889	34	6	40	869	11,071	4.5	12.5
62	5.7	40.2	849	34	5	34	830	10,202	4.0	12.0
63	5.1	42.8	810	35	4	29	791	9,372	3.6	11.6
64	4.7	45.4	771	35	4	25	752	8,581	3.2	11.1
65	4.4	48.2	732	35	3	21	713	7,829	2.9	10.7
66	4.2	51.2	694	36	3	18	675	7,116	2.6	10.3
67	3.9	54.6	655	36	3	15	636	6,441	2.3	9.8
68	3.5	58.3	616	36	2	12	597	5,805	1.9	9.4
69	3.1	62.3	578	36	2	10	559	5,208	1.7	9.0
70	2.8	66.7	540	36	1	8	522	4,649	1.5	8.6

Table 35. Marriage Table for Single Males, United States, 1940

Age (Years)	Per 1,000 alive and single at beginning of year of age		Of 100,000 Born Alive				Stationary Population		Per cent marrying for the first time in this year of age and all later years	Average number of years remaining before first marriage or death
	Number marrying during year	Number dying during year while single	Number living and single at beginning of year of age	Number dying during year of age while single	Number marrying for the first time		In year of age	In this year of age and all later years		
					During year of age	In this year of age and all later years				
(1)	(2)	(3)	(4)	(5)	(6)	(7)	(8)	(9)	(10)	(11)
0	–	52.4	100,000	5,238	–	86,905	95,591	2,448,026	86.9	24.5
1	–	5.5	94,762	524	–	86,905	94,453	2,352,435	91.7	24.8
2	–	2.9	94,238	273	–	86,905	94,093	2,257,982	92.2	24.0
3	–	2.0	93,965	189	–	86,905	93,867	2,163,889	92.5	23.0
4	–	1.6	93,776	152	–	86,905	93,697	2,070,022	92.7	22.1
5	–	1.5	93,624	136	–	86,905	93,556	1,976,325	92.8	21.1
6	–	1.3	93,488	121	–	86,905	93,428	1,882,769	93.0	20.1
7	–	1.2	93,367	111	–	86,905	93,312	1,789,341	93.1	19.2
8	–	1.1	93,256	103	–	86,905	93,204	1,696,029	93.2	18.2
9	–	1.1	93,153	99	–	86,905	93,103	1,602,825	93.3	17.2
10	–	1.1	93,054	98	–	86,905	93,005	1,509,722	93.4	16.2
11	–	1.1	92,956	100	–	86,905	92,906	1,416,717	93.5	15.2
12	–	1.1	92,856	105	–	86,905	92,804	1,323,811	93.6	14.3
13	0.0	1.2	92,751	114	0	86,905	92,694	1,231,007	93.7	13.3
14	.0	1.4	92,637	129	0	86,905	92,572	1,138,313	93.8	12.3
15	.0	1.6	92,508	145	4	86,905	92,434	1,045,741	93.9	11.3
16	.5	1.8	92,359	163	48	86,901	92,254	953,307	94.1	10.3
17	2.3	1.9	92,148	179	208	86,853	91,955	861,053	94.3	9.3
18	11.9	2.1	91,761	195	1,095	86,645	91,116	769,098	94.4	8.4
19	21.7	2.3	90,471	208	1,963	85,550	89,386	677,982	94.6	7.5
20	69.2	2.4	88,300	216	6,115	83,587	85,135	588,596	94.7	6.7
21	184.1	2.5	81,969	203	15,095	77,472	74,320	503,461	94.5	6.1
22	148.7	2.7	66,671	179	9,916	62,377	61,624	429,141	93.6	6.4
23	165.8	2.9	56,576	162	9,380	52,461	51,805	367,517	92.7	6.5
24	179.8	3.0	47,034	143	8,455	43,081	42,735	315,712	91.6	6.7
25	190.0	3.2	38,436	122	7,304	34,626	34,723	272,977	90.1	7.1
26	195.9	3.4	31,010	104	6,073	27,322	27,922	238,254	88.1	7.7
27	196.6	3.6	24,833	88	4,881	21,249	22,349	210,332	85.6	8.5
28	190.0	3.8	19,864	76	3,775	16,368	17,939	187,983	82.4	9.5
29	176.6	4.1	16,013	66	2,829	12,593	14,566	170,044	78.6	10.6
30	159.4	4.4	13,118	58	2,091	9,764	12,044	155,478	74.4	11.9
31	141.5	4.7	10,969	52	1,552	7,673	10,167	143,434	70.0	13.1
32	126.2	5.1	9,365	47	1,182	6,121	8,751	133,267	65.4	14.2
33	113.7	5.4	8,136	44	925	4,939	7,652	124,516	60.7	15.3
34	101.6	5.8	7,167	42	728	4,014	6,782	116,864	56.0	16.3
35	90.3	6.3	6,397	40	578	3,286	6,088	110,082	51.4	17.2
36	79.7	6.8	5,779	39	461	2,708	5,529	103,994	46.9	18.0
37	70.1	7.3	5,279	39	370	2,247	5,075	98,465	42.6	18.7
38	61.6	7.9	4,870	39	300	1,877	4,701	93,390	38.5	19.2
39	54.1	8.6	4,531	39	245	1,577	4,389	88,689	34.8	19.6
40	47.5	9.3	4,247	39	202	1,332	4,127	84,300	31.4	19.8
41	41.7	9.9	4,006	39	167	1,130	3,903	80,173	28.2	20.0
42	36.5	10.5	3,800	40	139	963	3,711	76,270	25.3	20.1
43	32.0	11.2	3,621	41	116	824	3,543	72,559	22.8	20.0
44	28.5	12.0	3,464	41	99	708	3,394	69,016	20.4	19.9
45	25.6	12.8	3,324	43	85	609	3,260	65,622	18.3	19.7
46	23.1	13.7	3,196	44	74	524	3,137	62,362	16.4	19.5
47	20.7	14.6	3,078	45	64	450	3,024	59,225	14.6	19.2
48	18.3	15.6	2,969	46	54	386	2,919	56,201	13.0	18.9
49	16.3	16.6	2,869	48	47	332	2,822	53,282	11.6	18.6
50	14.5	17.8	2,774	49	40	285	2,730	50,460	10.3	18.2
51	12.9	19.0	2,685	51	35	245	2,642	47,730	9.1	17.8
52	11.4	20.3	2,599	53	30	210	2,558	45,088	8.1	17.3
53	10.1	21.8	2,516	55	25	180	2,476	42,530	7.2	16.9
54	9.0	23.3	2,436	57	22	155	2,397	40,054	6.4	16.4
55	8.1	24.9	2,357	59	19	133	2,318	37,657	5.6	16.0
56	7.2	26.6	2,279	61	16	114	2,241	35,339	5.0	15.5
57	6.4	28.3	2,202	62	14	98	2,164	33,098	4.5	15.0
58	5.7	30.0	2,126	64	12	84	2,088	30,934	4.0	14.6
59	5.0	31.8	2,050	65	10	72	2,013	28,846	3.5	14.1
60	4.4	33.6	1,975	66	9	62	1,938	26,833	3.1	13.6
61	3.9	35.6	1,900	68	7	53	1,863	24,895	2.8	13.1
62	3.5	37.6	1,825	69	6	46	1,788	23,032	2.5	12.6
63	3.2	40.0	1,750	70	6	40	1,712	21,244	2.3	12.1
64	2.9	42.5	1,674	71	5	34	1,636	19,532	2.0	11.7
65	2.8	45.2	1,598	72	4	29	1,560	17,896	1.8	11.2
66	2.7	48.1	1,522	73	4	25	1,484	16,336	1.6	10.7
67	2.5	51.3	1,445	74	4	21	1,406	14,852	1.5	10.3
68	2.2	54.7	1,367	75	3	17	1,328	13,446	1.2	9.8
69	1.9	58.5	1,289	75	2	14	1,251	12,118	1.1	9.4
70	1.6	62.6	1,212	76	2	12	1,173	10,867	1.0	9.0

Table 36. Marriage Table for Single Females, United States, 1948

Age (Years)	Per 1,000 alive and single at beginning of year of age		Of 100,000 Born Alive				Stationary Population		Per cent marrying for the first time in this year of age and all later years	Average number of years remaining before first marriage or death
	Number marrying during year	Number dying during year while single	Number living and single at beginning of year of age	Number dying during year of age while single	Number marrying for the first time		In year of age	In this year of age and all later years		
					During year of age	In this year of age and all later years				
(1)	(2)	(3)	(4)	(5)	(6)	(7)	(8)	(9)	(10)	(11)
0	–	25.9	100,000	2,594	–	94,550	97,782	2,107,896	94.6	21.1
1	–	2.2	97,406	209	–	94,550	97,301	2,010,114	97.1	20.6
2	–	1.3	97,197	121	–	94,550	97,137	1,912,813	97.3	19.7
3	–	1.0	97,076	94	–	94,550	97,029	1,815,676	97.4	18.7
4	–	.8	96,982	74	–	94,550	96,945	1,718,647	97.5	17.7
5	–	.7	96,908	64	–	94,550	96,876	1,621,702	97.6	16.7
6	–	.6	96,844	56	–	94,550	96,817	1,524,826	97.6	15.7
7	–	.5	96,788	49	–	94,550	96,764	1,428,009	97.7	14.8
8	–	.5	96,739	45	–	94,550	96,716	1,331,245	97.7	13.8
9	–	.4	96,694	42	–	94,550	96,673	1,234,529	97.8	12.8
10	–	.4	96,652	40	–	94,550	96,633	1,137,856	97.8	11.8
11	–	.4	96,612	40	–	94,550	96,592	1,041,223	97.9	10.8
12	–	.4	96,572	42	–	94,550	96,550	944,631	97.9	9.8
13	0.0	.5	96,530	47	1	94,550	96,506	848,081	97.9	8.8
14	2.7	.5	96,482	52	263	94,549	96,325	751,575	98.0	7.8
15	9.8	.6	96,167	60	947	94,286	95,664	655,250	98.0	6.8
16	45.8	.7	95,160	65	4,355	93,339	92,950	559,586	98.1	5.9
17	74.5	.7	90,740	67	6,764	88,984	87,325	466,636	98.1	5.1
18	227.2	.7	83,909	61	19,067	82,220	74,345	379,311	98.0	4.5
19	212.8	.8	64,781	51	13,784	63,153	57,864	304,966	97.5	4.7
20	226.0	.9	50,946	44	11,516	49,369	45,166	247,102	96.9	4.9
21	301.3	.9	39,386	37	11,867	37,853	33,434	201,936	96.1	5.1
22	258.3	1.1	27,482	29	7,099	25,986	23,918	168,502	94.6	6.1
23	236.7	1.2	20,354	23	4,817	18,887	17,934	144,584	92.8	7.1
24	222.7	1.3	15,514	20	3,455	14,070	13,777	126,650	90.7	8.2
25	205.6	1.4	12,039	16	2,476	10,615	10,793	112,873	88.2	9.4
26	190.5	1.5	9,547	14	1,819	8,139	8,631	102,080	85.3	10.7
27	178.8	1.6	7,714	12	1,379	6,320	7,019	93,449	81.9	12.1
28	154.8	1.8	6,323	11	979	4,941	5,828	86,430	78.1	13.7
29	140.0	2.0	5,333	11	747	3,962	4,954	80,602	74.3	15.1
30	126.4	2.1	4,575	10	578	3,215	4,281	75,648	70.3	16.5
31	113.8	2.2	3,987	9	454	2,637	3,756	71,367	66.1	17.9
32	102.4	2.4	3,524	8	361	2,183	3,340	67,611	61.9	19.2
33	92.5	2.5	3,155	8	292	1,822	3,005	64,271	57.7	20.4
34	84.2	2.6	2,855	8	240	1,530	2,731	61,266	53.6	21.5
35	76.9	2.8	2,607	7	201	1,290	2,503	58,535	49.5	22.5
36	70.2	3.0	2,399	7	168	1,089	2,312	56,032	45.4	23.4
37	63.6	3.2	2,224	7	141	921	2,150	53,720	41.4	24.2
38	56.9	3.4	2,076	7	118	780	2,014	51,570	37.6	24.8
39	50.6	3.6	1,951	7	99	662	1,898	49,556	33.9	25.4
40	44.7	3.9	1,845	7	83	563	1,800	47,658	30.5	25.8
41	39.4	4.1	1,755	7	69	480	1,717	45,858	27.4	26.1
42	34.5	4.4	1,679	7	58	411	1,647	44,141	24.5	26.3
43	30.3	4.7	1,614	8	49	353	1,586	42,494	21.9	26.3
44	26.8	5.0	1,557	8	42	304	1,532	40,908	19.5	26.3
45	23.7	5.3	1,507	8	36	262	1,485	39,376	17.4	26.1
46	21.0	5.6	1,463	8	31	226	1,444	37,891	15.4	25.9
47	18.4	6.0	1,424	9	26	195	1,407	36,447	13.7	25.6
48	16.1	6.3	1,389	9	22	169	1,374	35,040	12.2	25.2
49	14.1	6.6	1,358	9	19	147	1,344	33,666	10.8	24.8
50	12.3	7.0	1,330	9	16	128	1,318	32,322	9.6	24.3
51	10.8	7.5	1,305	10	14	112	1,293	31,004	8.6	23.8
52	9.4	8.0	1,281	10	12	98	1,270	29,711	7.7	23.2
53	8.3	8.6	1,259	11	10	86	1,249	28,441	6.8	22.6
54	7.4	9.2	1,238	11	9	76	1,228	27,192	6.1	22.0
55	6.7	9.9	1,218	12	8	67	1,208	25,964	5.5	21.3
56	6.1	10.6	1,198	13	7	59	1,188	24,756	4.9	20.7
57	5.5	11.5	1,178	13	7	52	1,168	23,568	4.4	20.0
58	5.1	12.3	1,158	14	6	45	1,148	22,400	3.9	19.3
59	4.9	13.2	1,138	15	6	39	1,128	21,252	3.4	18.7
60	4.7	14.2	1,117	16	5	33	1,107	20,124	3.0	18.0
61	4.5	15.2	1,096	17	5	28	1,085	19,017	2.6	17.4
62	4.2	16.4	1,074	18	5	23	1,063	17,932	2.1	16.7
63	3.7	17.8	1,051	19	4	18	1,040	16,869	1.7	16.1
64	3.1	19.2	1,028	20	3	14	1,017	15,829	1.4	15.4
65	2.5	20.7	1,005	21	2	11	994	14,812	1.1	14.7
66	1.9	22.6	982	22	2	9	970	13,818	.9	14.1
67	1.4	24.8	958	24	1	7	946	12,848	.7	13.4
68	1.1	27.5	933	26	1	6	920	11,902	.6	12.8
69	.9	30.6	906	28	1	5	892	10,982	.6	12.1
70	.7	34.0	877	30	1	4	862	10,090	.5	11.5

Table 37. Marriage Table for Single Females, United States, 1940

| Age (Years) | Per 1,000 alive and single at beginning of year of age | | Of 100,000 Born Alive | | | | Stationary Population | | Per cent marrying for the first time in this year of age and all later years | Average number of years remaining before first marriage or death |
| | Number marrying during year | Number dying during year while single | Number living and single at beginning of year of age | Number dying during year of age while single | Number marrying for the first time | | In year of age | In this year of age and all later years | | |
					During year of age	In this year of age and all later years				
(1)	(2)	(3)	(4)	(5)	(6)	(7)	(8)	(9)	(10)	(11)
0	–	41.5	100,000	4,152	–	89,745	96,549	2,242,498	89.7	22.4
1	–	4.9	95,848	469	–	89,745	95,571	2,145,949	93.6	22.4
2	–	2.4	95,379	232	–	89,745	95,256	2,050,378	94.1	21.5
3	–	1.7	95,147	166	–	89,745	95,061	1,955,122	94.3	20.5
4	–	1.4	94,981	133	–	89,745	94,912	1,860,061	94.5	19.6
5	–	1.2	94,848	114	–	89,745	94,791	1,765,149	94.6	18.6
6	–	1.0	94,734	97	–	89,745	94,685	1,670,358	94.7	17.6
7	–	.9	94,637	86	–	89,745	94,594	1,575,673	94.8	16.6
8	–	.8	94,551	77	–	89,745	94,513	1,481,079	94.9	15.7
9	–	.8	94,474	72	–	89,745	94,438	1,386,566	95.0	14.7
10	–	.8	94,402	70	–	89,745	94,367	1,292,128	95.1	13.7
11	–	.8	94,332	72	–	89,745	94,296	1,197,761	95.1	12.7
12	–	.8	94,260	76	–	89,745	94,222	1,103,465	95.2	11.7
13	0.0	.9	94,184	85	0	89,745	94,141	1,009,243	95.3	10.7
14	.8	1.0	94,099	97	72	89,745	94,015	915,102	95.4	9.7
15	5.7	1.2	93,930	112	533	89,673	93,608	821,087	95.5	8.7
16	26.6	1.3	93,285	124	2,477	89,140	91,985	727,479	95.6	7.8
17	43.5	1.5	90,684	132	3,947	86,663	88,645	635,494	95.6	7.0
18	137.2	1.5	86,605	128	11,880	82,716	80,601	546,849	95.5	6.3
19	128.0	1.6	74,597	119	9,551	70,836	69,762	466,248	95.0	6.3
20	187.7	1.6	64,927	106	12,185	61,285	58,782	396,486	94.4	6.1
21	252.0	1.7	52,636	88	13,263	49,100	45,961	337,704	93.3	6.4
22	221.0	1.8	39,285	70	8,681	35,837	34,910	291,743	91.2	7.4
23	222.7	1.9	30,534	57	6,800	27,156	27,106	256,833	88.9	8.4
24	213.3	2.0	23,677	47	5,050	20,356	21,129	229,727	86.0	9.7
25	197.0	2.1	18,580	39	3,660	15,306	16,730	208,598	82.4	11.2
26	178.3	2.3	14,881	34	2,653	11,646	13,538	191,868	78.3	12.9
27	161.8	2.4	12,194	29	1,973	8,993	11,193	178,330	73.7	14.6
28	146.9	2.6	10,192	26	1,498	7,020	9,430	167,137	68.9	16.4
29	130.3	2.8	8,668	24	1,130	5,522	8,091	157,707	63.7	18.2
30	113.3	2.9	7,514	22	851	4,392	7,078	149,616	58.5	19.9
31	97.1	3.1	6,641	20	645	3,541	6,309	142,538	53.3	21.5
32	83.3	3.2	5,976	19	498	2,896	5,718	136,229	48.5	22.8
33	72.3	3.4	5,459	18	395	2,398	5,253	130,511	43.9	23.9
34	63.3	3.5	5,046	18	319	2,003	4,878	125,258	39.7	24.8
35	55.7	3.7	4,709	17	262	1,684	4,570	120,380	35.8	25.6
36	49.1	3.9	4,430	17	217	1,422	4,313	115,810	32.1	26.1
37	42.8	4.1	4,196	17	180	1,205	4,098	111,497	28.7	26.6
38	37.1	4.3	3,999	17	148	1,025	3,917	107,399	25.6	26.9
39	32.3	4.5	3,834	17	124	877	3,764	103,482	22.9	27.0
40	28.3	4.8	3,693	18	104	753	3,632	99,718	20.4	27.0
41	24.7	5.1	3,571	18	88	649	3,518	96,086	18.2	26.9
42	21.5	5.4	3,465	19	75	561	3,418	92,568	16.2	26.7
43	18.8	5.7	3,371	19	63	486	3,330	89,150	14.4	26.4
44	16.7	6.1	3,289	20	55	423	3,252	85,820	12.9	26.1
45	15.0	6.5	3,214	21	48	368	3,180	82,568	11.4	25.7
46	13.5	6.9	3,145	22	42	320	3,113	79,388	10.2	25.2
47	12.0	7.3	3,081	23	37	278	3,051	76,275	9.0	24.8
48	10.7	7.8	3,021	24	32	241	2,993	73,224	8.0	24.2
49	9.4	8.3	2,965	25	28	209	2,939	70,231	7.0	23.7
50	8.4	8.9	2,912	26	24	181	2,887	67,292	6.2	23.1
51	7.5	9.5	2,862	27	21	157	2,838	64,405	5.5	22.5
52	6.6	10.2	2,814	29	19	136	2,790	61,567	4.8	21.9
53	5.8	11.0	2,766	30	16	117	2,743	58,777	4.2	21.2
54	5.1	11.8	2,720	32	14	101	2,697	56,034	3.7	20.6
55	4.6	12.7	2,674	34	12	87	2,651	53,337	3.3	19.9
56	4.1	13.6	2,628	36	11	75	2,605	50,686	2.9	19.3
57	3.6	14.6	2,581	38	9	64	2,558	48,081	2.5	18.6
58	3.2	15.8	2,534	40	8	55	2,510	45,523	2.2	18.0
59	2.9	17.0	2,486	42	7	47	2,462	43,013	1.9	17.3
60	2.7	18.3	2,437	45	7	40	2,411	40,551	1.6	16.6
61	2.5	19.7	2,385	47	6	33	2,359	38,140	1.4	16.0
62	2.2	21.2	2,332	50	5	27	2,305	35,781	1.2	15.3
63	1.9	22.9	2,277	52	4	22	2,249	33,476	1.0	14.7
64	1.6	24.8	2,221	55	3	18	2,192	31,227	.8	14.1
65	1.2	26.9	2,163	58	3	15	2,133	29,035	.7	13.4
66	1.0	29.2	2,102	61	2	12	2,071	26,902	.6	12.8
67	.7	31.8	2,039	65	2	10	2,006	24,831	.5	12.2
68	.6	34.7	1,972	68	1	8	1,938	22,825	.4	11.6
69	.5	37.9	1,903	72	1	7	1,867	20,887	.4	11.0
70	.5	41.6	1,830	76	1	6	1,792	19,020	.3	10.4

mortality among the older single women has been greater than the increase in their nuptiality.

The average duration of life as a single person is the figure shown opposite age 0 in column 11 of Tables 34-37. In 1948, the average was 23.5 years for males and 21.1 years for females. In other words, newborn males, on the average, can expect to live about $2\frac{1}{2}$ years longer than females before marriage or death.[5]

Currently, the expectation of life as a single person drops to a low of about $4\frac{1}{2}$ years at age 18 for females and at age 21 for males. The values then rise until the early 40's, after which they decline without interruption. It is noteworthy that for females the expectation of life as a single person is greater at ages 34 through 55 than at birth—at age 42 the difference is as much as 5.2 years. For males, by contrast, the peak at mid-life is 6.1 years below the figure at birth.

REMARRIAGE TABLES FOR THE WIDOWED AND DIVORCED POPULATION

The chances of remarriage (per cent remarrying) and the expectation of life (average number of years remaining) as a widowed or divorced person are shown for 1948 and 1940 in Tables 38-41. These values were derived from the marriage and death rates shown in the left-hand columns of the tables. The basic data and method of computation are similar to those for the single population (see preceding sections). The figures corresponding to columns 4-9 in the tables for the single are not shown in the remarriage tables, since such values are not meaningful unless

[5]Another standard which may be used for this comparison is provided by the probable lifetime as a single person, which is the age at which half of the original members of the cohort have died or married. In other words, it is the age to which an infant born alive has just an even chance of surviving and remaining single. In computing this median duration of life as a single person, the deaths and marriages in the age interval in which the median age lies are assumed to be evenly distributed. In Tables 34-37, this measure is the age at which there are just 50,000 survivors in column 4. For 1948, this age is 22.7 years for males and 20.1 years for females; the comparable values for 1940 are 23.7 and 21.2 years, respectively. Evidently the median length of life as a single person is somewhat shorter than the average duration.

related to age at widowhood (or divorce) and years elapsed since the event.[6]

The accompanying tables are by attained age, which means that the values for a specific age refer to the experience of all widowed (or divorced) persons whose previous marriage was dissolved at that exact age or earlier. However, the remarriage rate is at a maximum shortly after widowhood or divorce (Chapter 5), and then declines rapidly with advance in duration. Thus, the per cent remarrying among newly widowed (or divorced) persons of a specific age would be somewhat greater than the figure shown for all persons of that attained age; for those who have been widowed (or divorced) for many years, the figure would be smaller than the value by attained age. For the same reason, the reverse relationship is true with regard to the average number of years remaining before remarriage or death.

Chances of Remarriage. Divorced men and women are more likely to remarry than widowed persons; and, except at the very young ages, the widowed have greater prospects of marriage than the single. At age 25, for example, the chances of eventual marriage are now better than 99 in 100 for divorcees, compared with about 93 in 100 for widows and 88 in 100 for single females. Among men of the same age, the chances per 100 are about 99, 97, and 93 for the respective marital classes.

The chances of marriage are at a maximum for widowed or divorced women in their late teens and for the men in their early twenties, and then decrease with advancing age. However, the decrease is more gradual for them than for the single population. Among men, for example, the chances remain above three in four through age 48 for the divorced (Table 40) and age 45 for widowers (Table 38), but only through age 32 for bachelors (Table 34). It is not until age 59 for widowers and age 64 for the divorced that the odds are more than two to one against their eventual remarriage.

The prospects of remarriage are very favorable for young widows and divorcees. In fact, up to

[6]Such American remarriage tables have been approximated for widows. See, for example, Robert J. Myers, "Further Remarriage Experience," *Proceedings of the Casualty Actuarial Society*, XXXVI:73, 1949.

Table 38. Remarriage Table for Widowed Males and Females, by Attained Age, United States, 1948

| Attained Age | Per 1,000 alive and widowed at beginning of year of age | | | | Per cent remarrying in this year of age and all later years | | Average number of years remaining before remarriage or death | |
| | Number remarrying during year | | Number dying during year while widowed | | | | | |
	Male	Female	Male	Female	Male	Female	Male	Female
17	4.3	48.7	2.0	1.7	95.9	97.2	8.1	6.4
18	9.9	97.4	2.7	1.9	96.1	97.2	7.2	5.7
19	19.8	111.6	3.5	2.2	96.3	97.1	6.2	5.3
20	63.2	163.2	4.2	2.5	96.6	97.0	5.4	4.9
21	126.7	206.6	4.8	2.8	96.8	96.7	4.7	4.8
22	162.9	233.3	5.5	3.0	96.9	96.2	4.4	4.9
23	182.7	242.4	5.7	3.1	96.9	95.4	4.2	5.3
24	199.2	240.8	5.9	3.2	96.9	94.3	4.0	5.9
25	212.6	231.9	6.0	3.2	96.8	92.9	3.9	6.6
26	222.9	219.1	6.1	3.3	96.7	91.1	3.9	7.5
27	230.3	205.9	6.4	3.4	96.5	89.0	3.8	8.5
28	233.9	190.0	6.7	3.6	96.3	86.5	3.9	9.6
29	233.9	168.6	7.1	3.7	96.0	83.7	4.0	10.8
30	231.5	145.2	7.4	3.9	95.6	80.8	4.1	12.0
31	228.1	123.2	7.5	4.1	95.2	77.9	4.2	13.0
32	225.0	106.9	7.7	4.3	94.7	75.1	4.3	13.8
33	222.6	97.9	8.0	4.5	94.2	72.5	4.5	14.4
34	220.0	94.0	8.2	4.6	93.4	69.8	4.6	15.0
35	216.7	92.8	8.6	4.8	92.6	67.0	4.9	15.6
36	212.0	91.9	8.9	5.0	91.5	64.0	5.1	16.3
37	205.4	88.8	9.4	5.2	90.2	60.7	5.4	16.9
38	195.7	83.3	10.0	5.5	88.8	57.2	5.8	17.6
39	183.2	76.7	10.6	5.7	87.1	53.6	6.2	18.3
40	169.5	69.8	11.3	6.1	85.3	50.1	6.5	18.9
41	156.6	63.3	12.1	6.4	83.5	46.6	6.9	19.4
42	146.2	57.7	12.9	6.8	81.6	43.3	7.2	19.8
43	139.2	53.5	13.8	7.2	79.6	40.2	7.4	20.2
44	134.4	50.1	14.7	7.7	77.5	37.1	7.7	20.5
45	130.7	47.2	15.6	8.1	75.3	34.0	7.9	20.7
46	127.1	44.3	16.5	8.5	72.9	31.0	8.2	20.9
47	122.4	41.0	17.5	9.0	70.3	28.0	8.5	21.0
48	116.5	37.0	18.5	9.4	67.5	25.2	8.8	21.1
49	109.9	32.7	19.4	9.8	64.6	22.5	9.1	21.1
50	103.1	28.3	20.4	10.2	61.6	20.1	9.3	21.0
51	96.6	24.3	21.6	10.8	58.5	18.0	9.6	20.8
52	90.7	21.0	22.8	11.4	55.4	16.1	9.8	20.5
53	85.8	18.6	24.1	12.0	52.2	14.5	10.0	20.2
54	81.5	16.8	25.4	12.6	49.1	13.0	10.1	19.8
55	77.6	15.4	26.6	13.3	45.8	11.7	10.3	19.4
56	73.4	14.2	27.9	14.0	42.5	10.5	10.4	19.0
57	68.7	13.0	29.0	14.8	39.1	9.3	10.6	18.5
58	63.0	11.6	30.8	15.8	35.7	8.3	10.7	18.0
59	56.5	10.4	32.6	16.9	32.5	7.3	10.7	17.5
60	50.0	9.3	34.4	18.0	29.4	6.4	10.7	17.0
61	43.9	8.3	36.3	19.3	26.7	5.6	10.6	16.5
62	39.1	7.4	38.2	20.6	24.2	5.0	10.5	15.9
63	36.0	6.7	40.3	21.9	22.0	4.3	10.4	15.4
64	34.2	6.2	42.3	23.2	19.9	3.8	10.2	14.8
65	32.9	5.8	44.3	24.6	17.9	3.2	10.0	14.2
66	31.6	5.3	46.6	26.3	15.8	2.8	9.8	13.7
67	29.5	4.8	49.1	28.3	13.7	2.3	9.6	13.1
68	26.3	4.2	52.2	31.0	11.7	1.9	9.3	12.5
69	22.4	3.6	55.5	34.0	9.8	1.5	9.1	12.0
70	18.4	3.0	59.0	37.2	8.2	1.2	8.8	11.4
71	14.8	2.4	62.8	40.8	6.9	.9	8.5	10.9
72	12.0	1.9	67.0	44.7	5.9	.7	8.2	10.3
73	10.3	1.5	72.0	49.0	5.1	.6	7.9	9.8
74	9.5	1.1	77.3	53.6	4.4	.4	7.5	9.3
75	9.0	.8	82.9	58.6	3.8	.4	7.2	8.8
76	8.6	.6	88.9	64.0	3.2	.3	6.9	8.4
77	7.8	.4	95.3	69.9	2.6	.2	6.5	7.9
78	6.6	.4	102.0	76.4	2.1	.2	6.2	7.5
79	5.3	.4	108.9	83.4	1.6	.2	5.9	7.0
80	3.9	.3	116.4	90.8	1.2	.2	5.6	6.6
81	2.7	.3	124.5	98.8	.9	.2	5.3	6.2
82	1.9	.3	133.4	107.4	.7	.1	5.0	5.9
83	1.4	.3	144.1	116.9	.6	.1	4.8	5.5
84	1.3	.3	155.8	127.0	.5	.1	4.5	5.2
85	1.2	.2	168.2	137.5	.5	.1	4.2	4.9
86	1.1	.2	181.1	149.0	.4	.1	4.0	4.6
87	1.1	.2	194.2	161.5	.4	.1	3.8	4.3
88	1.0	.2	207.5	174.9	.3	.1	3.6	4.0
89	.9	.2	221.1	189.3	.3	.0	3.4	3.8

Table 39. Remarriage Table for Widowed Males and Females, by Attained Age, United States, 1940

Attained Age	Per 1,000 alive and widowed at beginning of year of age				Per cent remarrying in this year of age and all later years		Average number of years remaining before remarriage or death	
	Number remarrying during year		Number dying during year while widowed					
	Male	Female	Male	Female	Male	Female	Male	Female
15	9.5	23.2	3.2	1.9	94.4	90.3	7.5	11.5
16	18.7	34.4	4.1	2.5	94.7	90.3	6.6	10.8
17	34.9	46.8	5.1	3.0	95.0	90.2	5.7	10.2
18	61.0	62.6	6.2	3.6	95.3	90.0	4.9	9.7
19	94.5	81.5	7.3	4.1	95.6	89.7	4.2	9.4
20	160.5	100.6	8.4	4.7	96.0	89.1	3.7	9.2
21	201.0	117.0	9.5	5.4	96.1	88.4	3.3	9.2
22	233.6	128.2	10.6	6.0	96.3	87.4	3.0	9.4
23	261.0	133.7	10.5	6.0	96.5	86.1	2.9	9.8
24	286.6	135.4	10.2	6.1	96.7	84.6	2.7	10.3
25	308.2	134.3	9.9	6.1	96.7	82.7	2.7	11.0
26	324.0	131.4	9.6	6.1	96.7	80.6	2.7	11.7
27	332.1	127.9	9.5	6.1	96.5	78.2	2.8	12.4
28	331.2	122.9	9.5	6.2	96.1	75.6	3.0	13.3
29	322.7	115.8	9.5	6.2	95.5	72.7	3.2	14.2
30	308.7	107.5	9.7	6.3	94.6	69.6	3.6	15.1
31	291.6	99.1	9.9	6.4	93.5	66.4	4.0	16.0
32	273.5	91.5	10.2	6.5	92.2	63.1	4.6	16.8
33	252.0	84.6	10.5	6.7	90.5	59.9	5.2	17.5
34	225.1	77.9	10.9	6.8	88.5	56.5	5.9	18.3
35	196.3	71.4	11.3	6.9	86.4	53.3	6.5	18.9
36	169.3	65.3	11.7	7.1	84.2	50.1	7.1	19.5
37	148.5	59.8	12.2	7.2	82.1	46.9	7.5.	19.9
38	136.1	55.0	12.6	7.3	80.2	43.9	7.9	20.3
39	129.7	50.8	13.0	7.5	78.2	40.9	8.2	20.7
40	126.6	47.0	13.5	7.7	76.1	38.1	8.5	20.9
41	124.3	43.6	14.2	8.0	73.7	35.3	8.7	21.1
42	120.1	40.3	14.9	8.4	71.2	32.6	9.1	21.2
43	113.8	37.3	15.8	8.8	68.4	30.0	9.4	21.3
44	107.3	34.6	16.7	9.3	65.5	27.6	9.7	21.3
45	100.7	32.2	17.7	9.8	62.5	25.2	10.0	21.2
46	94.2	29.9	18.7	10.3	59.5	23.0	10.3	21.1
47	87.9	27.5	19.8	10.8	56.4	20.8	10.6	21.0
48	81.5	25.1	20.9	11.4	53.4	18.8	10.8	20.8
49	75.0	22.7	22.1	11.9	50.4	16.9	11.0	20.6
50	68.8	20.3	23.3	12.6	47.5	15.2	11.1	20.3
51	63.1	18.2	24.7	13.3	44.8	13.6	11.2	20.0
52	58.6	16.3	26.1	14.0	42.2	12.1	11.2	19.6
53	55.6	14.7	27.5	14.7	39.7	10.8	11.2	19.2
54	53.9	13.4	29.0	15.5	37.2	9.7	11.2	18.8
55	52.7	12.3	30.5	16.4	34.7	8.6	11.1	18.3
56	51.4	11.2	32.1	17.3	32.1	7.6	11.1	17.8
57	49.1	10.2	33.6	18.3	29.4	6.6	11.1	17.3
58	45.3	9.0	35.2	19.5	26.7	5.8	11.0	16.8
59	40.7	7.9	36.8	20.7	24.1	5.0	10.9	16.3
60	35.8	6.8	38.5	22.1	21.7	4.3	10.8	15.8
61	31.3	5.8	40.2	23.5	19.6	3.8	10.6	15.2
62	27.8	5.1	41.9	25.1	17.8	3.3	10.4	14.7
63	25.8	4.5	44.3	26.7	16.1	2.9	10.2	14.1
64	24.9	4.2	46.9	28.6	14.5	2.5	9.9	13.6
65	24.3	3.9	49.6	30.5	13.0	2.2	9.6	13.0
66	23.6	3.7	52.6	32.7	11.4	1.8	9.3	12.5
67	22.2	3.4	55.9	35.1	9.8	1.5	9.1	11.9
68	19.7	3.0	59.3	38.2	8.2	1.2	8.8	11.4
69	16.5	2.5	63.1	41.7	6.8	1.0	8.5	10.8
70	13.2	2.0	67.1	45.5	5.6	.7	8.2	10.3
71	10.1	1.6	71.5	49.7	4.6	.6	7.9	9.8
72	7.9	1.2	76.3	54.4	3.9	.4	7.5	9.3
73	6.7	1.0	82.3	59.5	3.4	.3	7.2	8.8
74	6.2	.7	88.7	65.0	3.0	.2	6.8	8.4
75	6.0	.6	95.6	70.9	2.6	.2	6.5	7.9
76	5.9	.4	102.9	77.4	2.2	.1	6.2	7.5
77	5.5	.3	110.8	84.2	1.8	.1	5.9	7.1
78	4.8	.2	119.4	91.8	1.5	.1	5.6	6.7
79	3.8	.2	128.5	99.9	1.1	.1	5.3	6.3
80	2.9	.1	138.0	108.6	.8	.0	5.0	5.9
81	2.1	.1	148.1	117.7	.7	.0	4.7	5.6
82	1.5	.1	158.6	127.5	.5	.0	4.5	5.3
83	1.2	.1	170.1	138.1	.5	.0	4.2	5.0
84	1.1	.1	182.1	149.2	.4	.0	4.0	4.7

Table 40. Remarriage Table for Divorced Males and Females, by Attained Age, United States, 1948

Attained Age	Per 1,000 alive and divorced at beginning of year of age				Per cent remarrying in this year of age and all later years		Average number of years remaining before remarriage or death	
	Number remarrying during year		Number dying during year while divorced					
	Male	Female	Male	Female	Male	Female	Male	Female
17	66.0	460.6	1.9	0.8	99.0	99.8	3.6	1.6
18	314.6	483.8	1.9	1.0	99.2	99.8	2.8	1.6
19	185.1	492.4	2.4	1.1	99.1	99.7	2.9	1.6
20	173.6	490.9	2.8	1.3	99.2	99.7	2.5	1.6
21	390.6	483.3	2.7	1.3	99.3	99.7	1.9	1.7
22	419.0	473.4	2.8	1.3	99.3	99.7	1.8	1.8
23	438.1	458.3	3.0	1.4	99.3	99.6	1.8	1.9
24	446.1	435.0	3.1	1.5	99.2	99.5	1.7	2.1
25	446.7	407.1	3.3	1.6	99.2	99.4	1.8	2.3
26	443.4	378.8	3.4	1.7	99.1	99.2	1.8	2.5
27	439.4	354.8	3.6	1.8	99.1	99.0 •	1.8	2.7
28	433.7	336.3	3.9	2.0	98.9	98.8	1.9	3.0
29	424.1	320.6	4.2	2.1	98.8	98.5	2.0	3.2
30	411.9	306.5	4.5	2.3	98.7	98.1	2.0	3.5
31	398.7	292.6	4.7	2.4	98.5	97.5	2.1	3.9
32	386.1	277.8	5.1	2.5	98.2	96.8	2.2	4.3
33	374.2	261.5	5.4	2.7	98.0	95.9	2.4	4.8
34	362.0	244.7	5.9	2.8	97.6	94.8	2.5	5.3
35	349.2	227.9	6.4	3.0	97.1	93.5	2.7	5.9
36	335.5	211.5	7.0	3.2	96.5	91.9	2.9	6.6
37	320.6	196.2	7.7	3.4	95.7	90.1	3.1	7.2
38	303.7	182.1	8.5	3.6	94.8	88.1	3.4	7.9
39	284.7	169.0	9.4	3.9	93.7	85.8	3.7	8.6
40	265.0	156.7	10.3	4.2	92.4	83.4	4.0	9.3
41	245.7	145.0	11.2	4.5	90.9	80.7	4.4	10.0
42	228.3	133.7	12.1	4.8	89.3	77.8	4.7	10.6
43	212.8	122.7	13.2	5.2	87.5	74.8	5.0	11.2
44	198.6	112.2	14.2	5.6	85.6	71.7	5.3	11.8
45	185.6	102.4	15.3	5.9	83.5	68.5	5.6	12.3
46	173.6	93.5•	16.5	6.3	81.2	65.4	5.9	12.8
47	162.5	85.7	17.7	6.7	78.9	62.2	6.2	13.1
48	153.0	79.4	19.0	7.1	76.4	59.1	6.5	13.4
49	145.1	74.6	20.2	7.4	73.8	56.0	6.7	13.6
50	138.1	70.6	21.6	7.9	71.0	52.9	6.9	13.8
51	131.3	67.0	23.1	8.5	68.1	49.8	7.2	13.9
52	123.8	63.1	24.8	9.2	65.0	46.6	7.4	14.0
53	115.4	59.1	26.6	9.9	61.8	43.4	7.6	14.1
54	106.6	55.1	28.5	10.7	58.6	40.3	7.8	14.1
55	97.8	51.3	30.5	11.6	55.4	37.2	7.9	14.0
56	89.6	47.7	32.5	12.5	52.4	34.3	8.0	14.0
57	82.4	44.2	34.5	13.6	49.4	31.4	8.0	13.8
58	76.3	40.9	36.8	14.8	46.6	28.6	8.0	13.6
59	70.9	37.8	39.2	16.1	44.0	26.0	8.0	13.4
60	66.3	34.9	41.5	17.4	41.5	23.4	7.9	13.1
61	62.4	32.1	44.0	19.0	39.1	21.1	7.8	12.8
62	60.5	29.4	46.5	20.6	36.7	18.8	7.7	12.5
63	59.3	26.9	49.6	22.6	34.3	16.7	7.5	12.1
64	58.1	24.6	52.8	24.7	31.9	14.7	7.4	11.7
65	56.9	22.4	56.2	27.1	29.3	12.9	7.3	11.3
66	55.8	20.3	59.9	29.8	26.6	11.2	7.1	10.9
67	55.5	18.1	64.0	33.1	23.8	9.7	7.0	10.4
68	50.6	15.7	68.1	37.0	20.7	8.3	6.9	10.0
69	43.7	12.9	72.6	41.3	17.8	7.1	6.7	9.5
70	36.0	10.4	77.5	46.3	15.2	6.1	6.6	9.0
71	29.0	8.3	82.8	51.7	13.1	5.4	6.3	8.5
72	23.8	8.0	88.5	57.9	11.5	4.9	6.1	8.0
73	21.1	7.5	96.8	64.5	10.2	4.4	5.8	7.6
74	19.8	7.1	105.5	71.6	9.2	3.9	5.5	7.1
75	19.4	6.7	115.1	79.4	8.3	3.5	5.2	6.7
76	19.1	6.3	125.4	88.2	7.3	3.0	4.9	6.3
77	18.2	5.9	136.7	97.8	6.3	2.7	4.7	5.9
78	16.6	5.5	147.4	109.1	5.3	2.3	4.5	5.5
79	14.9	5.0	158.4	121.4	4.4	2.0	4.2	5.1

Table 41. Remarriage Table for Divorced Males and Females, by Attained Age, United States, 1940

| Attained Age | Per 1,000 alive and divorced at beginning of year of age | | | | Per cent remarrying in this year of age and all later years | | Average number of years remaining before remarriage or death | |
| | Number remarrying during year | | Number dying during year while divorced | | | | | |
	Male	Female	Male	Female	Male	Female	Male	Female
17	61.1	277.2	2.8	1.8	98.4	99.3	3.8	2.6
18	292.6	309.9	2.9	2.0	98.6	99.3	3.1	2.4
19	163.9	342.2	3.6	2.2	98.5	99.3	3.2	2.2
20	149.2	370.9	4.1	2.4	98.6	99.3	2.7	2.1
21	331.6	392.7	4.2	2.7	98.8	99.2	2.1	2.0
22	393.0	405.0	4.5	2.9	98.9	99.2	1.9	2.1
23	418.5	406.2	4.7	3.0	98.8	99.1	1.8	2.1
24	432.4	398.5	4.9	3.0	98.8	99.0	1.8	2.3
25	438.3	384.8	5.1	3.1	98.8	98.8	1.8	2.5
26	439.5	368.1	5.3	3.1	98.7	98.5	1.8	2.7
27	439.3	351.6	5.6	3.2	98.6	98.1	1.8	3.0
28	436.6	334.2	6.0	3.3	98.4	97.6	1.8	3.4
29	429.3	313.7	6.4	3.4	98.3	96.9	1.9	3.8
30	418.8	291.3	6.8	3.5	98.1	95.9	2.0	4.3
31	406.4	268.6	7.1	3.7	97.9	94.7	2.1	4.9
32	393.6	247.5	7.5	3.9	97.6	93.2	2.2	5.6
33	380.0	227.7	7.9	4.1	97.2	91.4	2.4	6.3
34	364.5	208.1	8.4	4.3	96.7	89.3	2.5	7.1
35	347.6	189.3	9.0	4.5	96.0	87.0	2.8	7.9
36	329.7	171.7	9.6	4.8	95.2	84.4	3.0	8.6
37	311.2	155.8	10.3	5.1	94.3	81.6	3.3	9.4
38	290.9	142.3	11.1	5.3	93.0	78.7	3.6	10.1
39	268.3	130.9	12.0	5.6	91.6	75.6	4.0	10.7
40	245.3	121.0	12.9	6.0	90.0	72.4	4.4	11.3
41	223.7	112.1	13.8	6.3	88.3	69.1	4.7	11.9
42	205.7	103.5	14.8	6.7	86.4	65.7	5.0	12.4
43	192.8	95.5	15.8	7.2	84.5	62.2	5.3	12.9
44	183.8	88.5	16.9	7.6	82.4	58.7	5.6	13.3
45	176.9	82.3	18.1	8.2	80.1	55.1	5.9	13.7
46	170.3	76.4	19.3	8.7	77.6	51.6	6.2	14.0
47	162.0	70.7	20.6	9.3	74.7	48.0	6.5	14.3
48	151.6	65.0	22.1	10.0	71.6	44.5	6.8	14.5
49	140.3	59.6	23.6	10.6	68.3	41.1	7.2	14.6
50	128.7	54.6	25.1	11.4	64.9	37.8	7.5	14.7
51	117.6	49.8	26.7	12.2	61.5	34.6	7.7	14.7
52	107.4	45.3	28.4	13.0	58.1	31.6	7.9	14.6
53	98.3	41.1	30.1	14.0	54.8	28.7	8.1	14.5
54	89.8	37.2	31.9	15.0	51.6	26.0	8.2	14.3
55	82.1	33.5	33.7	16.1	48.5	23.5	8.3	14.1
56	74.9	30.2	35.5	17.3	45.6	21.2	8.3	13.8
57	68.5	27.2	37.4	18.6	42.8	19.1	8.3	13.4
58	62.8	24.5	39.9	20.3	40.2	17.2	8.2	13.1
59	57.8	22.3	42.4	22.1	37.9	15.4	8.1	12.6
60	53.6	20.2	45.1	24.2	35.6	13.8	8.0	12.2
61	50.0	18.4	47.9	26.4	33.6	12.3	7.8	11.8
62	47.1	16.7	50.9	28.9	31.7	11.0	7.6	11.3
63	45.1	15.1	54.3	31.7	29.9	9.8	7.3	10.8
64	44.3	13.7	57.9	34.7	28.2	8.7	7.1	10.3
65	43.9	12.4	61.8	38.2	26.5	7.7	6.8	9.8
66	43.5	11.2	66.1	42.0	24.7	6.8	6.6	9.3
67	42.6	9.9	70.7	46.3	22.9	6.0	6.3	8.8
68	40.9	8.5	76.7	52.1	21.0	5.3	6.1	8.3
69	39.0	7.5	83.3	58.7	19.2	4.7	5.8	7.8
70	36.9	7.1	90.7	66.1	17.4	4.2	5.6	7.3
71	34.7	6.8	98.9	74.5	15.7	3.8	5.3	6.8
72	32.7	6.4	107.9	83.9	14.1	3.4	5.1	6.4
73	30.7	6.1	117.5	92.4	12.6	3.0	4.8	6.0
74	28.7	5.7	128.0	101.8	11.2	2.7	4.6	5.6
75	26.8	5.4	139.5	111.9	9.9	2.4	4.3	5.2
76	24.8	5.0	151.8	123.0	8.7	2.1	4.1	4.8
77	22.9	4.7	165.1	134.9	7.5	1.8	3.8	4.5
78	21.0	4.3	180.6	153.2	6.5	1.5	3.6	4.1
79	19.3	4.0	197.3	173.6	5.5	1.3	3.4	3.8

the early twenties, women are more likely to re-marry than men. Thereafter, men have the advantage, the chances of remarriage declining more rapidly for the women—especially among the widowed. By age 45, the ratio of the chances of remarriage for men as compared with women is 1.2 among the divorced, and as much as 2.2 among the widowed. Even at the 65th birthday a widower has a fairly good chance to remarry—about 18 in 100 eventually do, whereas for widows the chances are relatively small—only about 3 in 100.

Duration of Widowhood. The average number of years remaining before marriage or death varies according to the age of a widowed person. Among widows in 1948, for example, the figure dropped to a low of 4.8 years for those aged 21, then rose to a maximum of 21.1 years at ages 48-49, after which it declined continuously. It is noteworthy that the figure at its peak is equal to the expectation of life as a single person for females at birth.

The values fluctuate in a similar manner for widowers. However, because both marriage and death rates are higher among them, the expectation of life as a widowed person is much lower for men than for women at almost every period of life. In fact, at ages 27 through 53 the figure for widowers is less than one half of that for widows. Moreover, the expected duration of widowhood for men, which reaches no higher than 10.7 years at ages 58-60, falls below 10 years after age 65; women, by contrast, still have a decade of widowhood ahead of them even at their 72nd birthday.

The expected duration of widowhood changed somewhat between 1940 and 1948. As is evident from Tables 38 and 39, decreases occurred at ages 32-60 among men and after age 46 among women. At the other ages the figures increased, indicating that the rise in the marriage rate was not large enough to offset the contrary effects of the decline in mortality.

Duration of Life as a Divorced Person. The average number of years remaining before marriage or death—at any given age—is much lower for divorced men and women than for the widowed or the single. Among divorced males, the figure is currently under 2 years at ages 21-29 and reaches no higher than 8 years at age 57. Among the women, the figure is equally low at the younger ages, but it climbs to a much higher maximum in later life, namely, to about 14 years at ages 52-55.

The years remaining as a divorced person decreased between 1940 and 1948 for men at ages 35-60 and for women under age 56. By contrast, increases occurred for the older men and women. It is also noteworthy that Tables 40 and 41 indicate little or no change for men under age 35.

Chapter 7

THE TREND OF DIVORCE

MARRIAGE is a civil contract in the United States, but it differs from all other contracts in that it cannot be dissolved at the pleasure of the parties. In every divorce or annulment case, the state itself is a third and interested party.

The dissolution of a marriage by divorce differs in theory from the annulment of a marriage. The former presupposes that a valid, subsisting contract was entered into by the parties. Thus a divorce is a legal decree by a court of competent authority, which dissolves or partially suspends a legally recognized union for some cause that arose after the establishment of the marriage. An annulment of a marriage, on the other hand, is a legal decree that no valid marriage was contracted because of some condition which existed at the time of marriage. Divorce is statutory, however, and the statutes frequently grant this relief on grounds that would render a marriage void or voidable. Moreover, marriages which are void without legal process in some states may be annulled in others. In the absence of statute, a court of equity will annul a marriage for error, fraud, duress, or lunacy, since these are matters peculiar to equity jurisdiction.[1]

Currently, the term "divorce" generally refers to *divorce a vinculo matrimonii*, or absolute divorce from the bonds of matrimony, in contrast to *divorce a mensa et thoro*, or separation from bed and board. The first type of divorce puts an end to the marriage; the latter (also known as limited divorce) authorizes separate maintenance but leaves the marriage bond in full force.

Unless otherwise noted, all of the divorce statistics in this book refer to the total of absolute divorces, annulments, and dissolutions of marriage (Enoch Arden decrees in New York State).

[1]See, for example, John W. Morland, *Keezer on the Law of Marriage and Divorce*, Third Edition, The Bobbs-Merrill Company, Indianapolis, 1946.

EARLY HISTORY OF DIVORCE

Divorce is as old as the institution of the family itself. Among the Babylonians, for example, provisions for divorce were usually introduced into the marriage contracts of women who married without a dowry. Divorce was also not uncommon among other ancient civilizations such as the Hebrew, Greek, and Roman. In fact, among ancient peoples of all degrees of culture, marriage was considered a social institution, and as such the right of divorce was restricted only by social custom and law.

With the advent of the Christian era, ecclesiastical control over marriage and divorce gradually evolved. By the Middle Ages, the dogma of sacramental marriage had completely replaced the social contract theory throughout the Christian world. The doctrine of the indissolubility of marriage, however, even during the long reign of the Canon law, is said to have been never more than a utopian idea. According to Kitchin,[2] for example, the rule was never practiced except to keep women in subjection and men and women under the perpetual tutelage of the Church. Men, particularly the powerful or wealthy, could always obtain divorce or find some means of evading the rule even in the days when the Church was most powerful and had an opportunity of enforcing its doctrine. Moreover, since litigation over family troubles was a continuous source of revenue to the Church, all attempts to settle differences out of court were repressed. Consent to a divorce or even to a separation was treated as collusion or fraud, and was sufficient to prevent the granting of any remedy unless the parties were wealthy or powerful—in which case their consent was encouraged, as for example in the unsuccessful divorce negotiations between Henry VIII of England and Catherine of Aragon.

[2]Shepherd B. Kitchin, *A History of Divorce*, Chapman and Hall, Ltd., London, 1912, p. 81.

Since a marriage, once performed as a sacrament, could not be revoked, as is still true in the Roman Catholic Church, numerous causes were established for declaring a marriage null and void from its beginning on the ground that the conditions essential to a valid sacrament had not existed at the time of marriage. The impediments recognized by the Church for absolute dissolution of a marriage included defect of consent, impuberty, impotency, disparity of worship, and seven degrees of consanguinity, affinity, and spiritual relationship (those gained in baptism). In fact, according to the Thwings,[3] marriage regulations were so tangled at the beginning of the sixteenth century that for a sufficient consideration a canonical flaw could be found in almost any marriage. (Note, for comparison, the frequent recourse to annulments in New York State during recent decades.)

DIVORCE PRIOR TO THE CIVIL WAR

The Reformation, which had loosened the control of the Church, led to the gradual displacement of the sacramental theory of marriage in large areas of Western Europe. Although this view of marriage still prevailed in England—with all matrimonial litigation under the jurisdiction of the ecclesiastical courts—the American colonists rejected it from the start. As a result, matrimonial matters in the United States have always been subject to civil jurisdiction.

Despite numerous books on our early history, little information is available regarding family life and its disruption by separation, divorce, or annulment. It is known that as early as 1639 the Colony of Massachusetts Bay provided for divorce. Subsequently, such decrees were granted in some of the other colonies, such as by the Courts of Assistants in Connecticut, the Courts of Trials in Rhode Island, the Patroon's Courts of New Amsterdam, and also in the Colony of New York during its administration by the English.[4]

During the second half of the eighteenth century, in accord with English parliamentary practice, divorces were granted in some of the colonies by

legislative enactments for the accommodation of specific individuals.[5] Few of these legislative divorces were granted during the colonial period, but their number increased thereafter as the practice became established. In Pennsylvania, for example, 304 legislative decrees were granted between 1769 and 1873, with all but two after the War of Independence.[6]

Although there are many references in the literature to the concern and alarm over the high frequency of marital disruptions during our early history, it was not until the middle of the nineteenth century that any divorce statistics became available. However, even if adequate data were available for the earlier period, there is no doubt that they would markedly understate the actual rate at which marriages were broken. In the colonial period, it was not uncommon for men to abandon their wife in Europe and marry in America—a practice which probably continued, but at a lesser rate, up through the early years of the twentieth century. Similarly, during the 1800's, the frontier territories served as the meccas of the married who had deserted wife and family in the East.

DIVORCE SINCE 1860

In 1956 about 382,000 marriages were legally dissolved by divorce or annulment in the United States. Although this was a sharp drop from the peak year 1946, when close to 629,000 dissolutions occurred, it exceeded the number for every year prior to 1944. The long-term increase in the number of divorces has been due in part to the growth of our married population. Of even greater consequence, however, has been the upswing of the divorce rate which has risen with few interruptions during the past hundred years. Table 42 shows the trend since 1860.[7]

[3] Charles F. Thwing and Carrol F. B. Thwing, *The Family: An Historical and Social Study*, Lee and Shepard Publishers, Boston, 1887, pp. 83-84.

[4] Charles Cowley, *Our Divorce Courts*, Penhallow Printing Co., Lowell, Mass., 1879, pp. 11, 22.

[5] Matteo Spalletta, "Divorce in Colonial New York," *The New-York Historical Society Quarterly*, xxxix (4): 436-437, October, 1955.

[6] The practice of legislative divorce continued in some of the states until the turn of the century. For example, prior to 1897 nearly all divorces in Delaware were by legislative enactment. In Connecticut, nine absolute decrees were granted as late as the legislative sessions of 1889 to 1905.

[7] The number of decrees during 1860-1866 and 1940-1950 was estimated by the author. Those for the Civil War period were derived in relation to the published figure for 1867, on the assumption that the trend in the country as a whole

Table 42. Number of Absolute Divorces and Annulments, and Rates, United States, 1860-1956

Year	Divorce*	Rate per 1,000 Total Population	Rate per 1,000 Existing Marriages	Year	Divorce*	Annulment	Dissolution of Marriage†	Total Decrees Number	Total Decrees Rate per 1,000 Total Population	Total Decrees Rate per 1,000 Existing Marriages
1860	7,380	0.3	1.2	1909	79,671	§	–	79,671	0.9	4.5
1861	6,540	.2	1.1							
1862	6,230	.2	1.0	1910	83,045	§	–	83,045	.9	4.5
1863	6,760	.2	1.1	1911	89,219	§	–	89,219	1.0	4.8
1864	8,940	.3	1.4	1912	94,318	§	–	94,318	1.0	4.9
1865	10,090	.3	1.6	1913	91,307	§	–	91,307	.9	4.7
1866	11,530	.3	1.8	1914	100,584	§	–	100,584	1.0	5.0
1867	9,937	.3	1.5	1915	104,298	§	–	104,298	1.0	5.1
1868	10,150	.3	1.5	1916	114,000	§	–	114,000	1.1	5.5
1869	10,939	.3	1.6	1917	121,564	§	–	121,564	1.2	5.7
				1918	116,254	§	–	116,254	1.1	5.4
1870	10,962	.3	1.5	1919	141,527	§	–	141,527	1.3	6.5
1871	11,586	.3	1.6							
1872	12,390	.3	1.7	1920	167,105	3,400	–	170,505	1.6	7.7
1873	13,156	.3	1.7	1921	156,580	3,000	–	159,580	1.5	7.1
1874	13,989	.3	1.8	1922	148,815	2,795	41	151,651	1.4	6.6
1875	14,212	.3	1.8	1923	165,096	3,281	83	168,460	1.5	7.2
1876	14,800	.3	1.8	1924	170,952	3,310	125	174,387	1.5	7.2
1877	15,687	.3	1.9	1925	175,449	3,450	167	179,066	1.5	7.3
1878	16,089	.3	1.9	1926	180,853	3,616	209	184,678	1.6	7.4
1879	17,083	.3	2.0	1927	192,037	4,206	49	196,292	1.6	7.7
				1928	195,939	4,141	96	200,176	1.7	7.8
1880	19,663	.4	2.2	1929	201,468	4,307	101	205,876	1.7	7.9
1881	20,762	.4	2.3							
1882	22,112	.4	2.4	1930	191,591	4,228	142	195,961	1.6	7.4
1883	23,198	.4	2.4	1931	183,664	4,257	82	188,003	1.5	7.0
1884	22,994	.4	2.4	1932	160,338	3,830	73	164,241	1.3	6.1
1885	23,472	.4	2.3	1933	160,920	4,000	80	165,000	1.3	6.1
1886	25,535	.4	2.5	1934	198,840	5,000	160	204,000	1.6	7.4
1887	27,919	.5	2.7	1935	212,270	5,500	230	218,000	1.7	7.8
1888	28,669	.5	2.7	1936	229,600	6,100	300	236,000	1.8	8.3
1889	31,735	.5	2.9	1937	242,020	6,600	380	249,000	1.9	8.6
				1938	236,950	6,600	450	244,000	1.9	8.3
1890	33,461	.5	3.0	1939	243,580	6,900	520	251,000	1.9	8.4
1891	35,540	.6	3.1							
1892	36,579	.6	3.1	1940	256,692	7,440	590	264,722	2.0	8.7
1893	37,468	.6	3.1	1941	285,851	8,528	560	294,939	2.2	9.4
1894	37,568	.6	3.0	1942	310,869	9,650	810	321,329	2.4	10.0
1895	40,387	.6	3.2	1943	347,229	11,270	680	359,179	2.6	10.9
1896	42,937	.6	3.3	1944	398,818	13,020	780	412,618	3.0	12.3
1897	44,699	.6	3.4	1945	469,341	16,135	850	486,326	3.5	14.3
1898	47,849	.7	3.6	1946	605,754	22,056	950	628,760	4.4	18.2
1899	51,437	.7	3.7	1947	478,781	16,515	810	496,106	3.4	13.9
				1948	408,160	14,413	640	423,213	2.9	11.6
1900	55,751	.7	4.0	1949	379,922	13,400	478	393,800	2.6	10.6
1901	60,984	.8	4.2							
1902	61,480	.8	4.2	1950	371,309	13,200	418	384,927	2.5	10.2
1903	64,925	.8	4.3	1951‡	367,400	13,200	400	381,000	2.5	9.9
1904	66,199	.8	4.3	1952‡	378,600	13,000	400	392,000	2.5	10.0
1905	67,976	.8	4.3	1953‡	376,600	13,000	400	390,000	2.4	9.9
1906	72,062	.8	4.4	1954‡	365,900	12,700	400	379,000	2.3	9.5
1907	76,571	.9	4.5	1955‡	364,450	12,200	350	377,000	2.3	9.3
1908	76,852	.9	4.4	1956‡	369,300	12,400	300	382,000	2.3	9.3

*Figures for 1860-1919 and 1922-1939 include separations.   †New York State Enoch Arden decrees.   ‡Provisional.
§ Not available prior to 1920.

Note: Population excludes slaves prior to 1865; includes armed forces overseas during 1917-1919 and 1940-1956.
Source: Divorces, 1867-1919 and 1922-1932; annulments, 1926-1931; dissolutions, 1926-1931; total decrees, 1920-1921, 1932-1939, and 1951-1956; and total population; from various reports by the Bureau of the Census and the National Office of Vital Statistics. All other data were compiled or estimated by the author.

Immediately prior to the Civil War, the rate was only about 1.2 divorces annually per 1,000 existing marriages; by the turn of the century, it was up to 4 per 1,000; and since 1941 it has exceeded 9 per 1,000. At its peak in 1946 there were as many as 18.2 divorces for every 1,000 existing marriages, but the rate has since declined to 9.3. It is noteworthy that the current divorce rate is almost eight times that of 1860.

A similar pattern of change is obtained by relating divorces to the total population. This is not unexpected since the two series of divorce rates would diverge only to the extent that the married population grew at a lesser or greater rate than the total population. Thus, for the period 1930-1950, when the married population experienced the greater relative increase, the indicated rise in divorce was 38 per cent for the rate based on existing marriages compared with 56 per cent for the rate based on total population. By contrast, since 1950 (and for several years to come) the growth of the married population has closely paralleled that of the total population, with the result that both rates have indicated approximately the same relative change. It should also be noted

that either rate is usually adequate for measuring changes from one year to the next. However, since divorce can occur only among married persons, the rate based on existing marriages[8] is a more meaningful index of divorce and should be used whenever requisite population data are available.[9]

Although the divorce rate has followed a general upward course, there have been four major deviations from this trend. Three of these resulted from armed conflicts; the fourth, from the depression of the 1930's. The effects of these events on the divorce rate are reviewed in the sections that follow.

WAR AND THE DIVORCE RATE

War has a very pronounced effect on the divorce rate. Immediately after a conflict, the rate rises sharply and then falls off to the level of its prewar trend. This is well illustrated by the experience in the United States after the Civil War and the two World Wars.

A number of factors contribute to the postwar upsurge of divorce. Foremost is the large number of wartime marriages contracted after only a short acquaintance. Even those who enter into marriage on a more solid basis are subject to forces which tend to weaken the marital ties. For example, in cases of prolonged separation, the spouses may evolve diverse behavior patterns. Then too, the general difficulty of economic and social adjustment to postwar life leads to the

paralleled that in California (Sacramento County), Connecticut, Massachusetts, Minnesota (Hennepin County), New Hampshire, Ohio, and Vermont—areas which contributed one fifth of the nationwide total in 1867. The estimate of 8,940 divorces in 1864 can be compared with one other estimate for that year, namely, 8,551. However, no explanation is given for the latter figure, which was shown by Edwin B. Romig in *Recent Tendencies Toward Uniformity in Divorce Legislation*, Masters Essay, Sociology, Columbia University, February, 1917, p. 1.

The estimates for 1940-1950 (Table A19) were compiled from reports or statistics supplied by registrars of vital statistics for about one half of the states, and from local courts in the other states. For Kansas and Texas, the data were obtained from the State Judicial Councils; for Ohio, from the Secretary of State; for most of the counties in Missouri, from the Marriage and Divorce Committee of the Missouri Bar; for New Jersey, from the Chancery Division of the Superior Court; for North Carolina, from the Department of Justice and the Board of Public Welfare; for Nevada, from Mr. Joseph F. McDonald of the *Nevada State Journal*; and for the District of Columbia, from the Division of Procedural Studies and Statistics of the United States Courts. So far as possible, the data exclude separations and decrees nisi. Estimates have been included for courts from which data could not be obtained. For additional details, see Paul H. Jacobson, "Marital Dissolutions in New York State in Relation to Their Trend in the United States," *Milbank Memorial Fund Quarterly*, 28:25-42, January, 1950, particularly the footnotes on pages 27 and 29.

[8]Estimates of the annual number of existing marriages for 1860-1955 are given in Tables A6-7 (married males) and A22; projections to 1965 are shown in Table 46.

[9]In the past, due to the absence of annual estimates of the number of existing marriages, three other measures of the divorce rate have been used. These were the annual number of divorces in relation to (a) the total population aged 15 years and over; (b) the average number of marriages in the preceding ten years; and (c) the number of marriages during the same year. Obviously the results by the first two measures will conform closely to the trend of the rates shown in Table 42. However, nothing can be said in favor of the third measure, since there is little relationship between the marriages and divorces of a particular year. Moreover, the measure may be (and often has been) misinterpreted as representing the proportion of marriages terminating in divorce. In this connection, see I. M. Rubinow, *Some Statistical Aspects of Marriage and Divorce*, The American Academy of Political and Social Science, Pamphlet Series No. 3, Philadelphia, 1936, pp. 13-15.

failure of some marriages. There is also no doubt that a large number of postwar divorces occur among couples who have been living apart for many years. In fact, in some families a divorce may have been previously contemplated but postponed until a more opportune time—postwar years are generally periods of prosperity; remarriage prospects are favorable; and, in the midst

their prewar level, and they continued upward to a postwar peak of about 11,530 in 1866 (Table 42). Postwar reports[10] attributed the rise in divorce to the large number of imprudent and hasty marriages contracted during the war, mostly by soldiers home on leave; "the motive being on the woman's part, to get a share of the bounty, or the pension, if the husband should be killed."

Although the postwar upswing was short-lived—the rate dropping from 1.8 divorces per 1,000 existing marriages in 1866 to 1.5 per 1,000 in 1867—divorce soon resumed an upward course. By 1877, in fact, the rate exceeded the previous high and doubled it before the turn of the century.

Table 43. Divorces* and Divorce Rate by Month, United States, 1940-1950

Year	Jan.	Feb.	March	April	May	June	July	Aug.	Sept.	Oct.	Nov.	Dec.
					Number in Thousands†							
1940	21.7	19.9	23.1	23.9	23.9	22.3	21.0	20.3	22.8	20.8	21.3	23.8
1941	24.2	20.3	25.0	27.0	27.6	26.0	25.1	21.2	25.7	25.0	22.5	25.4
1942	24.7	22.1	28.4	25.9	27.7	28.3	28.4	24.9	29.9	29.0	25.3	26.8
1943	25.2	23.3	29.9	30.4	29.9	32.2	29.8	29.4	32.0	31.9	31.9	33.4
1944	29.8	30.6	34.0	34.9	37.8	39.2	32.7	33.4	33.9	38.7	35.0	32.7
1945	35.6	33.3	41.3	40.0	42.4	43.6	38.3	39.7	36.9	45.9	43.8	45.7
1946	49.4	50.3	58.1	59.5	58.0	56.1	51.9	46.3	47.3	56.5	48.1	47.4
1947	44.8	39.6	44.3	45.6	45.1	43.1	40.9	35.0	40.0	42.5	36.4	38.8
1948	35.9	32.1	39.4	37.7	37.1	37.9	34.7	29.6	33.7	36.2	36.0	32.9
1949	32.1	30.7	35.9	34.5	34.8	35.4	29.8	28.6	34.1	33.3	32.0	32.5
1950	29.3	29.2	35.4	30.9	36.3	35.6	29.5	28.9	33.3	34.4	32.6	29.6
					Rate per 1,000 Total Population							
1940	1.9	1.9	2.1	2.2	2.1	2.1	1.9	1.8	2.1	1.8	2.0	2.1
1941	2.1	2.0	2.2	2.5	2.4	2.4	2.2	1.9	2.3	2.2	2.0	2.2
1942	2.2	2.1	2.5	2.3	2.4	2.5	2.5	2.2	2.7	2.5	2.3	2.3
1943	2.2	2.2	2.6	2.7	2.6	2.9	2.6	2.5	2.8	2.7	2.8	2.9
1944	2.6	2.8	2.9	3.1	3.2	3.5	2.8	2.8	3.0	3.3	3.1	2.8
1945	3.0	3.1	3.5	3.5	3.6	3.8	3.2	3.3	3.2	3.8	3.8	3.8
1946	4.1	4.7	4.9	5.1	4.8	4.8	4.3	3.8	4.1	4.7	4.1	3.9
1947	3.7	3.6	3.6	3.9	3.7	3.6	3.3	2.8	3.4	3.5	3.1	3.1
1948	2.9	2.8	3.2	3.1	3.0	3.2	2.8	2.4	2.8	2.9	3.0	2.6
1949	2.6	2.7	2.8	2.8	2.8	2.9	2.4	2.3	2.8	2.6	2.6	2.5
1950	2.3	2.5	2.8	2.5	2.8	2.9	2.3	2.2	2.7	2.7	2.6	2.3

*Final decrees of absolute divorce and annulment, and dissolutions of marriage (Enoch Arden decrees) in New York.

†Independently rounded; hence the sums of monthly figures may differ slightly from the annual totals shown in Table 42.

Note: Rates are adjusted to annual basis; population includes armed forces overseas. Source: Estimated by the author.

World War I. The experience after the first world conflict was very much like that following the Civil War. In 1918, at the height of our participation, there was a slight recession from the long-term upswing, but immediately after the armistice divorces increased sharply. At its peak in 1920 there were 7.7 divorces per 1,000 existing marriages—one third above the high rate registered in 1917, the year we entered the war. Nor was the postwar pattern in our country unique. In fact, the rise in divorce at the end of the conflict was even more pronounced in the other major belligerent countries such as France, England, and Germany. Moreover, in all countries which sustained a postwar rise in divorce the rate fell off soon after 1920 but then resumed an upward trend.

of the large number of wartime marriages being dissolved, divorce among established families is also more likely to be accepted.

Civil War. The outbreak of hostilities in April, 1861, was followed by a decline in divorce, the number dropping from about 7,380 in 1860 to about 6,230 in 1862. Thereafter, the trend was reversed; by 1864 the number of divorces was one fifth above

World War II. The month-to-month record for the years 1940 through 1950 is shown in Table 43.[11]

[10]Theodore D. Woolsey, *Essay on Divorce*, Charles Scribner's Sons, New York, 1869, p. 223. See, also, the annual reports for 1867-68 and 1871-72 by the State Secretary of Ohio.

[11]See Tables A19-20 for the annual number of divorces and annulments by state in which granted.

It is evident that the up-swing in divorce in the United States not only continued, but actually accelerated, during the second world conflict and immediately there-after. In 1946 alone, a record total of close to 629,000 marriages were dissolved by divorce or annulment. This was $1\frac{1}{2}$ times the number only two years earlier and more than double the figure for 1941. In other words, the rise in the number of divorces between 1941 and 1946 exceeded the increase from the beginning of our history until 1941.

Although the divorce crest was reached in April, 1946, during which month almost 60,000 decrees became final, the decline there-after was more gradual than the prior upswing. Even as late as 1950, in fact, the monthly fig-ures were still well above those of the cor-responding months in 1941.[12] Moreover, as a result of our participation in the Korean conflict, it was not until 1955 that the rate dropped to its prewar level of less than $9\frac{1}{2}$ divorces annually for every 1,000 existing marriages (Table 42).

The upsurge in divorce, which started with World War II, was the greatest and most pro-longed in our history. In view of this fact, it is of interest to examine the trend of the divorce rate at various periods of married life. Table 44 shows these rates by five-year marriage-duration groups for the period from 1922 to 1955. The figures are based on estimates, by duration of marriage, of the number of absolute divorces and annulments in Table A21 and of existing marriages in Table A22.[13]

Table 44. Divorces per 1,000 Existing Marriages, by Duration of Marriage, United States, 1922-1955

Year	Total	Duration at Last Anniversary, in Years											
		0-4	5-9	10-14	15-19	20-24	25-29	30-34	35-39	40-44	20 and over	25 and over	30 and over
1922	6.6	11.4	9.2	6.4	4.3						2.2		
1923	7.2	12.3	10.4	6.9	4.6						2.4		
1924	7.2	12.4	10.8	7.0	4.7						2.4		
1925	7.3	12.5	11.2	6.8	4.8						2.3		
1926	7.4	12.8	11.6	6.8	4.8						2.3		
1927	7.7	13.5	12.1	7.2	5.1	3.7					2.4	1.8	
1928	7.8	13.7	12.2	7.4	5.2	3.7					2.4	1.8	
1929	7.9	13.8	12.4	7.7	5.1	3.8					2.5	1.8	
1930	7.4	13.2	11.5	7.6	4.8	3.6					2.3	1.6	
1931	7.0	12.7	10.9	7.4	4.6	3.4					2.1	1.5	
1932	6.1	11.2	9.6	6.4	4.0	2.9	2.0				1.8	1.3	.9
1933	6.1	11.4	9.5	6.3	4.1	2.9	2.1				1.9	1.4	1.0
1934	7.4	14.0	11.5	7.7	5.1	3.7	2.5				2.4	1.8	1.3
1935	7.8	14.8	12.0	8.2	5.4	3.8	2.4				2.4	1.8	1.5
1936	8.3	15.0	12.9	9.1	5.9	4.2	2.7				2.7	2.1	1.7
1937	8.6	15.3	13.3	9.4	6.2	4.5	3.0	2.1			2.9	2.2	1.8
1938	8.3	14.7	12.9	9.0	6.0	4.4	3.1	2.0			2.8	2.2	1.7
1939	8.4	14.8	13.0	9.2	6.1	4.6	3.6	2.1			2.9	2.2	1.5
1940	8.7	14.7	13.6	9.9	6.6	4.8	3.3	2.2			3.0	2.3	1.8
1941	9.4	15.3	14.7	11.0	7.5	5.5	3.6	2.9			3.4	2.6	2.0
1942	10.0	15.8	15.3	12.1	8.2	6.3	4.5	3.1	1.8		3.8	2.8	1.9
1943	10.9	17.6	16.0	13.3	9.1	6.9	4.8	3.3	2.1		4.0	2.9	2.1
1944	12.3	20.6	17.7	14.9	10.3	7.8	5.7	3.5	2.2		4.5	3.2	2.1
1945	14.3	26.5	20.4	16.8	10.7	8.5	5.8	3.7	2.4		4.6	3.3	2.2
1946	18.2	35.5	27.6	19.4	12.2	8.7	5.7	3.7	2.4		4.7	3.2	2.2
1947	13.9	25.8	20.3	14.5	10.6	7.8	5.5	3.4	2.1	1.5	4.2	3.0	1.9
1948	11.6	21.5	16.3	11.2	9.3	7.0	5.1	3.3	2.1	1.3	3.8	2.8	1.8
1949	10.6	20.1	14.3	10.1	8.1	6.6	4.6	3.0	1.9	1.2	3.6	2.5	1.7
1950	10.2	20.2	13.5	9.2	7.6	6.0	4.2	2.9	1.7	1.1	3.2	2.3	1.6
1951	9.9	19.7	13.8	9.0	7.4	5.7	4.3	2.8	1.6	1.1	3.1	2.3	1.5
1952	10.0	21.1	14.1	9.1	7.0	5.7	4.1	2.7	1.7	1.1	3.0	2.2	1.5
1953	9.9	21.9	13.8	8.6	6.7	5.5	4.0	2.4	1.6	1.1	2.9	2.1	1.4
1954	9.5	21.8	13.3	8.1	6.3	5.2	3.7	2.4	1.6	1.0	2.7	2.0	1.3
1955	9.3	22.2	12.9	8.0	6.1	5.1	3.6	2.4	1.5	1.0	2.7	1.9	1.3

Source: Tables A21 and A22. Data for 1951-1955 are provisional.

[12]There is no popular month for divorce in the sense that is true for marriage. The monthly variations that do occur result primarily from the dates and number of court sessions, loads on court calendars, and various aspects of state laws. Since many courts are not in session during the summer, the number of divorces is generally at its lowest level during those months, as is evident from Table 43. In 1950, for ex-ample, the daily average number of final decrees in August was almost one eighth below the average for the year.

[13]For details regarding the derivation of these estimates, see Paul H. Jacobson, "Total Marital Dissolutions in the United States: Relative Importance of Mortality and Divorce," in Studies in Population, George F. Mair, editor, Princeton University Press, 1949, pp. 3-15. The estimates shown in Tables A21-22 are more reliable than those previously published, due largely to the elimination of some inaccura-cies in the basic statistics and also because data for addi-tional areas have since become available.

It is apparent that the upswing in divorce during the 1940's was sharpest among those married less than five years—that is, essentially among those married during the war. The divorce rate within the first five years of marriage rose from 15.3 per 1,000 in 1941 to 35.5 in 1946, or by 132 per cent. The frequency of divorce increased also among persons whose marriage had lasted beyond the early, critical years, but the relative rise was progressively smaller for each successive five years of marriage. The divorce rate between 1941 and 1946 increased 88 per cent among those married 5-9 years, 76 per cent among those married 10-14 years, and 63 per cent among the marriages which had endured 15-19 years. For marriages of long duration—more than 30 years—the rate in 1946 was only 10 per cent higher than in 1941.

Generally, the divorce rate mounts rapidly to a maximum in the second to fourth year of marriage and then declines throughout the marital life span. During World War II and immediately thereafter, however, divorce became so widespread that marriages contracted as early as 1932 experienced their highest rate in 1946. Pronounced secondary peaks also occurred among marriages of longer standing. In many of these marriages, the spouses had been living apart for several years; in others, the marital ties may have been weakened even before the war.

Divorce declined sharply at every duration after 1946, but it was not until 1949 that the rate for any duration fell below the prewar level. At durations 0-4 years, moreover, the downswing halted far short of the 1941 mark. From 1949 to 1951 this rate remained virtually unchanged at about 20 per 1,000, or almost one third above that of 1941, and then moved upward again to about 22 per 1,000 by 1955.

Relative Instability of War and Postwar Marriages. From an analysis of divorces which occurred during the years 1922-1931, Hall[14] concluded that the incidence of divorce was higher for the postwar marriages of 1919 and 1920 than for the marriages of earlier or later years. This pattern for World War I and the years immediately thereafter is also evident from the duration-

specific divorce rates, classified by year of marriage, shown in Table 45. The latter are a more reliable index of the frequency of divorce than the approximate divorce ratios used by Hall.

In addition to confirming Hall's findings, the accompanying data indicate that the divorce rate at durations 5-9 years was higher for the marriages contracted in 1920 (12.7 per 1,000) than for any other group of persons married prior to 1931.

The question naturally arises whether we can generalize from the experience of World War I. Did the second world conflict repeat the pattern of the first; if not, how did World War II differ? The divorce rates shown in Table 45 throw some light on this question.

The data clearly indicate that the pattern of divorce was not alike for the marriages contracted during the two wars. In the second conflict, as in the first, the divorce rate at durations 0-4 years increased for each successive cohort of persons married after our entrance into the war. However, the highest incidence of divorce occurred among those married in 1944—at the height of the conflict—rather than among the postwar marriages, as was true a generation earlier. A ready explanation for this difference is not available. Aside from the fact that the time interval from our entrance into World War I until the postwar years 1919-1920 is about as long as the period between Pearl Harbor and the years 1944-1945, there does not appear to be any common denominator. Judged by the experience of the two world conflicts, therefore, it may be advisable to conclude that the frequency of divorce is disproportionately high both for wartime marriages as well as for those contracted immediately thereafter.

The two conflicts also differed in one other respect—the excess divorce rate among the recent war's marriages endured for no more than about five years, whereas for those who married immediately after World War I it lasted about ten years. In part, at least, this difference resulted from the long-term shift of the divorce peak to an earlier period in marriage. Around the turn of the century, the divorce rate was generally at a maximum for persons married four years; by the 1920's, it had been pushed ahead to about duration three years; and for the marriages contracted after 1943, the peak has occurred at durations one or two years. Divorce is not only more frequent

---

[14] Calvin Hall, "The Instability of Post-War Marriages," *Journal of Social Psychology*, 5:523-530, November, 1934.

today than generations ago, but it is also likely that it is resorted to sooner after marital difficulties arise.

DIVORCE AND THE ECONOMY

It is well known that the incidence of divorce, like that of marriage, closely follows the business cycle, running low in periods of depression and correspondingly high during years of prosperity. In general, however, the divorce rate is less sensitive to changes in economic conditions, due largely to the fact that a marriage cannot be dissolved as readily as it can be contracted. The relationship between business conditions and the divorce rate is well illustrated by the experience during the depression of the 1930's and its aftermath.

Immediately preceding the economic collapse in the United States, the divorce rate had climbed to a new peak of 7.9 per 1,000 existing marriages (Table 42). With the stock market crash on October 29, 1929, this uptrend was dramatically reversed. In the deepening depression that ensued, the rate dropped more than one fifth to a low of 6.1 per 1,000 in 1932 and 1933. As is evident from Table 44, divorce lessened in frequency at every stage of married life—the depression affecting even marriages which had endured more than twenty years. However, after the very nadir of the depression had passed, but before the business outlook had brightened materially, a new upswing in divorce raised the duration-specific rates to record levels.

That divorce should decline during periods of economic crisis is readily understandable. Divorce proceedings necessitate the expenditure of money, and even a relatively small attorney's fee and court costs can be a formidable barrier to a person who is unemployed or otherwise in financial distress. Moreover, matrimonial litigation is usually followed by alimony and other settlements. During the depression of the 1930's, monetary considerations also exerted a deterring influence on divorce in one other respect. Welfare assistance was more freely given to families than to individuals, and employment on relief projects was limited largely to persons with dependents.

Table 45. Divorces per 1,000 Existing Marriages, by Duration of Marriage, United States, Marriages Occurring During 1903-1951

Year of Marriage	Duration at Last Anniversary, in Years									
	0-4	5-9	10-14	15-19	20-24	25-29	30-34	35-39	40-44	45-49
1903	6.8	6.4	4.8	4.3	3.5	2.4	1.7	1.6	1.6	0.7
1904	7.1	6.5	5.0	4.5	3.5	2.3	1.9	1.6	1.5	.7
1905	7.5	6.7	5.3	4.7	3.7	2.3	2.0	1.8	1.4	.7
1906	7.5	6.7	5.6	4.6	3.7	2.3	2.0	2.0	1.3	.6
1907	7.4	6.6	5.7	4.5	3.6	2.3	2.0	2.1	1.4	
1908	8.0	7.1	6.2	4.8	3.5	2.5	2.4	2.2	1.1	
1909	8.5	7.7	6.8	4.8	3.4	2.9	2.8	2.3	1.2	
1910	8.5	8.0	7.0	5.0	3.4	3.0	3.0	2.2	1.0	
1911	8.6	8.6	6.8	5.0	3.4	3.1	3.2	2.2	1.1	
1912	8.8	9.0	6.8	5.0	3.4	3.2	3.4	1.9		
1913	9.0	9.2	7.1	4.8	3.7	3.3	3.5	1.8		
1914	9.3	10.0	7.0	4.7	4.0	3.7	3.5	1.6		
1915	10.1	10.2	6.8	4.5	4.3	4.3	3.4	1.7		
1916	11.1	10.1	7.1	4.6	4.4	4.8	3.4	1.7		
1917	11.2	10.2	7.3	4.6	4.6	5.1	3.2			
1918	12.0	11.3	7.2	5.3	5.2	5.6	3.0			
1919	12.3	11.4	7.1	5.8	5.8	5.7	2.9			
1920	12.5	12.7	7.2	5.5	5.9	5.2	2.5			
1921	12.2	12.1	7.1	6.0	6.5	5.0	2.5			
1922	11.8	11.5	7.6	6.8	7.6	4.8				
1923	12.5	11.3	8.1	7.1	7.9	4.5				
1924	13.1	11.0	8.6	7.5	8.1	4.2				
1925	13.4	10.9	9.0	8.4	8.0	4.1				
1926	13.6	10.9	9.2	9.2	7.3	3.9				
1927	13.3	11.0	9.6	9.8	6.7					
1928	12.6	11.7	10.0	10.4	6.4					
1929	12.1	12.2	10.4	10.4	5.8					
1930	12.0	12.2	11.1	9.7	5.3					
1931	12.9	13.4	13.5	9.9	5.5					
1932	14.4	14.8	16.6	9.2						
1933	15.4	15.2	17.6	8.4						
1934	14.5	14.9	15.7	7.5						
1935	14.2	14.8	14.0	6.9						
1936	14.6	16.0	12.8	6.7						
1937	14.8	17.5	10.6							
1938	15.6	18.8	9.6							
1939	16.6	20.5	9.2							
1940	16.5	20.3	8.8							
1941	18.0	19.1	8.7							
1942	23.4	15.6								
1943	25.5	14.1								
1944	26.9	13.4								
1945	26.4	13.6								
1946	23.8	14.3								
1947	19.7									
1948	19.5									
1949	20.3									
1950	20.3									
1951	21.4									

Note: Estimated by the author. Includes annulments. Data including experience for calendar years 1951-1955 are provisional.

The downswing in marriages during the depression (Table 2) also contributed to the decrease in divorces and annulments, but its effect was relatively minor. In fact, even if the annual number of marriages had continued unchanged after 1929, there would have been only 2½ per cent more marital dissolutions in 1932 and about 4 per cent more in 1933.

It is likely that some families were drawn closer together by the necessity of facing common problems. However, the rapid rise in the divorce rate shortly after the worst of the depression was passed makes it evident that this apparent cohesiveness often concealed a host of disillusionment, friction, and bitterness.

Stability of Depression Marriages. It is generally believed that fewer depression marriages are hasty and therefore that more of them succeed. In other words, couples who marry in hard times—unlike those who do so during wartime—are likely to make more intelligent selections because of longer courtship and other reasons. Whether or not this is generally true, however, depression couples are also likely to encounter innumerable obstacles at the very inception of their marriage—the period which is most critical even for persons who marry in normal times. It does not necessarily follow, therefore, that depression marriages are more enduring. In fact, the reverse appears to be true, judging by the divorce record for marriages contracted during the depression of the 1930's. As is evident from Table 45, the divorce rate at durations under 15 years increased for each successive cohort of marriages to a peak for those contracted in 1933, and then fell off.

RETROSPECT AND PROSPECT

The depression of the 1930's and the two world conflicts effected marked fluctuations of the divorce rate in the United States. Nevertheless, the long-term rise of divorce continued, though at a lesser rate of increase. The extent of the upswing can perhaps be best judged from a comparison of the experience for 1922, the low year after World War I, with that for 1955. Viewing this 33-year period as a whole, an upward trend in the divorce rate is evident at every stage of married life (Table 44). However, due largely to the shift of divorce to the earlier years of mar-

riage, the rise has been most pronounced at durations under five years, the rate almost doubling from 11.4 per 1,000 in 1922 to 22.2 in 1955. By comparison, increases of only about two fifths or less occurred for marriages which had endured beyond five years.

Although it is not possible to forecast with assurance the future trend of divorce, there is no doubt that, barring unforeseen crises, their annual number will resume an upward course. Some indication of the possible magnitude of this future rise is afforded by the data in Table 46. As is shown by Projection B, for example, should the duration-specific divorce rates increase in the future according to their annual average rise between 1922 and 1955, divorces would mount by one fifth to 457,000 in 1965. However, even if the rates remain unchanged at their 1955 level, the annual number of divorces would gradually move upward. In the latter case, Projection A, the divorce rate would continue downward from 9.3 per 1,000 existing marriages in 1955 to a low of 8.8 in 1963; according to Projection B, by contrast, the rate would rise from its present low point to 9.9 per 1,000 in 1965. Thus, despite the forthcoming upswing in the number of divorces, the rate is likely to remain well below its 1946 peak for many years to come.

Table 46. Marriages, Existing Marriages, and Divorces, United States, Projections to 1965

(Number in 1,000's; rate per 1,000 existing marriages)

Year	Marriages	Projection A			Projection B		
		Existing Marriages	Divorces Number	Rate	Existing Marriages	Divorces Number	Rate
1955	1,541	40,515	377	9.3	40,515	377	9.3
1956	1,585	41,050	377	9.2	41,040	381	9.3
1957	1,582	41,580	378	9.1	41,570	386	9.3
1958	1,597	42,090	380	9.0	42,070	391	9.3
1959	1,627	42,590	382	9.0	42,550	398	9.4
1960	1,657	43,120	385	8.9	43,070	405	9.4
1961	1,687	43,680	388	8.9	43,600	413	9.5
1962	1,735	44,240	392	8.9	44,140	421	9.5
1963	1,827	44,860	397	8.8	44,730	430	9.6
1964	1,888	45,540	404	8.9	45,380	441	9.7
1965	1,942	46,260	412	8.9	46,050	457	9.9

Note: Comparable data for earlier years are shown in Tables 2, 42, A6-7 (married males), and A22; existing marriages, including armed forces overseas, on July 1 of each year.

Projections: Marriages after 1956 parallel the expected growth of the male population aged 20-25 years.
Existing marriages, and divorces (including annulments), allow for no change in the 1955 rates of mortality and net in-migration. Projection A also assumes that the duration-specific divorce rates remain unchanged at their 1955 level; B, that the rise in the rates will equal the annual average increase since 1922.

Chapter 8

GEOGRAPHIC VARIATIONS AND
MIGRATORY DIVORCE

THE frequency of divorce varies markedly among the peoples of the world, ranging from total prohibition to the granting of dissolutions in response to a simple statement of desire or intention. Although neither extreme exists in the laws and regulations of any jurisdiction within the United States, there are pronounced differences in the divorce rate among the states and geographic areas of the country. In addition to legal processes, several other factors such as the social mores, religious proscriptions, and special conditions contribute to variations in divorce.[1]

Although absolute divorce represents the legal dissolution of an unsuccessful marriage, it is important to note that not all "broken" marriages end in divorce. In some countries, such as Brazil,[2] Ireland, Italy, and Spain, only limited divorces (separations) are permitted; in others, such as Chile, annulments are the primary means of legally dissolving a marriage. International comparisons of divorce are also influenced by the fact that in some countries consensual marriages are very frequent, and these do not require legal procedure for their dissolution.

In order to achieve more comparable data on marital dissolutions, the figures shown in this and other chapters refer to absolute divorce and annulment; however, some information on separations is given toward the end of this chapter.

[1]See, for example, Erik Allardt, "The Influence of Different Systems of Social Norms on Divorce Rates in Finland," *Marriage and Family Living*, XVII:325-331, November, 1955.

[2]Since Brazil became a republic in 1899, it has had four constitutions. Each one has specified that marriage is "indissoluble" and therefore that divorce is illegal. Thousands of couples have obtained "desquite," or legal separation decrees, in civil courts which do not permit remarriage. Despite increasing pressure to change the law, the Church has thus far successfully opposed such amendment of the constitution.

INTERNATIONAL DIFFERENCES

Divorce rates in many countries throughout the world have receded from the record highs reached immediately after World War II. Only in a few countries, however, has the rate returned to its prewar level. These facts are evident from a survey of divorce from 1900 to 1954 in 32 countries. The details are shown in Table 47.

The trend in most Western nations has been fairly similar to that in the United States. In general, the divorce rate swung upward during World War II and immediately thereafter. In Denmark, for example, the rate doubled, rising from 0.9 per 1,000 total population in 1935-1939 to 1.8 in 1946. The British Commonwealth nations, France, and several other European countries experienced even sharper increases during this period. An upswing in divorce also occurred in several Axis nations following the cessation of hostilities. In Germany, for instance, the rate in 1948 was more than double that which prevailed prior to the war. In Japan, too, divorce has been more frequent in the postwar years, reversing the downtrend which had been in evidence for the previous half century.[3]

In almost every country which experienced a rise in divorce immediately after the war, there has since been a decline. In France, for example, the rate dropped from 1.4 per 1,000 in 1947 to 0.8 in 1950-1954. In Canada the relative decrease has been equally as great—from 0.7 to 0.4. Declines of about the same magnitude have also been reported for England and Wales,

[3]During the nineteenth century, the divorce rate in Japan was among the highest in the world. Even as late as 1890, there were as many as 2.7 divorces for each 1,000 population. However, the Code of 1897 made divorce much more difficult to obtain than formerly. Moreover, with industrialization and the acquisition of Western customs the rate continued downward, reaching a low of 0.6 per 1,000 in the late 1930's.

Table 47. Divorces per 1,000 Population, Selected Countries, 1900-1954

Country	1900-1904	1905-1909	1910-1914	1915-1919	1920-1924	1925-1929	1930-1934	1935-1939	1940-1944	1945-1949	1950-1954†	1945	1946	1947	1948	1949
North and South America																
United States	0.8	0.9	1.0	1.1	1.5	1.6	1.5	1.8	2.4	3.4	2.4	3.5	4.4	3.4	2.9	2.6
Canada	0	0	0	0	.1	.1	.1	.2	.3	.5	.4	.4	.6	.7	.5	.5
Dominican Republic	*	*	*	*	*	*	*	.2	.2	.4	.4	.4	.4	.5	.5	.4
Guatemala	*	*	*	*	*	*	0	.1	.1	.1	.1	.1	.1	.1	.1	.1
Mexico	0	0	0	0	0	.1	.2	.2	.3	.4	.3	.4	.4	.4	.3	.3
Puerto Rico	*	*	*	*	*	*	1.6§	1.0§	1.4	1.7	1.9	1.6	1.9	1.7	1.5	1.6
Uruguay	*	*	*	*	.2§	.3	.2	.3	.3§	*	.6	*	*	*	*	*
Venezuela	*	*	*	*	0	0	0	.1	.1	.2	.2	.2	.1	.2	.2	.2
Europe																
Austria	0	0	0	*	*	*	*	.3	.9§	1.7	1.4	.7	1.9	1.9	2.0	1.8
Belgium	.1	.1	.2§	*	.4	.3	.3	.4	.3	.7	.5	.4	.7	.8	.8	.7
Bulgaria	.1§	*	*	*	*	.2	.2	.3	.3	*	.7§	*	*	*	*	*
Czechoslovakia	*	*	*	*	.4	.4	.4	.4	.4§	.9§	*	.6	1.0	.9	1.0	*
Denmark	.2	.3	.3	.3	.5	.6	.7	.9	1.1	1.7	1.5	1.4	1.8	1.7	1.7	1.7
England and Wales	0	0	0	0	.1	.1	.1	.1	.2	.9	.7	.4	.7	1.4	1.0	.8
Finland	0	.1	.1	.1	.2	.2	.3	.4	.6	1.2	.9	1.5	1.3	1.3	1.1	.9
France	.2	.3	.4	.2	.7	.5	.6	.6	.4	1.1	.8	.6	1.3	1.4	1.1	1.0
Germany	.2	.2	.3	.2	.6	.6	.6	.8	.8§	‡1.6§	1.1‡	*	1.1‡	1.7‡	1.9‡	1.7‡
Hungary	.1	.2§	*	.5	.8	.7	.5	.6§	*	*	1.2§	*	*	*	*	*
Netherlands	.1	.1	.2	.2	.3	.3	.4	.4	.4	.8	.6	.5	1.1	.9	.8	.7
Norway	.1	.1	.2	.2	.2	.3	.3	.4	.4	.7	.6	.6	.7	.7	.7	.7
Portugal	*	*	*	.1§	.1	.1	.1	.1	.1	.1	.1	.1	.1	.1	.1	.1
Romania	.2	.3	.4	.4§	.5	.4	.4	.6	.6	1.1§	*	.9	1.3	1.2	*	*
Scotland	0	0	.1	.1	.1	.1	.1	.1	.2	.5	.4	.4	.6	.5	.4	.5
Sweden	.1	.1	.1	.2	.2	.3	.4	.5	.7	1.0	1.2	1.0	1.0	1.0	1.0	1.1
Switzerland	.3	.4	.4	.4	.5	.6	.7	.8	.7	.9	.9	.9	1.0	.9	.9	.9
Africa, Asia, and Oceania																
Australia	.1	.1	.1	.1	.3	.3	.3	.4	.6	1.0	.8	1.0	1.0	1.1	.9	.8
Ceylon	*	*	.2§	.2	.2	.1	.1	.2	.2	.3	.2	.3	.3	.3	.2	.2
Egypt	*	*	*	*	*	*	*	3.4	4.0	4.0	3.5§	4.3	4.3	4.0	3.9	3.7
Israel♦	*	*	*	*	*	*	*	5.8	3.2	2.1	1.7	2.5	2.6	2.2	1.4	1.7
Japan	1.4	1.3	1.1	1.0	.9	.8	.8	.6	.7§	1.0§	.9	*	*	1.0	1.0	1.0
New Zealand	.1	.2	.2	.2	.4	.5	.4	.6	.7	1.2	.8	1.1	1.3	1.3	1.1	1.0
Turkey	*	*	*	*	*	*	.1	.2	.3	.3	.4	.3	.3	.4	.3	.4

0 Includes rates of less than 0.05 per 1,000.   *Not available.   †Provisional.   ‡Federal Republic.   ♦Jewish population.
§One or more years not available.

Note: Includes absolute divorces and annulments; so far as possible, excludes separations.

Source: United States, from Table 42; other countries, from yearbooks of the individual countries, annual reports of the International Statistical Institute, and United Nations Demographic Yearbooks.

Finland, Germany, and the Netherlands. Nevertheless, in these and in many other countries the frequency of divorce is now substantially above that for the years prior to World War II. In fact, in 13 of the countries under review the rate in 1950-1954 was at least double that in 1935-1939. Moreover, by the end of 1954 there had been little or no decline from the postwar peak in the Dominican Republic, Norway, Switzerland, Japan, or Turkey; in Puerto Rico and Sweden the rate was actually at a higher level.

The long-term rise of divorce in England and Wales is particularly noteworthy. Prior to World War I, legal dissolutions of marriage were comparatively rare; fewer than one divorce

occurred for every 20,000 population. By the outbreak of the second world conflict, the rate had increased manyfold but was still only about 0.1 per 1,000. During 1945-1949 the rate averaged 0.9 per 1,000, and since 1950 it has remained close to 0.7 per 1,000—or about seven times that of the prewar years. The upsurge of marital dissolutions in England and Wales during the past two decades has resulted in part, at least, from the more liberal divorce law of 1938.[4]

[4]Before 1857, absolute divorce required a private act of Parliament. From then until 1937, adultery was substantially the sole ground for divorce. Under the Herbert Act of 1937, which became effective in 1938, the grounds were extended to include persistent cruelty, willful desertion for at least

The sharp reduction of court costs and the improvement of economic conditions have also brought divorce within reach of many separated spouses.[5]

It is noteworthy that the divorce rate in England is now one fourth that of the United States, whereas a generation ago it was only about one sixteenth what we were then experiencing. In many other countries, too, the divorce rate has been increasing more rapidly than in the United States. In consequence, the disparity is much smaller today than before World War II or at the turn of the century. Nevertheless, our country continues to have one of the highest divorce rates in the world. Thus, of the 30 countries for which reasonably comparable data are available for 1950–1954 (Table 47), the rate in Egypt was 3.5 per 1,000— almost $1\frac{1}{2}$ times the rate of 2.4 in the United States. Our rate, in turn, exceeded by a considerable margin that of the next four ranking countries, namely, Puerto Rico (1.9), Israel (1.7), Denmark (1.5), and Austria (1.4).

GEOGRAPHIC DIFFERENTIALS IN THE UNITED STATES

Substantial increases in the divorce rate have been recorded in all areas of our country. The most pronounced rise, however, has occurred in the South Atlantic states. More liberal laws in the District of Columbia and in Florida resulted in sharp increases in divorce in these areas even prior to World War II. The rate has climbed even more rapidly in South Carolina since 1949, when the ban against absolute divorce was lifted.[6]

It is also noteworthy that the divorce rate in Delaware rose by 150 per cent between 1940 and 1950. Marked increases also occurred during this period in five other states, namely, Georgia (87 per cent), Mississippi (87 per cent), Alabama (81 per cent), New Mexico (70 per cent) and Arkansas (64 per cent). The divorce rates by state for the years 1940 through 1950, based on the author's data, are shown in Table 48. Comparable figures for earlier years have been published by the Bureau of the Census; the sources and limitations of these data are reviewed in the Introduction. Publications of the National Office of Vital Statistics also contain data for a varying number of states for the years since 1940.

The geographic pattern for divorce has remained relatively unchanged in recent decades, despite the variations in trend among the states. In general, the frequency of marital dissolutions tends to increase as one moves from east to west, and from north to south. Nevada, in 1950 as in previous years, was far ahead of all other states, with 55 divorces (and annulments) recorded for each 1,000 population. This figure, of course, does not reflect the divorce rate among long-term residents of that state. The great majority of Nevada decrees are granted to couples who temporarily migrate from other states to take advantage of the liberal divorce requirements. In 1950 relatively high rates also prevailed in most other western states, as well as in Florida, Oklahoma, Texas, and Arkansas. At the other extreme, the eastern states extending from Massachusetts to Pennsylvania; and South Carolina, Minnesota, Wisconsin, and the Dakotas had fewer than 1.5 dissolutions per 1,000 resident population.

---

three years, and incurable insanity after five years of confinement. In addition, a woman may obtain a divorce on proven charges of perversion against her husband.

[5] A law, effective October 1, 1950, provides free legal aid in bringing or defending high court action to all persons who do not earn more than £450 a year (somewhat more than $1,200). Even earlier, during World War II, Parliament passed legislation enabling noncommissioned servicemen to obtain legal aid for a divorce at a cost of only £5 (about $14); this compared with an average of about £70 ($196) for civilians.

For a comprehensive review of the laws and trend of divorce in England and Wales, see Griselda Rowntree and N. H. Carrier, "The Resort to Divorce in England and Wales, 1858-1957," *Population Studies*, 11:188-233, March, 1958.

[6] Prior to 1949, only annulments were granted in South Carolina. Since April, 1949, that state has had legislation permitting divorce on grounds of adultery, desertion, physi-

cal cruelty, or habitual drunkenness. Details are given in a later section of this chapter.

That not all legislation has a permanent effect on the level of divorce is evident from the experience in the state of Washington after its new law became effective on June 9, 1949. The number of absolute divorces and annulments in that state increased from 9,100 in 1948 to 10,900 in 1949, and then dropped to 10,000 in 1950 (Table A19). The temporary upswing in 1949 resulted from the fact that decrees are final when granted for actions started under the new law, whereas actions commenced under the former law still require an interlocutory period. In consequence, since June 9, 1949, the statistics include the prior law's interlocutory decrees which become final as well as final decrees granted under the new law.

Table 48. Absolute Divorces and Annulments per 1,000 Resident Population, by State, United States, 1940-1950

Geographic Division and State	1940	1941	1942	1943	1944	1945	1946	1947	1948	1949	1950
UNITED STATES	2.0	2.2	2.4	2.7	3.1	3.7	4.5	3.5	2.9	2.6	2.5
New England	1.1	1.3	1.4	1.3	1.6	1.8	2.6	2.2	1.7	1.5	1.5
Maine	1.8	2.0	2.1	2.3	2.7	3.2	4.8	3.4	2.6	2.3	2.4
New Hampshire	1.4	2.1	2.0	2.0	2.0	3.1	4.2	2.8	2.4	2.0	2.0
Vermont	1.2	1.2	1.4	1.5	1.7	2.1	3.0	2.1	1.4	1.5	1.8
Massachusetts	1.1	1.1	1.3	1.2	1.5	1.7	2.3	2.2	1.6	1.4	1.4
Rhode Island	.9	.9	1.0	1.0	1.2	1.5	2.0	2.0	1.0	1.3	1.2
Connecticut	1.0	1.2	1.3	1.1	1.3	1.5	2.0	1.7	1.4	1.4	1.3
Middle Atlantic	.9	.9	1.0	1.0	1.2	1.5	2.1	1.7	1.3	1.1	1.1
New York	.7	.8	.9	.9	1.0	1.3	1.8	1.3	1.0	.8	.8
New Jersey	.9	.9	1.1	1.0	1.2	1.4	1.7	2.0	1.5	1.2	1.1
Pennsylvania	1.0	1.1	1.2	1.3	1.5	1.8	2.7	2.0	1.8	1.5	1.4
East North Central	2.2	2.4	2.6	2.9	3.3	3.9	4.7	3.6	2.9	2.6	2.5
Ohio	2.4	2.6	2.7	3.0	3.5	4.1	5.0	3.6	3.3	2.8	2.8
Indiana	2.4	3.3	3.5	3.7	4.5	5.4	6.1	4.5	3.7	3.3	2.8
Illinois	2.3	2.4	2.6	3.0	3.2	3.8	4.5	3.7	3.0	2.7	2.6
Michigan	2.3	2.4	2.6	2.8	3.4	3.9	5.0	3.5	2.6	2.6	2.5
Wisconsin	1.1	1.3	1.3	1.5	1.8	2.2	2.5	1.9	1.5	1.4	1.4
West North Central	1.9	2.2	2.3	2.6	3.0	3.6	4.6	3.1	2.5	2.3	2.3
Minnesota	1.1	1.2	1.2	1.3	1.6	2.1	2.9	2.0	1.6	1.4	1.4
Iowa	1.9	2.1	2.0	2.3	2.7	3.3	4.0	2.7	2.2	2.1	2.1
Missouri	3.0	3.5	3.9	4.3	4.9	5.6	6.9	4.4	3.5	3.4	3.3
North Dakota	.8	.9	.8	.9	1.1	1.4	1.8	1.4	1.2	1.1	1.0
South Dakota	1.2	1.2	1.2	1.4	1.6	2.1	2.6	2.1	1.7	1.5	1.4
Nebraska	1.6	1.7	1.5	1.8	2.1	2.7	3.7	2.6	2.2	2.0	1.9
Kansas	2.1	2.4	2.4	2.7	3.0	4.0	5.0	3.6	2.8	2.4	2.6
South Atlantic	1.8	1.9	2.1	2.4	2.7	3.2	4.1	3.1	2.7	2.5	2.5
Delaware	.8	1.0	1.4	1.5	1.3	1.7	1.2	2.4	1.3	2.6	2.0
Maryland	1.7	2.1	2.6	2.6	2.8	3.1	3.7	2.9	2.6	2.1	2.0
Dist. of Columbia	1.9	2.0	2.0	1.8	1.4	2.1	2.6	2.3	2.2	1.9	2.0
Virginia	1.5	1.6	1.7	1.9	2.0	2.3	2.9	2.2	2.2	1.9	1.8
West Virginia	1.6	1.8	1.7	2.0	2.5	3.2	4.4	2.8	2.5	2.3	2.1
North Carolina	1.1	1.2	1.3	1.5	1.7	1.9	2.5	1.9	1.7	1.5	1.6
South Carolina	*	*	*	*	*	.1	.1	.1	.1	.5	1.1
Georgia	1.5	1.8	1.9	2.3	2.9	3.7	5.3	3.8	3.2	3.0	2.8
Florida	5.8	5.9	5.9	6.6	7.9	8.8	10.8	8.3	7.0	6.7	6.4
East South Central	1.8	2.1	2.3	2.9	3.6	4.2	5.1	3.6	3.2	2.9	2.7
Kentucky	2.0	2.4	2.4	3.0	3.6	4.0	5.3	4.1	3.4	3.0	2.8
Tennessee	1.9	2.1	2.3	3.0	3.9	4.5	5.1	3.4	2.8	2.6	2.4
Alabama	1.6	2.0	2.4	3.0	3.8	4.6	5.2	3.7	3.3	2.9	2.9
Mississippi	1.5	1.8	2.0	2.6	3.1	3.2	4.6	3.3	3.2	3.0	2.8
West South Central	3.5	3.9	4.3	4.7	5.4	6.3	7.0	5.4	4.7	4.6	4.4
Arkansas	2.8	4.1	4.9	4.2	5.7	7.0	7.9	5.7	5.2	5.3	4.6
Louisiana	1.4	1.6	2.1	2.3	2.6	2.8	2.3	2.0	1.8	1.7	1.7
Oklahoma	4.2	4.8	4.8	6.1	7.1	9.1	9.1	7.1	6.2	6.0	5.7
Texas	4.3	4.4	4.7	5.3	5.8	6.6	7.9	6.0	5.2	5.0	4.8
Mountain	4.2	4.4	5.2	6.1	7.0	8.7	11.1	8.0	6.7	6.2	5.3
Montana	3.0	3.1	3.1	3.9	3.7	5.0	6.2	4.6	3.9	3.5	3.3
Idaho	3.2	3.8	4.6	5.0	5.1	6.5	8.8	6.9	5.7	4.9	4.6
Wyoming	4.0	3.6	3.4	3.9	4.5	5.9	7.1	5.8	4.7	4.5	4.1
Colorado	2.5	2.1	2.5	2.5	3.2	3.8	5.7	4.2	3.7	3.5	3.1
New Mexico	2.3	2.3	2.8	3.7	4.4	5.8	6.9	5.4	4.4	4.5	3.9
Arizona	3.8	4.5	5.0	4.8	5.9	7.7	8.4	6.9	6.2	5.7	4.8
Utah	2.7	2.5	2.5	3.1	3.3	4.5	5.4	4.0	3.4	3.2	3.0
Nevada	49.0	53.6	62.8	73.6	83.5	100.8	143.9	92.3	72.3	67.8	55.0
Pacific	3.3	3.5	3.5	3.6	4.1	4.7	5.4	5.2	4.2	3.9	3.8
Washington	3.7	3.7	3.8	4.0	4.5	4.8	5.7	5.0	4.0	4.8	4.2
Oregon	3.3	3.9	4.3	4.8	5.6	6.7	7.7	5.1	4.6	4.0	4.0
California	3.3	3.4	3.3	3.3	3.9	4.5	5.0	5.2	4.2	3.7	3.7

*Less than 0.05.
Note: Based on number of absolute divorces and annulments in Table A19.

Nativity. Among the influences which contribute to the countrywide variation in the divorce rate is the relative number of foreign-born persons and their country of origin. Since the rate in the country from which they have emigrated is comparatively low, the foreign born are culturally less inclined to seek divorce in case of marital discord. The frequency of divorce is particularly low among new arrivals because of their general distrust of courts and language difficulties.

Religion. The strength of the prevailing religions, especially the Roman Catholic, is another important factor in geographic differentials. Although adequate data for measuring the rate of divorce and annulment in relation to religion are not available for the United States, there are indications that the recorded[7] rate for legal dissolutions is lower among Catholics than among the population as a whole.[8] However, it is possible that religious differentials have been decreasing. Various studies show that the frequency of interfaith marriages has been increasing,[9] and such mixed marriages are subject to a relatively high divorce rate.[10] The latter does not necessarily

---

[7]It is important to note that the recorded dissolution rate (absolute divorce and annulment) does not accurately reflect the relative stability of marriage, even in the restricted sense of "until death do us part." Not only is no account taken of informal unions which are "contracted" and "broken" among both legally married and single persons, but no allowance is made for desertion and separation. Desertions, for example, appear to be much more frequent among Catholics than among non-Catholics, according to data for the white population in Philadelphia. See Thomas P. Monahan and W. M. Kephart, "Divorce and Desertion by Religious and Mixed-Religious Groups," *American Journal of Sociology*, LIX:464, March, 1954.

[8]See, for example, Loren E. Chancellor and T. P. Monahan, "Religious Preference and Interreligious Mixtures in Marriages and Divorces in Iowa," *American Journal of Sociology*, LXI:233-239, November, 1955.

[9]John L. Thomas, "The Factor of Religion in the Selection of Marriage Mates," *American Sociological Review*, 16: 487-491, August, 1951.

[10]J. H. van Zanten and T. van den Brink, "Population Phenomena in Amsterdam," *Population*, August, 1938, pp. 35-37. A similar pattern is reported for Hamburg and Hungary.

This relationship is also shown by current data for the United States. In 1950 at the opening session of the twelfth annual convention of the American Catholic Sociological Society, the Very Rev. Arthur F. Bukowski, President of Aquinas College, reported that the divorce rate for mixed-Catholic marriages is 1⅓ times that for marriages in which both parties are Catholic.

---

reflect discord arising from differences in religious regulations and attitudes, since many mixed marriages are "forced" marriages, that is, they are contracted after premarital conception.

That Roman Catholics account for an appreciable proportion of absolute divorces is evident from data available for two areas of the country. Among persons divorced in Iowa during 1953, about $11\frac{1}{2}$ per cent reported their religious denomination as Catholic. In Montgomery County, Ohio, the stated church membership was given as Catholic for almost 8 per cent of the persons divorced during 1944-1950. It is also noteworthy that the Ohio data appear to indicate that the rise in the divorce rate immediately after World War II may have been greater for Catholics than for the population as a whole. Thus, of the total persons divorced, the proportion Catholic increased from 6.8 per cent in 1944 to 8.9 per cent in 1946 and then fell off to 6.6 per cent in 1950.

To date no comprehensive evaluation has been made of the differential in divorce by religion. Since a person's religion may change during his lifetime, such evaluation can be made only by means of a longitudinal study in which an initial cohort of marriages is classified according to the religion of the spouses and then the number dissolved by death, divorce, or annulment is recorded at each duration of marriage.

Race. The color or racial composition of the population also contributes to the geographic variations in divorce. Although statistics are available for only a few areas of the United States, national estimates based thereon indicate that in recent years the divorce rate has been higher among Negroes than among the white population. From 1939 to 1941, the number of divorces per 1,000 married males may have been higher for the white population than for the nonwhites. Thereafter, the divorce rate appears to have increased much more rapidly for the nonwhites, reversing the relationship. Between 1942 and 1950, in fact, the Negro rate averaged one fifth above the rate for the whites. These racial

---

T. Earl Sullenger also found a disproportionate number of absolute divorces granted to couples of mixed religious beliefs during 1922-1926. See his report entitled *A Study of Divorce and Its Causation in Douglas County, Nebraska*, Univ. of Nebraska Bulletin, March, 1927, p. 7 (second printing by Municipal University of Omaha, August, 1932).

differences in divorce are evident from Table 49, which was developed from data for areas[11] shown in Table A23.

Table 49. Divorces, Married Population, and Divorce Rate, by Color of Husband, United States, 1939-1950

Year	Number of Divorces* (1,000's)		Married Males† (1,000's)		Divorces per 1,000 Married Males		
	White	Nonwhite	White	Nonwhite	Total	White	Nonwhite
1939	233	18	27,162	2,733	8.4	8.6	6.6
1940	249	16	27,788	2,789	8.7	9.0	5.7
1941	274	21	28,471	2,858	9.4	9.6	7.3
1942	290	31	29,211	2,934	10.0	9.9	10.6
1943	316	43	29,942	3,008	10.9	10.6	14.3
1944	363	50	30,441	3,058	12.3	11.9	16.4
1945	441	46	30,842	3,100	14.3	14.3	14.8
1946	570	59	31,430	3,159	18.2	18.1	18.7
1947	445	52	32,376	3,255	13.9	13.7	16.0
1948	376	47	33,116	3,330	11.6	11.4	14.1
1949	348	46	33,754	3,396	10.6	10.3	13.5
1950	337	48	34,330	3,455	10.2	9.8	13.9

*Absolute divorces and annulments.
†Includes armed forces overseas.

Source: Estimated by the author; number of divorces, developed from data for areas shown in Table A23.

In the nineteenth century it was generally assumed that Negroes contributed divorces disproportionately to their numbers in the population. This opinion received a stamp of official status in 1889, when it was included in a government report on divorce.[12] In 1891, however, Willcox[13] showed that there was no relation between high divorce rates and density of Negro population, as had been contended in the 1889 Report. In a subsequent study, using Willcox's method, the government reversed its position and concluded that racial differences in the frequency of divorce could not be determined from available statistics.[14] More recently, population statistics classified by marital status have been used as the basis for conclusions regarding the relative rates

[11]For 1939 to 1950 inclusive, data on absolute divorces and annulments are available for areas which contain only a little more than 7 per cent of the country's white married males and about 16½ per cent of the nonwhite. Despite the approximate nature of these estimates, they are the best available evidence concerning racial differences in divorce.
[12]U.S. Commissioner of Labor, *A Report on Marriage and Divorce in the United States, 1867 to 1886*, Washington, 1889, p. 132.
[13]Walter F. Willcox, *The Divorce Problem, A Study in Statistics*, Columbia University Studies, 1891, pp. 30-32.
[14]Bureau of the Census, *Marriage and Divorce, 1867-1906*, Part I, Washington, 1909, pp. 21-22.

of divorce among the two races.[15] However, the use of these statistics for this purpose is erroneous; the data reflect differentials in mortality and remarriage as well as of divorce. Moreover, since the number of divorced persons has been markedly understated in decennial censuses (see Introduction) the racial differences in divorce derived from such data are also undoubtedly influenced by the relative accuracy with which persons report their marital status.

It is likely that divorce was relatively infrequent among Negroes up to the early years of this century, when desertion or informal separation was still their culturally accepted method for dissolving a marriage. This was especially the case in the rural South, but these practices were also carried along with the Negro in his migration to northern and urban centers. Even today, desertion or nonsupport is a common occurrence among Negroes in our large cities.[16] Apparently, economic considerations are an important factor in this situation. At any rate, the indications are that the divorce rate among the nonwhite population is very sensitive to the business cycle. As is evident from Table A23, from 1918 through 1928—years of relative prosperity—the divorce rate in Virginia was higher for nonwhites than for the white population. By contrast, between 1929 and 1940 the rate for the nonwhites was below that of the whites. In Mississippi, also, the relationship was reversed with the onset of the depression. In fact, the rate for Negroes dropped even more precipitously in Mississippi than in Virginia. Thus at the depth of the depression, in 1933, the rate for Negroes was only two fifths that of the whites in Mississippi, compared with about three fifths in Virginia.

The relatively greater upswing in the Negro divorce rate since World War II has also been due in large measure to economic factors. As a result of favorable opportunities for wartime and postwar employment, Negroes have gained financial security which has enabled them to

[15]Ernest R. Groves and William F. Ogburn, *American Marriage and Family Relationships*, Henry Holt and Co., New York, 1928, pp. 370-374.
William J. Goode, "Economic Factors and Marital Stability," *American Sociological Review*, 16:805, December, 1951.
[16]See, for example, the 37th Annual Report (1950) of the Municipal Court of Philadelphia, p. 161.

employ lawyers and to file divorce proceedings. For the men, legal divorce has been the means for safeguarding their earnings from a separated wife; women also have been interested in divorce rather than separation because of the possibilities of alimony and child support.

Urban-Rural Residence. The recorded divorce rate is higher in cities than in rural areas. This relationship has been established by European data and is also indicated by information available for the United States. Thus, in 1898-1902, the recorded divorce rate in counties containing a large city was about 6 per cent above the rate in counties composed of small cities and country districts. More recent data indicate that the differential has been widening.[17]

Although it would appear that divorce is resorted to more frequently by our urban population than by residents of rural communities, the available data are not appropriate for documenting this relationship. The recorded data relate to the legal residence of the plaintiff at the time the divorce action is initiated. By contrast, since either or both parties are likely to change their residence after a permanent separation, the statistics should be tabulated according to the place where the couple last lived together. Such changes in residence not only contribute to the geographic variations in divorce shown in Table 48, but also to the urban-rural differentials. Over the years, as our population has shifted from agricultural districts to rapidly growing urban areas, the stream of migrants has undoubtedly included a disproportionate number of separated persons. The reason for this is readily apparent. When a farm family is torn by marital discord, the husband or (more often) the wife leaves the home and usually the community too. The tendency is to move to a nearby village or to a large city in search of employment or other economic opportunity, and also to escape from neighbors and scenes which may recall painful memories.

[17]Bureau of the Census, *Marriage and Divorce, 1867-1906,* Part I, Washington, 1909, pp. 17-18 and 74.
Ibid., *Marriage and Divorce, 1924,* Washington, 1927, pp. 33-34.
It is noteworthy that in Iowa, where the excess rate for urban counties has long been the greatest in the country, the ratio between urban and rural divorce rates has increased markedly — from about three to one at the turn of the century to more than four to one after World War II.

MIGRATORY DIVORCE

Divorce and annulment in the United States are subject to the control of the states, each of which prescribes the residence requirements and other conditions under which its courts may take jurisdiction over matrimonial actions. State statutes also specify the grounds for the granting of a decree, the rights of remarriage, alimony, and related matters. Since there is considerable variation in these laws as well as in court practices, interstate migration for the purpose of obtaining a divorce has long existed in the United States. For a few states, this practice has been sufficiently marked to be readily apparent from their recorded divorce rates.

Nevada. Reno and Las Vegas apparently attract the largest number of persons who migrate for the purpose of securing a divorce. This is understandable since Nevada has liberal divorce laws; only six weeks' residence is necessary before bringing suit, the decree is final upon entry of the court's judgment, and either party may remarry at once. Moreover, in both cities, the furnished housekeeping rooms, hotel, and entertainment facilities are conducive to residence long enough to meet the legal requirements.

Nevada owes its origin and continuation as the divorce "capital" of the United States to the relatively short period of residence required before a suit may be filed. As early as 1861, the state's divorce code required a residence of only six months. However, it was not until 1909 that this lenient requirement was first exploited by divorce seekers from other states. In that year a New York lawyer who had moved to Nevada recognized the commercial possibilities of the Nevada law and inaugurated a successful advertising campaign in New York.

Nevada's residence requirement was increased to one year in 1913, but then changed back to six months in 1915. By the early 1920's, in consequence, the number of divorce decrees in Nevada had climbed above 1,000 annually. In 1927 the period of residence was reduced to three months, making it the lowest in any state. This was accompanied by a further upswing in the number of divorces granted—from 1,021 in 1926 to 1,953 in 1927 and to 2,595 in 1928.

In 1931, during the depression, Arkansas and

Idaho made unsuccessful bids for a major portion of Nevada's divorce business. On February 26 of that year Arkansas reduced its residence period from one year to three months,[18] and on March 3 Idaho enacted a 90-day law.[19] Nevada reacted almost instantaneously; by act of March 19, effective May 1, it prescribed the six-week requirement which has remained unchanged to date. Moreover, as a further concession to local business interests, the 1931 statute specified that the petitioner's testimony as to actual residence must be corroborated. Not only was Nevada's "trade" preserved by the new law but divorce decrees doubled, from 2,609 in 1930 to 5,260 in 1931. Although their number declined as the depression deepened, parallel to the downswing elsewhere in the country, they rose to new record highs in the 1940's (Tables 48 and A19). Currently about 10,000 decrees are granted annually in Nevada.

Until the 1930's Reno had almost a complete monopoly on the rapidly growing divorce business in Nevada. More recently Las Vegas has been attracting an increasing share of the total. About a century ago the site where Las Vegas now stands was used by the Mormons as a wagon station on the trail from Salt Lake City to the Pacific Coast. The little town was rarely in the news until after 1928, when it served as the railhead and business center for work on the Boulder Canyon Dam about twenty-five miles to the east. In 1936, with the Dam completed and the construction employees moving onward, Las Vegas actively stepped into the divorce field in order to offset a receding volume of business. These efforts were extremely successful, as is evident from the record of divorces granted in Las Vegas (Clark County). Their number increased from less than 100 annually prior to 1928 to more than 500 in the mid-1930's, passed the 1,000 mark in 1940, and now averages close to 4,000 annually. It is still surpassed by Reno, but by a very reduced margin. Prior to 1931 Reno (Washoe County) granted more than ten times as many decrees as Las Vegas. By 1940 the ratio had fallen to about 2 to 1; currently it is only 1.2 to 1. As in former

years, Reno is favored by New Yorkers[20] and persons from other eastern states, whereas Las Vegas attracts its patrons largely from Los Angeles and other parts of southern California. It is noteworthy that Las Vegas has continued to gain divorce business despite recent efforts to discourage it. The latter is not as paradoxical as it may seem. Las Vegas has built up a very lucrative business in gambling, entertainment, and "quickie" marriages, which attracts several million tourists each year and which is dependent on relatively fast turnover compared with the six weeks' residence required by divorce seekers.

Florida and Other States. Florida has attracted a relatively large number of divorce seekers since 1935, when its residence requirement was shortened to 90 days. As a result of this statute and also because of other liberal aspects of the state's laws, the number of divorces has climbed more rapidly in Florida than in the country as a whole. Florida decrees increased from 4,842 in 1934 to 5,167 in 1935 and to 7,002 in 1936; during 1955-1957 they averaged close to 20,000 annually. There are indications that most persons who come to Florida for a divorce are either relative newlyweds or else have been married for more than ten years. Miami and its environs have apparently obtained a large share of the total; however, the border and other northern areas also accommodate many persons who "migrate" from other states.[21]

Five other states also have liberal residence requirements. In Utah, three months' residence is necessary before divorce proceedings may be instituted; in Arkansas and Wyoming, 60 days; and in Idaho, only six weeks.[22] Alabama's divorce

---

[18]Residence in the state for three months before final judgment and two months before commencement of the action.

[19]At present the plaintiff need be a resident of Idaho for only six weeks.

[20]About three fifths of Nevada's divorce business in 1935 (largely Reno decrees) originated from New York and New Jersey. See Frank W. Ingram and G. A. Ballard, "The Business of Migratory Divorce in Nevada," *Law and Contemporary Problems*, 2:305, June, 1935. Although comparable estimates are not available for recent years, current newspaper reports make it evident that a much larger number of New Yorkers are divorced in Reno than in Las Vegas.

[21]Effective October, 1957, the residence required in Florida prior to filing for divorce was changed from ninety days to six months. This may result in a sharp reduction in the number of decrees, after the backlog of cases filed under the old law is cleared.

[22]John W. Morland, *Keezer on the Law of Marriage and Divorce*, Third Edition, The Bobbs-Merrill Co., Indianapolis, 1946.

law is even more noteworthy. The laws of most states specify a period of residence (generally, one year) before its courts may take jurisdiction in a divorce action. However, Alabama has no specified period, except in cases where the defendant is a nonresident or where the ground for divorce is voluntary abandonment. Moreover, since Alabama's 1945 law, even the latter exceptions are waived if one party is a resident and the other party submits to the jurisdiction of the court. The important thing is for one of the parties, usually the plaintiff, to prove to the satisfaction of the trial judge that he (or she) is a bona fide resident of the state. The typical evidence offered as proof of this allegation has been that the plaintiff resides at a specified address within the state and has applied for work in the state.[23] Thus, if a husband and wife agree to a divorce, it is now possible for one of them to come into Alabama and obtain a decree within a matter of days.[24]

Paris and Havana. Divorce seekers have not limited themselves to interstate migration, but have also sought decrees in foreign countries. In the period after World War I, hundreds of Americans were divorced in Paris. France does not compile divorce statistics by nationality, so that precise figures are not available. However, from personal observation, Bates[25] estimated that the number of decrees granted to our citizens increased from comparatively few in 1919 to more than 100 in 1922, and reached a peak of about 300 in 1926. Their number fell off thereafter as American newspapers began publishing the names of United States couples known to have been divorced in Paris, and the French government demanded proper evidence of a bona fide domicile. Divorces to Americans dropped below 200 in 1927, numbered less than 100 in 1928, and were fewer than 25 annually by 1934. It is noteworthy that the divorce "mill" in Paris was created by American lawyers to cater to wealthy New Yorkers and clients from other states, and that the "mill" collapsed only after it became extremely difficult to get the Paris courts to pass the American cases.

Havana is also said to have been a wealthy divorce resort during the 1930's. The law in Cuba required actual residence of only 30 days, and a "valid" divorce could be obtained within 90 days. However, there is no evidence that Havana ever succeeded in attracting more than a few divorce patrons from the United States.

Virgin Islands. For several years after the close of World War II, the American Virgin Islands attracted an increasing number of divorce seekers from the United States mainland. Prior to the war, the Virgin Islands rarely welcomed visitors. In fact, up to that time most persons in continental United States knew very little about the Islands.

The Virgin Islands have a very long history. Columbus first landed there on November 14, 1493, on his second voyage to the new world. Since that time, the Virgins have been under many flags. The three largest islands in the group—St. Croix, St. Thomas, and St. John—were acquired by Denmark in 1815 and sold to the United States for $25 million in 1917. Currently they are governed by the U.S. Department of the Interior; local administration is vested in a governor, appointed by the President of the United States, and in a legislative assembly.

In the mid-1940's, encouraged by the advances in air transportation which made the Islands only a short hop from the States, an official campaign was launched to attract tourists and expand local industry. At about the same time, a bid was made for the "quickie" divorce trade from the States. On December 18, 1944, the Eighth Legislative Assembly of the Virgin Islands passed a bill requiring residence of only six weeks before commencement of an action for divorce.[26] The law was approved by the acting governor and took effect on January 28, 1945, but at least two years elapsed before an appreciable number of divorce tourists took advantage of the new law.

[23] John D. Bonham, *Residence Required for Divorce in the United States*, Legislative Reference Service, Legislative Council of the State of Alabama, Montgomery, 1954, p. 5.

[24] It has been reported that, in Limestone County alone, several hundred of these "quickie" decrees have been granted in recent years — the majority to persons from New York. Limestone is a sparsely settled county in northern Alabama.

[25] Lindell T. Bates, "The Divorce of Americans in France," *Law and Contemporary Problems*, 2(3): 322-328, June, 1935.

[26] In 1950 the Puerto Rican legislature rejected a bill which would have reduced the residence requirement there from one year to six weeks.

The records of the District Court in the Virgin Islands do not show the race of persons in divorce suits, or any other information which can be used to identify applicants who resided in continental United States prior to their domicile in the Islands. However, their number may be approximated from the comparative trends of divorce in the two municipal divisions of the Islands, namely, St. Croix and St. Thomas.[27] The latter is relatively urbanized and has all kinds of shops, night spots, and a variety of hotel and tourist accommodations. Activities center almost completely around the mountain-enclosed city of Charlotte Amalie, where the Clerk of the District Court is located. St. Croix, by contrast, is pastoral and consists of large estates and sugar-cane plantations. Its two towns, Christiansted and Frederiksted, are small and lack the bustle of Charlotte Amalie. It is reasonable to assume, therefore, that St. Thomas would be the most likely Island to attract divorce seekers from the States. As a matter of fact, news reports and other information[28] confirm this assumption. Thus the general trend of divorce in St. Croix can be used as a yardstick for approximating the number of decrees that are granted to long-term residents of St. Thomas, or conversely, the extent to which St. Thomas decrees are granted to mainland residents. This procedure has been used in approximating the number of "migratory" divorces granted in the Virgin Islands; the estimates are shown in the right-hand column of Table 50.

The indications are that about 1,100 decrees were granted to persons from the States in the period from 1946 to 1956—the great majority on the grounds of incompatibility of temperament. Apparently, the number of "migratory" divorces rose from a very few in 1946 to more than 100 in 1949, and reached a peak of about 250 in 1952. Their number rapidly plunged downward, starting in 1953, when the United States Third Circuit Court of Appeals upheld a lower court ruling which had invalidated one of the Island decrees. The Circuit Court ruled that the plaintiff, although

[27]St. John, the most primitive of the three islands, has a population of less than 1,000 and is administered from St. Thomas.

[28]For example, in the early 1950's, one of the larger hotels on St. Thomas offered a special six-week rate of $498 to candidates for divorce, which included room, breakfast, and dinner.

Table 50. Number of Final Decrees of Absolute Divorce, Virgin Islands of the United States, 1940-1956

Year	Total	St. Thomas (Includes St. John)	St. Croix	Residents of Continental United States*
1940	34	16	18	0
1941	37	28	9	0
1942	49	34	15	0
1943	76	63	13	0
1944	63	45	18	0
1945	52	38	14	0
1946	90	64	26	10
1947	124	104	20	50
1948	143	132	11	80
1949	181	160	21	110
1950	271	244	27	190
1951	316	284	32	230
1952	343	310	33	250
1953	236	215	21	140
1954	123	90	33	20
1955	103	75	28	0
1956	129	100	29	20

*Decrees to persons who resided in continental United States prior to their domicile in the Virgin Islands.

Note: No annulments were granted during this period.

Source: Number of residents of continental United States, estimated by the author; all other data, from the Clerk of the District Court, St. Thomas, at Charlotte Amalie.

meeting the residence requirement, really had no intention of settling in the Islands as indicated in the suit. The final blow was struck on April 11, 1955, when the U.S. Supreme Court upheld the Island's District Court in refusing to grant divorces in the absence of domiciliary declarations. This decision was in accord with the laws in Nevada, Florida, and other states, which permit "quickie" divorces but require some form of declaration that the party obtaining the decree intends to remain in the state. By contrast, under the Virgin Islands' law, which was invalidated by the Supreme Court, the petitioner for a divorce was not required to declare intention to make a permanent home in the territory.

Mexico. Aside from Nevada and Florida, Mexico grants the largest number of "migratory" divorces to residents of the United States. Divorce has been permitted in Mexico since its constitution of 1917. As in the United States, the federal government of Mexico does not have jurisdiction over divorce; statutes are enacted by the state legislatures and vary markedly. Unlike the United States, however, one decision of the Supreme Court of Mexico does not have the force of precedent; for that result it is necessary for the Court to render five decisions on the same point. Thus there is always a question as to the validity of a decree issued by a regularly constituted court in Mexico. It is even more difficult to determine how many of the Mexican divorces obtained by our citizens would be recognized by the courts in the United States. Over the years, such divorces have been both rejected and accepted by our state courts. Some Americans, as a result, have been left in a legalistic "no man's land." For example, the New York Court of Appeals has long held that a wife who procures a "mail order" decree of divorce in Mexico has nothing but a scrap of paper, so long as her mate lives. This decision notwithstanding, the Court further held on March 2, 1950, that the husband's death converts that scrap of paper into a decree of disinheritance. On the other hand, the New York Supreme Court ruled on March 27, 1952, that Mexican divorces are valid when at least one of the parties appears personally in that country and the other is represented by authorized counsel—a position which has been taken by many of our states.

Questions as to the validity of Mexican divorces, and adverse criticism in both Mexico and the United States, have not deterred thousands of our citizens from obtaining such decrees. In some cases the parties remarry in Mexico and thus preclude the possibilities of prosecution for bigamy in the United States. In others, the Mexican decree is only the first or "quickie" means of dissolving a "broken" marriage; application for a divorce is also made at the place of usual residence in the United States—for example, in California, where more than one year is required to secure a final decree. For these and other reasons, Mexican decrees have retained their popularity among our citizens. In fact, the indications are that their number has been increasing.

As early as 1918, Yucatan State in southeastern Mexico succumbed to the urge to commercialize divorce, and enacted legislation to attract foreigners in search of "quickie" decrees. Since that time similar laws have been adopted in at least six other states: Campeche, bordering on Yucatan; Chihuahua, just below the Rio Grande; Morelos, south of Mexico City; Sonora,

contiguous to Arizona; Tamaulipas, the northernmost state on the Gulf of Mexico; and Tlaxcala, to the east of Mexico City. Table 51 shows the trend of divorce in these states, and in Mexico as a whole, for the years since 1926; comparable data are not available for earlier years.

The total number of divorces in Mexico has increased markedly in the past three decades, rising from less than 1,000 in 1926 to more than 12,000 in 1955. Most noteworthy are the trends in three states. In Tlaxcala, for example, the number of decrees jumped from three in 1933 to 100 in 1934, and then continued upward to a peak of 608 in 1941. In that year, however, the state legislature of Tlaxcala abolished its "quickie" divorce law. As a result, the number of decrees tumbled to only 26 in 1942, and has since remained close to that level.

Changes in divorce legislation have had an even greater impact on the number of decrees granted in Morelos State. Under the law which prevailed for two decades prior to 1952, divorce had become "big business" in the old resort town of Cuernavaca, the capital of Morelos, located 45 miles south of Mexico City. In uncontested cases, residence did not have to be established in the state, and a divorce could be obtained in a matter of days. The posting of a notice of intention on the walls of the courthouse or in the official gazette sufficed to establish jurisdiction, and if the spouse did not file an answer to the petition within three days the civil court could grant a divorce within twenty-four hours. As a result, numerous decrees were granted to nonresidents, many to New Yorkers and other citizens of the United States. In fact, the total number of decrees granted in Morelos reached a peak of 1,532 in 1946 and averaged 853 annually during 1947-1951. On June 12, 1952, however, a new law was enacted requiring actual residence in the state before a petition for divorce could be filed. This resulted in an immediate loss of the state's "mail order" divorce trade.[29] Decrees dropped from 622 in 1951 to 338 in 1952, and to about 70 annually thereafter (Table 51).

[29]Divorce by mail, in specific language, has never appeared in the statutes of any Mexican state. However, the provisions which permitted the attorney to post the notice of intention as well as to obtain the decree achieved this end.

Table 51. Absolute Divorces in Mexico, Number by State and Number to Couples from the United States, 1926-1955

Year	Total	State in Which Granted								Decrees to Couples with One or Both Spouses Born in the United States
		Campeche	Chihuahua	Morelos	Sonora	Tamaulipas	Tlaxcala	Yucatan	Other	
1926	977	66	35	52	90	45	1	163	525	230*
1927	1,141	93	60	54	172	58	1	82	621	230*
1928	1,291	69	68	85	203	51	0	109	706	280*
1929	1,409	72	52	195	194	45	0	130	721	360*
1930	1,626	51	126	202	180	34	0	143	890	410*
1931	1,606	24	123	236	107	47	3	87	979	357
1932	2,346	48	665	387	132	57	1	88	968	976
1933	3,472	32	1,475	396	99	56	3	168	1,243	1,684
1934	4,535	26	2,223	272	121	43	100	186	1,564	2,201
1935	4,752	28	1,849	157	102	266	215	120	2,015	1,772
1936	4,732	27	1,457	189	107	201	225	402	2,124	1,252
1937	4,472	37	1,291	118	96	236	251	400	2,043	1,149
1938	4,178	33	962	78	102	247	346	153	2,257	903
1939	4,539	33	923	100	111	312	552	129	2,379	832
1940	4,291	6	933	149	101	222	566	180	2,134	883
1941	5,179	19	1,067	285	110	284	608	174	2,632	1,045
1942	6,604	41	1,732	793	139	452	26	155	3,266	1,500
1943	7,972	24	3,160	599	166	479	22	207	3,315	2,309
1944	9,297	30	4,154	522	219	537	11	255	3,569	3,142
1945	9,602	20	3,919	1,234	231	441	20	223	3,514	2,997
1946	9,950	34	3,693	1,532	250	488	15	273	3,665	2,642
1947	8,693	27	2,744	1,377	281	532	14	260	3,458	1,754
1948	6,882	28	1,808	605	230	455	17	255	3,484	1,220
1949	6,777	43	1,640	656	202	503	25	237	3,471	1,040
1950	7,929	32	2,232	1,003	204	469	27	218	3,744	1,560*
1951	7,803	38	2,226	622	208	527	22	239	3,921	1,310*
1952	8,533	49	2,738	338	222	664	23	264	4,235	1,960*
1953	8,914	33	3,104	71	216	665	27	284	4,514	2,290*
1954	10,418	54	4,039	67	218	671	35	303	5,031	2,720*
1955	12,208	41	5,625	83	268	764	24	326	5,077	4,310*

*Estimated in whole or part by the author.

Source: Annual reports and unpublished data from Dirección General De Estadística, Departamento Técnico, Secretaría De Economía, México.

The record for Chihuahua is even more notable. That state has been the leading mecca for divorce seekers from other countries ever since its "quickie" laws were promulgated on January 15, 1932, and August 1, 1933. Moreover, the migratory divorce volume in Chihuahua has grown with the closing of the divorce centers in Tlaxcala and Morelos. The marked upswing of recent years may also have been influenced by the New York Supreme Court decision in 1952, which seemingly accepted the validity of certain Mexican divorces which had not previously been recognized by the New York courts.

The attraction of our citizens to Chihuahua is due in part to its liberal divorce laws. Proof of registration in the town where the plaintiff alleges residence—such registration can be made at the time of arrival—establishes the jurisdiction of the local court. Most citizens of the United States petition for a divorce on the grounds of incompatibility of character, and are able to secure their decree within three days to six weeks. Chihuahua is also popular because of its convenient location. Ciudad Juarez, the divorce "capital" in that state, is on the Rio Grande opposite El Paso, Texas, and is connected with the United States by three international bridges.

The total number of divorces granted in Chihuahua increased from less than 100 annually prior to 1930 to a peak of 2,223 in 1934 at the depth of the depression, which enhanced the appeal of the comparatively inexpensive Mexican decrees. An even higher peak was reached during World War II, when 4,154 decrees were granted in 1944 alone. More recently, after a postwar recession which dropped their number to a low of 1,640 in 1949, a third upsurge started. In 1955, the latest year for which statistics are available, an all-time record high of 5,625 divorces was granted in Chihuahua.

A considerable number of residents of the United States migrate to Mexico for a divorce. As is evident from the right-hand column of Table 51, Mexican decrees granted to couples with one or both spouses born in the United States have increased from about 230 in 1926 to more than 4,300 in 1955. These figures actually understate the totals to our residents, since they make no allowance for our foreign born (a very important factor in the earlier years) or for any of our citizens included under decrees granted to persons whose country of origin was reported as unknown (a frequent occurrence in the so-called mail-order cases where neither party appears). Allowing for these deficiencies, as well as for the absence of data prior to 1926, it is likely that more than 50,000 American couples were divorced in Mexico between 1918 and 1955.

Total Frequency. It is not possible to estimate precisely the total number of migratory divorces. These refer specifically to divorce seekers who migrate to evade the laws of their home state. However, the American people are highly mobile and move for a variety of reasons. Moreover, in cases of marital difficulty, it is not uncommon for one or both spouses to move to another state.

Around the turn of the century, divorce statistics classified by state of marriage were used to approximate the magnitude of migratory divorce. However, in addition to the limitations already noted, such measure fails to take into account the high frequency of nonresident marriages (Table 16). A more recent statistic—defendant's residence— also is deficient as an index of migratory divorce. Not only may the plaintiff supply false information, particularly if there is reason to avoid a contested action, but the defendant's whereabouts may actually be unknown.

Duplicate[30] and invalidated decrees further complicate the problem. However, there is every indication that the numerical importance of migratory divorces is relatively small. They probably

account for no more than 3 to 5 per cent of the total divorces annually.

SOUTH CAROLINA

South Carolina has a unique record with regard to legal dissolution of marriage. Divorces have been granted only since 1949; they were also permitted during a brief period after the Civil War, namely, from 1872 to 1878. In all other years, South Carolina was the only state in the Union which did not allow divorce. Moreover, even in the years when a marriage could be legally dissolved only through annulment, this means was resorted to only infrequently because the courts adhered strictly to the ecclesiastical grounds for such decrees.[31] Thus, throughout most of our history, the marriage contract was indissoluble in South Carolina, and could be terminated only by actual or presumed death. Proceedings for separation and alimony were always maintainable.[32] However, the indications are that few legal separations were sought in the courts—probably little more than a score annually even during the 1940's.

The Situation Prior to 1949. The family laws and mores of South Carolina, as well as their social and economic implications, have been the subject of both praise and criticism ever since the early years of our history. Since the details are readily available in the literature,[33] they will

---

[30]The number of duplicate decrees — divorces obtained from two jurisdictions — has probably increased in recent years, partly as a result of the adoption by several states of the Uniform Divorce Recognition Act. An example of such law is the one enacted by the state of Washington during 1949 which provides that:

A divorce obtained in another jurisdiction shall be of no force or effect in this state if both parties to the marriage were domiciled in this state at the time the proceeding for divorce was commenced.

Proof that a person obtaining a divorce from the bonds of matrimony in another jurisdiction was (a) domiciled in this state within twelve months prior to the commencement of the proceeding therefor, and resumed residence in this state within eighteen months after the date of his departure therefrom, or (b) at all times after his departure from this state and until his return maintained a place of residence within this state, shall be *prima facie* evidence that the person was domiciled in this state when the divorce proceeding was commenced.

[31]Solomon Blatt, Jr., and P. A. Sansbury, Jr., "Annulment of Marriage in South Carolina," *Year Book of the Selden Society*, 6:23-35, January, 1942.

James D. Sumner, Jr., "The South Carolina Divorce Act of 1949," *South Carolina Law Quarterly*, 3:255-256, March, 1951.

[32]Roy V. Rhodes, *Annulment of Marriage*, Parker and Co., Los Angeles, 1945, p. 355.

[33]James D. Sumner, Jr., *op. cit.*, pp. 258-259.

Schirmir (Jacob) Journal, April 29, 1845. Quoted in Rosser H. Taylor, *Ante-Bellum South Carolina: A Social and Cultural History*, Univ. of North Carolina Press, Chapel Hill, 1942, p. 66.

Joel P. Bishop, *New Commentaries on Marriage, Divorce, and Separation*, Vol. 1, T. H. Flood and Co., Chicago, 1891, pp. 24-26.

Albert L. James, "Liability of Husband for Wife's Tort," *Year Book of the Selden Society*, 3:39-41, January, 1939.

Isadore S. Bernstein, "Illegitimates and Inheritance," *Year Book of the Selden Society*, 7:39, June, 1943.

Carl N. Everstine, *Divorce in Maryland*, Legislative Council of Maryland, Research Report No. 25, Baltimore, February, 1946, pp. 10-11.

not be summarized here. Suffice it to say that, in former generations, South Carolinians were so strongly opposed to the legal dissolution of marriage that they evolved a "common law of their own." This included both social and legal recognition of extramarital family relationships—the law even prescribed the proportionate share of property which a (married) man could give to the woman who was not his lawful wedded wife.

South Carolina had a divorce law during the Reconstruction period, but it occasioned no rush to her courts. The constitution adopted in 1868 provided that "divorces from the bonds of matrimony shall not be allowed but by the judgment of a court as shall be prescribed by law." Four years later the legislature enacted the necessary statute. The law, which became effective on January 31, 1872, permitted divorce on the grounds of adultery or of willful desertion for two years (if caused by extreme cruelty or nonsupport). By the time the law was repealed on December 20, 1878, fewer than 200 decrees had been granted, as is evident from Table 52.

opinions gradually changed.[34] By the 1930's an appreciable number of South Carolinians were migrating to neighboring states for divorce, despite the questionable validity of such decrees. The uncertain legal effect of out-of-state divorces was clearly indicated in 1947 by one of the leading members of the Columbia (South Carolina) Bar.

> Since South Carolina grants no divorce,...no couple can obtain a valid divorce so long as both husband and wife retain their domiciles in this state....
>
> Our difficulty is with the client who wants to obtain a divorce in a state where neither he nor his wife is domiciled. Frequently he is unwilling to stay in that state even during the provided period of residence. Under the law his or her divorce is not valid. True, it may not be questioned. The state usually will not prosecute. Frequently the other spouse is estopped by participation or remarriage. Settlements relating to custody, property and support minimize the chances of unpleasant litigation. This merely means that the fraudulent divorcee usually gets by. But, in fact, his second marriage is not valid, and the children of this marriage not legitimate.[35]

Not all persons whose marriage was broken had the financial means or inclination to obtain a divorce by establishing a fictitious residence in another state. Some ignored the need for divorce and made new alliances without formality or by bigamous marriage. The records of social workers contain many illustrations of such marital tangles, as well as of some cases where a legal separation, which was possible, was thought to be a divorce and the parties remarried in good faith.

Table 52. Number of Absolute Divorces and Annulments, South Carolina, 1872-1956

Year	Divorce	Year	Annulment	Year	Annulment	Year	Total	Absolute Divorce	Annulment
1872	7	1926	10	1940	40	1949	1,100	980	120
1873	16	1927	6	1941	50	1950	2,250	2,170	80
1874	17	1928	8	1942	70	1951	2,330	2,240	90
1875	35	1929	8	1943	70	1952	2,400	2,310	90
1876	17	1930	13	1944	90	1953	2,500	2,400	100
1877	26	1931	19	1945	130	1954	2,480	2,360	120
1878	39	1932	29	1946	160	1955	2,720	2,600	120
				1947	140	1956	2,740	2,600	140
				1948	150				

Note: Data on annulments are not available prior to 1926, or for 1933-1939; divorce not permitted prior to 1872 or during 1879-1948.

Source: 1872-1878 and 1926-1932, from reports on marriage and divorce by the Bureau of the Census (divorce figures are also shown for 1869 and 1870, namely, 5 and 1, respectively; assuming that an error was not made in tabulation or publication, these data could be divorces granted without statutory authority, annulments, or separations); 1940-1950, from Tables A19-20; 1951, 1953-1956, from reports by the State Board of Health, with adjustments by the author for counties omitted from the state figures; 1952, estimated by the author.

The new state constitution of 1895 provided that "divorces from the bonds of matrimony shall not be allowed in this State," and this provision remained unaltered for more than a half century. For most of this period, it would appear that the public almost universally favored the ban against divorce. However, after the first World War,

The need for a divorce law had been discussed for many years, both in the General Assembly and among the people. There was a growing awareness that the prohibition of divorce did not promote the morals or welfare of the state or its people and that, if a reasonable divorce law was enacted, the state could exert control over its residents and

---

[34]H. C. Brearley, "A Note Upon Migratory Divorce of South Carolinians," *Law and Contemporary Problems*, 2:329, June, 1935.

[35]David W. Robinson, Jr., "Foreign Divorces: The Full Faith and Credit Clause," *Year Book of the Selden Society*, 8:29, April, 1947.

their property. During the 1940's, with the up-surge of divorce in the United States, a renewed drive to remove the ban against divorce in South Carolina was spearheaded by the South Carolina Bar Association. One of the reasons advanced for the change was that residents were obtaining divorces in other states, and that many of these decrees were based on perjured testimony as to domicile. For example, it has been stated that certain lawyers, for a fee of $60, would guarantee a divorce if their client would go to a boarding house in Augusta (Georgia), for example, leave his suitcase, and return to Augusta again only for the trial of the case.[36] Proponents also were concerned about the social aspects of the prevailing situation. Thus it was alleged that there were more people living in adultery or practicing bigamy in South Carolina than in all other states, and that it is a greater blotch on the escutcheon of South Carolina to atone bigamy than to oppose legal divorce.[37]

In the deliberations preceding the passage of the new law there is also some reference to the financial loss suffered by South Carolina because of its disposition to differ from other states.[38] No doubt economic considerations were an important factor underlying the favorable attitude of public officials and other leading citizens toward a change in the law. Until the 1930's most South Carolinians lived in rural areas and were dependent largely on agriculture and its by-products. More recently, industry has forged ahead of the farm in the number of jobs provided. With the state exerting a major effort to attract new industries and skilled workers, it is not surprising that South Carolina also saw the necessity of having divorce laws similar to those generally prevailing in other states. In other words, it is likely that the official backing for a change in the law was dictated more by necessity than by logic. Since the annulment statutes in South Carolina are not pliable, as are those in New York, for example, they could not act as a "safety valve," with the result that the proposal to adopt a divorce law received ready acceptance. There was some opposition to a change in the law, princi-pally from Catholic and Baptist Church sources. However, the fight was directed largely against amendment of the constitution, whereas the enabling divorce legislation was passed rather quickly. The sequence of events was as follows. The General Assembly at its 1947 session approved a joint resolution proposing that the state constitution be amended to provide for divorce.[39] Voters at the general election in 1948 approved the amendment, which was then ratified by the legislature on March 31, 1949 (R209, H1077). Within two weeks, the General Assembly passed the necessary enabling legislation setting forth the terms of the new statute, which became law with the governor's approval on April 15, 1949 (R319, H1174).

The Divorce Act of 1949. The provisions of South Carolina's divorce law are typical of those which generally prevail in other states.[40] Absolute divorces may be granted on four grounds, namely, adultery, desertion for a period of one year, physical cruelty, or habitual drunkenness.[41] Other important features provide that the plaintiff must have resided in the state at least one year prior to the commencement of a suit, and that a final decree cannot be granted before three months after the filing of a complaint. One other feature of the law is noteworthy. The original Act (Section 12) provided that on the granting of any final decree of divorce the wife shall thereafter be barred of dower in lands then owned or thereafter acquired by her former husband. Within a few months, however, this section was amended to also include the barring of dower in lands *formerly* owned by her ex-husband.

The Trend of Marital Dissolutions Since 1940. With the close of World War II, the number of annulments in South Carolina climbed to a peak of about 160 in 1946, and then fell off somewhat. Although this was only a fraction of the annual number of marital dissolutions in other states (Table A19), there is no doubt that it was an all-time record for South Carolina (Table 52). Starting with July, 1949, however, when final divorce

---

[36] South Carolina Bar Association, *Transactions of the 52nd Annual Meeting*, Columbia, 1946, pp. 17, 21.

[37] *Ibid.*, pp. 21, 23.

[38] *Ibid.*, p. 24.

[39] Joint Resolution No. 289, dated March 20, 1947, Acts and Joint Resolutions, General Assembly, South Carolina, 1947, *Statutes at Large*, pp. 725-726.

[40] For a detailed discussion of the 1949 Act, see James D. Sumner, *op. cit.*, pp. 259-302.

[41] The extent to which the statutory grounds have been used, and related data, are given in Chapter 9.

decrees were first issued, marital dissolutions increased sharply to new high levels. They totaled 1,100 in 1949, rose to 2,250 in 1950, and then followed a more gradual upswing. In 1956, the latest year for which data are available, 2,740 divorces and annulments were granted.

It is still too early to foretell the ultimate level of the divorce rate in South Carolina. With the large backlog of estranged couples and other long-standing marital tangles, it will take years for affairs to stabilize. Nevertheless, it is apparent that during the immediate future, at least, the rate will remain well below that of the country as a whole.

NEW YORK

Throughout our history, the recorded divorce[42] rate in New York State has been well below the national average. Since 1950, moreover, New York has had the lowest rate in the country; in prior years, South Carolina had that distinction. Currently the New York courts grant less than $2\frac{1}{2}$ per cent of the nation's total marital dissolutions, although the state contains almost a tenth of the country's population. In 1956 the rate in New York—about 0.5 decrees per 1,000 total population—was less than a fourth of the rate for the United States as a whole.

Trend of Marital Dissolutions. The recorded divorce rate in New York State has generally paralleled the trend of the rate in the country as a whole, especially since the turn of the century. Immediately after the Civil War the rate in New

[42]Reports by the Department of Labor and the Bureau of the Census contain detailed New York data for 1867-1906, 1916, and 1922-1932. Although divorces and separations were combined in these reports, each may be approximated from the tabulations by legal grounds. This procedure may also be used to distinguish the number of Enoch Arden decrees from annulments during 1926-1932, the only years for which such data were included in the government publications. The statistics for the period since 1940 (Table 53) show each of the four types of decrees separately, so that the total number of marriages legally dissolved is readily apparent. To maintain comparability in the trend of marital dissolutions over the entire period since 1867, the data for all years prior to 1940 (including published totals for 1936-1939) have been adjusted to allow for all types of decrees other than separations. Thus, unless otherwise indicated, all statements regarding divorce or marital dissolutions in New York State refer to the total of absolute divorces, annulments, and Enoch Arden decrees.

York was close to 0.2 per 1,000 total population. During the ensuing quarter century, the rate fluctuated without any definite upward or downward trend—a low point of little more than 0.1 per 1,000 being reached in 1877. After 1893, however, the divorce rate moved upward; it was 0.3 before World War I, 0.4 in the early 1920's, and 0.7 in 1940. At its peak in 1946, the rate was as high as 1.8 per 1,000. Further paralleling the trend for the United States, the rate for New York has since declined sharply.

In New York State, as in the country generally, there have been marked deviations from the long-term trend during financial crises and after armed conflicts. The effect of these phenomena on the dissolution rate in New York cannot be fully documented due to the absence of detailed data and also because of other factors such as fluctuations in the extent of migratory divorce. For example, Willcox explains the decrease in the New York rate during 1876-1878 as due to depressed economic conditions as well as to the large number of New Yorkers who flocked to Utah to take advantage of the liberal requirements in Utah's divorce law for those years.[43] Gaps in the New York data for the critical years during World War I and the depression of the 1930's do not enable us to examine the course of the rate during those periods. However, since the rate during 1937-1939 (0.7) was at a much higher level than during 1930-1932 (0.4), it is evident that there was an upward trend with improved economic conditions.

We are on much safer ground in evaluating the effect of World War II on the dissolution rate in New York. For this period, it is apparent from Table 48 that the trend in New York approximated the national pattern. In the nation, the rate in 1946 was two and one quarter times that for 1940, while in New York it was two and one half. Moreover, in both the nation and state, the rate in 1948 was about two fifths above the 1940 level. Thus the war and economic conditions of recent years have had the same effect on marital dissolutions in New York as in the other states.

Role of Annulments. Four types of matrimonial decrees may be granted in New York, namely, absolute divorce, dissolution of marriage,

[43]Walter F. Willcox, "A Study in Vital Statistics," *Political Science Quarterly*, 8:86, March, 1893.

Table 53. Number of Matrimonial Decrees, New York State, 1940-1956

Area and Type of Decree	1940	1941	1942	1943	1944	1945	1946	1947	1948	1949	1950
New York State											
Absolute divorce	7,150	7,600	7,920	7,640	9,080	10,860	14,960	11,960	9,310	6,773	6,604
Dissolution*	590	560	810	680	780	850	950	810	640	478	418
Annulment	2,280	2,730	2,890	2,900	3,380	4,430	8,350	5,680	4,840	4,313	4,599
Separation	570	600	660	610	780	830	920	1,070	1,040	1,010	852
New York City											
Absolute divorce	3,504	3,718	3,963	3,501	4,261	4,820	6,936	6,161	4,467	2,615	2,797
Dissolution*	262	327	418	451	520	554	630	571	474	343	306
Annulment	1,128	1,256	1,571	1,401	1,729	2,200	3,821	3,164	2,774	2,237	2,541
Separation	282	344	379	326	376	363	427	631	650	647	558
Buffalo†											
Absolute divorce	460	466	457	501	616	705	892	561	549	434	513
Dissolution*	166	93	203	70	79	90	73	34	31	20	26
Annulment	399	587	377	475	476	512	1,121	380	282	266	280
Separation	69	51	51	49	94	111	80	68	81	64	69
Rest of State‡											
Absolute divorce	3,186	3,416	3,500	3,638	4,203	5,335	7,132	5,238	4,294	3,724	3,294
Dissolution*	162	140	189	159	181	206	247	205	135	115	86
Annulment	753	887	942	1,024	1,175	1,718	3,408	2,136	1,784	1,810	1,778
Separation	219	205	230	235	310	356	413	371	309	299	225

	1951§	1952§	1953§	1954§	1955§	1956§
New York State						
Absolute divorce	6,350	6,150	5,800	5,400	4,800	4,750
Dissolution*	400	400	400	400	350	300
Annulment	4,500	4,500	4,300	3,950	3,750	3,600
Separation	950	950	900	900	900	850

*Enoch Arden decrees. †Erie County.
‡Includes allowance for a few counties which failed to supply data. §Provisional.
Note: The sum of absolute divorces, dissolutions, and annulments is the total number of marriages legally terminated.
Source: Compiled by the author.

annulment, and separation (Table 53). At this point, the presentation will be restricted to the first three of these actions—those that permanently dissolve a marriage; separations are considered in a later section.

Absolute divorce may be granted in New York for adultery only. From 1940 to 1948, these decrees averaged 9,600 a year. They reached a peak of almost 15,000 in 1946—double their number in 1940—but have since declined without interruption. In 1956, the latest year for which estimates are available, there were about 4,750 divorces—the smallest number since 1932. Divorces have also decreased as a proportion of the total marriages dissolved, from 71 per cent in 1940 to 55 per cent in 1956.

A marriage may also be dissolved in New York if a spouse is absent for five successive years and presumed to be dead. These dissolutions of marriage or Enoch Arden decrees, which are included in the divorce law of other states, averaged only 580 per year between 1940 and 1956, or less than one for every 13 decrees granted for adultery. Obviously, Enoch Arden decrees are too few to materially affect the total dissolution rate in the state.

In addition, a marriage may be annulled in New York. For the country as a whole, annulments constitute only a small proportion of the total legal dissolutions. Even at their peak in 1946, when about 22,000 were granted in the United States, they represented only 3.5 per cent of the total dissolutions (Table 42). In California and New York, however, annulments are of much greater relative importance. Thus, in California[44] annulments generally account for more than one ninth of all marriages dissolved. In New York they are an even larger, and growing, proportion of the total; about one quarter of the marital dissolutions during World War II, and since 1950 about two fifths. Moreover, for at least ten counties[45] in New York, the number of annulments now exceeds the number of absolute divorces. It is also noteworthy that during the 1950's, an average of 4,170 annulments per year have been

[44] The large number of annulments granted in California — more than in any other state — is due largely to its divorce law which requires a one-year interlocutory period before a decree becomes final.

[45] In 1950, these counties were Greene, Herkimer, Nassau, Oswego, Queens, Rensselaer, Richmond, Seneca, Suffolk, and Sullivan.

granted in New York State—almost one third of the total in the United States.

That annulment should be a method frequently used for terminating a marriage in New York is not surprising. The grounds for annulment provided by the state's law are relatively broad in scope. They include force, duress, fraud,[46] bigamy, incurable physical incapacity, non-age, want of understanding, and incurable insanity.

The New York data regarding annulment and divorce are not available by duration of marriage. However, since the great preponderance (about four fifths) of annulments in the country as a whole are granted in the first five years of marriage, it seems reasonable to assume that this is also the case for annulments granted in New York. Certainly, this would help to explain the fact that the dissolution rate in New York followed closely the United States trend in the war and early postwar years. In other words, it is likely that annulments served as the primary vehicle for dissolving unstable war marriages, and that divorces were used principally for dissolving marriages of longer duration.

The above assumptions are supported by the experience in Manhattan and The Bronx during 1950. As may be seen from Table A24, close to three fourths of the annulments were granted to couples married less than five years. By contrast, absolute divorces were distributed more evenly throughout the marital life span. Fewer than one fourth of the divorces were granted to persons in the first five years of marriage, and as many as three fifths to those at durations 5-19 years. It is also noteworthy that Enoch Arden decrees are concentrated largely in the later years of marriage; in fact, almost one half occurred after the twentieth year.

Although the three types of decrees for dissolving a marriage in New York differ markedly according to duration of marriage, their combined distribution is very much like that for legal dissolutions in the country as a whole (Table A21).

For 1950 the proportions at durations 0-4 years were 42 per cent in New York and 46 per cent in the United States; at 5-9 years they were 25 and 23 per cent, respectively.[47]

The situation in New York is also not unlike that for the country as a whole with regard to children affected by marital dissolutions. Minor children were involved in about one third of the total decrees granted in Manhattan and The Bronx during 1950; at durations 10-20 years, the proportion with children exceeded one half. The great majority of annulments in New York do not affect dependent children. Only about one eighth do, and these include children from former marriages. Children are also infrequently involved in Enoch Arden decrees—only one fourth report minor children, suggesting that in many cases the spouse has been absent for a long period of time. On the other hand, children are involved in about one half of the divorce actions. For additional details, including information on the number of children involved, see Table A24.

Although New York State now has the strictest divorce law in the country, the procedures in matrimonial actions are similar to those in other states. For example, as in the country as a whole, the wife is granted the decree in about three fourths of the marriages dissolved in New York. However, judged by the experience in Manhattan and The Bronx, the proportion varies markedly by type of decree. As is shown in Table 54, during 1946-50 wives obtained little more than three fifths of the Enoch Arden decrees but as many as four fifths of the absolute divorces. It is also evident that very few cases are contested. For divorce, the proportion is only about 4 per cent— and these generally involve contests over the custody of children or property settlement.

The New York Law. The divorce problem has been the subject of as much or more controversy in New York State than in any of the other legal jurisdictions in the United States. The state's divorce law dates back to March, 1787, when the legislature first established divorce on the

---

[46]Fraud, which is by far the most popular cause alleged in New York (as well as in California and many other states), is a general term covering a number of specific causes, such as misrepresentation of financial standing or of willingness to have children, deception as to character, etc. Bigamy and being under the legal age for marriage are also frequent grounds for annulment.

[47]The period at which marriages are dissolved varies considerably among the states. In 1948, for example, the dissolutions at durations 0-4 years ranged from less than one fourth of all decrees in Connecticut, New Jersey, and Vermont to more than one half in Iowa, Missouri, Oregon, Tennessee, and Wyoming.

Table 54. Contested Decrees, and Party to Which Granted, by Type of Matrimonial Decree, Manhattan and The Bronx in New York State, 1946-50

(Percentage of Total Decrees)

Contest; Party to Which Granted	Absolute Divorce	Dissolution of Marriage*	Annul-ment	Total†	Separa-tion
Contested	4.0	0.0	9.0	5.4	65.1
Not contested	96.0	100.0	91.0	94.6	34.9
Granted to wife	81.0	63.8	72.1	76.6	94.6
Granted to husband	19.0	36.2	27.9	23.4	5.4

*Enoch Arden decrees.
†Sum of absolute divorce, dissolution of marriage and annulment.

Source: Statistics compiled by the author from Supreme Court records.

grounds of adultery.[48] Over the years there have been some modifications and additions to the law. In the original act, for example, the defendant was forbidden to remarry. Today, remarriage may be permitted after three years. The problem of remarriage, however, is still important since many divorced New Yorkers remarry in Connecticut[49] and in other neighboring states.

The second basic step in constructing New York's matrimonial statutes occurred in 1813, when the Revised Laws originated the remedy of separations. This remedy was at first restricted to the wife, and it was not until 1880 that the right was definitely made applicable to husband and wife alike.[50] Other important changes in the New York laws include the authorization of annulments in 1830, the addition of Enoch Arden decrees in 1922,[51] and the liberalization of the residence requirements for all types of matrimonial actions. It is also noteworthy that, from 1811 to 1903, the legislature passed several bills dissolving individual marriages. A few of these were based on cruelty, abandonment, or other ground not available under the general statutes.[52]

[48]Charles R. and George Webster, *Laws of the State of New York*, Vol. 1, Albany, 1802, pp. 93-94.
[49]See, for example, Connecticut, *One Hundred and Second Registration Report*, Public Document No. 9, 1949, p. 59.
[50]Judicial Council of the State of New York, *Eighth Annual Report*, Legislative Document No. 16, 1942, pp. 354-355.
[51]*McKinney's Consolidated Laws of New York*, Annotated Book 14, Domestic Relations Law, Edward Thompson Co., Brooklyn, 1941; 1949-50 Supplement.
[52]Matteo Spalletta, "Divorce in Colonial New York," *The New-York Historical Society Quarterly*, xxxix(4):438, October, 1955.

The greatest advance in New York has undoubtedly come not through the evolution of the law itself, but rather through the fact that the courts have taken a more liberal attitude toward interpretation and application of the law. Official referees,[53] after taking testimony in undefended matrimonial suits, submit their recommendations to a justice. Generally, the courts accept these recommendations, almost without review. In fact, a decision by the Appellate Division on May 25, 1949, virtually stripped Supreme Court justices of authority to refuse an annulment, once a referee has made such a recommendation. The effects of this decision were offset somewhat in 1955 by legislative enactment of a three-year statute of limitations, from the time of discovery of fraud, in actions to annul a marriage on the basis of fraud.

The New York record for the past century at least includes repeated references to and evidence of fraud, perjury, collusion, and connivance in connection with matrimonial actions within the state. For example, Chancellor Kent, after a long career on the New York bench, stated that he believed that sometimes adultery was committed for the very purpose of obtaining a divorce because it could be secured on no other ground. During the 1930's, Judge Cohalan's determined fight against collusive divorce actions was widely publicized in the New York press. As a matter of fact, it has been common knowledge for several decades that the situation in New York has resulted in the appearance of a new remunerative occupation—that of the professional co-respondent. These conditions were brought into the spotlight again on November 30, 1948, when New York District Attorney Frank S. Hogan announced the arrest of members of a "divorce ring" on charges of perjury and subornation of perjury. Thereafter a grand jury investigation was launched of all uncontested matrimonial actions disposed of during the preceding two years.

The effects of the investigation on the volume of litigation were immediate and pronounced. Hundreds of uncontested cases on the New York

[53]Under the New York State constitution, judges are required to retire at the end of the year in which they reach their 70th birthday. Thereafter, they may serve until they are 76 as official referees, passing on civil actions referred to them by the courts.

Supreme Court calendar were adjourned at the request of counsel, many being taken to other jurisdictions. Due largely to these events, the number of marriages dissolved in Manhattan declined by two fifths within a year, from 2,777 in 1948 to 1,624 in 1949. Marked decreases were also recorded in the other boroughs of New York City—particularly in The Bronx, which is in the same judicial district as Manhattan. All in all, the number of decrees dropped about one third in New York City, but only one tenth in the upstate counties (Table 53). The effect of the perjury investigation was limited largely to absolute divorces in 1949; in 1950 both annulments and divorces increased slightly in New York City. In this connection, it is noteworthy that in 1949 the figures rose in two of the country's divorce centers with liberal residence requirements, namely, Miami and Reno.

The investigation confirmed what had long been suspected, namely, that fraud, perjury, and collusion are present in all types of matrimonial actions—including even those based on the so-called "Enoch Arden Law." The report of the Third Grand Jury for the November, 1948, term to the New York Court of General Sessions on March 6, 1951, concluded with a recommendation that a state commission be created "to study and analyze the problems relating to marriage, divorce, separation and annulment of marriage."

Attempts to amend and "liberalize" the New York divorce law have been made in various forms, both direct and indirect. New York took the initiative toward the end of the nineteenth century in petitioning for national uniform divorce legislation.[54] In the 1930's, unsuccessful attempts were made to amend the law directly in the state legislature. Since 1945, the Association of the Bar of New York City has sponsored and endorsed a number of suggested revisions of the law, but without success. In fact, even a proposal for a state commission to study the causes and effects of matrimonial problems, and to recommend changes in the law, was "killed" at various sessions of the state legislature between 1948 and 1955 before it was finally approved on March 22, 1956.

Migrant New Yorkers. Available statistics and numerous newspaper articles make it clear that New Yorkers often establish temporary residence in other states in order to secure divorce. No precise measure of the extent of these migratory divorces is available. On the basis of data on the place of marriage of those divorced in 1922, Cahen estimated that about 30 per cent of all divorces granted to New Yorkers were obtained outside the state.[55] This estimate is at best an educated guess since Cahen allowed for New York couples who migrate to other states to establish permanent residence, but did not take into account those citizens of other states who move to New York after marriage nor for the high proportion of couples who marry outside of their state of residence. Statistics for a series of years from 1916 to 1938, showing the place of divorce for persons remarrying in upstate New York, confirm Cahen's conclusion that a sizable proportion of New Yorkers secure divorce in other jurisdictions.[56] These data are similarly affected by migration, and also by the fact that many New Yorkers who go to Reno, for example, remarry there after their divorce. In the absence of valid information we can only speculate on the true extent of divorce among New Yorkers. Generally, it has probably been about one third to one half greater than the number recorded in New York State; currently, it may even be double, in view of the marked increase of Mexican divorces to Americans following the 1952 decision of the New York Supreme Court upholding the validity of certain Mexican decrees.[57]

Separations. It is probable that some persons, without the financial means of migrating to other jurisdictions, give up attempts to dissolve their "broken" marriage. Others take the "poor man's out" by deserting their family, or partially resolve their difficulties by securing a legal separation in the state.

Separations may be granted in New York on the grounds of extreme cruelty, desertion, or of nonsupport by husband. However, relatively few New

[54]N. Ruth Wood, "Marriage and Divorce Laws," *Women Lawyers' Journal*, 33:30, 1947.

[55]Alfred Cahen, *Statistical Analysis of American Divorce*, Columbia University Press, New York, 1932, p. 68.
[56]New York State Department of Health, *Fifty-eighth Annual Report*, vol. 2, page 262 for 1937, and earlier reports for years prior to 1937; unpublished data for 1938.
[57]See earlier section on Mexico.

Yorkers apply for these decrees. They averaged only 850 per year between 1940 and 1956, increasing from 570 in 1940 to almost 1,100 in 1947 and then receding to about 900 annually (Table 53).

Suits for separation are generally brought by the wife for permanent separate maintenance and support. Thus, it is not surprising that the great preponderance (about 95 per cent) of legal separations are granted to the wife (Table 54), and that about one half involve dependent children (Table A24). Also, since such decrees provide for property settlement and custody of the children—often preliminary to one of the spouses establishing residence for divorce in another state—about two thirds are generally contested. This contrasts sharply with the situation in actions to dissolve a marriage, the proportions contested being only 4 per cent for absolute divorce and 9 per cent for annulment (Table 54).

The low dissolution rate in New York has often been attributed to the state's large population of Catholics and the foreign born. This factor, however, does not appear to explain completely New York's divorce record. The population in Massachusetts, Illinois, and Pennsylvania also includes a large proportion of such persons, yet in each of these states the recorded divorce rate is higher than New York's (Table 48). In Massachusetts, for example, the rate during 1940-1950 was one and one-half times what it was in New York. Massachusetts, of course, has a more liberal divorce law; absolute decrees may be granted on seven different grounds.

The situation in New York also contrasts sharply with that in Virginia. In the latter the recorded rate of legally dissolved marriages is almost double the New York rate, and bed and board (separation) decrees average two and three-quarter times the number of separations granted in New York. For the country generally, however, there does not appear to be any relationship between the frequency of separation decrees and the dissolution rate. Census data on the marital status of the white population in the United States in 1940 also indicate no correlation between the proportions divorced and those separated in the individual states.

Separation decrees (divorce *a mensa et thoro*) are relatively infrequent in the United States. According to surveys by the author, covering the

period from 1940 to 1948, it is estimated that the number of legal separations in the country as a whole increased from about 6,000 in 1940 to a peak of 14,000 in 1946 and then declined to about 12,000 in 1948. For the latter year, this was equivalent to one separation decree for every 35 absolute divorces or annulments. Of course, legal separations are not the only kind which occur. More often, separations are informal—for example, by private agreement, or even by abandonment or desertion, with the husband usually the deserter. Some separations (legal and informal) eventually culminate in actions for absolute divorce. However, desertions are not always permanent; the deserter in many cases returns voluntarily to his family, perhaps only to repeat the performance in a later year.

Apparently, New Yorkers frequently resort to informal separations.[58] In the 1940 Census, for example, the proportion of the white women ever married (excluding widows) reported as living apart from their husband was one third greater in New York than in the country as a whole.[59]

Total Marital Disruptions. Census reports may be used as an index of marital disruption, but it is important to recognize certain limitations in the data. First, persons who are divorced or separated are likely to be attracted to large urban centers. New York City, especially, is a magnet for these people. Then too, the figures relate to persons divorced and not remarried, and are thus affected by geographic differences in the rate of remarriage. Finally, the data understate the true situation in New York since a sizable proportion of marital dissolutions in that state are by annulment, and the Bureau of the Census classifies as single those persons who report that their last marriage was annulled.

[58] Paul H. Jacobson, "Marital Dissolutions in New York State in Relation to their Trend in the United States," *Milbank Memorial Fund Quarterly*, 28:40-41, January, 1950.

[59] Desertions impose a heavy financial burden on the community. For example, based on New York City's experience during 1950, the National Desertion Bureau estimated that desertions cost the city more than $27,000,000 annually (half of its payments of aid to dependent children). The 1950 Report of Committee on Custody and Divorce to the New Jersey Supreme Court also highlighted this aspect of family breakdown. Most noteworthy is the conclusion on page 26 of Appendix B that "divorce is less of a factor in the background of children served by the State Board of Child Welfare, than is desertion or separation."

With these limitations in mind, we can consider the total frequency of marital disruptions in 1940 among white persons 15 years of age and over. The index used is the proportion divorced or separated of those ever married, excluding the widowed. Judged by this criterion, New York State was above the national average, even if the data are not inflated to allow for annullees. Among women, the age-adjusted proportion was 7.8 per cent in New York, as compared with 7.1 per cent in the United States as a whole. The disparity was even more pronounced among white men, 10.8 per cent in New York and 8.3 per cent in the United States.[60]

Thus, although the recorded divorce rate in New York is the lowest in the country, it is likely that annulments, migratory divorces, separations and desertions raise the total disruptions above the national average.

[60]For white women, 34 states had a smaller proportion divorced or separated than New York; for white men, 39 states.

Chapter 9

DIVORCE PROCEEDINGS

DIVORCE actions in the United States are conducted according to state requirements imposed by statute or recognized judicial precedent. Within this legal framework there may also be differences in procedure—even within a state—as a result of the wide range of discretion that may be exercised by justices in the interpretation and application of the law. The present chapter is devoted to several aspects of divorce litigation which can be described statistically. The first topic deals with applications for decrees, since suits for divorce (or annulment) start with the filing of a bill of complaint against the defendant.

APPLICATIONS AND THEIR DISPOSITION

The annual number of applications for divorce or annulment exceeds the number of final decrees by a considerable margin. In 1950, for example, about 541,000 applications were filed but during that same year not quite 385,000 decrees were granted. This corresponds to about 71 divorces per 100 applications, which is not much below the ratio for most years. In other words, for every three applications granted, there is usually one additional suit which does not end in divorce. Contrary to popular opinion, not all of the latter are denials nor are they all reconciliations. Denied petitions actually represent only a small fraction of the not-granted actions.[1] Moreover, in addition to reconciliations, suits may be withdrawn, dismissed for lack of prosecution, terminated because of the death of one of the parties, or remain pending because of failure to pay court

fees. It is also of interest that a large proportion of dismissed actions reappear in the courts.[2]

Until the mid-1920's the trend for decrees closely paralleled that for applications, the ratio between the two figures varying within a relatively narrow range. More recently the ratio has fluctuated markedly, as may be seen from Table 55. Most noteworthy was the upswing during the depression years from 1930 through 1933, when more than 80 divorces were granted annually for every 100 applications filed. In part, this was due to the fact that, as the depression deepened and new applications fell off, decrees continued to be granted on cases started months or even years earlier. It is also possible that, because of the expense involved, fewer suits were filed merely as a threat to "bring a spouse into line" or to obtain support money. Then too, persons who filed suit during the depression may have done so after greater forethought and therefore more of them pursued the action to termination. Regardless of the importance of these factors it is evident that during the depression there was a greater relative decrease in the number of applications than of decrees.

Plaintiff and Defendant. The wife is the plaintiff in almost three out of every four suits for divorce filed in American courts. For example, of the 423,213 final decrees in 1948, more than 297,000 or 70.3 per cent had been initiated by wives and fewer than 126,000 by husbands. As may also be ascertained from Table 56, for 1939 the proportion filed by wives was 73.8 per cent.

The proportionate number of suits brought by husbands and wives probably varies somewhat according to their relative ages. Among the marriages dissolved in Iowa, Nebraska, and Wisconsin during 1939, the wife was the plaintiff in

---

[1]According to statistics published by the Michigan Registrar of Vital Statistics, denied actions represented 4.5 per cent of the total suits not granted in that state during 1901-1928. In Ohio the annual reports of the Secretary of State for 1932-1940 indicate that the proportion denied was 7.2 per cent. Other states report figures as low as 1.7 per cent (Kansas, 1927-1950) and 3.7 per cent (Massachusetts, 1924-1948).

[2]Leon C. Marshall and G. May, *The Divorce Court*, The Johns Hopkins Press, Baltimore, Vol. 2 (Ohio), 1933, pp. 306-307.

Table 55. Number of Applications for Divorce, and Ratio of Decrees to Applications, United States, 1887-1950

Year	Applications (1,000's)	Divorces per 100 Applications	Year	Applications (1,000's)	Divorces per 100 Applications
1887	40	69.8	1920	237	71.9
1888	41	69.9	1921	212	75.3
1889	44	72.1	1922	204	74.3
			1923	230	73.2
1890	47	71.2	1924	228	76.5
1891	49	72.5	1925	242	74.0
1892	50	73.2	1926	240	76.9
1893	51	73.5	1927	254	77.3
1894	52	72.2	1928	265	75.5
1895	56	72.1	1929	272	75.7
1896	58	74.0			
1897	62	72.1	1930	242	81.0
1898	64	74.8	1931	233	80.7
1899	71	72.4	1932	196	83.8
			1933	201	82.1
1900	77	72.4	1934	261	78.2
1901	82	74.4	1935	280	77.9
1902	85	72.3	1936	296	79.7
1903	90	72.1	1937	311	80.1
1904	91	72.7	1938	309	79.0
1905	94	72.3	1939	318	78.9
1906	98	73.5			
1907	102	75.1	1940	348	76.1
1908	109	70.5	1941	394	74.9
1909	109	73.1	1942	414	77.6
			1943	487	73.8
1910	112	74.1	1944	558	73.9
1911	124	72.0	1945	676	71.9
1912	134	70.4	1946	815	77.1
1913	123	74.2	1947	628	79.0
1914	137	73.4	1948	565	74.9
1915	144	72.4	1949	544	72.4
1916	155	73.5			
1917	170	71.5	1950	541	71.2
1918	150	77.5			
1919	200	70.8			

Note: Data for 1920-1950 include annulments.

Source: Applications for 1887-1906, from the Bureau of the Census, with year unknowns distributed prorata; those for 1907-1950, estimated by the author from data for selected areas. Ratios of decrees to applications based on total decrees in Table 42.

Table 56. Party to Which Granted According to Plaintiff, Final Decrees of Absolute Divorce and Annulment, United States, 1939 and 1948

Plaintiff*	1939			1948		
	Number of Decrees	Per Cent Granted to		Number of Decrees	Per Cent Granted to	
		Husband	Wife		Husband	Wife
Husband	65,740	95.0	5.0	125,749	87.9	12.1
Wife	185,260	.5	99.5	297,464	1.8	98.2
Total	251,000	25.3	74.7	423,213	27.4	72.6

*The relatively small number of cases in which the plaintiff was neither the husband nor wife has been distributed prorata.

Source: Estimated by the author from data for selected areas.

75.6 per cent of those in which she was older than her husband, compared with 77.6 per cent if she was of the same age or younger.

The fact that the wife is usually the complaining spouse in divorce litigation is in part only the result of desertion or other intolerable conduct by the husband. Of much greater consequence is the availability of some grounds for divorce—for example, cruelty and neglect to provide are more readily applicable against the husband than against the wife. Moreover, where both parties desire the divorce it is customary for the wife to file the petition, because wives are more successful than husbands in obtaining a decree and also because applications by wives generally reflect less unfavorably upon the character of the parties.

The plaintiff is successful in all but a handful of suits that terminate in a final decree. However, men do not fare as well as women. In 1948, for example, wives were granted the decree in 12 per cent of the suits which had been brought by husbands, whereas husbands obtained only 2 per cent of the decrees in which the wife had been the plaintiff (Table 56).

Contests. Unlike other court litigation, suits for divorce or annulment are infrequently contested. Yet, by tradition, our state laws are based on the assumption that a constituted court must decide between one spouse who wants the marriage dissolved and the other who does not.

Answers are filed to about one seventh of all petitions (Table 57), but this does not necessarily reflect controversy over the granting of the decree. Often the defendant wishes to secure relatively favorable terms with respect to such

Table 57. Proportion Contested, Final Decrees of Absolute Divorce and Annulment, United States, 1887-1950

Period	Per Cent Contested	Period	Per Cent Contested	Period	Per Cent Contested
1887-91	14.6	1916	13.6	1931-35	13.0
1892-96	15.0			1936-40	13.4
1897-01	15.4	1922-25	14.0	1941-45	15.7
1902-06	15.9	1926-30	12.1	1946-50	14.8

Note: Data are not available for 1907-1915 and 1917-1921.

Source: Data for 1887-1932, from the Bureau of the Census; those for 1933-1950, estimated by the author from statistics for selected areas.

matters as alimony, disposition of property, or custody of children. Once this is accomplished, whether by formal or informal agreement, there is generally no further interest in continuing to oppose the action. The contesting of a suit may also be predicated on a desire to expedite the granting of the decree, or to assure its universal legality. The latter reason explains the relatively high proportion of decrees that are contested in Nevada and in the other so-called "divorce meccas." On the other hand, financial considerations tend to reduce the frequency of contests. In some states, the husband is required to pay the court costs and other expenses, including the fees of his wife's attorney, whether he is the plaintiff or defendant. Thus, if both parties want to be divorced, it may be less expensive if the wife makes the complaint, the husband does not answer, and the decree is granted by default.

Recipients of Decrees. For the past century, at least, wives have obtained the majority of divorces and annulments granted in the nation. Their share of the total has gradually increased from about 64 per cent in the years immediately after the Civil War to 72.5 per cent in 1950. However, the trend has not been uniformly upward. In the latter decades of the nineteenth century, the proportion granted to the wife remained relatively unchanged—it was still only 66 per cent during 1891-95. More recently, there has been a definite upswing, but this has been accompanied by marked fluctuations. During World War II, for example, the proportion granted to the wife fell from its all-time peak of

not quite 75 per cent in 1939 to about 71 per cent in 1943-1946. A similar decrease occurred during World War I, as may be seen from the left-hand panel of Table 58. In fact, the figures for the individual years indicate that the proportion was as low as 66 per cent in 1919 and 1920. By contrast, the proportion granted to the wife rose sharply during and immediately after the depression of the 1930's, climbing to about 73 per cent in 1931 and remaining at or above that level until Pearl Harbor.

The increase in the proportion of divorces granted to wives has been countrywide. Most pronounced has been the rise in the South. In the South Central states, for example, the proportion increased from 54.0 per cent during 1867-86 to 69.9 per cent during 1948, or by 15.9 per cent. The upswing was even greater along the South

Table 58. Per Cent of Absolute Divorces and Annulments by Party to Which Granted, and by Legal Ground, United States, 1867-1950

Period	Granted To		Legal Ground						
	Husband	Wife	Cruelty	Desertion	Adultery	Drunkenness	Neglect to Provide	Combinations	All Others
1867-70	36.0	64.0	12.4	35.4	26.4	3.0	1.6	13.4	7.8
1871-75	33.9	66.1	14.8	37.4	21.5	4.3	2.0	13.2	6.8
1876-80	34.3	65.7	15.8	38.8	19.3	4.3	2.4	12.3	7.1
1881-85	33.8	66.2	16.8	39.8	19.3	4.5	2.9	11.2	5.5
1886-90	34.7	65.3	18.3	39.9	18.0	3.9	2.9	10.5	6.5
1891-95	34.0	66.0	20.4	38.7	17.5	4.0	3.4	9.9	6.1
1896-00	33.3	66.7	22.1	38.8	16.1	3.7	3.9	9.2	6.2
1901-05	32.9	67.1	23.1	38.8	15.3	3.9	3.9	9.0	6.0
1906-10	31.9	68.1	24.4	37.3	14.6	4.1	4.3	9.3	6.0
1911-15	30.7	69.3	24.8	37.4	13.3	4.4	4.9	9.1	6.1
1916-20	32.6	67.4	27.8	36.9	12.1	2.7	4.2	8.7	7.6
1921-25	31.8	68.2	35.2	33.3	10.7	1.2	3.9	7.7	8.0
1926-30	28.7	71.3	39.9	29.9	8.4	1.7	4.0	6.2	9.9
1931	27.2	72.8	41.6	27.5	7.4	1.5	4.0	7.8	10.2
1932	26.5	73.5	42.0	27.5	7.1	1.3	4.1	7.8	10.2
1933	25.8	74.2	43.7	25.4	8.0	1.6	3.9	6.9	10.5
1934	26.5	73.5	44.3	25.9	7.0	1.7	3.8	6.8	10.5
1935	26.9	73.1	44.4	26.1	6.9	1.9	3.3	6.6	10.8
1936	27.0	73.0	44.0	26.9	6.7	2.2	3.0	6.3	10.9
1937	26.5	73.5	44.6	25.9	6.8	2.5	2.9	6.1	11.2
1938	25.7	74.3	45.9	25.6	6.7	2.5	2.6	5.7	11.0
1939	25.3	74.7	47.1	25.2	6.1	2.6	2.5	5.8	10.7
1940	26.0	74.0	47.8	25.1	6.2	3.0	2.4	5.0	10.5
1941	26.4	73.6	47.3	24.0	5.9	2.8	2.2	4.6	13.2
1942	27.4	72.6	47.7	25.2	6.0	2.7	2.1	3.8	12.5
1943	29.2	70.8	50.4	24.2	5.2	2.8	2.0	4.2	11.2
1944	29.0	71.0	51.9	22.4	5.4	2.7	1.8	4.7	11.1
1945	28.6	71.4	54.6	20.0	5.6	2.8	1.8	4.3	10.9
1946	29.2	70.8	54.6	17.8	5.8	2.9	1.8	4.1	13.0
1947	27.5	72.5	55.0	17.5	5.3	2.9	1.8	3.8	13.7
1948	27.4	72.6	55.0	17.8	4.5	2.9	1.6	3.5	14.7
1949	26.8	73.2	58.2	17.1	2.7	2.9	1.7	3.1	14.3
1950	27.5	72.5	58.7	17.6	2.7	2.9	2.1	1.7	14.3

Note: Figures for 1867-1930 are averages of annual proportions.

Source of basic data: 1867-1906, 1916, 1922-1932, from reports by the Bureau of the Census; all other years, from Table A25.

Atlantic, namely, 17.4 per cent. In the North and West, on the other hand, the increases averaged only about 5 per cent. As a consequence of these trends, the differences among areas have diminished, but the pattern of variations has remained relatively unchanged. In 1948, the latest year for which nationwide data are available, the proportion granted to the wife varied from a maximum of 77.0 per cent in the Pacific states to a low of 68.2 per cent in the South Atlantic.

The proportions granted to husbands and wives during 1948, by geographic division and state, are shown in the left-hand columns of Table 59. Most noteworthy are the details for North Carolina, Louisiana, and Mississippi, in each of which wives obtained slightly less than 60 per cent of the total decrees.[3] These states, and the South in general, have always had relatively low percentages. As late as 1916 the proportion of divorces granted to the wife was only a shade over one half in North Carolina and Mississippi. Moreover, during the nineteenth century, more divorces were granted to husbands than to wives in the latter states as well as in Alabama, Florida, South Carolina,[4] Virginia, and West Virginia. The record for the South reflects in part traditional customs and attitudes. Southern women have always had a lesser degree of social and economic independence than women in the North and West. It is only in recent decades that large numbers of southern women have been gainfully employed and have thus become less dependent on their husband for support. In addition, the "unwritten" laws, which provide many rights to husbands but not to wives, have been rapidly disappearing but they still have great weight among large segments of the southern population.

---

[3]Outside of the South, Nevada had the lowest proportion granted to wives, namely, 66.4 per cent. This was also well below the national average.

[4]The figures for South Carolina shown in Table 59 refer to annulments only, since absolute divorces were not granted until 1949. With the enactment of the new divorce law, the proportion of decrees granted to the wife increased from 64.7 per cent in 1948 to about 68 per cent in 1949 and 1950, or to the approximate level for the South Atlantic states as a whole. It is likely that the rise in South Carolina was offset in part by a decline in Georgia, which formerly attracted divorce migrants from South Carolina.

LEGAL GROUNDS

Every jurisdiction in the United States allows absolute divorce and annulment, but the grounds differ widely in number and phraseology. To highlight significant trends and to maintain comparability, the data for recent years have been grouped according to the seven categories used in former reports by the Commissioner of Labor and the Bureau of the Census. These are cruelty, desertion, adultery, drunkenness, neglect to provide, combinations, and all others.[5] The statistics are shown in Tables 58, 59 and A25.

Cruelty. For about the past one hundred years, cruelty has been steadily increasing in relative importance as a ground for divorce. In the late 1860's it accounted for only one eighth of the total decrees in the United States, and was outranked by both desertion and adultery. By 1890 cruelty had overtaken adultery and since 1922 it has been in first place. The proportion of marriages dissolved by our courts on the grounds of cruelty increased to one fifth in 1891-95, reached two fifths in 1927, and was close to three fifths in 1950 (Table 58).

Every jurisdiction except Maryland, New York, and North Carolina allows divorce on the grounds of cruelty. However, the statutes vary in language; they include extreme cruelty, repeated cruelty, intolerable cruelty, physical cruelty, intolerable severity, cruel and abusive treatment, cruel and inhuman treatment, cruel and barbarous treatment, attempt to take life, personal indignities rendering life intolerable, excesses and outrages, treatment endangering reason, treatment injuring health, violence endangering life, and the like.

Cruelty is most frequently alleged in the Pacific and Mountain divisions of the country. During 1948 it represented about 70 per cent of all decrees in these areas. Several states outside of the West reported even higher proportions, as is evident from Table 59. In fact, the figures for Iowa (87.9 per cent), Maine (86.6 per cent), Michigan (85.5 per cent) and Texas (85.3 per

---

[5]Some countries tabulate all grounds specified in a decree, with the result that the sum of the figures by grounds exceeds the total number of decrees. However, this procedure has not found favor in the United States.

Table 59. Per Cent of Absolute Divorces and Annulments by Party to Which Granted, and by Legal Ground, by State, United States, 1948

Geographic Division and State	Granted To		Legal Ground						
	Husband	Wife	Cruelty	Desertion	Adultery	Drunkenness	Neglect to Provide	Combinations	All Others
UNITED STATES	27.4	72.6	55.0	17.8	4.5	2.9	1.6	3.5	14.7
New England	24.2	75.8	66.7	17.7	3.3	4.0	1.9	2.9	3.5
Maine	24.0	76.0	86.6	7.2	1.1	1.8	2.5	.0	.8
New Hampshire	28.9	71.1	71.9	1.4	5.7	1.4	*	15.2	4.4
Vermont	30.0	70.0	43.3	5.2	5.8	*	18.5	5.2	22.0
Massachusetts	23.1	76.9	70.8	19.1	2.5	2.9	1.6	.0	3.1
Rhode Island	20.8	79.2	32.8	20.6	1.1	17.1	2.4	25.7	.3
Connecticut	25.3	74.7	51.6	31.2	6.4	6.8	*	.7	3.3
Middle Atlantic	28.4	71.6	34.9	26.1	25.4	*	*	.3	13.3
New York	24.3	75.7	*	4.3†	62.9	*	*	*	32.8
New Jersey	32.0	68.0	19.0	69.0	8.5	*	*	.0	3.5
Pennsylvania	30.4	69.6	69.4	27.4	1.2	*	*	.6	1.4
East North Central	25.5	74.5	45.7	19.7	1.2	3.0	2.1	4.5	23.8
Ohio	27.1	72.9	12.9	4.1	.5	.2	*	7.8	74.5
Indiana	25.5	74.5	64.6	6.6	3.0	6.9	7.8	8.1	3.0
Illinois	24.2	75.8	36.5	53.7	1.8	5.7	*	.0	2.3
Michigan	25.8	74.2	85.5	5.7	.1	.3	4.2	2.8	1.4
Wisconsin	23.1	76.9	80.8	6.5	.3	.5	1.1	5.4	5.4
West North Central	24.2	75.8	64.3	14.8	1.1	2.1	.8	8.2	8.7
Minnesota	30.3	69.7	64.0	25.2	2.1	3.0	*	3.8	1.9
Iowa	22.8	77.2	87.9	7.3	.6	1.6	*	.0	2.6
Missouri	23.0	77.0	72.5	18.4	1.5	2.4	*	.0	5.2
North Dakota	25.3	74.7	53.6	17.0	.7	.7	7.8	17.0	3.2
South Dakota	25.9	74.1	73.9	16.4	.6	1.0	5.0	.0	3.1
Nebraska	22.7	77.3	78.6	6.4	.5	.7	6.5	4.1	3.2
Kansas	23.6	76.4	10.8	8.3	.4	1.9	*	44.0	34.6
South Atlantic	31.8	68.2	34.5	35.2	5.4	9.0	.0	1.2	14.7
Delaware	30.8	69.2	19.0	68.0	6.7	4.1	.0	.0	2.2
Maryland	33.5	66.5	*	74.9	15.4	*	*	.0	9.7
Dist. of Columbia	39.6	60.4	7.6	55.5	8.2	*	*	.0	28.7
Virginia	35.6	64.4	.0	81.7	9.2	*	*	4.9	4.2
West Virginia	34.4	65.6	35.6	27.9	11.7	18.1	*	4.2	2.5
North Carolina	42.8	57.2	*	*	7.0	*	*	.0	93.0
South Carolina	35.3	64.7	*	*	*	*	*	*	100.0
Georgia	16.3	83.7	59.4	12.6	1.0	24.6	*	1.0	1.4
Florida	33.4	66.6	60.3	29.3	.8	8.2	*	.0	1.4
East South Central	30.7	69.3	50.3	24.4	4.6	4.2	.1	12.7	3.7
Kentucky	28.4	71.6	66.9	14.0	4.8	5.6	*	.0	8.7
Tennessee	24.7	75.3	47.4	.4	2.4	1.0	.0	46.0	2.8
Alabama	32.1	67.9	41.1	44.0	5.2	5.8	.4	2.6	.9
Mississippi	40.1	59.9	44.1	43.0	6.6	4.4	*	.0	1.9
West South Central	29.8	70.2	70.1	7.5	2.6	.3	.9	1.8	16.8
Arkansas	37.3	62.7	70.8	16.0	.6	1.1	*	1.1	10.4
Louisiana	40.2	59.8	4.5	8.9	19.4	.2	*	.0	67.0
Oklahoma	23.7	76.3	47.2	8.1	1.2	.9	4.6	3.2	34.8
Texas	28.8	71.2	85.3	5.2	1.6	*	*	1.7	6.2
Mountain	27.5	72.5	69.4	5.8	.5	1.2	6.4	.9	15.8
Montana	27.3	72.7	60.3	17.8	1.0	1.2	13.2	.0	6.5
Idaho	26.3	73.7	79.5	8.8	.4	1.0	5.9	.0	4.4
Wyoming	28.2	71.8	73.4	7.2	.4	.4	4.7	9.4	4.5
Colorado	18.1	81.9	82.9	3.2	.1	.2	7.3	1.6	4.7
New Mexico	28.7	71.3	.8	7.6	.0	.4	1.9	1.5	87.8
Arizona	25.6	74.4	74.0	7.0	.5	4.4	4.4	.7	9.0
Utah	20.0	80.0	59.4	7.6	3.4	5.1	18.1	.6	5.8
Nevada	33.6	66.4	78.6	2.3	.1	.1	4.7	.0	14.2
Pacific	23.0	77.0	71.1	9.1	.9	2.6	3.2	1.9	11.2
Washington	24.5	75.5	64.6	9.4	1.8	5.2	11.0	2.6	5.4
Oregon	24.3	75.7	85.1	12.2	.0	.2	*	.0	2.5
California	22.5	77.5	70.4	8.5	.8	2.4	2.0	2.0	13.9

*No law.   †Dissolutions of marriage (Enoch Arden decrees).

Source of basic data: Statistics compiled by the author from publications and surveys of state, county, and court offices; includes estimates for areas which failed to provide information.

cent) exceeded those for any other individual state.[6]

Desertion. This category includes statutes pertaining to abandonment, absence for a period of years, willful desertion, utter desertion, and the like. Only the state of North Carolina makes no provision for dissolutions on this ground. The period of desertion, where specified, varies from one to five years and must be uninterrupted during the prescribed period. In addition to absence for five years, New York requires that the party seeking relief make diligent search to discover the absent husband or wife and believe that the spouse is dead (Enoch Arden decree).

Desertion as a proportion of total decrees has decreased sharply in the United States, falling from a peak of about 40 per cent in the 1880's to less than 18 per cent at mid-century. In part, this reflects the shift of divorce to the earlier years of marriage, since desertion is a more frequently *alleged* cause among suits started at the later durations.[7]

Desertion still is a popular ground for dissolving a marriage. In fact, the number of decrees granted for desertion has been increasing throughout most of our history. They reached an all-time high of about 112,000 in 1946 (Table A25) and, even with the general decline in divorce since that year, they amounted to about 68,000 in 1950—a larger number than in any year prior to 1941.

Although desertion now ranks second in the country as a whole, it is the leading ground in seven states and the District of Columbia. In four of these, it accounted for more than two thirds of the total decrees during 1948, namely, Virginia (81.7 per cent), Maryland (74.9 per cent), New Jersey (69.0 per cent) and Delaware (68.0 per cent).

Adultery. Although adultery now is a ground

for divorce in all areas of the country, it is a relatively minor cause everywhere but in New York. The latter state awards almost half of all absolute divorces granted for adultery in the United States. Such decrees accounted for 62.9 per cent of all marital dissolutions in New York during 1948. By contrast, the next highest proportion was only 19.4 per cent for Louisiana; Maryland followed with 15.4 per cent, and West Virginia with 11.7 per cent.

Adultery was the second leading ground for divorce in the United States in the mid-1800's. Since that time it has rapidly declined in relative importance, falling from 26 per cent of all marital dissolutions in the 1860's to about 11 per cent after World War I, and now is less than 3 per cent.

Drunkenness. Currently, drunkenness is a ground for divorce in all but eight states[8] and the District of Columbia. The statutes include habitual or continued drunkenness, habitual or continued intemperance, habitual or continued intoxication, voluntary and excessive use of opium, morphine, chloral, chloroform, cocaine, and the like.

Drunkenness has long been one of the common grounds for divorce in the United States, but it has never accounted for a substantial proportion of the marital dissolutions. At their maximum in 1876, decrees for drunkenness represented no more than 5 per cent of the total. Nevertheless, there are some interesting aspects to the long-term trend. Most noteworthy is the experience during and after World War I.

With the outbreak of hostilities in Europe, the proportion of decrees attributed to alcoholism in the United States declined from 4.5 per cent in 1914 to 3.3 per cent in 1918, and then plunged downward to the all-time low of 1.0 per cent in 1921 and 1922. One factor in the postwar downswing was undoubtedly the start of the great experiment in national prohibition. The Wartime Prohibition Act became effective months after the Armistice, on July 1, 1919, followed by the 18th Amendment to the Constitution, and the National Prohibition Law of January 16, 1920. However, it is not possible to determine from the available data whether the decline in the number

---

[6] It is interesting to note the experience of South Carolina under its new divorce law. Available data for 1949 indicate that cruelty accounted for only little more than one fifth of the total decrees. By contrast, desertion was alleged in about one half of the cases. In addition, about one sixth were granted for drunkenness and one twentieth for adultery; the balance were annulments.

[7] The indications are that desertion actually occurs most frequently in the first year of marriage and thereafter declines with advance in duration. See, for example, Charles E. Clark and H. Shulman, *A Study of Law Administration in Connecticut*, Yale University Press, New Haven, 1937, pp. 157-159.

[8] Maryland, New Jersey, New York, North Carolina, Pennsylvania, Texas, Vermont, and Virginia.

of divorces attributed to drunkenness represented, even in part, a true decrease in the incidence of alcoholism or whether it merely reflected a shift toward grounds which met with less public opprobrium. Regardless of the true influence of prohibition, the proportion of decrees attributed to drunkenness tended to increase after 1922 but still was only 1.6 per cent in 1933, when the Amendment was repealed (December 5). In the next seven years the proportion followed a more definite upward course, but since 1940 has remained close to 3 per cent.

In only a few of the states which grant divorce on account of drunkenness is the statute frequently used. In 1948 almost 25 per cent of the decrees in Georgia were attributed to this ground.[9] The proportions were also relatively high in West Virginia (18 per cent) and Rhode Island (17 per cent). In all other states, it was 8 per cent (Florida) or lower.

Neglect to Provide. In about half of the states, neglect to provide is a ground for absolute divorce.[10] The statutes include nonsupport, willful neglect, refusal to provide, failure to provide, and the like. In 1948, this ground was most frequently alleged in Vermont and Utah, where it represented about 18 per cent of all marriages legally dissolved. Such decrees also constituted more than one tenth of the total in Montana (13 per cent) and Washington (11 per cent). For the country as a whole, however, nonsupport was a relatively minor ground in 1948, as it has been throughout our history. In fact, even at the depth of the depression of the 1930's the proportion was only 4 per cent, or approximately the level which had prevailed in the earlier years of the century. More recently the proportion has declined; it was about 2 per cent in 1950.

Combinations. This category includes all decrees reported to have been granted on two or more of the preceding grounds, or of one of the preceding together with at least one other ground. Combinations of grounds have decreased in rela-

tive importance, falling from 13 per cent of all dissolutions around 1870 to about 2 per cent at present. In part, this decline may reflect an improvement in the statistics, that is, the less frequent recording of the grounds alleged in the complaint in lieu of the ground on which the decree was granted.[11]

All Other Grounds. State statutes also provide a variety of other grounds for dissolving a marriage. These have been grouped into one category, "all others," and include, whether occurring separately or in combination, bigamy, fraudulent contract, loathsome disease, conviction for a felony or other infamous crime, impotency, insanity, imprisonment in penitentiary, incest, incompatibility, mental incapacity, gross neglect of duty, non-age, pregnancy before marriage, voluntary separation, and the like. It should be noted that all annulment decrees are included in this category.

These miscellaneous grounds, as a group, have greatly increased in relative importance, and now account for about one seventh of all decrees of absolute divorce and annulment in the country. Several factors have contributed to this upswing. Foremost has been the gradual admission in recent decades of voluntary separation as a ground for divorce. In 1948, the latest year for which nationwide data are available, about 13,300 decrees (3 per cent of the total) were attributed to this ground. The largest number—close to 6,000—were granted in North Carolina, where they accounted for 91 per cent of all decrees. The proportions were also relatively high in Louisiana (63 per cent), the District of Columbia (24 per cent), Vermont (20 per cent) and Nevada (14 per cent). In the other 13 states with such statutes,[12] less than one tenth of the dissolutions were granted on this ground.

Voluntary separation is one of the very few

[9]The relative importance of this ground in Georgia declined sharply after 1948, possibly due in part to the 1949 law in South Carolina which permits divorce for drunkenness.

[10]Neglect to provide is not a statutory ground for divorce in Oklahoma. However, the state courts have interpreted the statute "gross neglect of duty" to allow divorce for failure to support, and many decrees are granted on the latter ground.

[11]The plaintiff wishes to assure the granting of the decree and thus tends to "build up" the case by alleging several grounds; by contrast, the court procedure tends toward the one ground which is least difficult to prove. For example, in Ohio during 1930, only 24 per cent of the divorces were granted on two or more grounds, whereas multiple grounds had been alleged in 52 per cent of the petitions. See Leon C. Marshall and G. May, *op. cit.*, p. 310.

[12]Arizona, Arkansas, Idaho, Kentucky, Maryland, Minnesota, North Dakota, Rhode Island, Texas, Utah, Washington, Wisconsin, and Wyoming.

grounds for absolute divorce which is not based on the defendant's fault, but recognizes that it is for the best interests of society and of the parties themselves to allow dissolution of a marriage which has factually ceased to exist. Even more noteworthy in this respect is New Mexico's law, enacted in 1933, which permits divorce for incompatibility. That the statute has become popular is evident from the fact that almost seven eighths of the decrees in New Mexico are now granted on this ground.

Gross neglect of duty is also numerically important among the miscellaneous grounds, even though statutes exist in only three states. In 1948 it accounted for more than two thirds of all decrees in Ohio and for almost one third in Kansas and Oklahoma. The other specific grounds are used much less frequently. Bigamy, for example, was the ground for only 3,600 decrees of absolute divorce and annulment in the country as a whole.

Comment. It is well known that the legal grounds for divorce bear little relation to the causes underlying family dissolution. The grounds are merely the tests which the laws of a particular state accept as evidence that a marriage has failed. Often the actual cause is not a legal ground in the particular state in which the court action takes place. Even more frequently, the ground alleged in a complaint is the one which can be most easily established to the satisfaction of the court according to the statutes of the particular jurisdiction.[13]

Most grounds—particularly the popular ones, such as cruelty, desertion, and adultery—relate to what people do or have done. They are the symptoms or end results rather than the underlying causes of marriage failure. Very likely this is all that can be expected from judicial statistics. As John Milton pointed out in his *The Doctrine and Discipline of Divorce* during the seventeenth century, no court is capable of inquiring into "the secret reason of dissatisfaction between man and wife." In fact, attempts to probe deeply into the psychological and physiological causes may do more harm than good, by unnecessarily aggravating the sufferings of the parties. A multiplicity of studies have advanced numerous

[13]For examples of evidence advanced in support of alleged grounds, see Leon C. Marshall and G. May, *op. cit.*, Vol. 1 (Maryland), 1932, pp. 171 ff.

hypotheses and explanations for the social and individual situations which lead to divorce.[14] However, in most instances it may be nothing more than the fact that when the spark of love, of comradeship, and of mutual respect no longer exists in a marriage, the relationship has no further meaning for the couple concerned.

ALIMONY

In the course of the procedures for dissolving a marriage, the courts may also entertain motions relating to such incidental matters as alimony or division of property, custody and maintenance of the children, counsel fees, and court costs. Details regarding custody of children are given in Chapter 10; the remainder of this chapter is devoted largely to information on the support of the parties after divorce.

Years ago, under common law, a man became entitled to absolute ownership of the chattels and earnings of the woman he married. In the event that they were legally separated, the husband did not lose his marital rights in his wife's property with the result that she was left with no means of support. To prevent the wife from falling into a destitute state, the ecclesiastical courts upon granting a separation (divorce *a mensa et thoro*) ordered the husband to provide

[14]See, for example, Alfred Cahen, *Statistical Analysis of American Divorce*, Columbia University Press, New York, 1932, pp. 45 ff. Several of the studies reported by Dr. Cahen, as well as by others, have been based on attempts to deduce the underlying causes from information available in court records or in the files of lawyers, family organizations, and the like. Typical examples are the analyses by T. Earl Sullenger, "A Study of Divorce and Its Causation in Douglas County, Nebraska," *University of Nebraska Bulletin*, March, 1927, second printing by the Municipal University of Omaha, August, 1932, pp. 12-15, and by Harry C. Harmsworth and M. S. Minnis, "Non-Statutory Causes of Divorce: The Lawyer's Point of View," *Marriage and Family Living*, 17:316-321, November, 1955. Generally, financial matters, use of alcoholic beverages, and various aspects of sexual relations loom large as problem areas. However, such classifications contribute little to our understanding of divorce causation. They are largely different listings of the kinds of things people do or are interested in. In other words, it is only natural that, when married people disagree, they will quarrel over such matters. Thus, differences over finances, for example, merely indicate the nature of incidents which furnish the evidence in support of the statutory grounds for divorce.

money for his wife's maintenance. This was referred to as alimony, derived from *alimentum*, which literally means nourishment or sustenance.

In the United States an award similar to the provisions established by the ecclesiastical courts may be made when a marriage is dissolved, as well as in connection with a separation. These awards, ordered by civil courts according to state statute, are called alimony. In theory, however, they are not alimony when given after a divorce, since the husband's duty to support and maintain his wife was removed when the marriage was dissolved.

The amount of alimony is supposed to be reasonable according to the husband's wealth, and sufficient to provide the food, clothing, habitation, and other items necessary for the wife's sustenance. In general, alimony is predicated on the existence of a valid marriage. Thus it is not usual in cases of annulment. However, there are exceptions to this rule.[15] For example, a woman who obtains an annulment from a man on the ground of his prior subsisting marriage may be awarded alimony.

Since at common law the wife had no duty to support her husband, he is not entitled to alimony from his ex-wife unless it is specifically allowed by statute—which is the case today in twelve states.[16] Moreover, such awards are infrequent and, when made, they often consist of the division of the wife's property to provide for children in the father's custody. On the other hand, it is not unusual for alimony to be granted to the wife in cases in which the husband petitions for and obtains the divorce. Thus, if alimony is awarded, it almost always is to the wife.

Strictly speaking, alimony and property settlement are dissimilar. Unlike alimony, which is payable in installments during the joint lives of the parties, the total amount payable under a property division is fixed and ascertainable. Moreover, an order for property settlement is not subject to later modification as is a decree for alimony. Child support is also related, but different from alimony. It is founded on the fact that a father has the obligation to support his child during minority even if the child is awarded to someone else's custody, unless the divorce decree provides otherwise.

Frequency of Awards. Reliable information on the frequency of alimony and other forms of support is hard to come by. The most complete data are those formerly published by the Bureau of the Census. These indicate that 13.4 per cent of the divorces around the turn of the century (1887-1906) included requests for permanent alimony, but it was awarded in only 9.3 per cent of the cases. In 1916 it was demanded by 20.3 per cent and awarded in 15.4 per cent. According to the tabulations for 1922, the latest year for which nationwide data are available, alimony was decreed in 14.7 per cent of the divorces. These statistics relate to permanent alimony secured as an incident to the divorce suit. Since financial considerations are often made apart from the divorce proceeding, the figures understate the true frequency of alimony awards.

The data for recent years are even more deficient. For one thing, they are available for only a few areas; equally important, they have not been tabulated in a uniform manner and therefore are not strictly comparable. The figures for around 1939 and 1950 are shown in Table 60. It would appear that alimony or property settlement awards are now made in about one fourth of the marriages dissolved in the United States. The proportion varies considerably from state to state according to existing statutes, local customs, extent of migratory divorce,[17] and other factors.

Women are more likely to be awarded alimony if they obtain the divorce. During 1939, for

---

[15] Alimony in some form may be allowed in connection with annulment decrees in the District of Columbia and in nine states, namely, Connecticut, Iowa, New Hampshire, New Jersey, New Mexico, Oregon, Vermont, Virginia, and West Virginia. It may also be awarded for the duration of the interlocutory period in New York and until the final decree *(pendente lite)* in Wisconsin.

[16] Iowa, Massachusetts, New Hampshire, North Dakota, Ohio, Oklahoma, Oregon, Pennsylvania (only if husband is insane), Utah, Virginia, Washington, and West Virginia. A number of other states have statutes allowing provision for the husband out of the wife's property.

[17] An order to pay alimony cannot be imposed upon a nonresident defendant in a divorce suit, except as to property situated within the jurisdiction, unless he is summoned or voluntarily appears in court. See, for example, John W. Morland, *Keezer on the Law of Marriage and Divorce,* Third Edition, The Bobbs-Merrill Company, Indianapolis, 1946, p. 610. The low proportion of awards in states which attract divorce migrants may also be due, in part, to prior financial settlements which are not incorporated into the divorce action.

Table 60. Alimony or Property Settlement Awards as a Percentage of Absolute Divorces and Annulments, Selected Areas of the United States, Around 1939 and 1950

Area	Around 1939		Around 1950	
	Per Cent	Year	Per Cent	Year
Alabama	13.6	1939	*	*
Florida‡	10.7	1939	7.2	1949
Illinois‡	*	*	13.8	1948
Iowa	28.3	1939	25.5	1948
Kansas	35.1	1941-42†	48.4	1955-56†
Michigan	37.2	1939	*	*
Missouri	*	*	29.6	1950
Nebraska	42.2	1939	35.4	1952
Ohio	24.3§	1939-40†	43.7	♦
Oklahoma	21.3	1939	*	*
Virginia§	14.4	1941	12.1	1950
Wisconsin	40.5	1939	*	*
Wyoming	*	*	22.3	1949-50

*Not available. †Fiscal year. ‡Cook County only.
♦Cuyahoga County, fiscal year 1946-47 and Summit County, fiscal year 1948-49. §Alimony only.

Source of basic data: Published reports and surveys by the author.

example, alimony was allowed the wife in 30 per cent of the cases in which she was granted the decree, but in only 16 per cent of those in which the divorce was granted to the husband.[18] Requests for alimony are also allowed more frequently when the welfare of children is involved.[19]

Size of Awards. Every investigation has shown that the "alimony racket" exists largely in newspaper headlines concerning a few sensational cases. The fact is that the typical divorcee re-

[18]Based on data for Alabama, Florida, Iowa, Michigan, Nebraska, Oklahoma, and Wisconsin.
[19]Sam B. Warner, "San Francisco Divorce Suits," *California Law Review*, 9:180, March, 1921. Among the suits filed in 1913 and early 1914, alimony was received by almost two thirds of the women awarded custody of children, compared with less than one tenth of those without young children. See, also, Leon C. Marshall and G. May, *op. cit.*, Vol. 1, pp. 311-312 and Vol. 2, pp. 340-341. For example, among the decrees granted in Ohio during the second half of 1930, women awarded custody of children fared almost four times as well as did women without children.

ceives only a modest amount of alimony, and property settlement usually represents little more than a reasonable share of the household furnishings. For example, Marshall and May[20] reported that in Maryland and Ohio, around 1930, about one half of the periodic payment awards for alimony and child support totaled $33 or less monthly. The number of children to be supported had little effect on the size of the award, the amount per individual diminishing as the size of the family increased.

Since alimony and child support awards are governed, in part at least, by general economic conditions, their size has increased in recent years. Nevertheless, most amounts still are relatively small. In New Jersey, for example, one half of the payments ordered during 1949 was for less than $74 monthly.

Alimony transactions have become big business in the United States, their volume increasing steadily since the depths of the depression. In the Detroit area alone (Wayne County), more than $49 million in alimony and child support money was collected and paid out during the 1940's.[21] The receipts now exceed $10 million a year, or four times the annual payments in the period immediately prior to World War II. The increases have been equally large in many other metropolitan areas. Between 1940 and 1950, payments rose by 250 per cent in Cuyahoga County (includes Cleveland), by 517 per cent in Hamilton County (includes Cincinnati), and by 733 per cent in Sedgwick County (includes Wichita).

[20]*Ibid.*, Vol. 1, p. 312 and Vol. 2, p. 333.
[21]In Michigan, the collection of alimony and child support money is administered by the Office of the Friend of the Court. The agency was first established in Wayne County by court rule in 1918. A year later, it was extended by statute to all of the state's circuit courts. All payments are made directly to the court, rather than to the ex-wife. Thus, refusal to pay is automatic ground for contempt. However, when a man becomes financially embarrassed, the Friend of the Court can start procedures to reduce the size of the payments.

Chapter 10

CHILDREN IN DIVORCE

THE long-term rise of divorce has been accompanied by a torrent of articles on what is right and what is wrong with the American family. A recurrent theme has been the effect of divorce on children, and yet statistical documentation has been woefully inadequate. Few data concerning children affected by divorce have been available since 1932, and even those for earlier years were very limited in scope.[1] The present chapter extends the series of data formerly published by the Bureau of the Census, and also includes details on child custody, differentials in divorce by size of family and duration of marriage,[2] and orphanhood.

---

[1] The available statistics on children are subject to numerous deficiencies. State records may refer to all children regardless of age, children under a specified age, or to minor children (the age of which also varies according to the laws of the individual state). There is also variation in what is reported by the different courts within a state. In addition to the children of the present marriage, the figures may or may not include adopted children and stepchildren. Some courts include all living minors, others limit the number to those residing at home. Some report unmarried children over 21 years of age who live with their parents, and others include "prenatal children" covered by the decree. As a whole, the data now reported closely approximate, but undoubtedly understate, the number of children under 21 years of age in families dissolved by divorce.

It should also be noted that the recent statistics are not strictly comparable to those published by the Bureau of the Census for various years prior to 1933. Those for 1867-1886 are supposed to represent the number of children by the marriage, but it is likely that they relate largely to children affected by the decree. Moreover, the data cannot be used because of the relatively large number of decrees with no report as to children and the conflicting evidence as to whether the latter represent "no children" or omissions from court records of information regarding children. On the other hand, although the data for 1887-1906, 1916, and 1922-1932 also have their limitations, they appear to approximate the number of minor children affected by divorce.

[2] Preliminary findings were published in Paul H. Jacobson, "Differentials in Divorce by Duration of Marriage and Size of Family," *American Sociological Review*, 15:235-244, April, 1950.

GENERAL PATTERN

More children are affected by divorce than is generally realized. About 343,000 minor children were involved in the 377,000 final decrees of divorce and annulment during 1955, or roughly nine children for every ten marriages dissolved. However, close to 53 per cent of the divorced couples had no children. This means that about 47 per cent had children, and among them there was an average of 1.93 children per couple.

The proportion of divorces involving children varies considerably with the duration of marriage, as may be seen from Table 61, which summarizes the experience in 1948. The proportion with children rises from about 9 per cent for marriages ended in the first year to a maximum of 64 per cent in the 18th year. Beyond that duration, the proportion drops steadily, since an increasing number of the offspring have grown up or left home. It is noteworthy that children were involved in more than half of all decrees obtained by couples married 7 to 22 years. The fact that a majority of the total decrees—almost three fifths—did not involve children is explained largely by the heavy concentration of divorces and annulments[3] in the early years of marriage when couples are less likely to have children. About 55 per cent of the marriages dissolved in 1948 had endured for less than 7 years.

As might be expected, the average number of

---

[3] A couple with children may have their marriage annulled if they have legal grounds for an annulment. However, such decrees constitute only a small proportion of all dissolutions involving children in the country as a whole. Even in New York State, where they are much more frequent, only about one sixth of the decrees involving children are annulments (Table A24). At common law the children of an annulled marriage were considered illegitimate, but many states now have statutes which provide that the offspring of such marriages shall be legitimate. Some states have even modified their divorce law to include the grounds for annulment, in order to protect the interests of the offspring and parties to a marriage which is dissolved on such grounds.

Table 61. Decrees Involving Children and Number of Children, Absolute Divorces and Annulments by Duration of Marriage, United States, 1948

Duration of Marriage (Years)	Total Decrees	Decrees Involving Children		Children Involved		
					Ratio to	
		Number	Per Cent	Number	Total Decrees	Decrees with Children
Total	423,213	175,713	41.5	322,000	.76	1.8
0	31,448	2,931	9.3	3,785	.12	1.3
1	43,187	9,034	20.9	10,845	.25	1.2
2	45,224	13,862	30.7	16,622	.37	1.2
3	33,262	12,382	37.2	15,819	.48	1.3
4	27,909	12,006	43.0	16,633	.60	1.4
5	27,313	12,293	45.0	18,226	.67	1.5
6	23,646	11,525	48.7	18,490	.78	1.6
7	20,406	11,134	54.6	19,014	.93	1.7
8	17,368	9,459	54.5	17,460	1.01	1.8
9	14,671	8,009	54.6	15,790	1.08	2.0
10	13,051	7,271	55.7	15,064	1.15	2.1
11	11,990	6,903	57.6	14,454	1.21	2.1
12	11,102	6,552	59.0	14,033	1.26	2.1
13	9,612	5,821	60.6	12,676	1.32	2.2
14	8,780	5,363	61.1	12,295	1.40	2.3
0-4	181,030	50,215	27.7	63,704	.35	1.3
5-9	103,404	52,420	50.7	88,980	.86	1.7
10-14	54,535	31,910	58.5	68,522	1.26	2.1
15-19	33,582	20,968	62.4	51,160	1.52	2.4
20-24	23,511	12,151	51.7	30,697	1.31	2.5
25-29	14,528	5,266	36.2	12,235	.84	2.3
30-34	7,374	1,950	26.4	4,680	.63	2.4
35-39	3,363	642	19.1	1,555	.46	2.4
40 and over	1,886	191	10.1	467	.25	2.4

Source: Estimated by the author from statistics for a large number of states and counties.

AGE OF CHILDREN

The concentration of divorce-children in the early years of marriage means, obviously, that a large proportion of the children are relatively young. National data on this point are lacking, but statistics for several areas indicate that about two thirds of the children affected by divorce are under age 10. Marshall and May,[5] for example, in their investigations in Maryland and Ohio for the period around 1930, found that 63 per cent of the children were under 10 years of age—a much higher proportion than prevailed among children in the general population. More recent statistics for Multnomah County, Oregon[6] and Cook County, Illinois,[7] indicate that the proportion at ages under 10 has increased somewhat, to about 69 per cent. This increase in the proportion of younger children probably results from the relatively larger number of divorces now occurring in the early years of marriage. In other words, it is likely that the age distribution of children involved in divorce at each duration of marriage has changed little in recent decades.

children in families dissolved by divorce increases with the duration of marriage.[4] The average per parent couple rises from 1.2 children for marriages dissolved after the first year to a maximum of 2.5 at durations 20-24 years. The ratio of the number of children to the total number of divorces climbs rapidly to a peak of 1.5 at durations 15-19, and thereafter declines. The actual number of children involved, however, is at a maximum in a much earlier period of married life. In 1948 the divorces at durations 5-9 years accounted for almost 28 per cent of the total children.

TREND

The average number of children per divorce involving children has varied over a relatively narrow range. It declined gradually after the turn of the century to a low of 1.73 in 1933 and then followed a general upward course. In most years since 1940 the ratio has been at or above 1.87, the average which prevailed during the period 1887-1906. Even more marked has been the recent upswing in the proportion of decrees involving children, as may be seen from Table 62. From a minimum of 36 per cent in 1940, the proportion has climbed almost without

[4] The ratio in the first year of marriage, namely, 1.3 children per family with children, may be due in part to a relatively high divorce rate among the remarried with children of a previous marriage. Divorces following premarital pregnancy may also be a contributing factor. In this connection, see Harold T. Christensen and H. H. Meissner, "Studies in Child Spacing: III—Premarital Pregnancy as a Factor in Divorce," *American Sociological Review*, 18:641-644, December, 1953.

[5] Leon C. Marshall and G. May, *The Divorce Court*, The Johns Hopkins Press, Baltimore, Vol. 1 (Maryland), 1932, pp. 82-83 and Vol. 2 (Ohio), 1933, pp. 115-117.

[6] Read Bain, *et al.*, "Divorce and Children of Divorce," *Portland City Club Bulletin*, 30:350, June 17, 1949.

[7] Analysis by Judge Edwin A. Robson of 11,300 divorce cases heard by him in Superior Court from September, 1945, to July 2, 1948; and cases filed in Superior and Circuit Courts from 1940 to 1946.

interruption to about 47 per cent in 1955. As a result, the number of children per divorce has increased from 0.68 at the beginning of the second world conflict to 0.91 at present. This means that the annual number of children affected by divorce has risen more rapidly than has the number of divorces. In fact, each year since 1953 one third of a million children have been involved. Only at the close of World War II, when record numbers of divorces and annulments occurred, were more children affected. An all-time high of 471,000 children were involved during 1946, and the annual number was not much below 400,000 in 1945 and 1947.

One aspect of the experience during the depression of the 1930's is of special interest. Since divorce is generally more costly when children are involved, one might have expected a decline in the proportion with children. However, the opposite occurred; decrees involving children as a proportion of all decrees increased from 38.5 per cent in 1926-30 to 40.4 per cent in 1935.

CUSTODY OF CHILDREN

The great majority of minor children are entrusted to the custody of their mother, as may be seen from Table 63. Although the experience varies somewhat from area to area, the mother receives custody in close to four fifths of all cases and the father in only about one tenth. In the relatively few remaining cases, both parents are given custody for part of the time, or the children are awarded to a relative or guardian. The available data also indicate that there has been little if any change in the pattern of custody dispositions since before the turn of the century.

In most instances, children are awarded to the petitioner for divorce. Around 1930, for example, the proportion was close to 70 per cent in Maryland and about 75 per cent in Ohio. Available statistics for more recent years show a similar pattern. Plaintiffs were awarded 83 per cent of

Table 62. Decrees Involving Children and Number of Children, Absolute Divorces and Annulments, United States, 1887-1955

Period	Total Decrees	Decrees Involving Children		Children Involved		
		Number	Per Cent	Number (1,000's)	Ratio to	
					Total Decrees	Decrees with Children
1887-91	157,324	80,806	51.4	*	*	*
1892-96	194,939	99,723	51.2	*	*	*
1897-01	260,720	130,483	50.0	*	*	*
1902-06	332,642	159,450	47.9	*	*	*
1887-06	945,625	470,462	49.8	882	.93	1.87
1916	114,000	47,870	42.0	*	*	*
1922-25	673,564	255,975	38.0	467	.69	1.82
1926-30	982,983	378,690	38.5	676	.69	1.79
1931-35	939,244	375,023	39.9	653	.70	1.74
1936-40	1,244,722	478,322	38.4	867	.70	1.81
1941-45	1,874,391	703,691	37.5	1,417	.76	2.01
1946-50	2,326,806	960,006	41.3	1,786	.77	1.86
1951-55	1,919,000	870,800	45.4	1,640	.85	1.88
1931	188,003	73,539	39.1	130	.69	1.77
1932	164,241	65,484	39.9	114	.69	1.74
1933	165,000	66,000	40.0	114	.69	1.73
1934	204,000	82,000	40.2	143	.70	1.74
1935	218,000	88,000	40.4	153	.70	1.74
1936	236,000	91,000	38.6	162	.69	1.78
1937	249,000	99,000	39.8	177	.71	1.79
1938	244,000	95,000	38.9	171	.70	1.80
1939	251,000	98,000	39.0	177	.71	1.81
1940	264,722	95,322	36.0	180	.68	1.89
1941	294,939	106,539	36.1	202	.68	1.90
1942	321,329	119,429	37.2	229	.71	1.92
1943	359,179	132,779	37.0	277	.77	2.09
1944	412,618	156,718	38.0	323	.78	2.06
1945	486,326	188,226	38.7	386	.79	2.05
1946	628,760	251,060	39.9	471	.75	1.88
1947	496,106	203,006	40.9	380	.77	1.87
1948	423,213	175,713	41.5	322	.76	1.83
1949	393,800	164,300	41.7	310	.79	1.89
1950	384,927	165,927	43.1	303	.79	1.83
1951†	381,000	166,900	43.8	306	.80	1.83
1952†	392,000	173,500	44.3	320	.82	1.84
1953†	390,000	175,100	44.9	330	.85	1.88
1954†	379,000	177,300	46.8	341	.90	1.92
1955†	377,000	178,000	47.2	343	.91	1.93

*Not available. †Provisional.

Source of basic data regarding children: 1887-1932, from Bureau of the Census; 1933-1955, estimated by the author from statistics for selected areas. Data are not available for 1907-1915 and 1917-1921.

the children in Montana during 1948 and 71 per cent in New Jersey during 1949; in Missouri, the proportion was 80 per cent during 1948-1955. Apparently the proportion was also within this range in Tennessee during 1949, since in 81 per cent of the cases the children were awarded to the parent who was granted the divorce.

When the mother initiates the action for divorce or annulment, which is generally the case, it is all but universal to vest her with custody of the minor children. On the other hand, when

Table 63. Custody Disposition of Children Involved in Absolute Divorces and Annulments, Selected Areas of the United States at Various Periods from 1875 to 1957

Area and Period	Data Refer to	Per Cent Awarded to		
		Mother	Father	Other*
Connecticut (New Haven County), 1919-1932†	Cases	85.4	14.6	0.0
Illinois (Cook County), 1945-1948‡	Cases	85.7	9.0	5.3
Kansas, 1927-1939♦	Children	86.6	12.0	1.4
1940-1943	Children	86.6	11.1	2.3
1944-1946	Cases	83.3	11.1	5.6
1947-1950 (Sedgwick County)	Children	85.0	12.5	2.5
1957	Cases	86.6	8.3	5.1
Maryland, 1929§	Cases	68.3	10.2	21.5
Minnesota (Hennepin County), 1875-1899	Children	77.6	9.1	13.3
1900-1919	Children	76.3	9.3	14.4
1920-1939	Children	79.8	9.3	10.9
Missouri, 1948-1955	Cases	84.4	8.4	7.2
New Jersey, 1949	Cases	74.4	6.9	18.7
Ohio, 1900-1919	Cases	84.8	15.1	.1
1920-1939	Cases	83.4	12.9	3.7
1940-1942	Cases	80.8	13.4	5.8
1949 (Stark and Summit Counties)	Cases	87.3	12.7	.0
Tennessee, 1949	Cases	81.7	6.0	12.3

*Both parents, relatives, guardian, reserved, or not reported.
†Excludes divided awards, from C. E. Clark and H. Shulman, A Study of Law Administration in Connecticut, Yale Univ. Press, New Haven, 1937, pp. 160-161.
‡Superior Court only.
♦Excludes 1932, 1934, and 1936, for which data are not available.
§From L. C. Marshall and G. May, The Divorce Court, The Johns Hopkins Press, Baltimore, Vol. 1 (Maryland), 1932, p. 316.

Source of basic data: State or county reports, unless otherwise noted.

offices, but a few are vigorously contested even in the courtroom.

About four fifths of all divorce petitions are filed by the parent who has *de facto* custody of the children. Among the remaining fifth, the number of actions initiated by the father is approximately double the number by the mother, judging by the experience in New Jersey during 1949.

DIVORCE RATE BY SIZE OF FAMILY

It is widely believed that the presence of children in a family acts as a powerful deterrent to divorce. This view probably had its origin in the high proportion of divorces to couples without children, but it has also received undocumented support from our technical literature. For example, consider this statement in a published dissertation[9] from one of our leading universities:

...71 per cent of childless marriages in America end in divorce, while only 8 per cent of married couples with children eventually are divorced.

the father is the plaintiff, the children are as likely to be assigned to the mother as to the father (Table 64). This does not necessarily mean that our courts tend to favor the mother. In our society both parents have an equal claim upon the children.[8] However, many men recognize that their children will be better cared for by the mother. Moreover, when a couple separate, even if they disagree regarding the custody of the children, the tendency is for the children to stay with the mother. In consequence, most minor children are living with their mother at the time a divorce action is started, and the courts infrequently alter this arrangement. Nevertheless, disputes regarding child custody may be bitter and prolonged. Some are resolved in attorneys'

[8]For a review of the situation in primitive societies, see Kingsley Davis, "Children of Divorced Parents: A Sociological and Statistical Analysis," *Law and Contemporary Problems*, Summer, 1944, pp. 700-720.

Table 64. Custody Disposition of Children According to Plaintiff, Absolute Divorces and Annulments in Selected States

Plaintiff, State and Period	Per Cent of Cases Awarded to			
	Mother	Father	Other*	Unknown
Mother				
Maryland, 1929	85.1	2.4	3.3	9.2
Missouri, 1948-1955	92.6	2.5	2.6	2.3
New Jersey, 1949	86.0	1.1	.3	12.6
Ohio, 1930	85.9	2.2	4.5	7.4
Tennessee, 1949†	90.9	1.1	5.2	2.8
Father				
Maryland, 1929	25.3	30.3	7.0	37.4
Missouri, 1948-1955	53.3	32.0	6.3	8.4
New Jersey, 1949	45.0	24.0	4.7	26.3
Ohio, 1930	34.1	37.5	8.8	19.6
Tennessee, 1949†	32.3	32.3	26.8	8.6

*Both parents, relatives, or guardian.
†Refers to party granted the decree.

Source of basic data: L. C. Marshall and G. May, The Divorce Court, The Johns Hopkins Press, Baltimore, Vol. 1 (Maryland), 1932, p. 316 and Vol. 2 (Ohio), 1933, p. 346; and state reports.

[9]Alfred Cahen, *Statistical Analysis of American Divorce*, Columbia University Press, New York, 1932, p. 113.

Clearly, this would seem to indicate that the likelihood of divorce is nine times greater in childless marriages than in those with children. However, this ratio of nine is so much greater than that reported for other countries, namely, 2.0 for Amsterdam[10] in 1929-1932 and 2.2 for Sweden[11] in 1933, that it is desirable to review the statistical basis for the quotation. Actually, the statement is based on the erroneous assumption that if 17 per cent of American married women never bear children, 17 per cent of the marriages existing in 1928 had no children. Obviously, if 17 per cent of married women reach the end of their reproductive life span without ever having borne children, then the proportion childless among women in the early years of marriage is much greater than 17 per cent. Moreover, not all children survive. Also, at the later years of marriage, an increasing proportion of the children reach adulthood, marry, or leave their family for other reasons. Therefore the proportion of all existing marriages without children must have been much greater than 17 per cent. As a matter of fact, the figure in 1928 was about twice as large, according to estimates derived from available data.[12] Using these population estimates, and including annulments with the divorces, it is found that the divorce rate in 1928 was approximately 14.9 per 1,000 for the existing marriages without children and about 4.4 for those with children. In other words, the divorce rate was only 3.4 times greater for the "childless"—not 9 times greater.

At this point it may be appropriate to ascertain whether later data can throw any additional light on this question. Recent surveys by the Bureau of the Census[13] provide data from which it is possible to estimate the distribution of existing marriages according to number of children under 18.

The divorce data, however, refer largely to the number of children under 21 years of age. It is necessary, therefore, to translate the divorce data into their distribution by number of children under age 18. This was accomplished by means of the statistics by Marshall and May[14] on the age distribution of children in divorce according to marital duration. In making this adjustment, it was assumed that the ratio of the children under 18 to those under 21 at any one specified duration of marriage was independent of the number of children in a family.[15]

For 1948 the indications are that the divorce rate was 14.9 per 1,000 among marriages not involving children. This is 1.7 times the rate among those with children, which was 8.8 per 1,000. Since 1948 the decline in divorce has been somewhat greater among the "childless," with the result that the ratio dropped slightly to 1.6 in 1955. In other words, during recent years the rate among "childless" marriages has been less than double the rate among families with children, which is more like the situation of years ago in Amsterdam and Sweden, as previously noted.

Although the difference in the divorce rate between couples with and without children has diminished, the rate still varies inversely with the number of children in the family (Table 65). For

Table 65. Divorces and Annulments per 1,000 Existing Marriages, According to Size of Family, United States, 1928, 1948, and 1955

Year	Total	Without Children	With Children	Number of Children			
				One	Two	Three	Four or More
1928	7.8	14.9	4.4	7.4	4.3	2.8	1.5
1948	11.6	14.9	8.8	11.4	7.7	6.5	5.4
1955	9.3	11.9	7.4	10.9	6.8	5.2	4.1

Note: 1928 relates to children under age 21; 1948 and 1955, to children under 18. Data for 1955 are provisional.

Source: Estimated by the author.

[10] J. H. van Zanten and T. van den Brink, "Population Phenomena in Amsterdam," *Population*, August, 1938, p. 30.

[11] Carl-Erik Quensel, "Frequency of Divorce with Special Regard to the Number of Children," *Annex No. 6*, Statistical Institute in Lund, 1938, p. 202 (in Swedish).

[12] Total existing marriages from Table A22; distribution by number of children, derived from Bureau of the Census, *Types of Families in the United States, 1930*, released on August 5, 1935. The indications are that about 32 per cent had no dependent children under 21.

[13] Bureau of the Census, *Current Population Reports*, Series P-20 (various issues).

[14] Leon C. Marshall and G. May, *op. cit.*, Vol. 1, p. 81 and Vol. 2, p. 115.

[15] The ratio of children under 18 to children under 21 does not deviate substantially from unity until about the 20th year of marriage, when the frequency of divorce and the number of children fall off rapidly. Thus, although most divorces and annulments are reported by number of children under 21, it is unlikely that the accuracy of the data is materially affected by the adjustment.

couples without children, the divorce rate in 1955 was 11.9 per 1,000. Where one child was present, the estimated rate was 10.9 per 1,000. The figure thus continues to decrease, and in families with four or more children the rate was 4.1. Altogether, the rate for couples with minor children was 7.4 per 1,000.

Before drawing any conclusions from these rates, it is important to ascertain whether the differential results from the fact that "childless" marriages and those with children are of different composition with regard to duration. In other words, how does the divorce rate for the two groups compare at specified durations of marriage? These duration-specific rates are shown in Figure 7 and Table 66; the data relate to 1948, the only year for which such statistics are available. It is readily apparent that the differential in the divorce rate between "childless" couples

Table 66. Divorce Rate for Existing Marriages With and Without Children Under Age 18, According to Duration of Marriage, United States, 1948

(Includes annulments; rate per 1,000)

Duration (Years)	Without Children	With Children	Duration (Years)	Without Children	With Children
0	17.5	11.6	0-4	29.3	12.7
1	29.5	10.0	5-9	34.0	10.8
2	40.3	13.5	10-14	21.7	8.3
3	40.0	14.4	15-19	15.5	7.4
4	42.5	12.9	20-24	10.7	4.9
5	41.3	11.9			
6	35.7	10.8	25-29	5.6	4.2
7	30.6	11.0	30-34	3.4	3.1
8	30.0	10.4	35-39	2.1	2.2
9	28.9	9.8	40-44	1.3	1.3

Source: Estimated by the author.

and those with children is not uniform throughout married life. Rather, divorce is much more frequent among those without children in the early

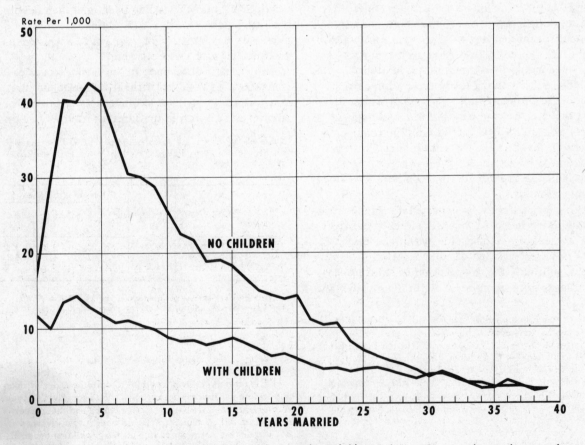

Figure 7. Divorce rate for existing marriages with and without children under age 18, according to duration of marriage, United States, 1948 (includes annulments)

years of marriage, and the differential diminishes rapidly thereafter. In 1948 the divorce rate for parent couples rose to a maximum of 14.4 per 1,000 in the fourth year of marriage, whereas the rate for couples without children reached a peak of 42.5 per 1,000 in the fifth year. The frequency of divorce among the "childless" fell off so rapidly thereafter that the ratio between the rates for the two groups dropped from $3\frac{1}{2}$ in the sixth year of marriage, to about 3 by the tenth year, and to little more than 2 by the fifteenth year. Indeed, after the 30th year the two rates were practically identical.

Thus it is evident that refinement of the divorce rates according to duration of marriage does not eliminate the differential between the "childless" and those with children. Rather, the duration-specific rates indicate that the differential itself varies with the period of married life. What effect other uncontrolled variables may have on the findings cannot be determined with any degree of accuracy. It is known, however, that somewhat fewer divorced spouses are from rural areas, where the fertility rate is comparatively high. Also, there are indications that the interval between separation and divorce is about one half year longer for "childless" couples than for those with children. Whether divorce rates corrected for the actual period of marriage prior to separation and for urban-rural residence would eliminate part or all of the differential cannot be answered from data now available. For the present, one can only point to Quensel's[16] estimates for Sweden, which show that the differential between the two groups was cut almost in half when he allowed for these variables.

The accompanying data indicate that the relative frequency of divorce is greater for families without children than for families with children. Yet, the presence of children is not necessarily a deterrent to divorce. It is likely that in most cases both divorce and childlessness result from more fundamental factors in the marital relationship. Moreover, while children may hold some marriages together, in others pregnancy itself and the additional strains involved may disintegrate rather than cement the marriage. It is also probable that some unsuccessful marriages are

not legally dissolved until the children have grown up. However, their number is undoubtedly less than is popularly believed in view of the small difference in the divorce rate between the two groups at the later years of marriage.

DIVORCE-CHILDREN AND ORPHANS

One of the most serious aspects of unsuccessful marriages is the damaging effect of conflicts between estranged parents on the lives of the children. For this reason the children of divorced parents, especially the younger ones, are the subject of great concern. However, the details concerning such children do not complete the picture of children deprived of the influence and support of a normal home life. In addition there are the children orphaned by the premature death of one of the parents and also those affected by separations resulting from marital discord, chronic illness, or other causes.

Despite the decline in mortality and the rise of divorce (Chapter 11), the annual number of new orphans still is somewhat greater than the number of children involved in divorce. In 1955, for example, about 350,000 children[17] under age 18 became orphaned during the year, whereas less than 340,000 children under 18 were affected by divorce.[18] Nevertheless, since divorce affects children at a younger age than does the death of a parent, the total number of divorce-children now exceeds the number of orphans by more than one fifth. In mid-1955 there were about 3.3 million children[19] under age 18, or 5.9 per cent of the total child population, whose parents had been divorced, and only 2.7 million orphans.

---

[17]Estimated by the author.

[18]Nationwide data are not available regarding children in families broken by separation or desertion. There is no doubt, however, that such children constitute a considerable proportion of the total children from all types of broken homes. See, for example, legal separations in New York (Table A24), criminal actions for desertion and nonsupport in Maryland (L. C. Marshall and G. May, *op. cit.*, Vol. 1, pp. 35, 74, 87), and desertion or nonsupport cases in Philadelphia (annual reports of the Municipal Court, Domestic Relations Division).

[19]Estimated by the author from statistics on children involved in divorce (Table 62) and available data on the age of children at the time of divorce, with allowance for mortality and for children affected by more than one divorce.

[16]Carl-Erik Quensel, *op. cit.*, p. 206.

Table 67. Orphans Under Age 18, by Type and Age, United States, 1920-1955

Year; Age	All Orphans	Father Only Dead	Mother Only Dead	Both Parents Dead
	Number (1,000's)			
1920	6,400	3,350	2,300	750
1930	5,050	2,700	1,900	450
1940	3,840	2,180	1,370	290
1949	2,930	1,890	960	80
1955	2,700	1,830	820	60
	Per Cent of Child Population			
1920	16.3	8.5	5.9	1.9
1930	11.7	6.3	4.4	1.1
1940	9.5	5.4	3.4	.7
1949	6.1	3.9	2.0	.2
1955	4.8	3.2	1.5	.1
	Per Cent of All Orphans, 1920			
Total	100.0	52.6	35.7	11.7
0-4	9.6	5.3	3.8	.4
5-9	25.0	13.5	9.6	1.9
10-14	38.4	20.0	13.6	4.9
15-17	27.0	13.8	8.7	4.5
	Per Cent of All Orphans, 1955			
Total	100.0	67.8	30.4	2.2
0-4	6.7	4.8	1.9	*
5-9	22.2	15.2	6.7	.4
10-14	37.8	25.6	11.5	.7
15-17	33.3	22.2	10.4	1.1

*Less than 0.05 per cent.

Source: Estimates by the Statistical Bureau of the Metropolitan Life Insurance Company and by the Social Security Administration, in *Social Security Bulletin*, March, 1955, p.18 and February, 1956 p. 11.

TRENDS IN ORPHANHOOD

The number of orphans has decreased absolutely as well as relatively in recent decades, due largely to the marked gains in survival at the child-rearing ages. The details are shown in Table 67. Around 1920, about 6.4 million children under 18 years of age—almost one in every six—had lost one or both natural parents by death. In 1955 only 4.8 per cent of the total child population were orphaned, the proportion ranging from less than 1 per cent in early life (under age 5) to about 13 per cent at ages 15-17.

In a previous section it was shown that the mother is usually entrusted with the custody of the children in marriages ended by divorce. Similarly children tend to remain with the mother in cases of separation or desertion. Mothers also bear the major burden of orphanhood. Thus, of the total orphans in 1955, almost 68 per cent had lost their father only, about 30 per cent had lost their mother only, and little more than 2 per cent were bereft of both parents.

CHANCES OF ORPHANHOOD

The risk of orphanhood increases with advance in the age of the parent. Currently, a white child born into an American family where the father is 25 years old has 44 chances in 1,000 of becoming a paternal orphan before reaching its 18th birthday. The chances rise to 101 per 1,000 if the father is 35 years of age at the birth of the child and to 231 per 1,000 if he is then age 45.

The incidence of orphanhood is much lower now than at the turn of the century for children born to relatively young parents; the details are shown in Figure 8. Where the father is 25 years of age at the time of the child's birth, the chances of paternal orphanhood before age 18 have been reduced by almost two thirds; where his age is 35, the reduction has been more than one third. However, for a

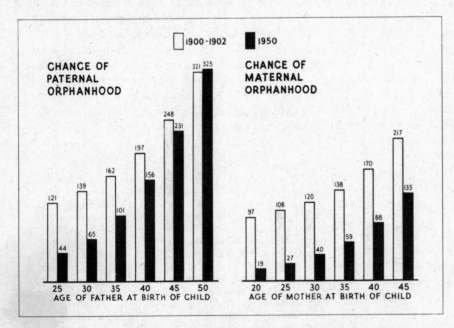

Figure 8. Chances in 1,000 that a newborn child will be orphaned before attaining age 18, white population, United States, 1900-1902 and 1950

child born to a father 45 years of age the risk of orphanhood is not much less now than it was a half century ago. Of the relatively few children born to fathers at age 50, about one third will become orphans before they are 18 years old.

The chances that a child will lose its mother are materially smaller than those of losing its father. Two factors account for this situation: age for age, the death rate is lower for mothers than for fathers; furthermore, the mother is generally several years younger than her mate. Yet, under current conditions 40 out of every 1,000 white children born to mothers at age 30 will be maternal orphans before reaching their 18th birthday. The chances increase to 88 per 1,000 when the mother is 40 years old at the child's birth. Around 1900 the risk of maternal orphanhood was much higher than it is at present, irrespective of the age of the mother.

Chapter 11

MORTALITY AND THE DURATION OF MARRIAGE

IT is widely believed that the disruption of family life in the United States has been increasing at a rapid rate for many years. This view probably has its origin in the marked upward trend of the divorce rate, but it errs by omitting from the reckoning the counterbalancing effect on family life of the decline in the death rate. The present chapter reviews the trend of mortality and its role in marital dissolutions, and considers the combined effect of death and divorce on the duration of marriage.

MORTALITY AND WIDOWHOOD

Current Pattern of Mortality by Marital Status. Married people experience a lower mortality than persons who remain single or those whose marriage has been broken by death or divorce. The married have an advantage at every age after 20 years, and particularly at the period of life when most families have young children in their care. The 1949-51 record for persons in the United States is shown in Table 68. In part, the lower death rate for married persons is due to the more healthful way of life that marriage provides. The higher mortality among the unmarried also reflects the reduced chances of marriage or remarriage for those with physical impairments or serious chronic illness.[1]

The differential in mortality between the married and the unmarried is larger among men than among women. Several causes exact an exceptionally heavy toll of life among unmarried men.[2] In the white population, for example, the tuberculosis death rate among the single, the widowed,

[1]A large part of the excess mortality attributed to the divorced may be fictitious, since their net undercount is undoubtedly greater in census enumerations than on death certificates. For further details, see the Introduction.

[2]Death rates by cause for 1949-51 have been published by the National Office of Vital Statistics in *Vital Statistics—Special Reports*, Vol. 39, No. 7. Comparable details for 1940 were published by I. M. Moriyama in Vol. 23, No. 7.

and the divorced is more than 4 times the rate among the married. The ratios are even larger before midlife; among widowers under age 45, it is almost 9 to 1. The death rate from pneumonia and influenza at ages 20-74 among widowers is $2\frac{1}{2}$ times that among husbands; the single and divorced are at a greater disadvantage. At ages 20-44, the unmarried fare even worse; their mortality from pneumonia and influenza being 5 to 6 times that of the married. For cirrhosis of the liver, prior to midlife the death rate among divorced men is nearly 9 times that among the married.

Accidents and other forms of violence likewise take a relatively heavier toll among unmarried men. The death rate from motor vehicle accidents at ages 20-44 is 4 times as high for widowers and divorced men as for the married. Particularly high is the frequency of suicide among the younger white men whose marriage had been broken. At ages 20-44, divorced men resort to suicide 5 times as frequently as do the married; for the widowed the ratio exceeds 6 to 1.

Trend of Mortality for the Married. The marked reduction in mortality since the turn of the century has benefited both sexes, but the gains have been much more pronounced for women than for men. Among the women, moreover, the married have done better than the unmarried. At ages 20 and over, the death rate for married women has been cut more than half—from 16.4 per 1,000 in 1900 to 7.5 per 1,000 in 1949-51, whereas for the unmarried the rate dropped only about two fifths. For men, the decline was less than one third among both the married and the unmarried.

The mortality record for husbands and for wives over the past half century is shown in the upper part of Table 69. For the first half of this period, the married men and women both experienced virtually the same relative decline in

Table 68. Deaths per 1,000 Population, by Marital Status, Sex and Age, United States, 1949-51

Age	Male					Female				
	Total	Single	Married	Widowed	Divorced	Total	Single	Married	Widowed	Divorced
All ages	11.1	5.5	12.2	70.3	26.0	8.3	3.9	5.9	41.4	8.9
Under 15	3.9	3.9	2.6	2.8	1.0	3.0	3.0	2.5	12.4	.0
15-19	1.4	1.4	1.6	2.0	2.3	.8	.7	1.0	4.8	1.6
20-24	1.9	2.2	1.5	5.8	3.4	1.0	1.2	.9	3.4	1.7
25-34	2.2	3.7	1.7	8.7	5.8	1.4	2.2	1.2	4.1	2.6
35-44	4.3	8.5	3.6	12.2	11.8	2.9	3.9	2.6	6.2	4.5
45-54	10.8	17.7	9.3	21.6	23.1	6.5	7.0	5.8	10.4	8.1
55-59	20.0	29.8	17.8	30.3	36.3	11.4	11.5	10.3	14.9	13.9
60-64	29.0	40.8	25.9	39.4	48.5	17.5	16.6	15.8	20.9	21.2
65-69	41.1	55.2	36.8	50.3	66.4	26.0	24.9	23.8	28.5	33.5
70-74	60.5	78.6	54.5	69.1	91.8	43.2	42.9	39.6	45.5	59.0
75-79	91.0	112.7	82.0	99.7	143.9	70.8	72.2	64.8	72.5	101.8
80-84	130.0	156.7	117.4	137.4	204.6	108.1	115.0	98.0	108.8	167.9
85 and over	216.0	204.8	189.9	231.3	310.7	192.7	188.1	147.2	197.0	214.5

Note: Excludes deaths and population in armed forces overseas.

Source of basic data: Number of deaths, from the National Office of Vital Statistics, with decedents of unknown age or status distributed by the author; population, from Table A5 and the 1950 Census.

mortality, about one fifth. In the second half, however, the downward trend for women was greatly accelerated.

Among both men and women every age group shared in the long-term reduction in mortality. The decrease was greatest in early adult life and lessened with advance in age. Especially large was the decline among young wives. At ages 20-34 their death rate dropped at least five sixths between 1900 and 1949-51. The reduction was nearly three fourths in the age range 35-44, and amounted to more than one half at 45-54. Even at ages 65 and over the decrease in mortality among married women was fully one third. Age for age, the women recorded larger declines than the men. The more favorable experience for women reflects the more pronounced drop in their death rate from tuberculosis, pneumonia, and a number of other diseases. Of special importance, and particularly at the earlier reproductive ages, has been the marked progress made in safeguarding pregnancy and childbirth. As recently as 1935, the maternal mortality rate in the United States was 58 per 10,000 live births; currently, it is less than 6 per 10,000.[3]

The reduced toll from maternity undoubtedly

[3]This notable achievement in life conservation has resulted from a variety of factors, including the increased utilization of medical and hospital services. See Paul H. Jacobson, "Hospital Care and the Vanishing Midwife," *Milbank Memorial Fund Quarterly*, 34:253-261, July, 1956.

Table 69. Deaths per 1,000 Population for the Married and Unmarried, by Sex and Age, United States, 1900-1951

Marital Status and Age	Male				Female			
	1900*	1924-28†	1940	1949-51	1900*	1924-28†	1940	1949-51
Married								
20 and over‡	17.4	14.3	13.4	11.7	16.4	12.9	9.9	7.5
20-24	5.0	3.4	2.2	1.5	7.9	4.7	2.1	.9
25-34	6.2	4.0	2.7	1.7	8.4	4.9	2.5	1.2
35-44	9.1	6.2	4.9	3.6	9.6	6.3	4.2	2.6
45-54	14.1	11.1	10.9	9.3	12.9	10.2	7.8	5.8
55-64	26.3	22.6	23.2	21.4	22.4	19.4	16.1	12.6
65 and over	71.5	65.3	62.9	57.3	58.7	53.0	45.7	37.4
Unmarried								
20 and over‡	29.3	24.2	22.9	21.1	21.5	17.7	15.1	12.2
20-24	7.3	4.3	2.9	2.2	5.5	3.6	2.1	1.2
25-34	11.7	6.5	5.1	3.9	7.5	4.9	3.5	2.4
35-44	18.2	12.9	10.5	9.4	11.0	7.6	6.0	4.6
45-54	25.9	21.2	20.4	19.6	17.7	13.7	11.2	8.9
55-64	41.6	37.2	37.4	36.1	31.9	25.7	21.5	17.1
65 and over	113.3	104.2	103.6	94.6	90.4	83.8	77.1	65.3

*Death Registration States. †Death Registration States of 1924.
‡Adjusted on basis of age distribution of total population in United States, 1940.

Note: Excludes deaths and population in armed forces overseas.
Source of basic data: Various reports by the Bureau of the Census and the National Office of Vital Statistics.

accounts, in good measure, for the greater improvement in the over-all death rate among married women than among the unmarried. In 1900 the married actually experienced the higher death rate at ages under 35; at 20-24 years the excess then amounted to no less than 44 per cent. This excess was gradually reduced, but it was not until after 1940 that married women showed the lower mortality. At ages 25-34 the disadvantage of the married was eliminated in the first half of the period under review, and converted into a distinct advantage in subsequent years.[4] Past the main childbearing period of life, at ages 45 and over, the ratio of mortality between the married and unmarried has decreased very little since 1900.

Widowhood. The chances that a wife will outlive her husband are dependent on the difference in their ages. According to the mortality experienced in the United States during 1950, the probability that the wife will be left a widow increases with the number of years that she is younger than her husband (Figure 9). Thus, where the spouses are the same age, the chances that the wife will

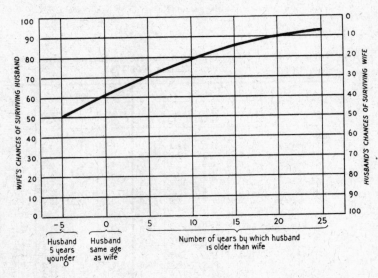

Figure 9. Chances in 100 that a married person will survive his or her mate, United States, 1950

outlive her husband are 60 in 100, but they rise to 70 where the husband is 5 years older, and to almost 80 if he is her senior by 10 years. Widowhood is practically a certainty for wives 20 or more years younger than their husband; the chances in such extreme instances are about 90 in 100. Only if the wife is at least 5 years older than her husband is it probable that she will pre-

decease him. Since the typical bride is younger than her groom (Table A13), most women outlive their husband.

As a result of the decrease in mortality prior to midlife, widowhood has been postponed to the older ages. At the same time, the greater improvement in survival for wives than for husbands has increased the chances that a wife will eventually be widowed.

During the 1890's, about 330,000 marriages a year were broken by the death of the husband or wife. In less than 56 per cent of these families the wife was the surviving spouse. Since that time the proportion has mounted almost without interruption. It reached 60 per cent by 1930 and 65 per cent by 1942. In 1956, when death dissolved 720,000 marriages, the proportion was almost 70 per cent.

Not only are more widows than widowers created each year, but the annual proportion who die or remarry is lower for widows than for widowers (Tables 28 and A29). In consequence, the number of widows has grown rapidly.[5] During the early years of this century widows were increasing by less than 80,000 annually; since 1930 the yearly rise has been close to 100,000. By mid-1958 there were about 8 million widows in the United States compared with only about $2\frac{1}{4}$ million widowers. In other words, widows now outnumber widowers by more than $3\frac{1}{2}$ to 1.

An appreciable proportion of the women who become widowed are still in the prime of life. Currently, the median age at which wives enter widowhood is about 56 years. A significant number are much younger; about one fifth of the new widows each year are under age 45. Thus most women have many years of life ahead of them after their husband dies.[6] About three quarters of all women at age 50 can expect to live 20 years longer; that many years of life also remain for one out of every two at age 60.

---

[4]During the nineteenth century married women probably were at a more pronounced disadvantage over a wider range of ages. In fact, among white persons of all marital classes as a group, through most of the childbearing period, females experienced a higher death rate than men. See Paul H. Jacobson, "An Estimate of the Expectation of Life in the United States in 1850," *Milbank Memorial Fund Quarterly*, 35:198-199, April, 1957.

[5]Fatalities among American servicemen overseas have also been a factor. Annual death rates for the period 1890-1950, which include the mortality among our armed forces overseas, are shown in Table A29.

[6]For the average number of years remaining before remarriage or death, see Tables 38-39.

RATE OF MARITAL DISSOLUTIONS

Role of Mortality. The long-term improvement in health conditions has contributed to the stability of American family life. In the 1860's, the annual marital dissolutions due to the death of the husband or wife averaged $31\frac{1}{2}$ per 1,000 existing marriages. With the ensuing reduction in mortality, this rate dropped to 26 per 1,000 in the 1900's and to less than $17\frac{1}{2}$ during 1954-56. Equally impressive has been the marked lessening of the annual fluctuations in the death toll (Table 70 and Figure 10).

the high level of mortality, and the marked annual fluctuations, during the 1800's. Since the turn of this century, with the quickened tempo of advances in environmental sanitation and in preventive and curative medicine, these diseases have been virtually eliminated as causes of death. Even so, the most pronounced deviation from the trend of marital dissolutions occurred as recently as 1918 during the influenza pandemic, when the rate from deaths shot up to 34 per 1,000—the highest since the post Civil War period. Deaths overseas of married men in our armed forces

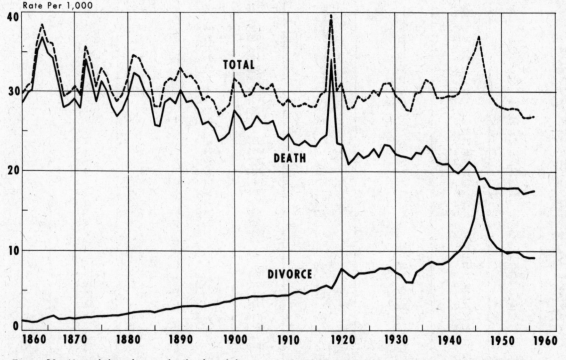

Figure 10. Marital dissolutions by death and divorce per 1,000 existing marriages, United States, 1860-1956 (rates from Table 70)

A century ago there still was little or no provision for safeguarding food and water supplies or for disposal of refuse or other waste products. Moreover, there were no controls against the infectious diseases, with the result that epidemics of smallpox, yellow fever, cholera, typhoid fever, and other contagions recurred at intervals and took a heavy toll of life. The records for a number of our cities[7] and states[8] provide ample evidence of

also contributed to the 1918 upswing, but to a much smaller extent than those from the pandemic. Indeed, the overseas deaths represented only 4 per cent of all marital dissolutions by death in that year. Fatalities among American married men outside of continental United States during

[7]John K. Gore, "On the Improvement in Longevity in the United States during the Nineteenth Century," *Proceedings*

of the Fourth International Congress of Actuaries, 1:30-54, 1904.

[8]Walter F. Willcox, *Introduction to the Vital Statistics of the United States, 1900 to 1930*, Bureau of the Census, Washington, 1933, Table XVI, pp. 99-100.

Table 70. Marital Dissolutions by Death and Divorce per 1,000 Existing Marriages, and Per Cent of Dissolutions by Divorce, United States, 1860-1956

Year	Dissolution Rate			Per Cent by Divorce†	Year	Dissolution Rate			Per Cent by Divorce†
	Total	Death*	Divorce†			Total	Death*	Divorce†	
1860	29.6	28.4	1.2	4.1	1909	28.3	23.9	4.5	15.8
1861	30.7	29.7	1.1	3.5					
1862	31.1	30.1	1.0	3.3	1910	29.1	24.6	4.5	15.6
1863	36.2	35.1	1.1	3.0	1911	28.2	23.5	4.8	16.9
1864	38.4	36.9	1.4	3.7	1912	28.2	23.3	4.9	17.5
1865	36.4	34.8	1.6	4.4	1913	28.5	23.8	4.7	16.3
1866	36.0	34.2	1.8	4.9	1914	28.2	23.2	5.0	17.7
1867	32.4	30.9	1.5	4.6	1915	28.2	23.1	5.1	18.0
1868	29.4	27.9	1.5	5.1	1916	29.6	24.1	5.5	18.4
1869	29.8	28.3	1.6	5.3	1917	30.2	24.6	5.7	18.8
					1918	39.6	34.2	5.4	13.6
1870	30.7	29.1	1.5	5.0	1919	30.1	23.5	6.5	21.6
1871	29.5	27.9	1.6	5.4					
1872	35.7	34.0	1.7	4.7	1920	31.0	23.3	7.7	24.8
1873	33.5	31.7	1.7	5.2	1921	27.8	20.8	7.1	25.4
1874	30.5	28.7	1.8	5.9	1922	28.1	21.5	6.6	23.5
1875	33.0	31.3	1.8	5.4	1923	29.5	22.3	7.2	24.3
1876	32.0	30.1	1.8	5.7	1924	28.8	21.6	7.2	25.1
1877	29.9	28.0	1.9	6.3	1925	29.3	22.0	7.3	25.0
1878	28.7	26.8	1.9	6.6	1926	30.2	22.8	7.4	24.5
1879	29.6	27.7	2.0	6.6	1927	29.5	21.7	7.7	26.2
					1928	31.0	23.3	7.8	25.1
1880	31.7	29.5	2.2	7.0	1929	31.1	23.2	7.9	25.3
1881	34.6	32.4	2.3	6.6					
1882	34.3	31.9	2.4	6.9	1930	29.6	22.2	7.4	25.0
1883	32.6	30.2	2.4	7.5	1931	28.9	21.8	7.0	24.4
1884	31.6	29.3	2.4	7.4	1932	27.8	21.7	6.1	22.0
1885	28.2	25.9	2.3	8.3	1933	27.6	21.5	6.1	22.0
1886	28.2	25.7	2.5	8.8	1934	29.8	22.4	7.4	24.9
1887	31.2	28.6	2.7	8.5	1935	30.0	22.2	7.8	26.0
1888	31.8	29.2	2.7	8.4	1936	31.5	23.2	8.3	26.4
1889	31.4	28.5	2.9	9.2	1937	31.1	22.5	8.6	27.7
					1938	29.3	21.1	8.3	28.3
1890	33.1	30.2	3.0	8.9	1939	29.3	20.9	8.4	28.6
1891	31.8	28.7	3.1	9.7					
1892	32.0	28.9	3.1	9.6	1940	29.5	20.9	8.7	29.3
1893	31.0	27.9	3.1	10.0	1941	29.5	20.1	9.4	31.9
1894	29.0	25.9	3.0	10.5	1942	29.8	19.8	10.0	33.6
1895	29.5	26.3	3.2	10.8	1943	31.3	20.4	10.9	34.9
1896	28.9	25.6	3.3	11.5	1944	33.5	21.2	12.3	36.8
1897	27.2	23.8	3.4	12.4	1945	34.9	20.6	14.3	41.1
1898	27.8	24.2	3.6	12.8	1946	37.2	19.0	18.2	48.9
1899	28.5	24.8	3.7	13.1	1947	33.1	19.2	13.9	42.0
					1948	29.7	18.1	11.6	39.0
1900	31.7	27.7	4.0	12.5	1949	28.5	17.9	10.6	37.2
1901	30.9	26.7	4.2	13.7					
1902	29.5	25.3	4.2	14.1	1950	28.1	17.9	10.2	36.2
1903	29.8	25.6	4.3	14.4	1951‡	27.8	17.9	9.9	35.6
1904	31.2	27.0	4.3	13.6	1952‡	27.9	17.9	10.0	36.0
1905	30.5	26.2	4.3	14.0	1953‡	27.8	17.9	9.9	35.5
1906	30.4	26.1	4.4	14.4	1954‡	26.7	17.2	9.5	35.5
1907	31.0	26.4	4.5	14.7	1955‡	26.7	17.4	9.3	34.9
1908	28.9	24.4	4.4	15.4	1956‡	26.8	17.5	9.3	34.6

*Includes deaths overseas during 1917-1919 and 1940-1956.   †Includes annulments.   ‡Provisional.

Source of basic data: Tables 42, A6-7 (married males), A22, A26-28; and 1956 estimates of existing marriages, and of deaths in the United States.

World War II were of greater magnitude, but even at their peak in 1944 they amounted to little more than 9 per cent of that year's total dissolutions by death.

Estimates of the annual number of deaths of married persons are shown in Tables A26-28. Those for deaths which occurred in continental United States were derived according to methods previously reported.[9]

In view of the sharp rise in the death rate during the influenza pandemic, it is noteworthy that the annual changes in the estimated number of deaths for married persons in the United States from 1916 to 1920 closely parallel the trend of deaths recorded in New York State.

Deaths Among Married Persons: 1916 Equals 100

Year	New York State (Recorded)	United States (Estimated)
1916	100.0	100.0
1917	104.6	103.9
1918	140.3	140.5
1919	101.6	101.1
1920	100.7	102.3

It should also be noted that the national estimates are lower than those previously published by Rubinow,[10] who assumed no differential in the death rate between the married and the unmarried. However, they are in essential agreement with those by Hauser and Jaffe.[11]

[9]Paul H. Jacobson, "Total Marital Dissolutions in the United States: Relative Importance of Mortality and Divorce," in *Studies in Population*, George F. Mair, editor, Princeton University Press, 1949, pp. 3-15; and *Some Statistical Patterns of Marriage in the United States*, Ph.D. dissertation, Faculty of Political Science, Columbia University, 1952, pp. 152-157.

Mortimer Spiegelman, "Mortality in Relation to Widowhood," *Proceedings of the American Philosophical Society*, 80:548, 1939.

[10]I. M. Rubinow, *Some Statistical Aspects of Marriage and Divorce*, Pamphlet Series No. 3, The American Academy of Political and Social Science, Philadelphia, 1936, pp. 16-19 (number of deaths of married persons from 1910 to 1930).

[11]Philip M. Hauser and A. J. Jaffe, "The Extent of the Housing Shortage," *Law and Contemporary Problems*, 12:3-15, Winter, 1947. This paper contains estimates of the number of families broken by death, 1930-1945. The estimates for 1939-1943 and 1945 appear to be somewhat too high. For example, the 1940 estimate includes the deaths of divorced persons and of all persons of unknown marital status.

Trend of Total Marital Dissolutions. Willcox[12] was the first American demographer to take cognizance of the fact that a marriage may end "naturally" by the death of either spouse or "civilly" by divorce or annulment. He and a number of subsequent researchers considered the problem in terms of the relative importance of death and divorce, but only with a view toward estimating the probability that a marriage would end in divorce. No one, apparently, has considered quantitatively the total effect on the family of the long-term upward trend of divorce and the downward course of mortality. In other words, what has been the trend of the combined rate of marital dissolutions resulting from death and divorce?

The trend of marital dissolutions for the years 1860 to 1956 is shown in Figure 10. It is apparent that the annual disruptions by divorce have increased from about 1 per 1,000 existing marriages in the early 1860's to 9 per 1,000 in 1956. At the same time, however, the rate of dissolutions because of the death of the husband or wife has dropped by an even greater amount. In consequence, the annual rate of total marital dissolutions is lower now than it was 100 years ago; the combined rate has declined from an annual average of 33 per 1,000 in the 1860's to about 27 per 1,000 at present.[13]

By 1915 the combined rate of marital dissolutions had fallen to about 28 per 1,000 existing marriages. This downswing reflected the long-term decline in mortality. In sharp contrast was the explosive rise in marital dissolutions in 1918, caused almost entirely by the influenza pandemic which struck in the autumn of that year. The rate of dissolutions in 1918 jumped to almost 40 per 1,000—the highest point in the 100-year period under review. This pandemic experience provides a measure of the extent to which recurrent plagues must have disrupted family life in earlier eras of history.

[12]Walter F. Willcox, *The Divorce Problem*, Ph.D. dissertation, Faculty of Political Science, Columbia University, 1891, pp. 16, 19; *Introduction to the Vital Statistics of the United States, 1900 to 1930*, pp. 50-51 and 124; and *Studies in American Demography*, Cornell University Press, 1940, pp. 348-349.

[13]A similar trend is evident from 1880 forward for Amsterdam in the Netherlands. See J. H. van Zanten and T. van den Brink, "Population Phenomena in Amsterdam," *Population*, August, 1938, p. 10.

From 1919 until the beginning of World War II, the rate of marital dissolutions fluctuated somewhat, but showed no definite upward or downward trend. It is noteworthy, however, that during the depression year 1933 the rate dropped to 27.6 per 1,000—one of the lowest points of the entire series. Throughout World War II, marital dissolutions rose rapidly as a result of the mounting divorce rate, and reached a high of 37 per 1,000 in 1946. Thereafter, however, the divorce rate receded so sharply that by 1949 the total dissolution rate was already below the prewar level.

Although the annual dissolution *rate* has fallen to a record low, since 1948 the *number* of dissolutions has remained relatively unchanged at a level well above that which prevailed prior to World War II. In 1956 there were about 1.1 million marriages broken by death or divorce, or 22 per cent more than in 1940.

Relative Importance of Death and Divorce. Death dissolves more marriages than does divorce and annulment. However, the contribution of mortality to the total of marital dissolutions has decreased, whereas that of divorce has increased.[14] This may be seen from the figures in the right-hand column of Table 70. Prior to 1868, divorce accounted for less than 5 per cent of the total annual marital dissolutions. Since then the proportion has risen with few interruptions.[15] It reached 10 per cent in 1893, passed 20 per cent by 1919, and has exceeded 30 per cent since 1941. The highest proportion occurred in 1946, when almost as many marriages were dissolved by divorce as by death. In 1956, the latest year for which data are available, about 34½ per cent of all marital dissolutions resulted from divorce.

The ratio, divorce as a proportion of the total annual marital dissolutions, was once thought to be a reliable index of the probability that a marriage would end in divorce. Actually, however, it overstates the chances of divorce (or annulment), as may be seen from a comparison of the figures

for 1948 and 1955 in Table 70 with the corresponding figure in Tables 71 and 72. The overstatement is the net effect of two factors. First, the long-term trend of new marriage formations has been upward. Second, the divorce rate is highest in the early durations of marriage (the more recent and larger marriage cohorts) whereas the death rate is highest at the later durations (the older and smaller cohorts).

DURATION OF MARRIAGE

The chances of celebrating successive wedding anniversaries, the probability that a marriage will end in divorce, the average number of years of married life remaining, and related information are shown for 1955 and 1948 in Tables 71 and 72.

Divorce Rates. Column 2 in each table shows the annual number of marriages dissolved by divorce per 1,000 marriages existing at the beginning of each year of duration. The rates are based on absolute divorces and annulments in the United States during 1948 and 1955 (Table A21) and on existing marriages including the population in the armed forces overseas during those years (Table A22). The figures for individual durations were derived largely by interpolation of the data grouped in five-year intervals. At the early durations, where the rate changes rapidly, divorces and existing marriages by single years of duration were used so far as was necessary to provide a smooth blend with the values obtained by interpolation. In the absence of reliable detail for marriages of very long standing, the rate after duration 52 years was assumed to decrease linearly to zero at the 80th anniversary.

The frequency of divorce and annulment rises rapidly after the first few months of marriage, reaches a maximum during the third year, and thereafter declines. In 1955, for example, the rate decreased from a high of 25.4 per 1,000 at duration 2 years to 9.6 per 1,000 at duration 10, and to less than 5 per 1,000 after duration 22 years. A few marriages are dissolved by divorce even after the 40th anniversary. However, in a large proportion of these cases, the husband and wife have lived apart for years. Although the divorce rates were generally higher in 1948 than in 1955, the reverse was true at durations under

---

[14]The United States is not unique in this respect; most countries have experienced a long-term rise in the proportion of marriages ended by divorce. See, for example, the annual statistical reports of Finland, Germany, Norway, Sweden, and Switzerland.

[15]See, for comparison, Alfred Cahen, *Statistical Analysis of American Divorce*, Columbia University Press, 1932, pp. 29-31; I. M. Rubinow, *op. cit.*, p. 20; and Walter F. Willcox, *Studies in American Demography*, p.348.

Table 71. Duration of Marriage Table for Total Population, United States, 1955

Duration (Years)	Per 1,000 marriages existing at beginning of year of duration, number dissolved during year by		Of 100,000 Marriages Contracted				Stationary Population		Per cent dissolved by divorce in this year of duration and all later years	Average number of years of marriage remaining before dissolution by divorce or death
	Divorce	Death	Number existing at beginning of year of duration	Number dissolved by divorce		Number dissolved by death during year of duration	In year of duration	In this year of duration and all later years		
				During year of duration	In this year of duration and all later years					
(1)	(2)	(3)	(4)	(5)	(6)	(7)	(8)	(9)	(10)	(11)
0	18.1	4.9	100,000	1,810	24,855	490	99,092	3,149,079	24.9	31.5
1	25.1	5.0	97,700	2,452	23,045	489	96,230	3,049,987	23.6	31.2
2	25.4	5.1	94,759	2,407	20,593	483	93,314	2,953,757	21.7	31.2
3	22.1	5.2	91,869	2,030	18,186	478	90,615	2,860,443	19.8	31.1
4	18.8	5.3	89,361	1,680	16,156	474	88,284	2,769,828	18.1	31.0
5	15.9	5.4	87,207	1,387	14,476	471	86,278	2,681,544	16.6	30.7
6	13.9	5.5	85,349	1,186	13,089	469	84,522	2,595,266	15.3	30.4
7	12.5	5.5	83,694	1,046	11,903	460	82,941	2,510,744	14.2	30.0
8	11.3	5.7	82,188	929	10,857	468	81,490	2,427,803	13.2	29.5
9	10.9	6.0	80,791	881	9,928	485	80,108	2,346,313	12.3	29.0
10	9.6	6.4	79,425	762	9,047	508	78,790	2,266,205	11.4	28.5
11	8.2	6.8	78,155	641	8,285	531	77,569	2,187,415	10.6	28.0
12	7.5	7.1	76,983	577	7,644	547	76,421	2,109,846	9.9	27.4
13	7.0	7.5	75,859	531	7,067	569	75,309	2,033,425	9.3	26.8
14	6.6	7.8	74,759	493	6,536	583	74,221	1,958,116	8.7	26.2
15	6.4	8.2	73,683	472	6,043	604	73,145	1,883,895	8.2	25.6
16	6.2	8.7	72,607	450	5,571	632	72,066	1,810,750	7.7	24.9
17	6.0	9.4	71,525	429	5,121	672	70,975	1,738,684	7.2	24.3
18	5.8	10.4	70,424	408	4,692	732	69,854	1,667,709	6.7	23.7
19	5.6	11.5	69,284	388	4,284	797	68,692	1,597,855	6.2	23.1
20	5.5	12.8	68,099	375	3,896	872	67,476	1,529,163	5.7	22.5
21	5.3	14.1	66,852	354	3,521	943	66,204	1,461,687	5.3	21.9
22	5.1	15.2	65,555	334	3,167	996	64,890	1,395,483	4.8	21.3
23	4.8	16.2	64,225	308	2,833	1,040	63,551	1,330,593	4.4	20.7
24	4.5	17.0	62,877	283	2,525	1,069	62,201	1,267,042	4.0	20.2
25	4.1	17.8	61,525	252	2,242	1,095	60,852	1,204,841	3.6	19.6
26	3.8	18.6	60,178	229	1,990	1,119	59,504	1,143,989	3.3	19.0
27	3.5	19.5	58,830	206	1,761	1,147	58,154	1,084,485	3.0	18.4
28	3.2	20.6	57,477	184	1,555	1,184	56,793	1,026,331	2.7	17.9
29	3.0	21.6	56,109	168	1,371	1,212	55,419	969,538	2.4	17.3
30	2.7	22.8	54,729	148	1,203	1,248	54,031	914,119	2.2	16.7
31	2.5	24.2	53,333	133	1,055	1,291	52,621	860,088	2.0	16.1
32	2.3	25.8	51,909	119	922	1,339	51,180	807,467	1.8	15.6
33	2.1	27.6	50,451	106	803	1,392	49,702	756,287	1.6	15.0
34	1.9	29.7	48,953	93	697	1,454	48,180	706,585	1.4	14.4
35	1.8	32.0	47,406	85	604	1,517	46,605	658,405	1.3	13.9
36	1.6	34.4	45,804	73	519	1,576	44,980	611,800	1.1	13.4
37	1.5	36.9	44,155	66	446	1,629	43,308	566,820	1.0	12.8
38	1.4	40.1	42,460	59	380	1,703	41,579	523,512	.9	12.3
39	1.3	43.4	40,698	53	321	1,766	39,789	481,933	.8	11.8
40	1.2	46.9	38,879	47	268	1,823	37,944	442,144	.7	11.4
41	1.1	50.6	37,009	41	221	1,873	36,052	404,200	.6	10.9
42	1.0	54.4	35,095	35	180	1,909	34,123	368,148	.5	10.5
43	.9	58.5	33,151	30	145	1,939	32,167	334,025	.4	10.1
44	.8	62.8	31,182	25	115	1,958	30,191	301,858	.4	9.7
45	.7	67.3	29,199	20	90	1,965	28,207	271,667	.3	9.3
46	.6	71.6	27,214	16	70	1,949	26,232	243,460	.3	8.9
47	.5	75.9	25,249	13	54	1,916	24,285	217,228	.2	8.6
48	.5	79.8	23,320	12	41	1,861	22,384	192,943	.2	8.3
49	.4	83.9	21,447	9	29	1,799	20,543	170,559	.1	8.0
50	.3	88.0	19,639	6	20	1,728	18,772	150,016	.1	7.6

Table 72. Duration of Marriage Table for Total Population, United States, 1948

Duration (Years)	Per 1,000 marriages existing at beginning of year of duration, number dissolved during year by		Of 100,000 Marriages Contracted				Stationary Population		Per cent dissolved by divorce in this year of duration and all later years	Average number of years of marriage remaining before dissolution by divorce or death
	Divorce	Death	Number existing at beginning of year of duration	Number dissolved by divorce		Number dissolved by death during year of duration	In year of duration	In this year of duration and all later years		
				During year of duration	In this year of duration and all later years					
(1)	(2)	(3)	(4)	(5)	(6)	(7)	(8)	(9)	(10)	(11)
0	16.5	5.5	100,000	1,650	29,062	550	99,121	2,987,855	29.1	29.9
1	20.7	5.5	97,800	2,024	27,412	538	96,519	2,888,734	28.0	29.5
2	24.7	5.6	95,238	2,352	25,388	533	93,796	2,792,215	26.7	29.3
3	23.8	5.7	92,353	2,198	23,036	526	90,991	2,698,419	24.9	29.2
4	21.2	5.8	89,629	1,900	20,838	520	88,419	2,607,428	23.2	29.1
5	19.3	5.9	87,209	1,683	18,938	515	86,110	2,519,009	21.7	28.9
6	16.6	6.0	85,011	1,411	17,255	510	84,051	2,432,899	20.3	28.6
7	15.4	6.1	83,090	1,280	15,844	507	82,197	2,348,848	19.1	28.3
8	14.6	6.2	81,303	1,187	14,564	504	80,458	2,266,651	17.9	27.9
9	13.9	6.5	79,612	1,107	13,377	517	78,800	2,186,193	16.8	27.5
10	12.3	6.9	77,988	959	12,270	538	77,240	2,107,393	15.7	27.0
11	11.3	7.2	76,491	864	11,311	551	75,784	2,030,153	14.8	26.5
12	11.1	7.6	75,076	833	10,447	571	74,374	1,954,369	13.9	26.0
13	10.6	8.0	73,672	781	9,614	589	72,987	1,879,995	13.0	25.5
14	10.2	8.4	72,302	737	8,833	607	71,630	1,807,008	12.2	25.0
15	9.9	8.8	70,958	702	8,096	624	70,295	1,735,378	11.4	24.5
16	9.6	9.3	69,632	668	7,394	648	68,974	1,665,083	10.6	23.9
17	9.2	10.0	68,316	629	6,726	683	67,660	1,596,109	9.8	23.4
18	8.7	10.7	67,004	583	6,097	717	66,354	1,528,449	9.1	22.8
19	8.3	11.5	65,704	545	5,514	756	65,054	1,462,095	8.4	22.3
20	7.8	12.3	64,403	502	4,969	792	63,756	1,397,041	7.7	21.7
21	7.3	13.3	63,109	461	4,467	839	62,459	1,333,285	7.1	21.1
22	6.9	14.2	61,809	426	4,006	878	61,157	1,270,826	6.5	20.6
23	6.5	15.3	60,505	393	3,580	926	59,846	1,209,669	5.9	20.0
24	6.1	16.4	59,186	361	3,187	971	58,520	1,149,823	5.4	19.4
25	5.7	17.5	57,854	330	2,826	1,012	57,183	1,091,303	4.9	18.9
26	5.3	18.8	56,512	300	2,496	1,062	55,831	1,034,120	4.4	18.3
27	5.0	20.1	55,150	276	2,196	1,109	54,458	978,289	4.0	17.7
28	4.6	21.5	53,765	247	1,920	1,156	53,064	923,831	3.6	17.2
29	4.2	23.0	52,362	220	1,673	1,204	51,650	870,767	3.2	16.6
30	3.9	24.6	50,938	199	1,453	1,253	50,212	819,117	2.9	16.1
31	3.5	26.3	49,486	173	1,254	1,301	48,749	768,905	2.5	15.5
32	3.2	28.3	48,012	154	1,081	1,359	47,256	720,156	2.3	15.0
33	2.9	30.4	46,499	135	927	1,414	45,725	672,900	2.0	14.5
34	2.7	32.8	44,950	121	792	1,474	44,153	627,175	1.8	14.0
35	2.4	35.3	43,355	104	671	1,530	42,538	583,022	1.5	13.4
36	2.2	38.0	41,721	92	567	1,585	40,883	540,484	1.4	13.0
37	2.0	40.8	40,044	80	475	1,634	39,187	499,601	1.2	12.5
38	1.8	43.8	38,330	69	395	1,679	37,456	460,414	1.0	12.0
39	1.7	47.0	36,582	62	326	1,719	35,692	422,958	.9	11.6
40	1.6	50.3	34,801	56	264	1,750	33,898	387,266	.8	11.1
41	1.4	53.8	32,995	46	208	1,775	32,085	353,368	.6	10.7
42	1.3	57.5	31,174	41	162	1,793	30,257	321,283	.5	10.3
43	1.1	61.4	29,340	32	121	1,801	28,424	291,026	.4	9.9
44	.9	65.5	27,507	25	89	1,802	26,594	262,602	.3	9.5
45	.7	69.8	25,680	18	64	1,792	24,775	236,008	.2	9.2
46	.5	74.0	23,870	12	46	1,766	22,981	211,233	.2	8.8
47	.3	78.1	22,092	7	34	1,725	21,226	188,252	.2	8.5
48	.3	81.8	20,360	6	27	1,665	19,525	167,026	.1	8.2
49	.3	85.8	18,689	6	21	1,604	17,884	147,501	.1	7.9
50	.2	89.7	17,079	3	15	1,532	16,312	129,617	.1	7.6

3 years. This results from the long-term shift of divorce to the earlier years of marriage, and may be due in part to a reduction in the interval between separation and divorce.

Mortality Rates. Column 3 in each table shows the annual number of marriages dissolved by death per 1,000 marriages existing at the beginning of each year of duration. The rates, which allow for the experience among our armed forces overseas, are based on existing marriages during 1948 and 1955 (Table A22) and on deaths of husbands and wives during those years. The dissolutions by death according to duration of marriage are approximations; they were derived in part from (a) deaths of married persons in 1948 and 1955, classified by age and sex, (b) married population in the United States during 1948, classified by age, sex, and duration of marriage,[16] and

(c) married population in the United States during 1953, classified by age, sex, and year of marriage.[16] The resulting death rates are higher than those which would be obtained by the methods previously used by Cahen and by Monahan.[17]

In the early years of marriage, death constitutes a much smaller hazard to the continuity of family life than does divorce. This may be seen from Figure 11, which is based on the experience in 1955. At durations 1 and 2 years, the rate of dissolutions from the death of either husband or wife is about 5 per 1,000, or only one fifth that from divorce. In fact, it is not until duration 13 years that death exceeds divorce as a cause of marital disruption. Beyond that year of marriage, death takes an increasing toll and the frequency of divorce continues to decline.

The combined effect of death and divorce is

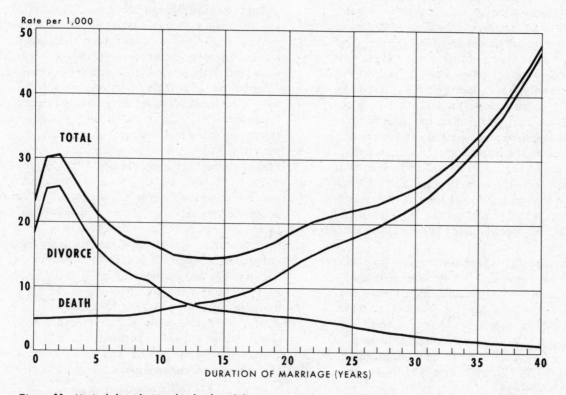

Figure 11. Marital dissolutions by death and divorce per 1,000 existing marriages, by duration of marriage, United States, 1955 (rates from Table 71)

[16]Bureau of the Census, *Current Population Reports*, Series P-20, No. 23, pp. 12-13 and No. 50, p. 13.

[17]Alfred Cahen, *op. cit.*, p. 121.
Thomas P. Monahan, "The Changing Probability of Divorce," *American Sociological Review*, 5:538, August, 1940.

also noteworthy, as is evident from the upper-most line in the accompanying figure. The total dissolution rate rises rapidly to a peak of 30.5 per 1,000 in the third year of marriage (duration 2 years), declines through the 11th year, after which it continues at about the level of 15 per 1,000 until the 19th year is reached. At the later durations, the rate increases steadily, virtually paralleling that for deaths alone. However, not until the 35th year of marriage does the total dissolution rate exceed that among newlyweds.

Number Existing at Beginning of Year of Duration. Column 4 of Tables 71 and 72 shows the number of marriages still existing at each attained duration out of an original cohort of 100,000 among which the divorce and death rates at each duration of marriage are exactly those shown in columns 2 and 3. In other words, the figures represent the marriages which have escaped dissolution by both divorce and death. The losses due to these causes at each duration are shown in columns 5 and 7.

The chances that a cohort of marriages will survive between specified wedding anniversaries can be readily determined from the figures in column 4. According to the 1955 table, out of every five marriages contracted, four would reach the tenth anniversary, three the silver anniversary, and one the golden anniversary. Similarly, among the marriages which have attained the 10th anniversary, one in two may be expected to continue for at least 29 years longer. Those which have survived for 25 years have an equal chance of celebrating 19 additional anniversaries.

The probability of celebrating most marriage milestones was somewhat smaller according to conditions in 1948. However, the reverse is true with regard to the first five years of married life, as may be seen from a comparison of Tables 71 and 72. For example, the proportion that would continue to duration 3 years was 92.4 per cent in 1948 compared with 91.9 per cent in 1955.

Probability of Divorce. These figures are shown in column 10 under the heading, "Per cent dissolved by divorce in this year of duration and all later years." They represent the proportion of marriages at a particular duration which would subsequently be dissolved by divorce or annulment

according to the divorce and death rates in columns 2 and 3. The figures are calculated from the accumulated number dissolved by divorce (column 6) divided by the number of existing marriages (column 4).

The chances that a newly contracted marriage will eventually end in divorce or annulment is relatively high in the United States. They are 25 in 100 according to conditions during 1955 and 29 in 100 for those of 1948. Judged by the later table, one out of every ten marriages will be legally dissolved within the first five years of marriage[18] and one of six within the first eleven years. Although the probability of divorce lessens with each advance in duration of marriage, it exceeds 10 in 100 through the 11th anniversary and remains above 5 in 100 until the 22nd. Moreover, not until after the 37th year does the likelihood of divorce drop below 1 in 100.

Expected Duration of Marriage. These figures are shown in column 11 under the heading "Average number of years of marriage remaining before dissolution by divorce or death." In order to arrive at these values, it is first necessary to compute the total time (in years) spent within each year of duration by the marriages surviving from the initial cohort of 100,000. The figures in column 8 for any one year of duration, except the first,[19] are midway between the existing marriages at the beginning and end of that year of duration (column 4). Column 9 is constructed by accumulating the figures in column 8, and represents the total number of years of marriage lived by the survivors of the initial cohort after attaining a specified wedding anniversary. This cumulated number (of years) for a particular duration divided by the number of marriages existing at that duration (column 4) gives the average remaining marital lifetime.

The average lifetime of a marriage is the figure shown opposite duration 0 in column 11 of the accompanying tables. The data indicate that the average increased about $1\frac{1}{2}$ years between

[18]This measure is computed by summing the figures in column 5 from duration 0 through duration 4, and dividing by the initial cohort of 100,000.

[19]Because divorces and annulments are not uniformly distributed over the first twelve months of marriage, the stationary population (column 8) for duration 0 years was computed from the number of marriages existing at the beginning of each month of duration.

1948 and 1955. Currently, newlywed couples may look forward to 31.5 years,[20] on the average, before their marriage is dissolved by divorce or death.

The number of years of marriage remaining decreases very little between the first and fourth anniversaries, due to the high rate of dissolutions from divorce and annulment during this period of marriage. According to the experience in 1955 (Table 71), the average is 31.2 years at durations 1 and 2, and it still is as high as 31.0 years at duration 4. Thereafter, however, the figure declines steadily with each advance in duration. There are 25.6 years remaining, on the average, at the 15th anniversary and 19.6 years at the 25th. At the golden wedding anniversary, the typical couple can look forward to 7.6 additional years of married life.

Another standard which may be used for measuring the lifetime of a marriage is its probable duration—the duration to which a newly contracted marriage has just an even chance of surviving. This value is also known as the median duration of marriage, since it is the duration at which half of the initial cohort of marriages has been dissolved by divorce or death. In computing this measure, the divorces and deaths in the duration interval in which the median duration lies are assumed to be uniformly distributed. The median in Tables 71-72 (pages 145-146) is the duration at which there are exactly 50,000 marriages remaining in column 4. This duration is 33.3 years for 1955 and 30.6 years for 1948. Evidently the probable duration of marriage is somewhat longer than its expected duration.

Potential Years of Marriage. If all marriages continued until the death of one of the spouses, the average couple who married in 1955 could look forward to 39.4 years together. This is 7.9 years longer than the *actual* expected duration, which allows for the probability of divorce and annulment as well as of mortality. Table 73 shows for every 5th wedding anniversary the potential years of marriage remaining and the years lost because of divorce and annulment, according to conditions

Table 73. Potential Years of Marriage, and Years Lost by Divorce, Total Population, United States, 1955

Duration (Years)	Potential Years of Marriage*	Years Lost by Divorce	Duration (Years)	Potential Years of Marriage*	Years Lost by Divorce
0	39.4	7.9	20	23.5	1.0
5	35.3	4.6	25	20.2	.6
10	31.3	2.8	30	17.0	.3
15	27.3	1.7	35	14.0	.1

*Average number of years of marriage remaining if marriages were dissolved by death only. Computed as per Table 71, using 0's in column 2 and the death rates in column 3.

prevailing in 1955. It is evident that the number of years lost as a result of divorce lessens rapidly after the early period of marriage; by the 20th anniversary it amounts to only one year.

Variations by Age at Marriage. The values in Tables 71-73 relate to the total experience for married persons of varying ages who have attained a specific duration of marriage. However, the experience for persons who married very early in life and for those who married at an advanced age undoubtedly differs from that of the total group, most of whom married within a relatively narrow range of ages. Thus it would be useful to have tables which take into account the ages of the spouses as well as the duration of marriage. Unfortunately, the absence of requisite data preclude the construction of such tables for American marriages.

There are indications that the divorce rate varies according to the age disparity between husband and wife. In Iowa during 1937-1948, for example, the ratio of divorces to marriages for husbands at least 25 years older than their wife was approximately double that for spouses with a smaller age differential. More precise information for other countries shows that the divorce rate is also relatively high for marriages in which the wife is much older than her husband. In Sweden during 1919-1922, when the rate was 1.4 per 1,000 for all existing marriages, it was more than double that figure for the marriages where the husband was at least 15 years younger than his spouse as well as for those where he was her senior by 25 years or more.[21] Statistics

[20]It is interesting to note that this figure corresponds to that for France during 1928-1933. See Pierre Depoid, "New Tables Relative to the French Population," *Bulletin de la Statistique Générale de la France*, 27:269-324, January-March, 1938.

[21]Carl-Erik Quensel, "Frequency of Divorce with Special Regard to the Number of Children," *Annex No. 6*, Statistical Institute in Lund, 1938, p. 200 (in Swedish).

for Amsterdam,[22] covering various periods from 1905 to 1932, and for France[23] during 1930-1932, reveal a similar pattern.

Even more conclusive is the evidence regarding the role of mortality in determining the probable length of marriage for couples of specified ages. This may be seen from Table 74, which was derived from the mortality experienced by the total

Table 74. Chances in 1,000 of Joint Survival for 10, 25, or 50 Years, White Population, United States, 1955 and 1900-02

Age of Male	Years of Joint Survival								
	10	25	50	10	25	50	10	25	50
	Female Four Years Younger			Female Same Age as Male			Female Two Years Older		
	1955								
17	978	932	539	977	927	501	977	923	476
19	977	924	480	977	918	438	976	913	413
21	977	914	419	976	906	375	976	901	350
23	977	902	357	976	892	314	975	886	289
25	976	886	296	975	875	254	973	867	228
27	974	867	237	972	853	195	971	845	170
29	971	843	181	968	827	142	966	817	120
31	967	815	131	963	797	97	960	785	79
33	961	783	88	956	762	61	953	749	47
35	953	746	55	947	723	34	944	707	25
37	943	704	32	937	678	18	933	660	12
39	932	658	17	924	627	9	919	607	6
	1900-02								
17	899	699	267	887	683	235	882	675	216
19	887	681	229	877	666	197	873	659	179
21	878	664	192	869	650	161	865	643	144
23	870	648	157	862	634	127	859	627	111
25	862	631	123	856	617	96	853	609	82
27	855	614	92	849	598	68	846	588	56
29	847	594	65	842	576	45	839	564	36
31	840	571	42	835	550	28	832	536	21
33	833	545	26	828	520	15	824	504	11
35	825	515	14	820	487	8	816	470	5
37	817	482	7	810	451	3	805	432	2
39	807	445	3	798	411	1	792	390	1

white population of the United States. As the figures indicate, the probabilities of joint survival for a period of 50 years are very favorable for young couples, but decrease rapidly with advance in age. Thus, for the man aged 21 who marries a girl four years younger than himself, the chances

[22]J. H. van Zanten and T. van den Brink, "Population Phenomena in Amsterdam," *Population*, August, 1938, pp. 24-29.

[23]Pierre Depoid, "Mortalité par État Matrimonial: Dissolution des Unions Suivant la Durée et L'Age Combiné des Deux Époux," *Journal de la Société de Statistique de Paris*, April, 1938, pp. 100-101.

are now better than 2 out of 5 that both will survive to the golden anniversary. However, in cases of marriage at ages 29 or later, the corresponding chances are less than 1 out of 5. Of course, the likelihood of celebrating a silver wedding anniversary is very much greater. In fact, even for men who marry as late as age 35, the chances are better than 7 in 10. This is more favorable than the comparable chances for teen-agers who married around the turn of the century.[24]

The figures in the accompanying table approximate the chances that both parties to a marriage will survive to the 10th, 25th, or 50th anniversary. Since a large proportion of marriages are dissolved by divorce or annulment (Tables 71-73), mere survival to these anniversaries does not necessarily imply their celebration.

Pattern for Remarriages. With the high divorce rates of recent years, attention has been focused on the relatively large proportion of divorces granted to persons who had been previously divorced. This situation has been referred to in the literature as a drift toward serial or sequential polygamy,[25] which is not unlike the term "successive polygamy" first used shortly after the Civil War.[26] The question naturally arises whether remarriages are more likely to end in divorce or annulment than are first marriages. Although this question cannot be answered conclusively, it would appear that the remarriages are the less stable. Thus data for Iowa and Missouri indicate that remarried persons account for a disproportionate share of the total divorces and annulments. In Iowa, for example, where remarrying brides and grooms constituted only one sixth of the total marriages during 1937-1949, persons married more than once accounted for one fourth of all divorces and annulments. In

[24]For information regarding the joint expectation of life for couples of various age combinations, according to mortality conditions for the white population of the United States in 1939-1941, see "Length of Married Life Increases," *Statistical Bulletin* (Metropolitan Life Insurance Company), February, 1944, p. 7.

[25]Thomas P. Monahan and L. E. Chancellor, "Statistical Aspects of Marriage and Divorce by Religious Denomination in Iowa," *Eugenics Quarterly*, 2:170, September, 1955.

Paul H. Landis, "Sequential Marriage," *Journal of Home Economics*, 42:628, October, 1950.

[26]Anon., "Frequent Divorce in New England," *American Quarterly Church Review*, 20:234, July, 1868.

other words, the ratio of divorces to marriages was about two thirds higher for the remarried. Moreover, the ratio rises substantially for each higher order of remarriage.

How accurately does the ratio of divorces to marriages measure the frequency of divorce? Since remarriages have been increasing in importance during recent years, at any point of time the proportion remarried among all existing marriages is smaller than the proportion remarrying among the marriages being started. For this reason alone, the true rate of divorce— the annual number of divorces and annulments per 1,000 existing remarriages—would be greater than that indicated by the ratio of divorces to remarriages. It may be that the duration-specific divorce rates for remarriages are almost twice those for all marriages. On the assumption that this approximates the true situation, the chances that a remarriage will end in divorce have been computed for 1955. In addition to using double the divorce rates shown in column 2 of Table 71, the duration-specific death rates in column 3 have been advanced by 12 years to allow for the higher average age at which remarriages occur.[27] According to these conditions, 41 out of every

[27] Based on ages of grooms, United States, 1948.

100 remarriages would be dissolved by divorce or annulment. In other words, the chances of divorce are almost two thirds greater for remarriages than for all marriages. Moreover, the remarriages endure for a shorter period of time, on the average; their probable duration is only 17.2 years, or about 16 years less than that for all marriages. It is also noteworthy that the chances are less than 2 in 5 of reaching the silver anniversary and only little more than 3 in 100 of celebrating the golden anniversary.

Celebrants of Silver and Golden Anniversaries. So much has been made of our high divorce rate that we tend to overlook the fact that an increasing number of marriages have endured to the 25th and later anniversaries. For example, the number of existing marriages at durations 25-29 years increased from 2.3 million in 1932 to about 3.1 million in 1955 (Table A22). Equally noteworthy, in 1955 about 690,000 couples celebrated the silver anniversary and 110,000 the golden anniversary. Couples reaching these happy occasions will continue to grow in the years ahead. The number of marriages attaining the 25th anniversary will rise to 770,000 by 1960 and exceed 880,000 in 1965; those celebrating the golden anniversary will increase to 130,000 in 1960 and to 160,000 five years later.

APPENDIX NOTES

1. SECOND MARRIAGE CEREMONIES

Within two years after marriage in Bronx or New York counties (New York State),[1] almost 3 per cent of the couples had a second ceremony; at the end of three years the proportion was 4 per cent. In a few cases the original marriage was performed by a religious officiant and the second ceremony by a clergyman of a different faith or by a civil official. Much more frequently, the records revealed a civil ceremony followed by a religious one. Thus the frequency of second ceremonies was determined largely by the proportion of marriages initiated by a civil ceremony— about one fourth may ultimately be followed by a religious ceremony. The actual experience was about 11 per cent within two years of marriage and almost 18 per cent within three years. If this is typical of the national experience, and since one fourth of all marriages in the country are now performed by civil ceremony, it would indicate that close to 6 per cent of all marriages in the United States are followed by a second ceremony.

In Bronx and New York counties there is a definite policy for handling second marriage ceremonies. If the license for the original marriage was issued in the county, the second ceremony record is filed under the original registration number and apparently is not included in the marriage statistics. However, whether or not all such cases were identified by the City Clerk was not determined, since this would require intensive search of the files and indexes for about nine years.

A second ceremony record for a marriage which originally took place in a different jurisdic-

tion is relatively infrequent. In The Bronx, for example, at the start of September, 1951, they constituted about one fifth of all second ceremony records in the 1948 files. These, however, were registered and counted as original marriages. All ten cases discovered among the records in the sample were by religious officiants. The initial marriage for one case occurred in Tarrytown, New York; five in other states; and four in Europe.

Judged by this experience, it is likely that the overstatement of marriages due to second ceremonies may vary from as little as 0.5 per cent in states with good record systems to almost 6 per cent in those with poor systems. The proportion may be relatively high in states, such as California, from which a large number of residents "migrate" to marry by civil ceremony in neighboring states.

2. MARRIAGE LICENSE: BOTH PARTIES APPLY IN PERSON

Many states require only one party to appear at the marriage bureau when applying for a license, despite definite and worthwhile advantages to be gained by requiring both parties to appear. The more important of these are to lessen the possibility of fraud and to increase the accuracy of the personal particulars of both parties.

The first of these advantages is worthy of further comment. It seems strange that in our country where there has been almost continuous demand for restrictive divorce legislation as a "means toward better marriages," the educational value of information on marriage records has been all but overlooked. For example, there are indications that the divorce rate is relatively high among the remarried who have dependent children from a previous marriage. Indeed, some remarriages may fail simply because the

[1]Based on an investigation by the author of more than 2,000 records of marriage licenses issued and used during 1948. For information on the situation in New Jersey, see Thomas P. Monahan, *The Pattern of Age at Marriage in the United States*, Stephenson-Brothers, Philadelphia, 1951, Vol. I, p. 182.

spouse was not "aware" of the dependent children until some time after the marriage. With remarriages now constituting a sizable proportion of total marriages, it is evident that an item calling for such information would be a valuable addition to the marriage record. Yet, not one jurisdiction required any information on children of a previous marriage until August 29, 1951, when the following regulation became effective in Ohio:

In case either party has been previously married the application shall include the names of the parties to any such marriage, any minor children, and if divorced the jurisdiction, date and case number of the decree.

The requirement that both parties appear and make application could be waived in certain special circumstances, primarily when one of the parties is unable to appear by reason of illness or other physical disability. In such cases, however, the disability should be documented by affidavit of a practicing physician, and the absent party should make and cause to be filed an affidavit setting forth the information required of marriage applicants.

3. ADJUSTMENT OF DIVORCED POPULATION

As the first step, account was taken of the fact that our nation's divorce statistics overstate the number of American men and women who are divorced each year. The author's estimates of the amount of this overstatement, by decades, are as follows:

Decade	Husbands	Wives
1860–1869	190	170
1870–1879	890	780
1880–1889	2,620	2,700
1890–1899	6,070	5,800
1900–1909	13,000	12,000
1910–1919	25,000	22,000
1920–1929	44,000	41,000
1930–1939	55,000	53,000
1940–1949	30,000	29,000

For the years prior to 1940, the estimates represent largely the exclusion of separations, which are included in the published divorce statistics. The Bureau of the Census has reported that separations (limited decrees) constituted less than 1 per cent of the total of absolute and limited decrees in their statistics for 1887-1906. According to surveys by the author, there were almost 12,000 legal separations in the United States during 1948. This means that they amounted to almost 2.8 per cent of the total of absolute and limited decrees in that year. The number of separations in other years was estimated on the assumption that there were none prior to 1860, and that thereafter the proportion increased linearly to the figure for 1887-1906 and then to that for 1948. However, no allowance was necessary for the 1940's, since the divorce data exclude separations (Table 42).

The estimates also allow for the fact that some divorces are granted in the United States while the spouse resides in a foreign country. This component was derived from statistics by the Bureau of the Census showing the number of libelees residing outside the state in which the decree was granted during 1887-1906, 1916, and 1922, and the number of libelees in a foreign country during 1922. An arbitrary allowance was also made for duplicate and voided decrees. Their number is not believed to have been too significant prior to World War II; however, they represent a large proportion of the total estimate for the 1940's.

As the second step, the number of divorced men and women was estimated as of January 1, 1860, on the assumption that the relationship between the number of divorced persons reported in the 1890 Census to the number of persons divorced in 1889 was the same in 1860. (Since there were few divorced persons in 1860, even a relatively large error in this estimate would have only a negligible effect on estimates of their numbers in later years.) Their number for subsequent years was then derived by allowing for net in-migration, new divorces, remarriages, and deaths. For this purpose, divorced male and female in-migrants were each assumed to increase linearly from zero in 1860 to 100 in 1900, and one tenth of the decennial figures shown in Table A3 was used for later years. The annual number of remarriages and deaths was derived from the unadjusted annual remarriage and death rates for 1900-1950, with the average annual rate for 1900-1909 used as the rate for the years prior to 1900.

APPENDIX TABLES

Table A1. Live Births by Sex, United States, 1900-1950

(Number in 1,000's)

Year	Male	Female	Year	Male	Female	Year	Male	Female
1900	1,282	1,214	1917	1,514	1,430	1934	1,230	1,166
1901	1,291	1,223	1918	1,516	1,432	1935	1,219	1,158
1902	1,305	1,236	1919	1,408	1,332	1936	1,207	1,148
1903	1,317	1,247	1920	1,516	1,434	1937	1,238	1,175
1904	1,329	1,259	1921	1,571	1,484	1938	1,280	1,216
1905	1,343	1,272	1922	1,481	1,401	1939	1,265	1,201
1906	1,356	1,284	1923	1,495	1,415	1940	1,313	1,246
1907	1,367	1,295	1924	1,531	1,448	1941	1,387	1,316
1908	1,380	1,308	1925	1,497	1,412	1942	1,537	1,452
1909	1,396	1,322	1926	1,459	1,380	1943	1,593	1,511
1910	1,426	1,351	1927	1,441	1,361	1944	1,509	1,430
1911	1,442	1,367	1928	1,374	1,300	1945	1,467	1,391
1912	1,458	1,382	1929	1,327	1,255	1946	1,754	1,657
1913	1,473	1,396	1930	1,345	1,273	1947	1,960	1,857
1914	1,523	1,443	1931	1,286	1,220	1948	1,866	1,771
1915	1,522	1,443	1932	1,252	1,188	1949	1,872	1,777
1916	1,523	1,441	1933	1,185	1,122	1950	1,863	1,769

Note: Adjusted for underregistration; total births for 1900-1908 and sex distribution for 1900-1934, estimated by the author.

Source of basic data: National Office of Vital Statistics, *Vital Statistics–Special Reports*, Vol. 37, No. 7, p. 154 for births by sex during 1935-1950 and Vol. 33, No. 8, p. 141 for total births during 1909-1934.

Table A2. Net Increase of Immigrant Aliens, by Sex and Marital Status, United States, 1900-1951

(Number in 1,000's)

Year Ended June 30	MALE					FEMALE				
	Total	Single	Married	Widowed	Divorced	Total	Single	Married	Widowed	Divorced
1900	223.0	146.1	74.9	1.9	0.1	106.0	75.5	25.9	4.5	0.1
1901	214.0	144.7	67.3	1.9	.1	131.0	88.4	37.1	5.4	.1
1902	339.0	222.5	113.5	2.9	.1	154.0	103.5	44.1	6.3	.1
1903	434.0	286.8	143.3	3.8	.1	211.0	140.6	61.8	8.5	.1
1904	314.0	219.9	91.0	3.0	.1	220.0	148.6	62.3	9.0	.1
1905	514.0	339.4	170.0	4.5	.1	254.0	171.0	72.6	10.3	.1
1906	486.0	330.2	151.2	4.5	.1	283.0	190.5	80.8	11.6	.2
1907	637.0	424.4	206.9	5.6	.1	296.0	200.2	83.6	12.1	.2
1908	164.0	140.8	21.2	2.0	.1	223.8	153.0	61.5	9.2	.1
1909	341.2	229.8	108.2	3.1	.1	184.8	127.2	50.0	7.6	.1
1910	581.2	341.2	234.9	5.0	.1	257.9	172.3	74.4	11.1	.1
1911	331.1	244.5	83.0	3.5	.1	251.8	174.1	66.7	10.9	.2
1912	254.0	198.6	52.7	2.6	.1	250.9	174.5	65.1	11.2	.2
1913	556.3	361.5	191.5	3.2	.1	333.4	226.6	92.0	14.5	.2
1914	556.5	342.0	210.6	3.9	.1	358.6	244.5	97.1	16.8	.3
1915	18.9	35.1	− 17.0	.7	*	103.7	69.5	28.2	5.9	.1
1916	75.6	51.9	22.3	1.3	*	93.5	57.1	30.6	5.6	.1
1917	126.1	83.4	40.3	2.3	.1	103.1	63.5	32.9	6.7	.1
1918	− 9.5	.9	− 10.7	.3	*	25.5	16.3	7.3	1.9	.1
1919	− 17.9	20.2	− 39.2	1.0	*	35.5	20.4	12.0	3.1	.1
1920	9.9	103.2	− 95.7	2.3	.1	131.8	85.0	35.7	11.0	.2
1921	260.3	233.0	24.2	3.0	.1	297.2	201.8	74.8	20.4	.3
1922	6.5	48.4	− 42.5	.6	.1	104.3	84.3	9.7	9.9	.3
1923	252.8	170.8	78.5	3.3	.2	188.7	119.3	56.7	12.2	.5
1924	365.9	245.4	115.7	4.5	.3	264.2	152.9	95.8	14.8	.7
1925	92.4	86.9	3.9	1.5	.1	109.2	68.8	33.7	6.3	.3
1926	115.6	95.3	18.9	1.4	.1	111.9	71.2	34.4	5.9	.5
1927	142.6	110.6	30.2	1.6	.1	119.2	73.4	39.2	6.3	.4
1928	111.2	92.3	17.6	1.2	.1	118.6	72.8	39.5	5.8	.5
1929	95.6	82.7	11.9	.8	.1	114.9	70.3	39.3	4.8	.5
1930	84.5	69.5	14.1	.8	.1	106.6	63.1	38.2	4.9	.4
1931	− .2	8.0	− 8.2	− .1	*	35.5	20.2	12.9	2.2	.2
1932	− 52.9	− 22.6	− 28.4	−1.9	− *	− 14.8	− 5.3	− 8.2	− 1.3	.1
1933	− 42.6	− 18.9	− 22.5	−1.2	− *	− 14.4	− 5.2	− 8.2	− 1.1	*
1934	− 12.4	− 4.1	− 8.0	− .3	− *	2.1	.5	1.2	.3	.1
1935	− 10.4	− 2.6	− 7.4	− .3	− *	6.5	3.1	3.0	.2	.1
1936	− 7.0	− 1.1	− 5.6	− .2	− *	7.5	3.5	3.5	.4	.1
1937	5.2	4.7	.6	− .1	.1	18.3	8.6	8.5	.9	.2
1938	14.5	9.6	4.8	*	.1	28.1	14.5	11.7	1.6	.4
1939	22.8	12.2	10.3	.1	.2	33.5	15.3	15.5	2.2	.5
1940	19.7	8.9	10.6	*	.2	29.6	11.5	15.6	2.0	.5
1941	12.3	4.7	7.3	.1	.2	22.4	8.3	11.9	1.8	.4
1942	7.6	3.1	4.2	.2	.1	13.9	5.0	7.3	1.4	.2
1943	7.0	2.9	3.9	.2	.1	11.6	4.4	5.9	1.1	.2
1944	8.7	3.5	4.8	.3	.1	14.2	5.3	7.4	1.3	.3
1945	9.6	4.4	4.8	.3	.2	21.0	8.0	11.3	1.3	.4
1946	17.0	8.9	7.5	.4	.2	73.5	13.3	57.8	1.8	.7
1947	39.4	22.4	15.5	1.1	.4	85.4	29.9	47.6	6.1	1.8
1948	55.8	32.1	21.7	1.4	.6	93.9	33.7	50.5	7.6	2.0
1949	67.4	36.5	28.9	1.5	.4	96.3	33.7	55.0	6.3	1.4
1950	104.8	55.1	46.9	2.0	.8	116.8	47.6	59.4	7.7	2.1
1951	86.5	44.7	39.1	1.6	1.0	93.1	38.5	46.2	6.4	2.0

*Less than 50 persons.

Note: Minus sign (−) denotes excess of departures over admissions. Individual figures have been independently rounded; hence the sums of parts may differ slightly from the totals.

Source of basic data: U.S. Immigration and Naturalization Service for immigrant aliens admitted, by sex, 1900-1909, and by sex and marital status, 1910-1951; for emigrant aliens departed, by sex, 1908-1917, and by sex and marital status, 1918-1951; all other figures, estimated by the author.

Table A3. Net Increase of Population Through Migration, by Sex and Marital Status, United States, 1900-1950

(Number in 1,000's)

Intercensal Period Ended	MALE					FEMALE				
	Total	Single	Married	Widowed	Divorced	Total	Single	Married	Widowed	Divorced
April 15, 1910	2,646	1,992	626	27	1	1,535	1,212	256	66	1
January 1, 1920	1,104	1,076	13	14	1	1,435	1,045	317	72	1
April 1, 1930	1,624	1,412	185	25	2	1,676	1,087	467	116	6
April 1, 1940	− 201	− 62	−142	−	3	150	70	36	36	8
April 1, 1950	1,023	513	473	27	10	937	331	522	67	17

Note: Minus sign (−) denotes excess of departures over admissions.

Source: Estimated by the author from Table A2 and data on the movement of nonimmigrant aliens and citizens.

Table A4. Population in the Armed Forces Overseas, by Marital Status According to Age and Sex, United States, April, 1950

(Number in 1,000's)

Sex and Age	Total	Single	Married	Widowed	Divorced
Male Total	433.0	289.7	122.2	4.3	16.8
Under 20	83.0	82.0	.7	.1	.1
20 − 24	169.0	139.7	25.5	.6	3.2
25 − 29	75.0	37.5	32.6	.6	4.2
30 − 34	58.0	18.9	33.7	.8	4.5
35 − 39	27.0	7.0	16.8	.7	2.5
40 − 44	13.0	2.9	8.1	.6	1.4
45 − 49	5.0	1.0	3.0	.4	.6
50 − 54	2.0	.4	1.1	.3	.2
55 − 59	1.0	.2	.5	.2	.1
Female Total	2.5	1.8	.3	.2	.2

Note: Individual figures have been independently rounded; hence the sums of parts may differ slightly from the totals.

Source: Estimated by the author from sample counts by age, and by marital status, of the male and female armed forces abroad (Bureau of the Census, *1950 Census of Population*, Vol. II, Part 1, Washington, 1953, pp. 89, 97) and the age distribution of the male armed forces overseas (*Current Population Reports*, Series P-25, No. 98, pp. 7, 15).

Table A5. Population 14 Years Old and Over, by Marital Status According to Age and Sex, United States, April, 1950

(Number in 1,000's)

Sex and Age	Total	Single	Married	Widowed	Divorced
Male Total	55,311.6	14,518.1	37,399.6	2,302.2	1,091.7
14	1,089.5	1,079.9	6.6	1.7	1.3
15 – 19	5,311.3	5,135.8	165.7	5.0	4.9
20 – 24	5,606.3	3,316.5	2,229.3	9.1	51.3
25 – 29	5,972.1	1,426.6	4,425.1	15.7	104.7
30 – 34	5,624.7	745.9	4,739.7	21.2	117.8
35 – 39	5,517.5	560.4	4,787.8	36.9	132.4
40 – 44	5,070.3	458.7	4,414.3	60.0	137.3
45 – 49	4,526.4	397.3	3,901.2	94.1	133.8
50 – 54	4,128.6	346.2	3,507.2	152.4	122.9
55 – 59	3,630.0	301.6	3,013.3	215.0	100.1
60 – 64	3,037.8	262.9	2,406.8	291.2	76.9
65 – 69	2,424.6	213.1	1,793.2	363.6	54.7
70 – 74	1,628.8	136.3	1,098.4	363.3	30.9
75 – 79	992.5	80.4	584.4	312.8	14.9
80 – 84	514.3	38.3	247.2	223.0	5.8
85 and over	236.8	18.3	79.3	137.3	2.0
Female Total	57,042.4	11,454.3	37,503.8	6,710.8	1,373.5
14	1,049.7	1,042.0	6.9	.6	.2
15 – 19	5,305.3	4,405.8	878.0	5.2	16.2
20 – 24	5,875.5	1,910.0	3,843.3	25.2	96.9
25 – 29	6,270.2	838.8	5,215.0	57.5	158.9
30 – 34	5,892.3	550.5	5,073.6	92.0	176.2
35 – 39	5,728.8	482.5	4,892.0	156.1	198.2
40 – 44	5,133.7	427.8	4,260.6	254.4	190.9
45 – 49	4,544.1	362.4	3,624.4	391.4	165.8
50 – 54	4,143.5	323.4	3,105.9	577.6	136.6
55 – 59	3,605.1	280.8	2,488.5	738.9	96.9
60 – 64	3,021.6	248.4	1,812.3	897.0	64.0
65 – 69	2,578.4	218.5	1,258.7	1,061.2	40.0
70 – 74	1,783.1	162.2	651.4	950.1	19.5
75 – 79	1,135.9	108.1	279.6	739.8	8.4
80 – 84	635.1	59.8	90.0	482.1	3.2
85 and over	340.1	33.1	23.7	281.7	1.5

Note: Individual figures have been independently rounded; hence the sums of parts may differ slightly from the totals.

Source: Sample estimates of marital status according to age adjusted by the author to complete counts of age, and of marital status; basic data from Bureau of the Census, 1950 *Census of Population*, Vol. II, Part 1, Washington, 1953, pp. 90, 97, 179.

Table A6. Population by Sex and Marital Status, United States, 1890-1950

(Number in 1,000's on July 1 of Each Year)

Year	MALE Total	Single Under 15	Single 15 and Over	Married	Widowed	Divorced	FEMALE Total	Single Under 15	Single 15 and Over	Married	Widowed	Divorced	Divorced Population (Adjusted) Male	Divorced Population (Adjusted) Female
1890	32,292	11,340	8,765	11,312	826	49	30,764	10,981	6,323	11,213	2,175	72	120	116
1891	32,952	11,527	8,938	11,569	872	46	31,410	11,177	6,458	11,462	2,244	69	128	124
1892	33,611	11,714	9,105	11,833	915	44	32,055	11,373	6,586	11,718	2,310	68	135	131
1893	34,269	11,901	9,271	12,097	957	43	32,701	11,569	6,716	11,973	2,375	68	142	137
1894	34,928	12,088	9,444	12,359	995	42	33,347	11,765	6,852	12,228	2,434	68	147	143
1895	35,586	12,275	9,614	12,625	1,029	43	33,994	11,961	6,989	12,487	2,488	69	153	148
1896	36,244	12,462	9,772	12,901	1,063	46	34,641	12,157	7,114	12,755	2,541	74	160	155
1897	36,901	12,650	9,923	13,184	1,092	52	35,288	12,353	7,237	13,032	2,586	80	168	163
1898	37,558	12,837	10,076	13,467	1,118	60	35,936	12,549	7,360	13,309	2,629	89	176	171
1899	38,215	13,024	10,223	13,751	1,146	71	36,584	12,745	7,479	13,586	2,673	101	186	180
1900	38,869	13,206	10,353	14,041	1,185	84	37,226	12,936	7,577	13,873	2,726	114	199	193
1901	39,649	13,384	10,576	14,378	1,223	88	37,936	13,109	7,739	14,195	2,774	119	214	208
1902	40,480	13,567	10,804	14,761	1,255	93	38,680	13,287	7,889	14,561	2,820	123	227	220
1903	41,263	13,725	11,013	15,148	1,280	97	39,369	13,440	8,015	14,930	2,857	127	237	230
1904	42,082	13,885	11,242	15,541	1,312	102	40,083	13,596	8,151	15,304	2,900	132	245	239
1905	42,968	14,060	11,498	15,955	1,347	108	40,852	13,767	8,307	15,691	2,949	138	255	248
1906	43,836	14,225	11,727	16,390	1,378	116	41,600	13,927	8,436	16,096	2,996	145	267	259
1907	44,679	14,377	11,926	16,842	1,408	126	42,321	14,075	8,531	16,515	3,045	155	279	271
1908	45,595	14,553	12,172	17,295	1,438	137	43,114	14,246	8,667	16,940	3,096	165	293	284
1909	46,546	14,742	12,436	17,757	1,462	149	43,945	14,430	8,834	17,362	3,142	177	309	298
1910	47,554	14,966	12,670	18,278	1,485	155	44,852	14,648	8,996	17,818	3,205	185	321	311
1911	48,292	15,162	12,785	18,682	1,506	157	45,576	14,842	9,097	18,180	3,267	190	331	323
1912	49,020	15,369	12,881	19,085	1,524	161	46,311	15,045	9,191	18,547	3,331	197	341	338
1913	49,961	15,653	12,999	19,602	1,545	162	47,266	15,324	9,316	19,011	3,413	202	344	345
1914	50,889	15,945	13,099	20,111	1,570	164	48,229	15,611	9,447	19,467	3,498	206	345	349
1915	51,571	16,168	13,137	20,500	1,596	170	48,978	15,830	9,535	19,831	3,568	214	348	357
1916	52,238	16,393	13,140	20,901	1,625	179	49,728	16,051	9,591	20,219	3,642	225	355	367
1917	52,933	16,617	13,105	21,366	1,652	193	50,480	16,272	9,594	20,659	3,719	236	366	376
1918	53,316	16,838	12,966	21,605	1,703	204	51,234	16,490	9,668	20,988	3,841	247	375	382
1919	53,658	16,863	13,051	21,769	1,753	222	51,405	16,515	9,634	21,094	3,901	261	393	397
1920	54,295	17,069	13,076	22,124	1,775	251	52,171	16,713	9,626	21,603	3,942	287	426	424
1921	55,292	17,372	13,236	22,613	1,796	275	53,250	17,015	9,730	22,194	4,000	311	459	454
1922	55,891	17,584	13,277	22,937	1,805	288	54,164	17,229	9,887	22,667	4,055	326	482	475
1923	56,864	17,782	13,486	23,465	1,830	301	55,086	17,416	10,024	23,183	4,122	341	500	494
1924	57,987	18,001	13,754	24,054	1,856	322	56,126	17,618	10,197	23,750	4,198	363	523	520
1925	58,820	18,164	13,944	24,492	1,877	343	57,012	17,755	10,376	24,219	4,273	389	550	552
1926	59,590	18,255	14,148	24,916	1,904	367	57,809	17,835	10,547	24,654	4,354	419	580	589
1927	60,402	18,341	14,366	25,363	1,934	398	58,636	17,916	10,715	25,103	4,446	456	616	633
1928	61,100	18,362	14,588	25,750	1,968	432	59,401	17,926	10,920	25,512	4,545	498	660	684
1929	61,684	18,327	14,778	26,110	2,002	467	60,086	17,872	11,115	25,905	4,652	542	702	737
1930	62,297	18,245	15,050	26,477	2,028	497	60,780	17,753	11,403	26,293	4,751	580	743	789
1931	62,726	18,138	15,303	26,725	2,043	517	61,314	17,665	11,647	26,562	4,832	608	779	837
1932	63,070	17,982	15,589	26,910	2,064	525	61,770	17,530	11,935	26,766	4,915	624	803	875
1933	63,384	17,790	15,857	27,132	2,086	519	62,195	17,348	12,212	27,006	5,002	627	807	895
1934	63,726	17,584	16,021	27,503	2,100	518	62,648	17,143	12,383	27,389	5,096	637	807	913
1935	64,110	17,412	16,096	27,961	2,112	529	63,140	16,966	12,464	27,855	5,197	658	811	938
1936	64,459	17,219	16,157	28,416	2,122	545	63,594	16,762	12,533	28,310	5,302	687	819	968
1937	64,790	17,016	16,184	28,899	2,127	564	64,035	16,552	12,565	28,792	5,408	718	829	999
1938	65,235	16,893	16,225	29,403	2,131	583	64,590	16,424	12,603	29,298	5,513	752	841	1,033
1939	65,713	16,797	16,286	29,895	2,133	602	65,166	16,317	12,659	29,791	5,612	787	855	1,069
1940	66,352	16,711	16,307	30,577	2,145	612	65,770	16,226	12,614	30,415	5,708	807	866	1,102
1941	66,920	16,714	16,094	31,329	2,166	617	66,482	16,219	12,448	31,194	5,804	817	878	1,135
1942	67,597	16,820	15,828	32,145	2,185	619	67,263	16,298	12,232	32,016	5,895	822	875	1,153
1943	68,546	17,136	15,615	32,950	2,209	636	68,194	16,572	12,028	32,759	5,992	843	884	1,178
1944	69,378	17,313	15,633	33,499	2,235	698	69,020	16,775	12,006	33,222	6,110	907	953	1,258
1945	70,035	17,578	15,452	33,942	2,258	805	69,893	16,989	11,957	33,674	6,253	1,020	1,077	1,389
1946	70,631	17,855	14,980	34,589	2,259	948	70,757	17,220	11,623	34,406	6,338	1,170	1,235	1,551
1947	71,946	18,656	14,328	35,631	2,268	1,063	72,180	17,994	10,971	35,488	6,432	1,295	1,350	1,674
1948	73,130	19,339	13,976	36,446	2,274	1,095	73,502	18,654	10,630	36,357	6,523	1,338	1,382	1,718
1949	74,335	20,035	13,768	37,150	2,286	1,096	74,853	19,327	10,440	37,114	6,620	1,352	1,383	1,737
1950	75,530	20,745	13,588	37,785	2,305	1,107	76,153	20,000	10,285	37,777	6,718	1,373	1,380	1,749

Note: Estimated by the author. Includes armed forces overseas during 1917-1919 and 1940-1950. For method of adjusting divorced population, see Appendix Note 3.

Table A7. Population Under Age 15, Married Persons, and Marriage Eligibles, by Sex, United States, 1860-1889

(Number in 1,000's on July 1 of Each Year)

Year	MALE				FEMALE			
	Total	Under Age 15	Married	Marriage Eligibles	Total	Under Age 15	Married	Marriage Eligibles
1860	16,119	6,481	6,029	3,609	15,394	6,294	5,998	3,102
1861	16,528	6,601	6,100	3,827	15,823	6,410	6,069	3,344
1862	16,936	6,721	6,153	4,062	16,252	6,526	6,120	3,606
1863	17,343	6,841	6,202	4,300	16,683	6,642	6,169	3,872
1864	17,749	6,961	6,255	4,533	17,114	6,759	6,221	4,134
1865	18,154	7,081	6,346	4,727	17,547	6,875	6,312	4,360
1866	18,558	7,202	6,482	4,874	17,980	6,991	6,447	4,542
1867	18,961	7,322	6,641	4,998	18,415	7,107	6,605	4,703
1868	19,363	7,442	6,804	5,117	18,850	7,223	6,768	4,859
1869	19,764	7,562	6,968	5,234	19,287	7,339	6,931	5,017
1870	20,175	7,689	7,137	5,349	19,730	7,462	7,100	5,168
1871	20,711	7,890	7,306	5,515	20,227	7,660	7,268	5,299
1872	21,248	8,092	7,465	5,691	20,724	7,857	7,427	5,440
1873	21,785	8,294	7,624	5,867	21,221	8,054	7,585	5,582
1874	22,323	8,496	7,796	6,031	21,717	8,252	7,757	5,708
1875	22,861	8,698	7,966	6,197	22,212	8,449	7,927	5,836
1876	23,400	8,900	8,128	6,372	22,707	8,646	8,089	5,972
1877	23,940	9,102	8,296	6,542	23,201	8,844	8,257	6,100
1878	24,481	9,303	8,480	6,698	23,693	9,041	8,440	6,212
1879	25,022	9,505	8,674	6,843	24,186	9,238	8,633	6,315
1880	25,575	9,704	8,878	6,993	24,687	9,432	8,835	6,420
1881	26,242	9,867	9,087	7,288	25,300	9,586	9,041	6,673
1882	26,912	10,031	9,307	7,574	25,909	9,741	9,256	6,912
1883	27,581	10,194	9,544	7,843	26,519	9,896	9,488	7,135
1884	28,252	10,357	9,776	8,119	27,127	10,050	9,714	7,363
1885	28,924	10,521	10,016	8,387	27,734	10,205	9,950	7,579
1886	29,596	10,684	10,282	8,630	28,342	10,359	10,212	7,771
1887	30,269	10,848	10,531	8,890	28,948	10,514	10,456	7,978
1888	30,943	11,011	10,764	9,168	29,553	10,668	10,682	8,203
1889	31,618	11,174	11,012	9,432	30,157	10,823	10,923	8,411

Note: Estimated by the author.

Table A8. Unmarried Population 14 Years Old and Over, by Sex and Age, United States, 1900-1950

(Number in 1,000's on July 1 of Each Year)

Year	MALE										FEMALE									
	14 & over	14	15-19	20-24	25-34	35-44	45-54	55-64	65-74	75 & over	14 & over	14	15-19	20-24	25-34	35-44	45-54	55-64	65-74	75 & over
1900	12,408	786	3,717	2,863	2,464	1,037	608	420	308	205	11,192	775	3,393	1,990	1,581	889	785	770	633	376
1901	12,683	796	3,784	2,925	2,516	1,066	631	435	318	212	11,418	786	3,451	2,023	1,615	916	807	787	648	385
1902	12,959	807	3,857	2,987	2,568	1,092	652	448	330	218	11,630	798	3,512	2,056	1,640	937	825	800	666	396
1903	13,208	818	3,927	3,046	2,610	1,115	671	461	337	223	11,808	809	3,570	2,079	1,658	956	840	811	680	405
1904	13,486	830	4,002	3,112	2,658	1,140	693	474	348	229	12,002	819	3,631	2,104	1,679	975	859	824	695	416
1905	13,795	842	4,084	3,184	2,715	1,167	719	489	360	235	12,226	832	3,699	2,135	1,707	996	880	838	712	427
1906	14,076	855	4,164	3,252	2,762	1,189	740	502	370	242	12,421	844	3,764	2,158	1,724	1,016	898	850	729	438
1907	14,327	867	4,242	3,310	2,797	1,207	760	515	380	249	12,587	856	3,825	2,177	1,736	1,030	914	859	741	449
1908	14,627	880	4,325	3,376	2,851	1,232	785	532	391	255	12,797	869	3,894	2,200	1,757	1,050	934	872	759	462
1909	14,941	894	4,409	3,445	2,904	1,261	811	551	403	263	13,036	883	3,964	2,230	1,785	1,076	958	888	777	475
1910	15,221	911	4,489	3,498	2,946	1,286	836	567	417	271	13,285	899	4,033	2,257	1,814	1,101	986	908	795	492
1911	15,369	921	4,517	3,502	2,970	1,309	861	585	428	276	13,463	909	4,060	2,269	1,838	1,124	1,013	932	814	504
1912	15,499	933	4,541	3,496	2,987	1,330	886	604	439	283	13,640	921	4,085	2,277	1,860	1,149	1,040	958	832	518
1913	15,653	947	4,578	3,493	3,004	1,352	910	625	452	292	13,867	936	4,120	2,291	1,889	1,178	1,073	990	855	535
1914	15,795	962	4,608	3,484	3,018	1,375	935	648	466	299	14,102	951	4,156	2,303	1,921	1,210	1,107	1,023	879	552
1915	15,877	974	4,617	3,453	3,023	1,395	961	669	478	307	14,279	962	4,167	2,309	1,944	1,237	1,138	1,056	899	567
1916	15,928	984	4,618	3,416	3,017	1,415	985	687	491	315	14,431	973	4,176	2,305	1,963	1,262	1,166	1,085	918	583
1917	15,943	993	4,638	3,376	2,992	1,424	1,000	701	500	319	14,534	985	4,179	2,292	1,965	1,276	1,187	1,113	938	599
1918	15,847	974	4,628	3,247	2,954	1,447	1,028	727	515	327	14,752	996	4,190	2,300	1,997	1,311	1,227	1,152	963	616
1919	16,023	997	4,629	3,248	2,989	1,488	1,058	751	529	334	14,793	997	4,155	2,277	2,000	1,330	1,250	1,179	978	627
1920	16,119	1,017	4,661	3,245	2,993	1,503	1,059	769	537	335	14,864	1,009	4,214	2,235	2,007	1,336	1,251	1,202	988	622
1921	16,351	1,044	4,790	3,276	2,995	1,504	1,065	781	554	342	15,076	1,035	4,300	2,237	2,023	1,342	1,265	1,226	1,016	632
1922	16,434	1,064	4,888	3,277	2,957	1,484	1,063	786	568	347	15,327	1,059	4,396	2,248	2,038	1,350	1,285	1,256	1,050	645
1923	16,704	1,087	5,012	3,341	2,966	1,486	1,062	804	591	355	15,568	1,081	4,493	2,265	2,047	1,355	1,298	1,284	1,086	659
1924	17,041	1,109	5,154	3,434	2,986	1,489	1,068	825	613	363	15,862	1,104	4,614	2,298	2,056	1,363	1,315	1,314	1,125	673
1925	17,286	1,122	5,252	3,489	2,987	1,494	1,084	850	635	373	16,159	1,121	4,717	2,337	2,060	1,379	1,342	1,349	1,161	693
1926	17,554	1,135	5,353	3,549	2,988	1,507	1,107	873	657	385	16,454	1,134	4,799	2,382	2,071	1,400	1,373	1,383	1,200	712
1927	17,848	1,150	5,455	3,621	2,986	1,528	1,134	896	680	398	16,763	1,146	4,882	2,437	2,076	1,427	1,409	1,418	1,235	733
1928	18,153	1,165	5,542	3,697	2,978	1,557	1,173	921	704	416	17,120	1,157	4,958	2,511	2,082	1,466	1,453	1,460	1,273	760
1929	18,422	1,175	5,608	3,771	2,962	1,590	1,212	941	728	435	17,471	1,162	5,014	2,596	2,095	1,508	1,499	1,498	1,311	788
1930	18,764	1,189	5,671	3,853	2,982	1,629	1,255	966	759	460	17,904	1,170	5,071	2,685	2,132	1,560	1,552	1,546	1,359	829
1931	19,052	1,189	5,700	3,917	3,033	1,653	1,281	1,006	785	488	18,257	1,170	5,098	2,726	2,188	1,598	1,590	1,605	1,410	872
1932	19,373	1,195	5,717	3,982	3,105	1,681	1,314	1,050	816	513	18,651	1,177	5,124	2,764	2,258	1,641	1,635	1,672	1,464	916
1933	19,667	1,205	5,731	4,040	3,172	1,703	1,345	1,090	844	537	19,033	1,192	5,155	2,803	2,324	1,676	1,674	1,737	1,515	957
1934	19,861	1,222	5,754	4,081	3,206	1,700	1,360	1,118	864	556	19,327	1,211	5,191	2,824	2,367	1,693	1,703	1,783	1,561	994
1935	19,983	1,246	5,791	4,104	3,211	1,680	1,367	1,133	882	569	19,551	1,232	5,234	2,832	2,388	1,698	1,720	1,818	1,603	1,026
1936	20,082	1,258	5,848	4,113	3,210	1,661	1,371	1,143	898	580	19,767	1,245	5,290	2,839	2,405	1,700	1,739	1,845	1,649	1,055
1937	20,123	1,248	5,917	4,107	3,200	1,635	1,370	1,146	913	587	19,921	1,230	5,349	2,836	2,414	1,698	1,758	1,860	1,695	1,081
1938	20,187	1,248	5,986	4,103	3,187	1,618	1,367	1,152	928	598	20,093	1,225	5,395	2,837	2,428	1,703	1,773	1,875	1,747	1,110
1939	20,257	1,236	6,047	4,111	3,180	1,606	1,364	1,156	948	609	20,268	1,210	5,429	2,845	2,446	1,714	1,790	1,893	1,804	1,137
1940	20,288	1,224	6,089	4,163	3,146	1,587	1,347	1,155	963	614	20,323	1,194	5,415	2,832	2,436	1,717	1,796	1,912	1,859	1,162
1941	20,086	1,209	6,044	4,140	3,061	1,551	1,326	1,157	974	624	20,248	1,179	5,350	2,761	2,381	1,713	1,809	1,949	1,908	1,198
1942	19,823	1,192	5,953	4,136	2,961	1,509	1,300	1,153	983	636	20,111	1,162	5,270	2,678	2,310	1,697	1,818	1,980	1,956	1,240
1943	19,636	1,177	5,864	4,121	2,900	1,483	1,288	1,156	998	649	20,005	1,142	5,187	2,598	2,249	1,692	1,834	2,015	2,007	1,281
1944	19,711	1,146	5,867	4,077	2,915	1,498	1,311	1,189	1,036	672	20,139	1,116	5,115	2,556	2,235	1,724	1,892	2,090	2,085	1,326
1945	19,628	1,115	5,683	4,037	2,917	1,516	1,340	1,228	1,085	707	20,322	1,092	5,033	2,516	2,227	1,764	1,953	2,173	2,175	1,389
1946	19,282	1,097	5,501	3,946	2,838	1,495	1,330	1,238	1,106	731	20,204	1,074	4,911	2,434	2,164	1,757	1,967	2,216	2,233	1,448
1947	18,751	1,094	5,534	3,708	2,684	1,424	1,268	1,204	1,092	743	19,756	1,059	4,759	2,291	2,041	1,706	1,927	2,208	2,259	1,506
1948	18,424	1,081	5,408	3,603	2,561	1,398	1,258	1,220	1,119	776	19,539	1,049	4,603	2,151	1,950	1,699	1,933	2,255	2,321	1,578
1949	18,229	1,082	5,320	3,542	2,515	1,384	1,237	1,224	1,124	801	19,456	1,045	4,500	2,087	1,899	1,689	1,930	2,286	2,368	1,652
1950	18,089	1,092	5,219	3,489	2,463	1,381	1,231	1,237	1,145	832	19,427	1,052	4,405	2,002	1,849	1,693	1,940	2,328	2,429	1,729

Note: Estimated by the author. Includes armed forces overseas during 1917-1919 and 1940-1950.

Table A9. Married Population, by Sex and Age, United States, 1900-1950

(Number in 1,000's on July 1 of Each Year)

Year	MALE 14 & over	14	15-19	20-24	25-34	35-44	45-54	55-64	65-74	75 & over	FEMALE 14 & over	14	15-19	20-24	25-34	35-44	45-54	55-64	65-74	75 & over
1900	14,041	1	38	790	3,807	3,872	2,821	1,658	818	236	13,873	4	417	1,740	4,310	3,474	2,225	1,179	442	82
1901	14,378	1	39	813	3,901	3,965	2,892	1,693	834	240	14,195	4	424	1,781	4,408	3,558	2,277	1,204	454	85
1902	14,761	1	41	843	4,008	4,067	2,971	1,736	849	245	14,561	4	434	1,828	4,519	3,650	2,339	1,234	466	87
1903	15,148	1	42	874	4,121	4,164	3,050	1,776	869	251	14,930	4	443	1,878	4,630	3,740	2,402	1,263	480	90
1904	15,541	1	43	904	4,236	4,263	3,131	1,820	887	256	15,304	4	453	1,929	4,744	3,832	2,466	1,291	493	92
1905	15,955	1	45	935	4,354	4,367	3,217	1,867	907	262	15,691	4	463	1,979	4,858	3,930	2,535	1,321	506	95
1906	16,390	1	46	968	4,483	4,473	3,306	1,916	928	269	16,096	4	473	2,033	4,981	4,027	2,609	1,351	520	98
1907	16,842	1	48	1,009	4,618	4,580	3,397	1,966	949	274	16,515	4	485	2,088	5,105	4,127	2,684	1,385	536	101
1908	17,295	1	49	1,044	4,746	4,690	3,492	2,019	973	281	16,940	4	496	2,143	5,231	4,230	2,763	1,419	550	104
1909	17,757	1	50	1,076	4,879	4,801	3,592	2,073	997	288	17,362	4	507	2,193	5,355	4,333	2,843	1,453	566	108
1910	18,278	1	53	1,115	5,026	4,926	3,703	2,136	1,022	296	17,818	3	519	2,246	5,491	4,448	2,929	1,490	581	111
1911	18,682	1	58	1,142	5,119	5,028	3,794	2,193	1,045	302	18,180	4	529	2,278	5,601	4,544	2,993	1,524	593	114
1912	19,085	1	63	1,167	5,211	5,130	3,889	2,249	1,066	309	18,547	4	537	2,309	5,711	4,645	3,060	1,560	604	117
1913	19,602	2	67	1,200	5,330	5,266	4,007	2,319	1,095	316	19,011	4	550	2,350	5,851	4,768	3,145	1,605	618	120
1914	20,111	2	73	1,229	5,443	5,397	4,126	2,390	1,125	326	19,467	4	558	2,388	5,988	4,894	3,230	1,651	630	124
1915	20,500	2	77	1,247	5,516	5,501	4,223	2,452	1,149	333	19,831	5	567	2,409	6,096	4,998	3,298	1,690	641	127
1916	20,901	2	82	1,266	5,590	5,607	4,322	2,518	1,174	340	20,219	5	574	2,436	6,207	5,106	3,372	1,736	653	130
1917	21,366	3	87	1,292	5,678	5,732	4,429	2,589	1,206	350	20,659	5	586	2,469	6,330	5,227	3,454	1,788	667	133
1918	21,605	3	92	1,267	5,656	5,828	4,522	2,650	1,231	356	20,988	5	590	2,481	6,421	5,328	3,519	1,829	679	136
1919	21,769	3	95	1,268	5,686	5,897	4,550	2,675	1,239	356	21,094	5	588	2,468	6,442	5,372	3,547	1,852	683	137
1920	22,124	3	98	1,287	5,784	6,033	4,575	2,733	1,255	356	21,603	6	609	2,474	6,633	5,511	3,618	1,916	698	138
1921	22,613	3	99	1,311	5,919	6,160	4,660	2,799	1,298	364	22,194	6	631	2,500	6,811	5,658	3,730	1,987	729	142
1922	22,937	3	101	1,329	5,986	6,222	4,724	2,859	1,340	373	22,667	5	647	2,521	6,945	5,766	3,826	2,052	760	145
1923	23,465	2	102	1,364	6,133	6,348	4,784	2,952	1,397	383	23,183	5	668	2,555	7,084	5,880	3,924	2,122	795	150
1924	24,054	2	106	1,410	6,294	6,479	4,861	3,053	1,454	395	23,750	5	692	2,609	7,221	6,008	4,032	2,197	830	156
1925	24,492	2	105	1,432	6,376	6,574	4,958	3,141	1,499	405	24,219	5	710	2,647	7,301	6,132	4,138	2,264	862	160
1926	24,916	2	104	1,449	6,441	6,682	5,058	3,224	1,540	416	24,654	5	720	2,683	7,366	6,256	4,248	2,324	887	165
1927	25,363	2	104	1,471	6,486	6,815	5,183	3,301	1,573	428	25,103	5	731	2,729	7,401	6,403	4,367	2,384	914	169
1928	25,750	1	104	1,487	6,482	6,955	5,319	3,362	1,601	439	25,512	5	735	2,776	7,411	6,560	4,486	2,434	933	172
1929	26,110	1	102	1,501	6,466	7,101	5,455	3,402	1,630	452	25,905	4	736	2,827	7,418	6,719	4,595	2,475	952	179
1930	26,477	1	100	1,510	6,480	7,219	5,586	3,441	1,669	471	26,293	4	730	2,868	7,447	6,862	4,702	2,522	973	185
1931	26,725	1	99	1,501	6,512	7,245	5,652	3,527	1,701	487	26,562	4	717	2,860	7,507	6,917	4,773	2,597	995	192
1932	26,910	1	97	1,484	6,548	7,238	5,705	3,607	1,727	503	26,766	4	701	2,846	7,574	6,941	4,827	2,665	1,012	196
1933	27,132	1	95	1,473	6,603	7,226	5,771	3,687	1,759	517	27,006	4	686	2,836	7,651	6,966	4,895	2,735	1,032	201
1934	27,503	1	95	1,479	6,697	7,240	5,875	3,779	1,804	533	27,389	4	685	2,853	7,752	7,008	4,995	2,822	1,062	208
1935	27,961	1	97	1,495	6,814	7,272	6,001	3,875	1,856	550	27,855	4	691	2,886	7,861	7,063	5,121	2,913	1,100	216
1936	28,416	1	98	1,510	6,926	7,303	6,133	3,964	1,915	566	28,310	4	698	2,913	7,964	7,118	5,252	2,997	1,140	224
1937	28,899	1	101	1,524	7,043	7,350	6,269	4,048	1,980	583	28,792	4	709	2,943	8,066	7,184	5,388	3,079	1,187	232
1938	29,403	1	104	1,538	7,162	7,413	6,406	4,129	2,053	597	29,298	4	717	2,975	8,175	7,267	5,531	3,154	1,237	238
1939	29,895	1	105	1,553	7,272	7,493	6,524	4,213	2,120	614	29,791	3	719	3,010	8,279	7,364	5,659	3,224	1,287	246
1940	30,577	1	109	1,621	7,441	7,625	6,632	4,315	2,199	634	30,415	3	730	3,075	8,421	7,493	5,780	3,313	1,346	254
1941	31,329	2	117	1,724	7,629	7,770	6,729	4,435	2,268	655	31,194	4	757	3,182	8,619	7,658	5,895	3,418	1,396	265
1942	32,145	2	126	1,848	7,823	7,919	6,838	4,558	2,349	682	32,016	4	789	3,294	8,818	7,825	6,020	3,529	1,457	280
1943	32,950	3	136	1,953	8,049	8,073	6,938	4,670	2,423	705	32,759	4	813	3,392	8,998	7,979	6,138	3,631	1,513	291
1944	33,499	3	140	1,986	8,238	8,189	7,005	4,747	2,473	718	33,222	5	815	3,443	9,125	8,094	6,211	3,692	1,542	295
1945	33,942	4	141	2,004	8,339	8,297	7,067	4,829	2,525	736	33,674	5	811	3,479	9,251	8,210	6,283	3,757	1,575	303
1946	34,589	5	142	2,060	8,503	8,440	7,142	4,935	2,596	766	34,406	6	824	3,565	9,448	8,379	6,381	3,855	1,631	317
1947	35,631	5	158	2,122	8,789	8,679	7,259	5,100	2,701	818	35,488	6	857	3,694	9,721	8,611	6,516	4,015	1,724	344
1948	36,446	6	167	2,234	9,016	8,883	7,315	5,220	2,757	848	36,357	6	894	3,806	9,968	8,814	6,600	4,128	1,782	359
1949	37,150	6	168	2,241	9,147	9,089	7,395	5,369	2,843	892	37,114	7	882	3,830	10,165	9,024	6,698	4,266	1,859	383
1950	37,785	7	168	2,278	9,283	9,280	7,458	5,481	2,903	927	37,777	7	888	3,851	10,330	9,215	6,785	4,379	1,919	403

Note: Estimated by the author. Includes armed forces overseas during 1917-1919 and 1940-1950.

Table A10. Population 14 Years Old and Over, by Marital Status According to Age and Sex, United States, Including Armed Forces Overseas, 1940 and 1948

(Number in 1,000's)

Age	MALE					FEMALE				
	Total	Single	Married	Widowed	Divorced	Total	Single	Married	Widowed	Divorced
	April, 1940†									
Total	50,705	17,676	30,259	2,144	626	50,549	13,936	30,090	5,700	823
14	1,218	1,217	1.2	.1	*	1,188	1,184	3.4	.1	.1
15 – 19	6,199	6,092	105	1.0	1.0	6,153	5,424	714	6	9
20 – 24	5,756	4,155	1,575	8	18	5,895	2,781	3,026	33	56
25 – 29	5,485	1,976	3,438	21	49	5,646	1,288	4,185	72	101
30 – 34	5,088	1,054	3,926	37	71	5,172	762	4,156	128	126
35 – 39	4,755	727	3,882	61	85	4,800	536	3,912	220	132
40 – 44	4,424	559	3,682	95	89	4,369	415	3,519	318	117
45 – 49	4,211	472	3,519	136	83	4,046	349	3,168	433	96
50 – 54	3,753	413	3,073	192	75	3,504	305	2,569	559	71
55 – 59	3,012	325	2,407	222	57	2,833	246	1,902	635	49
60 – 64	2,398	252	1,838	266	41	2,331	216	1,353	730	32
65 – 69	1,896	195	1,363	308	30	1,911	179	889	823	20
70 – 74	1,271	126	825	303	16	1,299	124	446	720	9
75 and over	1,239	112	622	493	11	1,404	127	249	1,023	5
	July, 1948									
Total	54,870	15,055	36,446	2,274	1,095	55,896	11,678	36,357	6,523	1,338
14	1,087	1,079	6	1.4	1.1	1,055	1,048	6	.5	.2
15 – 19	5,575	5,399	167	4	5	5,497	4,581	894	6	16
20 – 24	5,837	3,541	2,234	9	53	5,957	2,028	3,806	27	96
25 – 29	5,999	1,509	4,367	17	106	6,157	891	5,050	60	156
30 – 34	5,578	781	4,649	25	123	5,761	568	4,918	99	176
35 – 39	5,348	564	4,608	42	134	5,524	471	4,689	168	196
40 – 44	4,933	453	4,275	67	138	4,989	409	4,125	268	187
45 – 49	4,499	393	3,867	103	136	4,497	349	3,582	405	161
50 – 54	4,074	342	3,448	161	123	4,036	308	3,018	579	131
55 – 59	3,510	292	2,904	217	97	3,467	265	2,386	724	92
60 – 64	2,930	248	2,316	290	76	2,916	234	1,742	879	61
65 – 69	2,306	199	1,701	353	53	2,412	198	1,170	1,007	37
70 – 74	1,570	129	1,056	355	30	1,691	150	612	911	18
75 and over	1,624	126	848	630	20	1,937	178	359	1,389	11

*25 persons.

†Independently rounded; hence the sums of parts may differ slightly from the totals.

Source: Population residing in the United States during 1940, from the Bureau of the Census; all other data, estimated by the author.

Table A11. States with Central Files of Marriage and Divorce Records, and Year Originated (as of August, 1958)

(The custodian is the State Registrar,
Department of Health, unless otherwise noted)

State	Year Originated		State	Year Originated	
	Marriage	Divorce		Marriage	Divorce
Alabama	1936	1908	Nebraska	1909	1909
Arizona	–	–	Nevada	–	–
Arkansas	1917	1923	New Hampshire	1858	1850
California	1905	–	New Jersey	1879	1795(f)
Colorado	–	–	New Mexico	–	–
Connecticut	1897	1947	New York	1880(g)	–
Delaware	1913	1934	North Carolina	–	1958
District of Columbia (b)	1811	1800	North Dakota	1925	1949
Florida	1927	1927	Ohio	1949	1949
Georgia	1952	1952	Oklahoma	–	–
Idaho	1907	1947	Oregon	1906	1925
Illinois	–	–	Pennsylvania	1906	1943(a)
Indiana	–	–	Rhode Island	1853	–
Iowa	1880	1907	South Carolina	1950	–
Kansas	1913	1951	South Dakota	1905	1905
Kentucky	1958	1958	Tennessee	1945	1945
Louisiana(c)	1937	1918	Texas	–	–
Maine	1892	1892	Utah	1919	1954
Maryland	1914	1914	Vermont	1856	1861
Massachusetts(d)	1842	(e)	Virginia	1871	1918
Michigan	1867	1897	Washington	–	–
Minnesota	(h)	–	West Virginia	1921(a)	–
Mississippi	1926	1926	Wisconsin	1852	1907
Missouri	1948	1948	Wyoming	1941	1941
Montana	1943	1943			

(a) File incomplete.
(b) The custodian is the Clerk of the U.S. District Court.
(c) Excludes New Orleans.
(d) The custodian is the Secretary of the Commonwealth.
(e) A law enacted in 1952 requires annual reporting of the names and addresses of persons divorced and the date of the decree.
(f) The custodian is the Clerk of the Chancery Division, Superior Court, at Trenton.
(g) Excludes New York City.
(h) A law effective in 1958 requires monthly reporting of names, addresses, ages, and date of marriage.

Note: Several states had earlier laws, but these were generally ineffective or never enforced.
Source: State reports and statutes, and correspondence from state registrars.

Table A12. Estimated Number of Marriages in the United States and Number Reported in Selected Areas, 1860-1867

Area	1860	1861	1862	1863	1864	1865	1866	1867
United States — Number	256,000	232,000	236,000	256,000	282,000	334,000	354,000	357,000‡
— Rate per 1,000 population§	9.3	8.2	7.9	7.7	8.2	9.4	9.7	9.6‡
Northeast								
Vermont	2,179	2,188	1,962	2,007	1,804	2,569	3,001	2,857
Massachusetts	12,404	10,972	11,014	10,873	12,513	13,051	14,428	14,451
Rhode Island	1,748	1,533	1,450	1,618	1,844	1,896	2,318	2,344
Connecticut	4,036	3,757	3,701	3,467	4,107	4,460	4,978	4,779
New York — New York City	4,088	2,846	2,909	3,218	3,222	2,816	5,792	7,513
New Jersey	3,065	2,682	3,389	4,599	5,007	5,689	5,355	6,127
Pennsylvania — Philadelphia	4,479†	4,417	4,662	5,474	6,752	6,864	7,087	6,084
North Central								
Ohio	22,251	19,540	19,300	20,881	22,198	30,479	29,230	28,231
Illinois	14,148	*	*	*	*	*	*	*
Minnesota — Hennepin County	83	97	82	76	77	147	215	214
Missouri — St. Louis County	1,667	*	*	*	*	*	2,019	*
South								
Maryland	3,703	*	*	*	*	*	*	*
District of Columbia	815	927	1,390	1,821	2,052	2,065	2,002	1,905
Virginia — Norfolk and Richmond	159	256	358	307	361	492	604	686
Georgia — Bibb and Fulton Counties	264	195	162	210	196	301	327	421
Kentucky — Jefferson County	960	645	703	856	1,050	1,328	1,142	1,181
Alabama — Jefferson and Mobile Counties	421	415	356	451	403	697	643	913
Mississippi — Hinds County	107	86	57	34	42	140	133	118
— Lowndes County	93	*	*	*	*	58	272	252
— Other	2,333	*	*	*	*	*	*	*
Texas — Dallas	66	86	44	25	56	118	130	122
West								
California — Sacramento, San Diego and Santa Barbara Counties	101	125	216	334	200	191	204	225
— Other	2,520	*	*	*	*	*	*	*

*Not available.   †First half of year estimated by the author.
‡From the National Office of Vital Statistics.
§Population excludes estimated number of slaves; with slaves included, rates are: 1860 — 8.1, 1861 — 7.2, 1862 — 7.1, 1863 — 7.5, 1864 — 8.1.
Note: Data compiled by the author from state reports and surveys of local registration offices. The figures are believed to be incomplete for several areas; also, in the Confederate States marriages of slaves were not registered prior to 1865.

Table A13. Per Cent Distribution of Marriages by Difference in Age Between Groom and Bride, by Age of Groom and by Age of Bride, United States, 1948

(Total for each horizontal line = 100%)

Age (Years)	Number of Years Groom YOUNGER than Bride								Same Age	Number of Years Groom OLDER than Bride													
	15 or more	10-14	6-9	5	4	3	2	1	Same Age	1	2	3	4	5	6	7	8	9	10	11-14	15-19	20-24	25 or more
Total	0.2	0.6	1.8	1.0	1.3	1.9	3.0	5.0	9.6	10.9	11.3	12.3	8.8	7.1	5.2	4.2	3.2	2.4	2.0	4.6	2.2	0.9	0.5
Groom																							
Under 18		1.7	.6	2.4	2.3	4.3	6.9	16.6	30.9	22.0	9.0	3.3											
18 – 19	.1	.2	.8	.8	.9	2.2	4.9	11.6	26.7	26.0	15.6	7.7	2.2	.3									
20 – 24	.1	.3	1.2	.7	1.1	1.8	3.1	5.5	11.9	14.9	16.5	19.2	11.3	7.2	3.5	1.2	.4	.1					
25 – 29	.2	.6	2.2	.9	1.3	2.2	2.9	3.9	6.6	7.6	8.6	9.7	10.3	10.6	9.3	9.1	6.3	3.8	2.3	1.6			
30 – 34	.2	1.3	3.1	1.5	2.0	2.1	2.4	3.5	5.6	5.2	5.9	6.6	6.4	7.2	7.2	6.8	6.9	5.8	5.9	12.8	1.6		
35 – 39	.2	1.1	2.7	1.6	1.6	2.2	2.9	4.4	6.3	4.6	5.7	5.8	5.5	5.1	5.0	5.4	6.0	5.0	4.8	14.8	8.3	1.0	
40 – 44	.3	1.1	2.8	1.8	1.8	1.9	2.6	4.5	4.5	5.6	5.4	5.5	5.4	5.7	4.7	4.5	4.7	4.4	4.8	14.1	9.7	3.8	.4
45 – 49	.2	.9	1.7	.9	1.4	1.4	2.2	2.9	4.5	3.9	5.0	5.1	4.7	4.2	4.7	5.4	5.1	3.9	4.9	15.8	12.0	6.2	3.0
50 – 54	.6	1.4	2.7	1.1	1.6	1.7	1.6	1.7	4.4	4.3	3.7	3.7	4.2	6.3	4.4	4.6	4.2	4.0	5.1	16.7	11.6	6.6	3.8
55 – 59	.6	.7	2.3	1.4	2.2	1.3	2.5	2.4	2.5	2.9	4.2	3.1	3.8	3.6	3.4	4.0	5.3	4.5	4.4	16.9	14.7	7.2	6.1
60 – 64		.3	1.8	.8	.9	1.4	1.6	1.8	2.4	4.0	4.9	4.0	4.3	3.8	5.0	4.7	3.4	4.5	4.9	17.3	11.6	9.5	7.1
65 – 69		.1	.9	.2	.3	.6	2.0	2.4	3.6	3.7	4.1	4.0	4.5	4.1	4.3	2.9	3.3	3.4	4.1	15.8	16.9	8.2	10.6
70 – 74			.5		.4	.9	1.1	3.4	4.1	2.9	3.8	5.1	4.9	4.9	6.1	4.7	4.0	4.6	5.5	10.5	11.9	10.8	9.9
75 and over			.1	.9		.9	.3	1.8	.7	2.2	2.6	4.9	2.0	2.3	3.9	2.6	5.6	3.5	3.5	13.0	18.6	17.9	12.7
Bride																							
Under 16									.1	2.1	6.0	11.6	17.0	11.7	18.8	8.9	6.1	7.4	2.1	6.2	.8	1.1	.1
16 – 17								.1	2.2	6.8	13.1	14.7	17.8	16.8	8.6	6.0	3.9	2.9	1.8	3.5	1.1	.5	.2
18 – 19						.1	.2	1.5	6.9	9.9	15.4	23.8	12.1	8.1	5.8	4.5	3.3	2.3	1.7	2.9	.9	.4	.2
20 – 24				.2	.3	1.1	3.1	6.6	13.9	15.9	12.8	10.5	8.1	6.6	4.9	3.8	2.8	1.8	1.7	3.5	1.5	.5	.4
25 – 29		.1	2.4	2.3	3.6	5.2	6.7	7.8	10.7	9.2	8.0	7.3	5.9	5.4	4.1	3.7	3.0	2.7	2.2	5.2	2.8	1.1	.6
30 – 34		1.5	6.9	2.9	3.9	5.0	5.3	6.1	8.0	6.7	6.8	6.3	5.0	4.5	4.0	3.7	3.6	2.6	2.7	7.2	4.0	2.2	1.1
35 – 39	.4	3.1	8.3	3.2	3.6	3.8	4.7	5.9	8.0	5.6	6.2	5.6	5.1	4.7	3.7	3.4	3.3	2.4	2.8	7.9	5.6	1.6	1.1
40 – 44	1.2	4.3	8.4	3.2	2.3	3.4	3.1	5.8	5.8	6.2	4.8	5.7	4.7	3.7	3.3	4.1	3.7	3.2	3.5	10.4	5.2	2.9	1.1
45 – 49	1.7	3.8	5.1	3.5	3.8	2.3	4.0	5.3	6.0	4.9	5.6	4.2	4.6	6.6	4.7	4.0	3.8	3.0	3.2	9.9	6.3	2.5	1.2
50 – 54	1.3	3.3	4.9	1.8	2.8	2.8	3.4	3.7	7.3	6.7	5.2	5.0	4.6	4.2	4.2	5.0	3.9	4.0	3.7	11.8	7.2	2.9	.3
55 – 59	.9	4.4	6.5	3.0	5.1	3.6	4.1	3.9	4.6	5.1	7.7	4.6	6.0	4.5	4.7	4.1	3.7	3.0	4.0	9.8	3.9	2.4	.4
60 – 64	2.6	3.4	7.5	4.2	3.0	2.6	3.6	4.1	4.5	7.2	7.2	7.0	6.9	6.3	6.6	2.8	3.8	4.1	3.3	4.0	4.7	.3	.3
65 – 69	4.6	7.4	8.7	2.6	2.7	3.0	6.3	7.0	9.0	6.2	5.9	6.0	6.5	4.7	5.1	3.1	2.5	2.0	1.8	4.3	.4	.2	
70 and over	8.8	3.0	10.8	2.4	2.1	3.8	5.1	9.1	9.1	8.2	8.9	10.6	3.0	3.0	2.3	2.9	3.2	1.1	.6	1.4	.5	.1	

Source of basic data: Publications, and surveys by the author of state, county and city marriage records.

Table A14. Median Age of Marital Partner, by Race According to Age of Groom and Age of Bride, United States, 1940

Age of Groom (Years)	Median Age of Bride		Age of Bride (Years)	Median Age of Groom	
	White	Negro		White	Negro
15 – 19	18.0	17.7	Under 15	21.7	20.8
20 – 24	21.3	19.6	15 – 19	22.9	22.8
25 – 29	23.5	23.4	20 – 24	24.7	24.9
30 – 34	27.0	27.0	25 – 29	28.9	30.0
35 – 39	30.4	29.5	30 – 34	34.0	35.2
40 – 44	34.4	33.9	35 – 39	39.6	40.5
45 – 49	39.1	37.1	40 – 44	45.6	46.9
50 – 54	44.1	40.8	45 – 49	50.9	51.6
55 – 59	47.9	44.4	50 – 54	55.7	57.5
60 – 69	53.9	49.4	55 – 59	60.2	61.3
70 – 79	61.4	54.5	60 – 69	65.7	65.1

Note: Excludes interracial marriages.
Source of basic data: Statistics for a collection of states, from Bureau of the Census, *Vital Statistics — Special Reports*, Vol. 17, No. 22, p. 414.

Table A15. Grooms and Brides by Previous Marital Status, Marriages in the United States, 1900-1950

(Number in 1,000's)

Year	GROOM			BRIDE		
	Single	Widowed	Divorced	Single	Widowed	Divorced
1900	620	73	16	627	59	23
1901	649	76	17	655	61	26
1902	679	78	19	684	65	27
1903	717	80	21	723	66	29
1904	715	79	21	719	66	30
1905	742	79	21	745	67	30
1906	797	75	23	798	65	32
1907	830	82	25	834	69	34
1908	750	82	25	755	68	34
1909	786	84	27	794	67	36
1910	830	87	31	839	69	40
1911	838	85	32	841	73	41
1912	881	89	35	888	74	43
1913	895	88	38	898	74	49
1914	900	86	39	901	73	51
1915	884	81	43	884	71	53
1916	941	90	45	938	79	59
1917	1,000	93	51	991	86	67
1918	854	97	49	847	88	65
1919	976	117	57	968	108	74
1920	1,079	125	70	1,069	117	88
1921	973	121	70	967	111	86
1922	952	111	71	948	100	86
1923	1,034	117	79	1,028	108	94
1924	991	113	81	986	104	95
1925	993	112	83	991	102	95
1926	1,007	110	86	1,007	99	97
1927	1,004	109	88	1,004	98	99
1928	985	108	89	987	96	99
1929	1,026	112	95	1,031	98	104
1930	935	102	90	940	89	98
1931	881	93	87	888	80	93
1932	818	83	81	824	71	87
1933	919	88	91	926	76	96
1934	1,096	98	108	1,107	82	113
1935	1,114	96	117	1,122	83	122
1936	1,144	99	126	1,156	83	130
1937	1,210	102	139	1,220	88	143
1938	1,105	93	133	1,114	82	135
1939	1,166	95	143	1,178	83	143
1940	1,342	99	155	1,349	89	158
1941	1,419	102	175	1,427	93	176
1942	1,455	108	209	1,458	103	211
1943	1,264	106	207	1,267	102	208
1944	1,144	101	207	1,147	98	207
1945	1,270	106	237	1,266	111	236
1946	1,824	129	338	1,813	144	334
1947	1,565	115	312	1,557	126	309
1948	1,411	107	293	1,402	116	293
1949	1,211	98	270	1,205	107	269
1950	1,292	99	276	1,279	109	279

Note: Individual figures have been independently rounded; hence the sums of parts may differ slightly from the annual totals shown in Table 2.

Source: Compiled by the author from statistics for selected areas; 1948, based on nationwide data.

Table A16. Grooms and Brides by Previous Marital Status and Age, Marriages in the United States, 1940 and 1948

Age	GROOM				BRIDE			
	Total	Single	Widowed	Divorced	Total	Single	Widowed	Divorced
1940 Total	1,595,879	1,341,879	99,000	155,000	1,595,879	1,348,879	89,000	158,000
Under 15	6	6			881	876		5
15–19	43,926	43,825	46	55	357,714	354,033	416	3,265
20–24	648,862	637,679	2,351	8,832	683,897	651,415	4,475	28,007
25–29	454,166	418,539	8,287	27,340	282,845	230,682	9,649	42,514
30–34	192,413	146,361	11,449	34,603	117,741	69,875	12,154	35,712
35–39	96,166	54,922	9,916	31,328	60,755	24,541	13,503	22,711
40–44	54,511	21,610	12,095	20,806	35,467	9,404	13,092	12,971
45–49	37,582	10,158	12,529	14,895	23,576	4,345	12,056	7,175
50–54	25,434	4,917	11,824	8,693	14,740	2,075	9,265	3,400
55–59	17,596	2,175	11,232	4,189	8,863	925	6,529	1,409
60–64	10,811	924	7,797	2,090	4,860	482	3,824	554
65–74	12,251	661	9,666	1,924	4,237	189	3,800	248
75 and over	2,155	102	1,808	245	303	37	237	29
1948 Total	1,811,155	1,410,796	107,205	293,154	1,811,155	1,402,413	116,175	292,567
Under 15	13	13			2,901	2,875	11	15
15–19	112,785	112,037	20	728	530,284	520,276	396	9,612
20–24	760,894	731,086	1,625	28,183	649,780	584,293	7,005	58,482
25–29	404,889	341,115	4,401	59,373	253,239	172,567	13,406	67,266
30–34	184,960	119,775	6,324	58,861	131,530	63,495	11,310	56,725
35–39	113,750	53,038	9,509	51,203	89,800	31,502	15,401	42,897
40–44	72,810	26,160	10,637	36,013	57,750	14,747	15,908	27,095
45–49	51,104	13,176	13,413	24,515	38,179	6,678	16,767	14,734
50–54	39,860	7,922	15,414	16,524	24,120	3,021	12,430	8,669
55–59	27,810	3,683	15,487	8,640	15,279	1,516	9,509	4,254
60–64	18,273	1,509	11,919	4,845	9,530	994	6,660	1,876
65–74	20,395	1,121	15,344	3,930	8,003	389	6,755	859
75 and over	3,612	161	3,112	339	760	60	617	83

Source: Compiled by the author — 1948, from nationwide data; 1940, from statistics for selected areas.

Table A17. Per Cent Remarried Among Native White and Negro Married Women Living with Husband, by Age, United States, 1910 and 1940

Age	1940		1910	
	Native White	Negro	Native White	Negro
15–74	9.4	18.5	6.6	16.8
15–19	1.9	3.0	.5	1.5
20–24	3.6	6.6	1.5	5.2
25–29	6.1	12.7	3.3	11.8
30–34	8.6	18.8	5.4	17.6
35–39	10.4	22.6	7.5	21.0
40–44	11.3	25.7	8.9	25.7
45–49	11.8	26.3	9.8	25.6
50–54	12.4	25.9	10.4	27.7
55–64	12.8	26.2	10.9	27.2
65–74	13.7	26.6	13.5	29.4

Source of basic data: Bureau of the Census, *Population, Differential Fertility, 1940 and 1910 — Fertility by Duration of Marriage*, Washington, 1947, pp. 323-326, excluding women not reporting on children ever born.

Table A18. Legal Age for Marriage, by State (as of August, 1958)

State	With Consent		Without Consent		State	With Consent		Without Consent	
	Male	Female	Male	Female		Male	Female	Male	Female
Alabama	17	14	21	18	Nebraska	18	16	21	21
Arizona	18	16	21	18	Nevada	18	16	21	18
Arkansas	18	16	21	18	New Hampshire	14	13	20	18
California	18	16	21	18	New Jersey	18	16	21	18
Colorado	16	16	21	18	New Mexico	18	16	21	18
Connecticut	16	16	21	21	New York	16	16	21	18
Delaware	18	16	21	18	North Carolina	16	14	18	18
District of Columbia	18	16	21	18	North Dakota	18	15	21	18
Florida	18	16	21	21	Ohio	18	16	21	18
Georgia	17	14	21	18	Oklahoma	18	15	21	18
Idaho	15	15	18	18	Oregon	18	15	21	18
Illinois	18	16	21	18	Pennsylvania	16	16	21	21
Indiana	18	16	21	18	Rhode Island	18	16	21	21
Iowa	16	14	21	18	South Carolina	16	14	18	18
Kansas	18	16	21	18	South Dakota	18	15	21	21
Kentucky	16	14	21	21	Tennessee	16	16	21	21
Louisiana	18	16	21	21	Texas	16	14	21	18
Maine	16	16	21	18	Utah	16	14	21	18
Maryland	18	16	21	18	Vermont	18	16	21	18
Massachusetts	18	16	21	18	Virginia	18	16	21	21
Michigan	18	16	18	18	Washington	14	15	21	18
Minnesota	18	16	21	18	West Virginia	18	16	21	21
Mississippi	17	15	21	21	Wisconsin	18	15	21	18
Missouri	15	15	21	18	Wyoming	18	16	21	21
Montana	18	16	21	21					

Source: State reports and statutes.

Table A19. Number of Final Decrees of Absolute Divorce and Annulment by State in Which Granted, United States, 1940-1950

Geographic Division and State	1940	1941	1942	1943	1944	1945	1946	1947	1948	1949	1950
UNITED STATES	264,722	294,939	321,329	359,179	412,618	486,326	628,760	496,106	423,213	393,800	384,927
New England	9,682	10,873	11,908	11,345	13,310	15,350	22,724	20,010	15,373	14,411	14,027
Maine	1,558	1,740	1,768	1,837	2,190	2,523	3,981	2,929	2,276	2,107	2,175
New Hampshire	707	1,023	982	933	934	1,409	2,063	1,437	1,260	1,062	1,040
Vermont	426	433	491	502	526	646	1,032	749	520	565	678
Massachusetts	4,595	4,895	5,511	5,253	6,430	7,003	10,347	10,084	7,653	6,855	6,515
Rhode Island	653	666	739	771	951	1,155	1,531	1,540	817	1,011	907
Connecticut	1,743	2,116	2,417	2,049	2,279	2,614	3,770	3,271	2,847	2,811	2,712
Middle Atlantic	23,704	25,675	28,043	27,704	32,207	37,940	58,922	48,224	39,844	32,950	32,055
New York*	10,020	10,890	11,620	11,220	13,240	16,140	24,260	18,450	14,790	11,564	11,621
New Jersey	3,884	3,985	4,523	4,384	5,167	5,640	7,762	9,074	6,934	5,826	5,434
Pennsylvania	9,800	10,800	11,900	12,100	13,800	16,160	26,900	20,700	18,120	15,560	15,000
East North Central	58,553	65,867	69,890	76,128	88,382	103,426	134,328	103,516	87,392	79,479	77,019
Ohio	16,500	18,000	18,700	20,500	24,100	28,500	37,600	28,100	25,800	22,000	22,152
Indiana	8,400	11,500	12,200	12,900	15,600	18,400	22,500	17,000	14,500	13,100	11,200
Illinois	18,000	19,000	21,000	23,000	25,000	29,000	37,000	31,000	26,000	23,375	22,878
Michigan	12,054	13,317	14,085	15,259	18,356	21,133	29,158	21,386	16,017	16,274	15,979
Wisconsin	3,599	4,050	3,905	4,469	5,326	6,393	8,070	6,030	5,075	4,730	4,810
West North Central	26,140	29,268	30,215	32,849	36,841	44,853	59,952	41,444	33,584	31,844	31,786
Minnesota	2,964	3,310	3,196	3,240	3,975	5,346	7,822	5,720	4,690	4,220	4,085
Iowa	4,778	5,144	4,777	5,265	6,138	7,667	9,886	6,743	5,609	5,482	5,404
Missouri	11,220	13,200	14,900	15,800	17,400	19,600	26,000	17,000	13,520	13,300	13,200
North Dakota	523	527	472	507	576	748	1,041	835	683	639	589
South Dakota	793	744	678	843	904	1,198	1,547	1,240	1,030	921	924
Nebraska	2,085	2,143	1,892	2,294	2,548	3,294	4,656	3,306	2,752	2,582	2,554
Kansas	3,777	4,200	4,300	4,900	5,300	7,000	9,000	6,600	5,300	4,700	5,030
South Atlantic	31,581	35,662	39,165	46,388	52,794	61,575	81,046	62,187	55,153	52,468	53,306
Delaware	208	288	391	426	369	498	348	727	415	821	637
Maryland	3,143	4,036	5,102	5,446	5,923	6,520	8,188	6,483	5,842	4,790	4,771
Dist. of Columbia†	1,340	1,510	1,730	1,650	1,200	1,800	2,350	2,000	1,850	1,500	1,600
Virginia	4,100	4,466	5,201	5,941	6,544	7,204	9,248	7,018	7,081	6,167	5,941
West Virginia	2,964	3,400	3,200	3,500	4,300	5,500	8,100	5,300	4,800	4,400	4,200
North Carolina	3,900	4,300	4,700	5,500	5,900	6,800	9,100	7,100	6,500	5,880	6,361
South Carolina	40	50	70	70	90	130	160	140	150	1,100	2,250
Georgia	4,700	5,640	6,060	7,600	9,300	11,400	17,200	12,500	10,500	10,000	9,513
Florida	11,186	11,972	12,711	16,255	19,168	21,723	26,352	20,919	18,015	17,810	18,033
East South Central	19,145	22,451	25,276	31,641	37,822	42,927	55,018	40,034	35,127	32,135	30,943
Kentucky	5,850	6,750	6,850	8,050	9,350	10,500	14,700	11,500	9,500	8,650	8,250
Tennessee	5,600	6,200	6,900	9,000	11,200	13,000	15,800	10,730	9,130	8,500	7,828
Alabama	4,444	5,670	7,200	8,740	10,530	12,700	15,023	10,800	9,800	8,700	8,800
Mississippi	3,251	3,831	4,326	5,851	6,742	6,727	9,495	7,004	6,697	6,285	6,065
West South Central	45,900	51,800	57,420	64,054	70,604	82,822	95,960	74,700	67,100	65,100	63,530
Arkansas	5,400	8,000	9,600	7,800	10,000	12,300	14,200	10,400	9,500	9,800	8,800
Louisiana	3,200	3,900	5,400	6,000	6,400	6,700	5,800	5,100	4,800	4,450	4,600
Oklahoma	9,800	10,900	10,700	13,400	14,600	18,500	19,300	15,200	13,000	12,680	12,700
Texas	27,500	29,000	31,720	36,854	39,604	45,322	56,660	44,000	39,800	38,170	37,430
Mountain	17,297	18,043	21,487	26,665	29,808	36,683	49,410	36,691	31,557	30,314	27,308
Montana	1,700	1,700	1,600	1,900	1,745	2,380	3,212	2,439	2,090	1,995	1,951
Idaho	1,664	1,900	2,200	2,500	2,700	3,300	4,500	3,600	3,149	2,773	2,696
Wyoming	1,000	900	850	970	1,100	1,409	1,815	1,500	1,266	1,259	1,190
Colorado	2,800	2,400	2,800	2,900	3,600	4,200	6,800	5,200	4,650	4,500	4,200
New Mexico	1,200	1,150	1,400	2,000	2,300	3,124	3,877	3,160	2,631	2,884	2,655
Arizona	1,900	2,200	2,600	3,300	3,600	4,600	5,200	4,500	4,300	4,100	3,600
Utah	1,500	1,360	1,433	1,982	1,995	2,651	3,434	2,545	2,199	2,166	2,107
Nevada	5,533	6,433	8,604	11,113	12,768	15,019	20,572	13,747	11,272	10,637	8,909
Pacific	32,720	35,300	37,925	42,405	50,850	60,750	71,400	69,300	58,083	55,099	54,953
Washington	6,400	6,700	7,300	8,200	9,500	10,500	13,000	11,100	9,100	10,900	10,000
Oregon	3,600	4,140	4,725	5,905	6,850	8,400	10,300	6,900	6,450	5,668	6,120
California	22,720	24,460	25,900	28,300	34,500	41,850	48,100	51,300	42,533	38,531	38,833

*Includes dissolutions of marriage (Enoch Arden decrees).
†Includes estimate for limited decrees made absolute.

Note: Compiled by the author from publications and surveys of state, county, and court offices; includes estimates for areas which failed to provide information.

Table A20. Number of Annulments by State in Which Granted, United States, 1940-1950

Geographic Division and State	1940	1941	1942	1943	1944	1945	1946	1947	1948	1949	1950
UNITED STATES	7,440	8,528	9,650	11,270	13,020	16,135	22,056	16,515	14,413	13,400	13,200
New England	119	181	137	141	165	239	390	301	273	231	222
Maine	8	13	13	5	14	13	16	12	16	7	13
New Hampshire	9	14	13	5	12	19	23	29	30	22	29
Vermont	3	1	2	4	1	3	11	2	4	2	–
Massachusetts	93	135	97	109	118	170	276	244	183	168	150
Rhode Island	–	–	–	–	20	34	64	14	–	32	30
Connecticut	6	18	12	18	20	34	64	14	40	32	30
Middle Atlantic	2,430	2,890	3,060	3,080	3,590	4,760	8,810	6,095	5,164	4,607	4,905
New York	2,280	2,730	2,890	2,900	3,380	4,430	8,350	5,680	4,840	4,313	4,599
New Jersey	100	110	120	130	150	250	350	315	244	204	216
Pennsylvania	50	50	50	50	60	80	110	100	80	90	90
East North Central	431	479	569	591	618	760	1,081	798	667	692	587
Ohio	60	65	70	80	90	100	150	100	90	90	80
Indiana	92	100	100	110	130	200	210	160	100	120	67
Illinois	150	150	170	150	130	150	300	200	180	175	156
Michigan	59	74	119	131	138	160	221	168	147	157	139
Wisconsin	70	90	110	120	130	150	200	170	150	150	145
West North Central	215	248	306	288	312	415	542	429	355	303	291
Minnesota	7	16	6	11	14	20	14	25	32	25	36
Iowa	39	46	69	45	49	61	86	61	42	43	37
Missouri	66	78	87	92	102	115	152	99	79	103	85
North Dakota	13	14	15	16	20	30	40	30	20	4	9
South Dakota	7	10	12	14	15	20	30	20	18	7	10
Nebraska	57	54	87	76	77	118	152	126	104	66	64
Kansas	26	30	30	34	35	51	68	68	60	55	50
South Atlantic	509	551	625	778	880	1,070	1,362	1,100	1,033	894	815
Delaware	1	1	–	6	6	12	10	10	4	4	7
Maryland	24	32	46	53	76	90	153	111	105	97	89
Dist. of Columbia	45	35	41	45	53	68	81	76	79	52	74
Virginia	94	115	126	165	186	202	282	197	188	180	181
West Virginia	50	40	30	60	70	80	120	80	70	65	60
North Carolina	50	55	60	70	75	86	116	120	97	97	80
South Carolina	40	50	70	70	90	130	160	140	150	120	80
Georgia	80	100	100	100	100	150	200	150	130	100	56
Florida	125	123	152	209	224	252	240	216	210	179	188
East South Central	119	153	175	199	224	251	359	269	253	207	195
Kentucky	40	48	50	55	65	75	117	89	100	50	50
Tennessee	40	50	60	70	80	90	119	87	66	70	60
Alabama	27	27	30	35	40	50	70	60	52	50	50
Mississippi	12	28	35	39	39	36	53	33	35	37	35
West South Central	532	620	695	760	1,034	1,133	1,228	1,020	784	801	874
Arkansas	25	30	35	40	124	49	58	90	64	101	83
Louisiana	47	100	140	150	160	194	150	130	120	100	100
Oklahoma	200	200	200	200	350	430	450	280	200	250	329
Texas	260	290	320	370	400	460	570	520	400	350	362
Mountain	475	416	513	503	507	646	837	804	663	624	624
Montana	70	66	76	100	92	128	146	134	93	65	82
Idaho	35	30	30	30	32	37	61	49	43	12	31
Wyoming	20	16	17	25	10	20	22	20	20	22	20
Colorado	220	170	230	160	160	200	290	250	180	200	200
New Mexico	30	27	31	42	45	56	62	67	52	70	65
Arizona	40	40	60	70	80	105	140	120	115	107	110
Utah	20	22	24	26	28	30	36	94	100	93	76
Nevada	40	45	45	50	60	70	80	70	60	55	40
Pacific	2,610	2,990	3,570	4,930	5,690	6,861	7,447	5,699	5,221	5,041	4,687
Washington	100	150	180	180	230	270	325	215	185	152	130
Oregon	70	80	90	100	100	91	172	124	100	94	86
California	2,440	2,760	3,300	4,650	5,360	6,500	6,950	5,360	4,936	4,795	4,471

Note: Compiled by the author from publications and surveys of state, county, and court offices; includes estimates for areas which failed to provide information.

Table A21. Number of Absolute Divorces and Annulments by Duration of Marriage, United States, 1922-1955

Year		Duration at Last Anniversary, in Years										
	Total	0-4	5-9	10-14	15-19	20-24	25-29	30-34	35-39	40-44	45-49	Balance
1922	151,651	61,658	39,663	22,427	12,840							15,063
1923	168,460	67,870	45,260	24,720	14,070							16,540
1924	174,387	69,360	47,160	25,795	14,590							17,482
1925	179,066	69,900	51,080	25,420	15,043							17,623
1926	184,678	71,309	54,336	25,754	15,075							18,204
1927	196,292	75,898	57,113	27,833	15,974	9,909						9,565
1928	200,176	76,758	58,368	28,548	16,588	10,136						9,778
1929	205,876	77,793	60,454	30,090	16,893	10,493						10,153
1930	195,961	74,209	55,678	30,507	16,001	9,979						9,587
1931	188,003	70,128	52,872	30,700	15,511	9,573						9,219
1932	164,241	60,348	47,098	26,856	13,638	8,203	4,711					3,387
1933	165,000	59,990	46,750	26,760	14,270	8,430	4,900					3,900
1934	204,000	73,510	57,160	33,040	18,060	10,800	5,900					5,530
1935	218,000	80,030	59,870	35,250	19,400	11,200	5,900					6,350
1936	236,000	84,590	63,560	39,050	21,970	12,680	6,600					7,550
1937	249,000	91,930	63,550	40,980	23,140	13,840	7,240	4,070				4,250
1938	244,000	92,940	59,870	39,550	22,510	13,510	7,650	3,950				4,020
1939	251,000	95,520	60,930	40,520	23,300	14,280	9,090	4,250				3,110
1940	264,722	97,340	65,120	43,750	25,380	15,540	8,450	4,400				4,742
1941	294,939	106,250	73,520	48,040	28,820	18,120	9,500	5,800				4,889
1942	321,329	113,970	81,050	51,110	31,860	20,710	11,900	6,300	2,700			1,729
1943	359,179	131,820	89,450	54,850	35,120	23,080	12,800	6,800	3,200			2,059
1944	412,618	155,700	100,720	61,300	40,070	26,280	15,360	7,500	3,400			2,288
1945	486,326	198,510	117,590	70,160	41,570	28,410	16,000	7,900	3,700			2,486
1946	628,760	274,890	163,840	83,810	46,630	29,170	16,100	8,000	3,750			2,570
1947	496,106	210,230	124,780	66,800	39,310	26,380	15,600	7,580	3,350	1,520		556
1948	423,213	181,030	103,404	54,535	33,582	23,511	14,528	7,374	3,363	1,424		462
1949	393,800	173,170	92,820	50,540	29,620	22,460	13,380	6,760	3,140	1,280		630
1950	384,927	176,040	88,200	47,690	28,800	20,660	12,160	6,730	2,830	1,210		607
1951	381,000	165,600	94,100	48,480	29,350	19,610	12,440	6,860	2,790	1,240		530
1952	392,000	166,450	102,080	51,230	29,650	18,980	12,130	6,500	3,060	1,340	440	140
1953	390,000	165,120	103,510	50,280	30,020	18,120	12,020	6,080	2,900	1,360	450	140
1954	379,000	160,360	102,000	47,960	29,350	17,480	11,100	6,090	2,890	1,240	410	120
1955	377,000	160,670	99,920	47,780	29,010	17,680	11,020	6,000	3,000	1,340	440	140

Note: Estimated by the author from reports by the Bureau of the Census and the National Office of Vital Statistics, and data for states and counties. Data for 1951-1955 are provisional.

Table A22. Existing Marriages by Duration of Marriage, United States, 1922-1955

(Number in 1,000's on July 1 of Each Year)

Year	Total	Duration at Last Anniversary, in Years										Balance
		0-4	5-9	10-14	15-19	20-24	25-29	30-34	35-39	40-44	45-49	
1922	22,937	5,396	4,292	3,522	3,005							6,722
1923	23,465	5,498	4,337	3,583	3,056							6,991
1924	24,054	5,607	4,383	3,665	3,079							7,320
1925	24,492	5,585	4,545	3,715	3,116							7,531
1926	24,916	5,567	4,690	3,762	3,146							7,751
1927	25,363	5,613	4,719	3,842	3,161	2,678						5,350
1928	25,750	5,623	4,792	3,874	3,213	2,722						5,526
1929	26,110	5,631	4,872	3,911	3,285	2,741						5,670
1930	26,477	5,624	4,862	4,035	3,331	2,774						5,851
1931	26,725	5,533	4,856	4,153	3,373	2,801						6,009
1932	26,910	5,375	4,912	4,175	3,446	2,816	2,330					3,856
1933	27,132	5,251	4,944	4,242	3,479	2,865	2,370					3,981
1934	27,503	5,268	4,971	4,315	3,513	2,931	2,387					4,118
1935	27,961	5,395	4,989	4,316	3,620	2,972	2,416					4,253
1936	28,416	5,631	4,919	4,312	3,720	3,008	2,441					4,385
1937	28,899	5,993	4,774	4,359	3,730	3,070	2,454	1,940				2,579
1938	29,403	6,317	4,654	4,379	3,780	3,092	2,496	1,972				2,713
1939	29,895	6,467	4,674	4,399	3,837	3,118	2,553	1,984				2,863
1940	30,577	6,641	4,784	4,427	3,835	3,211	2,586	2,009				3,084
1941	31,329	6,927	4,992	4,370	3,828	3,296	2,615	2,030				3,271
1942	32,145	7,232	5,313	4,238	3,865	3,298	2,666	2,041	1,506			1,986
1943	32,950	7,480	5,589	4,122	3,875	3,334	2,680	2,075	1,530			2,265
1944	33,499	7,557	5,681	4,121	3,879	3,374	2,694	2,122	1,537			2,534
1945	33,942	7,501	5,774	4,180	3,898	3,358	2,768	2,146	1,555			2,762
1946	34,589	7,746	5,947	4,331	3,834	3,337	2,836	2,165	1,570			2,823
1947	35,631	8,164	6,136	4,605	3,706	3,361	2,834	2,204	1,578	1,044		1,999
1948	36,446	8,423	6,344	4,879	3,616	3,372	2,869	2,221	1,613	1,070		2,039
1949	37,150	8,621	6,473	5,018	3,660	3,394	2,916	2,247	1,664	1,090		2,067
1950	37,785	8,696	6,535	5,162	3,767	3,447	2,918	2,331	1,702	1,122		2,105
1951	38,473	8,414	6,835	5,382	3,956	3,433	2,926	2,417	1,743	1,158		2,209
1952	39,035	7,878	7,261	5,612	4,247	3,357	2,973	2,436	1,799	1,188	703	1,581
1953	39,540	7,532	7,503	5,819	4,509	3,293	2,999	2,482	1,826	1,230	735	1,612
1954	40,025	7,359	7,671	5,935	4,626	3,336	3,030	2,533	1,856	1,279	754	1,646
1955	40,515	7,247	7,742	5,989	4,757	3,436	3,087	2,538	1,938	1,312	783	1,686

Note: Estimated by the author from number of married males; and cohorts of marriages traced to successive anniversaries by allowing for net in-migration of married men, absolute divorces, annulments, and deaths of husbands and wives. Data for 1951-1955 are provisional. Includes armed forces overseas during 1940-1955.

Table A23. Divorces per 1,000 Married Males, by Color, Selected Areas of the United States, 1918-1950

Year	Virginia	
	W	N
1918	3.6	6.9
1919	4.9	9.0
1920	5.9	8.9
1921	5.6	7.1
1922	4.2	4.7
1923	4.6	5.7
1924	4.6	6.4
1925	5.0	5.9
1926	5.1	5.4
1927	4.9	5.7

Year	Virginia		Mississippi	
	W	N	W	N
1928	4.9	5.2	7.3	7.9
1929	5.2	4.8	7.9	7.9
1930	5.4	5.2	7.2	6.2
1931	5.2	4.5	6.2	3.5
1932	4.3	3.2	6.1	2.9
1933	4.6	2.6	6.4	2.7
1934	5.9	3.7	7.6	3.5
1935	6.4	4.2	7.4	3.5
1936	6.8	4.7	7.3	3.8
1937	6.8	4.6	8.2	4.6
1938	6.6	4.7	8.6	3.9

Year	Virginia		Mississippi		Arkansas		North Carolina*		Iowa		Ohio†		Other‡	
	W	N	W	N	W	N	W	N	W	N	W	N	W	N
1939	6.5	6.2	8.8	3.9					7.8	18.6			5.6	8.2
1940	7.4	6.0	9.2	4.3					7.9	24.8				
1941	7.2	8.3	9.6	6.3			6.4	3.3	8.4	27.5				
1942	7.5	11.8	10.1	7.9			6.3	5.2	7.7	27.9				
1943	7.7	15.0	11.6	12.9			7.1	6.4						
1944	8.4	15.4	12.8	15.5			7.3	7.2	9.7	29.7	19.1	29.0		
1945	9.3	15.0	14.4	13.2	28.4	23.6	8.3	7.5	12.0	28.0	21.7	27.4		
1946	11.7	18.5	21.2	17.3	32.5	27.4	11.0	9.5	15.3	46.9	29.9	48.4		
1947	8.4	14.8	15.4	12.9	23.6	20.3			10.3	35.8	20.0	33.8		
1948	8.3	13.9	13.5	13.7	21.6	17.8	12.0	4.5	8.5	25.1	17.5	30.7		
1949	7.0	12.1	12.5	13.1	22.3	17.8	10.8	7.3	8.2	26.9	14.8	25.8	12.4	24.1
1950	6.5	11.9	12.6	11.6					8.1	24.2	14.0	28.1	12.3	23.0

*Figures for 1948 and 1949 refer to Mecklenburg County only.
†Montgomery County only.
‡Figures for 1939 refer to Nebraska and Wisconsin; those for 1949 and 1950 to Missouri.

Note: W and N refer to white and nonwhite, respectively.
Source: Absolute divorces and annulments, from reports and unpublished data; married males, estimated by the author.

Table A24. Number of Matrimonial Decrees and Children Under Age 21, by Type of Decree and Duration of Marriage, Manhattan and The Bronx in New York State, 1950

Duration of Marriage (Years)	Absolute Divorce			Annulment			Dissolution of Marriage*			Total †			Separation		
	Total Decrees	Decrees Involving Children	Total Children Involved	Total Decrees	Decrees Involving Children	Total Children Involved	Total Decrees	Decrees Involving Children	Total Children Involved	Total Decrees	Decrees Involving Children	Total Children Involved	Total Decrees	Decrees Involving Children	Total Children Involved
Total	1,286	654	1,073	1,027	135	158	189	48	69	2,502	837	1,300	180	89	138
0	23	5	7	139	4	5	–	–	–	162	9	12	–	–	–
1	48	15	17	219	16	16	–	–	–	267	31	33	1	–	–
2	47	13	15	181	24	24	–	–	–	228	37	39	–	–	–
3	87	37	46	130	20	21	–	–	–	217	57	67	6	2	2
4	85	44	55	92	16	17	–	–	–	177	60	72	4	1	2
5	65	32	39	63	10	11	–	–	–	128	42	50	4	–	–
6	85	46	61	59	10	12	1	–	–	145	56	73	2	2	3
7	101	61	95	28	6	7	3	1	1	132	68	103	3	2	2
8	71	42	59	24	4	5	4	1	1	99	47	65	3	2	4
9	85	44	69	23	4	5	5	1	1	113	49	75	3	3	5
0-4	290	114	140	761	80	83	–	–	–	1,051	194	223	11	3	4
5-9	407	225	323	197	34	40	13	3	3	617	262	366	15	9	14
10-14	211	127	235	44	12	20	44	13	19	299	152	274	9	7	17
15-19	166	104	224	17	9	15	42	15	23	225	128	262	8	5	10
20-24	134	73	133	5	–	–	39	16	23	178	89	156	5	3	5
25-29	51	9	14	3	–	–	21	1	1	75	10	15	3	–	–
30-34	18	2	4	–	–	–	19	–	–	37	2	4	–	–	–
35-39	9	–	–	–	–	–	8	–	–	17	–	–	1	–	–
40-44	–	–	–	–	–	–	3	–	–	3	–	–	–	–	–
Unknown	–	–	–	–	–	–	–	–	–	–	–	–	128	62	88

*Enoch Arden decrees.
†Sum of absolute divorce, annulment, and dissolution of marriage.

Source: Compiled by the author from Supreme Court records.

Table A25. Number of Absolute Divorces and Annulments by Party to Which Granted, and by Legal Ground, United States, 1907-1915, 1917-1921, 1933-1950

(Number in 1,000's)

Year	Granted To		Legal Ground						
	Husband	Wife	Cruelty	Desertion	Adultery	Drunken- ness	Neglect to Provide	Combina- tions	All Others
1907	24.9	51.7	18.1	29.5	11.6	3.4	2.9	6.5	4.6
1908	24.6	52.3	19.1	28.7	11.0	3.1	3.4	7.3	4.3
1909	25.0	54.7	19.6	29.0	11.4	3.0	3.7	8.3	4.7
1910	25.9	57.1	20.5	30.0	11.6	3.6	4.0	7.9	5.5
1911	28.3	61.0	22.2	32.6	12.6	3.7	3.9	8.6	5.7
1912	29.5	64.8	23.6	36.1	12.4	4.3	3.9	8.5	5.5
1913	28.2	63.1	22.9	34.4	12.2	4.2	5.0	8.3	4.4
1914	30.0	70.6	24.1	37.3	13.5	4.5	5.1	9.1	7.0
1915	31.2	73.1	26.2	39.3	13.2	4.2	5.8	9.3	6.3
1917	38.1	83.5	32.5	45.0	14.1	4.2	5.1	11.2	9.5
1918	37.9	78.3	31.0	43.1	14.0	3.8	4.5	9.8	10.0
1919	48.3	93.3	39.9	52.6	17.8	3.1	6.1	12.5	9.4
1920	57.8	112.7	49.7	62.1	22.2	2.2	6.7	14.3	13.4
1921	53.1	106.5	49.4	56.8	19.2	1.6	5.9	12.4	14.3
1933	42.6	122.4	72.0	41.9	13.2	2.6	6.5	11.3	17.4
1934	54.1	149.9	90.3	52.9	14.3	3.5	7.7	13.8	21.5
1935	58.6	159.4	96.8	57.0	15.1	4.1	7.2	14.5	23.5
1936	63.7	172.3	103.9	63.4	15.8	5.1	7.2	14.8	25.8
1937	66.0	183.1	111.1	64.6	16.8	6.1	7.2	15.1	28.1
1938	62.7	181.3	112.0	62.6	16.3	6.1	6.4	13.9	26.8
1939	63.4	187.6	118.3	63.2	15.2	6.6	6.2	14.6	26.9
1940	68.7	196.0	126.7	66.4	16.4	7.9	6.3	13.1	27.9
1941	77.7	217.2	139.6	70.8	17.3	8.2	6.5	13.6	39.0
1942	88.2	233.1	153.2	81.0	19.2	8.6	6.7	12.2	40.5
1943	104.8	254.4	180.9	86.8	18.6	10.0	7.1	15.1	40.7
1944	119.8	292.9	214.3	92.5	22.1	11.2	7.6	19.2	45.7
1945	138.9	347.4	265.6	97.2	27.0	13.6	8.9	20.9	53.2
1946	183.7	445.1	343.3	111.7	36.2	18.1	11.2	25.9	82.4
1947	136.5	359.6	273.0	86.8	26.5	14.3	8.9	18.8	67.9
1948	115.8	307.4	232.6	75.4	19.1	12.5	7.0	14.8	61.7
1949	105.7	288.1	229.1	67.5	10.7	11.5	6.6	12.0	56.4
1950	106.0	278.9	225.8	67.9	10.2	11.0	8.1	6.5	55.4

Note: Individual figures have been independently rounded; hence the sums of parts may differ slightly from the annual totals shown in Table 42.

Source: Estimated by the author from trends in selected areas; 1948, from nationwide surveys.

Table A26. Number of Deaths in the United States, by Sex and Marital Status, 1890-1955

(Number in 1,000's)

Year	MALE					FEMALE				
	Total	Single	Married	Widowed	Divorced	Total	Single	Married	Widowed	Divorced
1890	642	403	190	48	1.0	569	325	151	92	0.9
1891	621	387	185	49	1.0	550	311	147	92	.9
1892	638	394	191	52	1.1	564	315	152	97	1.0
1893	626	384	188	53	1.1	553	305	150	97	1.0
1894	591	360	178	52	1.1	522	285	142	94	.9
1895	609	368	185	55	1.2	539	291	148	100	1.0
1896	602	361	183	57	1.2	532	284	147	101	1.0
1897	571	340	175	55	1.2	504	265	140	98	1.0
1898	589	348	181	59	1.3	520	271	145	104	1.0
1899	612	358	189	63	1.4	540	278	151	110	1.1
1900	696	405	216	74	1.6	614	312	173	128	1.3
1901	686	394	216	75	1.8	592	296	168	127	1.4
1902	664	376	212	74	2.0	565	278	162	124	1.5
1903	677	379	219	77	2.3	583	282	168	132	1.7
1904	728	402	239	85	2.8	621	295	181	144	2.0
1905	718	391	239	86	3.1	613	286	180	145	2.2
1906	732	393	246	89	3.4	612	280	181	149	2.4
1907	760	403	259	95	3.8	626	282	186	156	2.6
1908	707	369	244	90	3.8	595	263	178	151	2.7
1909	703	362	246	91	4.1	589	255	178	153	2.8
1910	742	377	263	98	4.6	614	261	187	163	3.1
1911	710	354	256	96	4.7	592	247	183	160	3.1
1912	711	348	261	97	4.9	588	240	184	161	3.2
1913	739	356	276	103	5.4	605	242	192	168	3.4
1914	723	342	274	102	5.5	598	234	192	168	3.5
1915	722	335	278	103	5.8	602	231	196	172	3.6
1916	773	356	297	113	6.5	637	241	207	185	3.9
1917	792	358	310	117	6.9	651	241	215	192	4.1
1918	1,029	465	398	157	9.5	840	287	312	237	5.2
1919	717	318	282	110	6.9	632	216	228	184	4.1
1920	728	322	284	115	7.3	657	223	232	197	4.4
1921	658	284	262	105	6.8	586	196	208	179	4.0
1922	687	290	279	110	7.3	601	197	213	186	4.3
1923	722	299	299	117	7.8	633	204	225	199	4.6
1924	713	288	301	116	7.9	612	194	218	196	4.6
1925	729	289	312	119	8.3	621	191	226	200	4.7
1926	769	301	332	128	9.0	653	197	237	214	5.1
1927	731	277	323	122	9.2	616	180	229	202	5.1
1928	782	289	351	132	10.6	659	188	248	218	5.8
1929	790	285	360	134	11.5	661	185	248	222	6.2
1930	766	271	351	132	11.9	632	174	237	215	6.3
1931	753	259	351	131	12.3	619	166	233	213	6.5
1932	738	247	349	129	12.7	618	162	234	215	6.8
1933	737	240	354	130	13.3	605	155	230	213	6.9
1934	773	244	377	137	14.5	624	156	238	223	7.5
1935	771	237	382	137	15.1	621	152	238	224	7.8
1936	821	245	409	150	17.1	658	156	249	244	8.6
1937	809	238	406	148	17.5	642	151	244	239	8.6
1938	765	220	387	142	16.9	616	142	232	234	8.5
1939	769	210	394	147	18.1	619	135	232	242	9.6
1940	791	211	407	154	19.0	626	135	230	252	9.3
1941	785	211	404	151	19.4	613	133	225	245	9.2
1942	780	208	403	150	20.0	605	129	222	244	9.2
1943	817	217	421	159	21.2	642	136	233	263	9.9
1944	790	202	415	152	20.4	621	128	228	256	10.0
1945	788	190	426	152	20.3	614	121	227	255	10.3
1946	786	187	429	150	19.9	610	119	224	256	10.6
1947	818	186	455	157	20.4	627	120	228	267	11.1
1948	821	195	440	159	27.8	623	123	220	268	12.0
1949	821	190	445	159	27.4	622	120	220	271	11.9
1950	828	183	454	162	28.2	625	115	220	278	12.1
1951	845	186	465	165	29.4	637	117	222	285	12.6
1952	854	185	473	165	31.3	643	118	222	290	12.9
1953	867	185	483	166	33.2	650	118	223	296	13.2
1954	846	179	471	163	32.3	635	115	216	291	12.7
1955	873	182	485	172	33.0	656	117	219	307	12.9

Note: Individual figures have been independently rounded; hence the sums of parts may differ slightly from the totals.
Source: Data for 1935-1940, 1943, and 1949-1951, from the National Office of Vital Statistics, with decedents of unknown status distributed; all other figures estimated by the author.

Table A27. Number of Deaths, by Sex and Marital Status, United States Armed Forces Overseas,* 1917-1919 and 1940-1956

Year	Male					Female
	Total	Single	Married	Widowed	Divorced	
1917	350	200	140	10	–	–
1918	73,000	41,560	29,480	1,820	140	–
1919	5,330	3,040	2,150	130	10	–
1940	137	67	70	–	–	–
1941	3,340	2,050	1,260	10	20	–
1942	29,000	19,050	9,700	80	170	10
1943	42,350	24,780	17,180	120	270	30
1944	161,460	93,910	66,130	450	970	60
1945	112,420	66,350	45,110	300	660	120
1946	7,439	2,999	4,300	30	110	20
1947	1,848	748	1,060	10	30	6
1948	1,315	535	750	10	20	2
1949	1,284	524	730	10	20	2
1950	11,441	7,721	3,600	20	100	17
1951	14,524	10,624	3,400	100	400	14
1952	7,112	4,712	2,070	60	270	13
1953 †	8,909	5,919	2,570	80	340	4
1954	3,015	1,865	980	40	130	8
1955	1,646	976	570	20	80	4
1956	1,614	964	550	20	80	4

*Includes 5,663 deaths of merchant marine personnel between December, 1941, and September, 1945.

†Includes about 3,100 declared dead under Missing Persons Act.

Note: Estimated by the author; based on data from the National Office of Vital Statistics, the various branches of the armed forces, War Shipping Administration, Veterans Administration, Metropolitan Life Insurance Company, and Bureau of the Census.

Table A28. Number of Deaths of Married Persons, United States, 1860-1889

(Number in 1,000's)

Year	Number	Year	Number	Year	Number
1860	171	1870	208	1880	262
1861	181	1871	204	1881	294
1862	185	1872	254	1882	297
1863	218	1873	242	1883	288
1864	231	1874	224	1884	286
1865	221	1875	249	1885	259
1866	222	1876	245	1886	264
1867	205	1877	232	1887	301
1868	190	1878	227	1888	314
1869	197	1879	240	1889	314

Note: Estimated by the author.

Table A29. Deaths per 1,000 Population, by Sex and Marital Status, United States, 1890-1950

Year	MALE					FEMALE				
	Total	Single	Married	Widowed	Divorced	Total	Single	Married	Widowed	Divorced
1890	19.9	20.0	16.8	58.5	20.4	18.5	18.8	13.5	42.3	12.5
1891	18.8	18.9	16.0	55.7	21.7	17.5	17.6	12.8	40.8	13.0
1892	19.0	18.9	16.1	56.7	25.0	17.6	17.5	12.9	41.8	14.7
1893	18.3	18.1	15.5	55.3	25.6	16.9	16.7	12.5	40.9	14.7
1894	16.9	16.7	14.4	52.1	26.2	15.7	15.3	11.6	38.7	13.2
1895	17.1	16.8	14.6	53.6	27.9	15.9	15.3	11.8	40.1	14.5
1896	16.6	16.2	14.2	53.2	26.1	15.4	14.7	11.5	39.7	13.5
1897	15.5	15.0	13.3	50.6	23.1	14.3	13.5	10.7	37.9	12.5
1898	15.7	15.2	13.4	52.7	21.7	14.5	13.6	10.9	39.4	11.2
1899	16.0	15.4	13.8	55.1	19.7	14.8	13.7	11.1	41.2	10.9
1900	17.9	17.2	15.4	62.4	19.0	16.5	15.2	12.5	47.0	11.4
1901	17.3	16.4	15.0	61.0	20.5	15.6	14.2	11.8	45.7	11.8
1902	16.4	15.4	14.3	59.0	21.5	14.6	13.1	11.1	44.1	12.2
1903	16.4	15.3	14.5	60.3	23.7	14.8	13.1	11.3	46.1	13.4
1904	17.3	16.0	15.4	64.7	27.5	15.5	13.6	11.8	49.6	15.2
1905	16.7	15.3	14.9	63.5	28.7	15.0	12.9	11.4	49.3	15.9
1906	16.7	15.1	15.0	64.7	29.3	14.7	12.5	11.2	49.6	16.6
1907	17.0	15.3	15.4	67.2	30.2	14.8	12.5	11.3	51.1	16.8
1908	15.5	13.8	14.1	62.5	27.7	13.8	11.5	10.5	48.9	16.4
1909	15.1	13.3	13.8	62.4	27.5	13.4	11.0	10.2	48.7	15.8
1910	15.6	13.6	14.4	66.1	29.7	13.7	11.0	10.5	50.9	16.8
1911	14.7	12.7	13.7	63.4	29.9	13.0	10.3	10.0	48.9	16.3
1912	14.5	12.3	13.7	63.8	30.4	12.7	9.9	9.9	48.3	16.2
1913	14.8	12.4	14.1	66.3	33.3	12.8	9.8	10.1	49.2	16.8
1914	14.2	11.8	13.6	64.8	33.5	12.4	9.3	9.9	48.1	17.0
1915	14.0	11.4	13.6	64.5	34.1	12.3	9.1	9.9	48.2	16.8
1916	14.8	12.1	14.2	69.5	36.3	12.8	9.4	10.3	50.9	17.3
1917	15.0	12.1	14.5	70.9	35.8	12.9	9.3	10.4	51.6	17.4
1918	20.7	17.0	19.8	93.2	47.3	16.4	11.0	14.8	61.6	21.1
1919	13.5	10.7	13.1	63.0	31.1	12.3	8.2	10.8	47.2	15.7
1920	13.4	10.7	12.8	64.8	29.1	12.6	8.5	10.8	50.0	15.3
1921	11.9	9.3	11.6	58.4	24.7	11.0	7.3	9.4	44.7	12.9
1922	12.3	9.4	12.2	61.1	25.3	11.1	7.3	9.4	45.9	13.2
1923	12.7	9.5	12.7	63.7	25.9	11.5	7.4	9.7	48.4	13.5
1924	12.3	9.1	12.5	62.3	24.5	10.9	7.0	9.2	46.6	12.7
1925	12.4	9.0	12.7	63.6	24.2	10.9	6.8	9.3	46.7	12.1
1926	12.9	9.3	13.3	67.1	24.5	11.3	6.9	9.6	49.0	12.2
1927	12.1	8.5	12.7	63.1	23.1	10.5	6.3	9.1	45.4	11.2
1928	12.8	8.8	13.6	66.9	24.5	11.1	6.5	9.7	47.9	11.6
1929	12.8	8.6	13.8	67.1	24.6	11.0	6.4	9.6	47.7	11.4
1930	12.3	8.1	13.3	65.3	23.9	10.4	6.0	9.0	45.3	10.9
1931	12.0	7.7	13.1	64.2	23.8	10.1	5.7	8.8	44.1	10.7
1932	11.7	7.4	13.0	62.6	24.2	10.0	5.5	8.7	43.8	10.9
1933	11.6	7.1	13.1	62.3	25.6	9.7	5.2	8.5	42.6	11.0
1934	12.1	7.3	13.7	65.2	28.0	10.0	5.3	8.7	43.7	11.8
1935	12.0	7.1	13.7	65.1	28.5	9.8	5.2	8.5	43.1	11.8
1936	12.7	7.4	14.4	70.5	31.3	10.3	5.3	8.8	46.0	12.5
1937	12.5	7.2	14.0	69.6	31.0	10.0	5.2	8.5	44.1	12.0
1938	11.7	6.6	13.2	66.5	28.9	9.5	4.9	7.9	42.4	11.3
1939	11.7	6.4	13.2	68.8	30.1	9.5	4.7	7.8	43.1	12.2
1940	11.9	6.4	13.3	71.9	31.0	9.5	4.7	7.6	44.1	11.5
1941	11.8	6.5	12.9	69.7	31.5	9.2	4.7	7.2	42.2	11.3
1942	12.0	6.9	12.9	68.5	32.5	9.0	4.5	6.9	41.4	11.2
1943	12.5	7.4	13.3	71.9	33.7	9.4	4.7	7.1	44.0	11.7
1944	13.7	9.0	14.4	68.4	30.6	9.0	4.5	6.9	41.8	11.0
1945	12.9	7.8	13.9	67.4	26.1	8.8	4.2	6.7	40.8	10.1
1946	11.2	5.8	12.5	66.4	21.1	8.6	4.1	6.5	40.4	9.0
1947	11.4	5.7	12.8	69.3	19.2	8.7	4.1	6.4	41.6	8.6
1948	11.2	5.9	12.1	69.8	25.4	8.5	4.2	6.1	41.1	9.0
1949	11.1	5.6	12.0	69.6	25.0	8.3	4.0	5.9	41.0	8.8
1950	11.1	5.6	12.1	70.3	25.6	8.2	3.8	5.8	41.3	8.8

Note: Includes deaths and population in armed forces overseas during 1917-1919 and 1940-1950; the small number of female deaths overseas are included with the single.
Source of basic data: Tables A6, A26, A27.

INDEX